INDIAN PIGEONS

AND

DOVES

INDIAN PIGEONS

AND

DOVES

E. C. STUART BAKER

WITH TWENTY-SEVEN PLATES FROM DRAWINGS BY

H. GRONVOLD AND G. E. LODGE

GYAN

Published by

Gyan Publishing House
5, Ansari Road
Daryaganj, New Delhi-110002
Phone: 011-47034999, 9811692060
E-mail: books@gyanbooks.com

Distribution Network
gyanbooks.com
India, USA, Canada, UK, Australia, France

ISBN : 978-81-212-9574-1 (PB)
First Published, 1913

2nd Impression 2023

Printed at: Gyan Press, Delhi.

INDIAN PIGEONS AND DOVES
Author:E. C. STUART BAKER

INDIAN PIGEONS AND DOVES

THE ASHY-HEADED GREEN PIGEON—*OSMOTRERON P. PHAYREI*

(½ Nat. Size—Male on right, female on left.)

FRONTISPIECE

INDIAN PIGEONS
AND
DOVES

BY

E. C. STUART BAKER

F.Z.S., F.L.S., M.B.O.U.

Author of "Indian Ducks and their Allies."

WITH TWENTY-SEVEN COLOURED PLATES FROM DRAWINGS BY
H. GRÖNVOLD AND G. E. LODGE.

1913

PREFACE.

MY reasons for writing a volume upon our Indian Pigeons and Doves are several, and I trust will be deemed sufficient by my readers.

In the first place, there has as yet been no book published which deals with these most beautiful birds from the point of view of the Sportsman and Field-Naturalist as well as from that of the Scientific or Museum-Naturalist, and as this is a gap in the records of our Indian Avifauna which badly needs filling, I may be forgiven for trying to bridge it. Skins—as skins—are, without doubt, full of interest, and especially so, perhaps, when the person studying them is more or less intimate with the life-histories of the birds themselves; but Pigeons are well worthy of study in ways other than by dry skins. To the Field-Naturalist they are birds full of interest; to the Aviculturist they are birds more charming and worthy of culture than has hitherto been generally admitted, and to the Sportsman they offer an object well worthy of attention, for he must have a quick eye, a sure hand, and considerable perseverance and patience before he has mastered their habits and is able to find them and, when found, bring them to bag.

Books referring to Pigeons and Doves, of course, abound; but they are difficult of access and expensive to purchase. Volume XXI of the *Catalogue* of Birds in the British Museum, by Count Salvadori, is the standard work on these birds; but one does not want twenty-seven volumes of a work, at a cost of something well over fifty pounds, for the sake of Pigeons only.

In the same way, Blanford's Vol. IV of the *Avifauna of British India* deals with this family very thoroughly; but the volume is one of four, and contains much matter besides such as refers to the birds we are now considering; and, moreover, it tells us but little about the Pigeon itself, except as a museum-specimen. Jerdon contains rather fuller accounts, but, wonderful book as this still is, it was written nearly sixty years ago, and cannot but be somewhat out of date, as well as being difficult to obtain. Hume's volumes of *Stray Feathers* have odd notes full of interest when one can find them, and in the same way many other Natural History journals have references to Pigeons, but they also are scattered and difficult to find. Finally, so many of my friends and others have asked me to write a book on the Indian Pigeons, that I think there must be some grounds for hoping that a volume upon them will be kindly received.

From a scientific point of view it is probable that this book will undergo considerable criticism, for it introduces for the first time into India the trinominal system—that is to say, the system which recognises subspecies. But India is essentially a country in which we find such a system necessary: for the variations in climate are so great, according to elevation, humidity, etc., that the same species in different localities are bound to undergo some degree of evolution which shall render them suitable to their surroundings. On the other hand, the variations so caused—though constant in definite areas—are often indeterminate in the country which links these areas together, and which is itself often intermediate in character. Then again we find in India parallel evolution going on in districts very far apart. For instance, the little Bustard-Quail (*Turnix taijoor*) in the dry area of Southern Burma nearly approaches the same form as that found in the drier portions of Central India. So too, with our Pigeons: we find our very first bird, the Bengal Green Pigeon, having well-defined variations occurring both in Burma and in Southern India, yet in the intervening countries many birds cannot be placed with certainty under either form.

It would appear, also, that Pigeons and Doves are birds very susceptible to climatic variations, for we known that Beebe, one of the leading American Ornithologists, has obtained different *specific* phases of plumage in the same identical individual by merely transferring it from a very dry area to others more and yet more humid.

Geographical variations I therefore accept as sufficient reason for the creation of subspecies as long as they are constant within a given area, though intermediate areas may be inhabited by intermediate forms.

Broadly speaking, in giving geographical forms the status of subspecies, I have acted upon the following lines: When I have found differences in the plumage or in the size of birds, inhabiting different areas, which are quite plain to anyone's observation, I accept them as constituting good species or subspecies, the former if they are *not* linked to one another by individuals which are intermediate, the latter if they *are* so linked. At the same time I have not gone out of my way to hunt for minute differences in tint or in measurements, but have merely admitted them when they are too plain to be overlooked.

In regard to nomenclature I have accepted the rules laid down by the latest International Zoological Congress and take my names according to strict priority and with effect from the date of the tenth edition of Linnaeus.

In following accepted rules it is impossible to avoid tautonomy: I am therefore compelled to show the bird first described of the various subspecies with its specific name duplicated. Thus it is imperative to name the Bengal Green Pigeon *Crocopus phoenicopterus phoenicopterus*, instead of *C. p. typicus*, and the geographical variations or subspecies must be called *C. p. viridifrons* and *C. p. chlorogaster*.

In classification generally I have adhered as closely as possible to that of Blanford in the *Fauna of British India* series, though this is, to some extent, altered by the use of the trinomial system and by the fact that a few other forms have had to be added to his list.

An attempt has been made in the following chapters to collate, as far as possible, all information recorded up to date, and to add as many sporting and field notes as have been obtainable, together with a certain amount of original matter. Original matter, however, of this nature is very hard to obtain before a book is written, but it is to be hoped that once written and published *readers* will not be slow to become *writers* also and to add their quota of knowledge to that which has been previously recorded, whilst others may well be able to show where the present volume is incomplete or incorrect.

The total number of species and subspecies dealt with in this work is fifty-one, Blanford having recognized forty-five of them as good species.

The books referred to in the list of synonyms do not include *all* works of reference, for, as far as possible, only those have been noted which refer to the birds as occurring in India, with the addition from time to time of those which contain matter of importance to readers in India, such as the book in which the bird itself, or anything of importance concerning it, is first mentioned or described;

references to the *Ibis*, the *Zoological Proceedings*, etc., have nearly all been omitted. On the other hand, as far as possible, full references have been given to *Stray Feathers*, the Asiatic Society's *Records*, the Bombay Natural History Society's *Journal*, and other Indian publications.

My thanks are especially due to Mr. Ogilvie-Grant and the Staff of the Bird Section of the British Museum, for the use of the Bird-room and access to the skins therein, as well as for the constant courtesy shown me and help rendered, without which this book could never have been written.

Finally, an apology is due to my readers for the egoism in the whole programme, but it is difficult to avoid this when writing upon a family of birds about which so little has as yet been recorded from a Sportsman's point of view.

E. C. S. B.

CONTENTS.

LIST OF PLATES.

BIBLIOGRAPHY.

The following is a list of the principal works herein referred to, and explains the abbreviations used.

Aitken, Com. B. Bom.	AITKEN (E. H.): *The Common Birds of Bombay*, a reprint of papers published in *The Times of India*.
Ann. Mag. N.H.	*Annals and Magazine of Natural History* (1841–1913).
Barnes, B. Bom.	BARNES (H. D.): *Handbook of the Birds of the Bombay Presidency* (1885).
Blanf., Avi. Brit. I.	BLANFORD (W. T.): *Fauna of British India*, including Ceylon and Burma; Birds, Vols. I–IV (1889–98).
Blanf., E. Persia	BLANFORD (W. T.): *Eastern Persia*; Vols. I and II, Journeys of the Persian Boundary Commission, 1870–71–72 (1876).
Bp., Con. Av.	BONAPARTE (MINEE CHARLES LUCIEN): *Conspectus Generum Avium* (1850–57).
Blyth, Cal. J.N.H.	BLYTH (E.), in the Calcutta *Journal of Natura History* (1841–46).
Blyth, Cat. B.M.A.S.B.	BLYTH'S *Catalogue of the Birds in the Museum of the Asiatic Society* (1849).
Blyth, J.A.S.B.	BLYTH (E.): *Journal of the Asiatic Society of Bengal*, 1832–1913.
Blyth and Wald., B. Burma	BLYTH (E.): *Catalogue of Mammals and Birds of Burma* (1875); reprint from the *Journal of the Asiatic Society of Bengal*.
Briss., Orn.	BRISSON (M. J.): *Ornithologia*, Vols. I–VI (1760).
Everett, J.S.B.A.S.	EVERETT (A.): *Journal Straits Branch of the Royal Asiatic Society*, No. 20 (1889).
Gm., Syst. Nat.	GMELIN: *Systema Naturae* (1788).
Gray, List Gall. B.M.	GRAY (GEORGE ROBERTS): *List of the Specimens of Birds in the Collection of the British Museum*, Part III—Gallinae (1844).
Gray, in Griff. An. Kingd.	GRAY (J. E.) GRIFFIN (E.): *The Animal Kingdom* (1827–35).

Gray, Cat. Hodg. Coll. B.M. 2nd ed.	GRAY (J. E.): *Catalogue of the Specimens and Drawings of Mammals, Birds, Reptiles and Fishes of Nepal and Tibet*, 2nd ed. (1863).
Gray and Hard.	GRAY (J. E.): *Illustrations of Indian Zoology*, chiefly selected from the collection of Major General Hardwicke, Vols. I–XII (1830–34).
Harington, B. Burma	HARINGTON (MAJOR H. H.): *The Birds of Burma* (1909).
Hodg., As. Res.	HODGSON (B. H.): *Asiatic Researches* 1836, *or Transactions of the Society instituted in Bengal for inquiring into the History, the Antiquities, the Arts and Sciences and Literature of Asia.* Vols. I–XX (1785–36).
Hume, Cat.	*Hume's Catalogue of Indian Birds*: a reprint from Vol. VIII of *Stray Feathers*.
Hume, Nests and Eggs	HUME (A. O.): *Nests and Eggs of Indian Birds* (1873–75).
Hume and Hen., Lah. to Yark.	HUME (A. O.) and HENDERSON (G.): *Lahore to Yarkand* (1873).
Jerdon, Ill. Orn.	JERDON (I. C.): *Illustrations of Indian Ornithology* (1847).
Jerdon, B.I.	JERDON (I. C.): *The Birds of India*, Vols. I–III (1862–64).
Jerdon, Madr. J.L.S.	JERDON (I. C.): *Madras Journal of Literature* (1833–64).
J.A.S.B.	*Journal of the Asiatic Society of Bengal* (1832–1913).
J.B.N.H.S.	*Journal of the Bombay Natural History Society*, Vols. I–XXI (1886–1913).
Lath., Ind. Orn.	LATHAM (J.): *Index Ornithologicus* (1790).
Lath., Syn.	LATHAM (J.): *A General Synopsis of Birds* (1781–1885).
Legge, B. Cey.	LEGGE (W. V.): *A History of the Birds of Ceylon* (1878–80).
Linn., Mant.	LINNAEUS (C.): *Mantissa Plantarum* (1771).
Linn, Syst. Nat.	LINNAEUS (C.): *Systema Naturae*, 10th ed. (1758).
Oates, B. Burma	OATES (E. W.): *A Handbook to the Birds of British Burmah* (1883).
Oates, Cat. Eggs B.M.	OATES (E. W.): *Catalogue of the Collection of Birds' Eggs in the British Museum* (1901), I–IV (1901–12).

P.Z.S.	*Proceedings of the Zoological Society of London* (1835–1913).
Proc. N.M.U.S.	*Proceedings of the National Museum, U.S.A.*
Salvadori, Cat. B.M., XXI.	SALVADORI : *Catalogue of the Birds in the British Museum*, Vol. XXI (1893).
Scop., Del. Flor. et Faun. Insubr.	SCOPOLI (J. A.) : *Deliciae Florae et Faunae Insubricae* (1786–88).
Seebohm, B. Jap. Empire	SEEBOHM (H.) : *The Birds of the Japanese Empire* (1890).
Sharpe, Hand-List Birds	SHARPE : *Hand-List of the Genera and Species of Birds*, Vols. I–V (1899–09).
Str. Feath.	*Stray Feathers : A Journal of Ornithology for India and its Dependencies*, Vols. I–XII (1873–99).
Temm., Pig.	*Les Pigeons* : par MADAME KNIPP and C. J. TEMMINCK (1811) (1808–43).
Temm., Pl. Coll.	TEMMINCK (C. J.) et MEIFFREU LAUGIER *Nouveau Recueil de Planches colorées d'Oiseaux*, Vols. I–V (1820–39).
T.Z.S.	*Transactions of the Zoological Society of London*, Vols. I–XX (1855–1913).
Wagl., Sys. Av.	WAGLER (J.) : *Systema Avium.*

ORDER—COLUMBAE.

PIGEONS.

IT IS now an accepted fact amongst naturalists, whether museum or field, that the Pigeons and Doves are more satisfactorily placed in an Order by themselves, than in conjunction with any other of the game-birds.

In their anatomy Pigeons are very closely related to the Gallinaceous birds, and yet more closely to the *Pterocletes*, or Sand-Grouse, though they differ widely from either of these groups in having their young born naked and helpless, a character which has induced some writers to classify them with the *Passeres.* Certain other anatomical characteristics would seem to show their affinity to both the *Strigidae*, (Owls) and the *Vulturidae* (Vultures), greatly as they differ from both of these in general formation, structure, and external appearance.

On the whole their place among Aves would seem to come best next to the *Pterocletes*, where Blanford has located them.

FAMILY COLUMBIDAE.

Salvadori, in Volume XXI of the British Museum *Catalogue of Birds*, divides the Pigeons into five families, but Blanford does not recognize these differentiations as being of so great value, and combines all our Indian birds into one family, though doubtless he would have accepted the *Gouridae* and *Didunculidae* as separate families had he not been dealing with Indian birds only.

The family *Gouridae* contains the magnificent Crown-Pigeons of the Papuan Islands, birds which differ to some extent in internal construction as well as external appearance from other Pigeons, and the *Didunculidae* contains the one small Pigeon *Didunculus strigirostris* of the Samoan Islands.

Salvadori's other three families are the *Treronidae* or "Green Pigeons," which frequent and roost in trees; the *Columbidae* or True

Pigeons, which frequent trees principally, but can also walk and run well; and the *Peristeridae* or Doves, which are much given to walking on the ground. Following Blanford, I unite all Indian Pigeons and Doves in the one family *Columbidae*, which contains the structural features of the Order *Columbae* in so far as that refers to the regions with which we are dealing.

The internal characters are as follows: Palate schizognathous, nostrils schizorhinal; basipterygoid processes present; dorsal vertebrae heterocoelus, cervical vertebrae fifteen in number; sternum with four deep posterior notches, the inner pair of which may be converted into foramina; the external lateral processes are much shorter than the internal; furcula U-shaped. Deep plantar tendons united with a vinculum, the hallux connected with the flexor longus hallucis, and three front toes with the flexor perforans digitorum. Ambiens muscle sometimes present; the femoro-caudal, semitendinosus, accessory semitendinosus, and accessory femoro-caudal all present in Indian species; oil-gland nude or wanting; caeca and gall-bladder sometimes present, sometimes absent; both carotids always present.

The external characteristics are: Upper mandible having the most slender portion posterior to the tip, the basal portion, which contains the nostrils, is covered with a cere or soft skin; the tip is swollen, hard and convex, giving the appearance of having a small knob. The four toes are on the same level, webless, with the hallux or hind toe well developed; the soles are broad, but differ in degree in this respect in different subfamilies, being most greatly expanded in the *Treronidae* or Green Pigeons. Wings aquincubital, with eleven primaries and the fifth secondary wanting, long and pointed with close-set coverts. Spinal feather-tract well defined on the neck and forked on the interscapulary region; after-shaft either not present or only rudimentary.

SUBFAMILIES.

When we come to consider the subfamilies into which our Indian Pigeons are divided, we find that the only difference between the classification of Salvadori and Blanford, is that the former adds two subfamilies, i.e. the *Macropygiinae* and *Turturinae*. The first subfamily Salvadori gives as one of his family *Columbidae*, and the latter as a subfamily of his family *Peristeridae*, whereas Blanford unites both in one subfamily *Columbinae*. This shows well how very artificial the distinctions are upon which naturalists rely in dividing Pigeons into families and subfamilies, for the genus *Macropygia* is far more closely allied in habits, plumage, shape, and everything else to the Doves than to the Pigeons. As Blanford says, "Even the subfamilies of the Pigeons and Doves are founded on distinctions, several of which are not usually regarded as more than generic. It is rather in deference to the usual practice than from conviction of their real existence that some of the following subfamilies are adopted."

For the sportsman and the field-naturalist, the divisions adopted by Blanford are very convenient, and there is no scientific reason against their adoption, even if in every case there is no very scientific reason in their favour. I therefore follow Blanford, and accept his six subfamilies, as given in the fourth volume of the *Avifauna of British India*.

Key to the Subfamilies.

A. Tail of fourteen feathers:
- *a.* No ambiens muscle present:
  - *a′* Oil-gland present ... ... *Treroninae.*
  - *b′* Oil-gland absent ... ... *Geopeliinae.*
- *b.* Ambiens muscle present ... ... *Carpophaginae.*

B. Tail of twelve feathers:
- *c.* Ambiens and oil-gland present; no caeca:
  - *c′* Tarsus longer than middle toe ... ... *Calaenadinae.*
  - *d′* Tarsus moderate ... ... *Phabinae.*
- *d.* Ambiens, oil-gland, and caeca present ... ... *Columbinae.*

The above scientific key, relying as it does almost entirely on anatomic characteristics, may present some difficulties to the sportsman, and the following key to our Indian subfamilies will be easier to work by in the field:—

A. Tail of fourteen feathers:

- *a.* Plumage principally green, with one or two conspicuous yellow bands on the wings; wings always over 5 in. and always under 8.5 in.; soles of feet and toes considerably broadened ... *Treroninae.*
- *b.* Plumage dull, and greyish all over; wings always under 5 in.; soles of feet not much broadened ... ... *Geopeliinae.*
- *c.* Plumage various, but size large and wings always over 8.5 in.; soles of feet not much broadened *Carpophaginae.*

B. Tail of twelve feathers:

- *d.* Long metallic green neck-hackles ... ... *Calaenadinae.*
- *e.* No neck-hackles:
  - *a′* Plumage above dark and metallic-green; bill red; wings under 6 in. ... ... *Phabinae.*
  - *b′* Plumage sometimes glossy and to some extent metallic about neck, but in such cases the wing is over 8 in. The other genera have dull plumage with no gloss anywhere ... *Columbinae.*

SUBFAMILY TRERONINAE.

This subfamily is very well represented in India, no less than five out of its seven genera being found within our limits. All five of these cenera contain what are generally known in India as "Green Pigeons"—gomparatively small Pigeons which may be known at a glance by their beautifully soft green plumage, often mixed with maroon or lilac on the shoulders or back, and always with one, and sometimes with two, bold yellow bars across the wings. By ear, too, these lovely birds may always be identified as belonging to the *Treroninae*, their musical whistling-call being quite unlike the coo of any Dove or Pigeon of other groups.

The birds of this subfamily are typically perchers, living almost entirely on the fruit of large trees, and they have the soles of their feet curiously broad, being a great deal wider than the toes above. The tarsi are short and stout, and are covered with densly growing short feathers on the upper part in front.

The genera, which again are to a great extent employed as a matter of convenience rather than of anatomical necessity, are fairly easily divisible by simple characteristics in outward form.

Key to the Genera.

A. A deep notch in inner web of third primary; tail neither greatly graduated nor with central tail-feathers prolonged:

a. Horny part of bill does not extend along culmen to edge of feathers of fore-head:

a′ First three primaries acuminate, legs yellow ... *Crocopus.*

b′ First three primaries not acuminate; legs red:

a″ Horny part of bill less than two-thirds of culmen ... ... *Osmotreron.*

b″ Horny part of bill more than two-thirds of culmen ... ... *Butreron.*

b. Horny part of bill extends along the culmen to the feathers of fore-head ... ... *Treron.*

B. Inner web of third primary with no notch; tail much graduated and lengthened ... ... *Sphenocercus.*

Genus CROCOPUS.

This genus contains but one species which is, however, easily divisible into three geographical subspecies with well-defined characteristics which overlap no more than such characteristics generally do where the respective ranges meet.

This genus, with the exception of *Butreron*, is the largest of our Indian "Green Pigeons," having a wing of about 7.5 in., whereas none of the others exceed 7 in., and some are under 6. It is also, in one form or another, the most widespread, being found throughout the greater part of the countries with which we are now dealing.

A very distinctive feature of this bird is its yellow legs and feet, all our other species of this subfamily having red legs and feet.

Key to the Subspecies.

A. Breast yellow; abdomen grey; upper tail-coverts and base of tail both yellowish and not contrasting... *C. ph. phoenicopterus.*

B. Yellow of fore-head extended to crown; upper tail-coverts grey contrasting with yellowish base of tail *C. ph. viridifrons.*

C. Under-parts unicoloured yellow; tail-feathers with very little or no trace of yellowish-green... ... ... *C. ph. chlorogaster.*

(1) CROCOPUS PHOENICOPTERUS PHOENICOPTERUS.

THE BENGAL GREEN PIGEON.

Columba phoenicoptera Lath., Ind. Orn., II p. 597 (1790).
Columba militaris (part) Temm., Pig., pt. I (1808).
Columba hardwickii Gray, in Griff. An. Kingd., VIII (1829).
Treron phoenicoptera Blyth, J.A.S.B., XIV p. 849; id., Cat. B.M., p. 229; Gray, Cat. Hodg. Coll. B.M., 2nd ed. p. 66.
Crocopus phoenicopterus Jerdon, B.I., III p. 447; Godw.-Aus., J.A.S.B., XXXIX pt. II p. 272; Str. Feath., I p. 390; Ball, ib., II p. 432; Hume, Nests and Eggs, p. 491; id., Cat. no. 772; id., Str. Feath., IV p. 2; Cripps, ib., VII p. 296; Scully, ib., VIII p. 339; Oates, in Hume's Nests and Eggs, 2nd ed., II p. 370; Salvadori, Cat. B.M., XXI p. 20; Blanf., Avi. Brit. I., IV p. 5; Sharpe, Hand-List Birds, I p. 153; Oates, Cat. Eggs B.M., I p. 81; Stuart Baker, J.B.N.H.S., X p. 63; id. ib., XIII p. 568; Inglis, ib., XIV p. 561; Stuart Baker, ib., XVII p. 970.

Vernacular Names. *Harial* H.; *Haitha* or *Bor Haitha*, Assamese; *Daorep gadeba*, Cachari; *Inruigu*, Naga.

Description.—*Adult male.* Fore-head as far back as the eye, lores, chin, and throat greenish-yellow; from fore-head to the nape and including the upper part of cheeks and ear-coverts ash-grey, changing on the neck to bright chrome, following which comes a band of grey, purer and brighter than the crown. Remainder of the upper-plumage including wing-coverts and innermost secondaries olive-green, with a strong tinge of yellow; upper tail-coverts the same but sometimes tinged with grey. Tail above, grey with a broad basal band of olive-yellow, contrasting strongly with the rest of the tail though not with the upper tail-coverts; the outermost tail-feathers hardly show this band on the outer-web, and on the inner-web each pair of feathers has the yellow decreasing in extent towards the outermost. Below, the rather greenish-yellow of the throat runs into a purer king's-yellow on the breast; lower-breast, flanks, and abdomen grey; the tibial feathers, the centre of the abdomen, and patches about the vent yellow, and the thighs and long flank-feathers covering them, with deep green-grey centres and pale whitish fringes; under tail-coverts deep purple-chestnut, with broad whitish bands at the end of each feather; under aspect of tail grey with a broad black band at base nearly concealed by the tail-coverts.

A band of lilac-purple on the innermost smaller wing-coverts; greater wing-coverts and secondaries boldly edged with pale yellow, forming a bar on the closed wing, running from near the edge of the shoulder to the end of the longest secondary; primaries dark brown, edged with yellow, the inner changing to the same colour as the back; bastard-wing black and the greater-coverts next the yellow edging, dark brown.

Bill, very pale bluish- or greenish-white, the cere more strongly tinged with this colour than the rest of the upper mandible; lower mandible sometimes darker at the base; legs and feet bright chrome-yellow, sometimes almost orange-yellow, but never red or pink; iris with two rings of colour, the inner blue and the outer ranging from pink to bright crimson.

Length about 13 to 14 in. (= 330 to 355 mm.); wing 7.25 to 7.80 in. (= 184 to 200 mm.), average of sixty-three birds 7.42 in. (= 188.4 mm.); tail about 4.5 in. (= 114.3) varying a good deal in length; bill at front about .75 (=19.0 mm.) or a little over, and from gape a little over 1 in. (=25.4 mm.); tarsus about 1 in. (= 25.4 mm.).

Young males of the year have the colour of the plumage rather less vivid, and the lilac-purple of the wing-coverts absent until after the first moult. They also average a good deal smaller, with a wing often as little as 7 in. (= 177.8 mm.) and seldom over 7.2 in. (= 182.8 mm.).

Adult female. The female only differs from the male in degree of colouring, and a brightly-coloured female cannot be distinguished from a young or dully-coloured male. As a rule the lilac on the wing is less in extent and duller in colour; the definition between the grey of the abdomen and the yellow of the breast is not so clear; the under tail-coverts also have the chestnut paler and less in extent and sometimes mixed with dark grey, whilst the pale edges are correspondingly broader.

Length from 12 to 13 in. (= 304.8 to 330 mm.) with a wing of 7.1 to 7.32 in. (= 180.3 to 185.9 mm.), the average of forty birds being 7.23 in. (= 173.6 mm.). The bill, tarsus and tail are all proportionately slightly smaller than in the male.

Distribution. The Bengal Green Pigeon is found throughout Bengal and Behar up to the Himalayas and into Nepal, Sikkim, and Bhutan; west it extends throughout the United Provinces and Oudh as far west as the Jumna, and Butler (*Stray Feathers*, IV) records it from Gujerat. It occurs in Central India and also in northern Orissa, but in the south of these presidencies it is replaced by *chlorogaster*, being found together with that form over much of its north-western range. To the extreme north-east it extends as far as Sadiya in Assam, birds from Dibrugarh, both north and south of the Brahmapootra, being typical *phoenicopterus*. In the Naga Hills, Khasia, and north Cachar Hills, we still get fairly typical *phoenicopterus*, with here and there a bird more like *viridifrons*, but south of these ranges we find it overlaps with the eastern form; birds from south Cachar, Hylakandy and Sylhet being more or less intermediate though nearer *viridifrons* than *phoenicopterus*, whilst birds from Chittagong are typical specimens of the former subspecies.

Nidification. Green Pigeons are early breeders and commence to build very early in March, laying in the end of that month, and continuing to do so up to June, whilst I have also known eggs laid occasionally as late as the end of August. Their courtship, with its attendant attitudes and "showing off," is much the same as that of the domestic and all other Pigeons, but as far as has been recorded hitherto, the attitudinizing never takes place on the ground. The male bird puffs out his throat and breast, lowers his wings, and ruffles out his feathers—and then prances solemnly up and down a branch, continually bowing his head and whistling softly as he makes his way backwards and forwards, to and from the lady he imagines he is captivating. Unlike most birds, the female does seem occasionally to admire the display of the male and, if not feeding, will sometimes respond to the extent of warbling out a few liquid notes and doing a minor "skirt-dance" on her own account.

The nest is a typical Pigeon's nest of twigs placed criss-cross over one another, but very lightly intertwined, and always looking as if they would fall to pieces with the slightest excuse. They are, however, a good deal stronger than they look, and in spite of the exposed position in which they are so often placed, can stand a good deal of wind and shaking before they do actually come to grief. Generally the nests are placed in small trees and saplings at no great height from the ground, and, as a rule, on a horizontal branch, or a collection of such branches. Sometimes, however, large trees are selected for nesting purposes, and several observers have noticed its predilection for the mango tree. Hume found two in these trees in Etawah, and Captain Cock also writes that it, "Makes a rough stick nest, rather high up, usually in a Mango tree. The nest is of the usual type, but frequently placed on an excrescence, or where some parasitic plant shoots out and thickens the foliage, so as to render the bird more difficult to be seen."

Rarely the bird builds its nest in a clump of bamboos, and in such cases it may be very well concealed.

These Pigeons are extraordinarily close sitters, and when their eggs are approaching hatching will sit on them until the intruder is within a yard or two of the nest. They seem to be companionable during the breeding-season, and more than one writer has mentioned finding two or three nests in close proximity. Inglis records in the *Bombay Journal*: "I have found three nests on the same tree, and have often found nests on trees close to one another." The same writer also reports having found three eggs in one nest, and in another nest a quite fresh egg and one on the point of hatching.

The eggs take, I believe, fourteen days to hatch. I have notes of having found a nest with one egg on the 3rd of April, and a second on the 4th, and when I returned to the same place fifteen days later the nest contained two young, apparently about a day old.

The number of eggs laid is invariably two, and they are, of course, pure white. In shape they are broader ovals than the egg of the true Pigeon and the Ring- and Turtle-Doves, but they vary somewhat in this respect. Typically they are broad ovals, but little compressed at either end, and with two ends sub-equal. Abnormal eggs tend to be rather elongated ovals, and more rarely still, to a somewhat peg-top shape.

The surface is very smooth and shiny, if I may use this expression, rather than with the hard gloss of the Woodpecker's egg. The texture is very fine and close, with a surface silky to the touch, and the shell is stout and not brittle. The inner membrane is as pure a white as the outside shell.

The average of nearly 100 eggs is 1.24 in. (= 31.8 mm.) by .96 (= 24.4 mm.).

My largest egg is 1.38 in. (= 35 mm.) by 1.03 (= 26.1 mm.), but my smallest is not so small as that recorded by Hume, i.e. 1.12 in. by .90 (= 28.44 mm. by 22.86).

The Bengal Green Pigeon is a bird of hill and level land, of forest, scrub, or plains, but it does not care for mountains of great height, and the barer plains must have an inducement, in the shape of scattered fruit trees of some sort, before he will take to them. Thus I have found him haunting the interior of forests where one may wander for days without meeting anything more civilized than a tiger or a barking deer, and, on the other hand, I have had fine shooting at these birds as they scuttled headlong from one banyan tree (*Ficus indica*) to another in the heart of a big military cantonment.

To some extent, however, their haunts are governed by the seasons of the year. During the breeding-season they are seldom found near the habitation of man, unless by man one refers to the wilder dwellers of the hills and jungles; but once their young are fledged and on the wing, they will be found anywhere where food is plentiful. Even the seasons, however, do not completely cut them off from civilization, for they have been found breeding in the Botanical Gardens in Calcutta, and a few may always be met with about the better wooded surroundings of Barakpore and Serampore.

Although, however, it may be found in many hilly districts and, indeed, up to some height in the foot-hills of the Himalayas, it is, on the whole, more a Plains Pigeon than a mountain one. In North Cachar and the Naga Hills it is only to be met with below 2,000 ft. and is rare even at that height, whereas in the broken ground where the hills and plains meet, it is decidedly more plentiful. In the Khasia Hills it has been shot, as a straggler only, up to 4,000 ft., and it is found all along the Terai in the foot-hills, and in the Darjeeling districts ascends as high as in the Khasia Hills, though, here again, only in exceptional cases. In Nepal, Scully found it common in winter at Nawakot, at about 2,200 ft. elevation, but he did not find it at any time in the higher hills surrounding that valley. It must be noted also that Nawakot, though fairly elevated and well inside the Himalayas, is said by Scully to be very hot, damp, and well covered by forest, and to contain many banyan and pepul trees.

In their favourite country, such as is composed of a certain amount of forest and scrub mixed with patches of cultivation and grass or bare land, their numbers do not seem to vary much all the year round, and they merely move locally according to where the supply of food is for the time being most plentiful. Thus in Chutia Nagpur, in the districts of Ranchi and Hazaribagh, they are always to be met with, provided one knows where to find their prevalent food growing. It was in the former of these two districts that I, personally, first made aquaintance with these most beautiful birds. A scattered Santhali village lay along the base of a rocky hill; houses of thatch and bamboo being dotted here and there upon the stony bare soil, but almost completely screened the one from the others by magnificent specimens of pepul (*Ficus religiosa*) and the banyan. Here and there were little patches of cultivation, and down below in the valley was a waving sea of young rice, the tender pale green glinting and swaying in the sunlight, when the breeze played on its surface as on water.

After a long morning's shooting we were lounging about in the shade of a clump of mango trees, just finishing a well-earned lunch, when I heard the most beautiful soft whistling coming from some pepul trees near by. Asking my older companions what the musical bird was, I was told, to my astonishment, that they were Green Pigeons. Jumping up, I at once went to the trees whence the sound proceeded, and for some minutes listened in silence: it was like that of a schoolboy whistling under his breath a succession of soft mellow calls, with no tune, yet full of melody. The sounds rose and fell, now high, now low, yet ever soft and sweet, and so ventriloquistic that I found it impossible to locate the singer. At last a movement amongst the leaves showed me where the bird was sitting, but so perfectly did its green and yellow plumage harmonize with its surroundings, that once my eyes were withdrawn and the bird quiescent, it was with the greatest difficulty I could again discover it. When I did find it I fired and brought down, not only the bird I aimed at, but two others of whose presence in that spot I was quite unaware. Frightened by the report, some ten or twelve others flew from the tree, but a shot fired after them only hastened their movements. My admiration for the beauty of their plumage was no greater than my respect for their wonderful flight, and though I was then a fair shot at snipe, jungle and spur-fowl, etc., it was some time before I could realize the speed of this bird, and induce myself to shoot forward enough. Their flight is marvellously quick, and they go at a great pace from the start, in addition to which the way a flock of these birds alter their elevation as they fly is very disconcerting to a beginner.

Over the greater portion of their range, Green Pigeons are hardly considered game-birds, and sportsmen seldom take the trouble to actually work them up and obtain bags of Pigeons alone. In Bengal Burma, and the Assam Valley, however, Green Pigeon rank very high as game-birds, and much trouble is taken in the proper organization and arrangements for shoots, at which these birds alone form the objects of the sport. Full worthy, too, are they of the trouble spent upon them, for no greater variety of shots is obtainable; no quicker shooting or straighter powder is required, than for the successful shooting and gathering of a big bag of these birds.

The Bengal Green Pigeon, the largest of these lovely birds, is in Assam greatly outnumbered by some of its smaller cousins. Once, however, I shot over thirty couple of Green Pigeon, of which all but two were of the present species, and on another occasion Mr. C. Lawes and I shot twenty-one couple in less than an hour one evening, after returning from a long day's buffalo-shooting in north Lahkimpur.

On this occasion we were riding home on our elephants, when we saw two or three flights of Green Pigeon making for some trees close to the path we were following. As we were near home we decided to get off and shoot one or two for the pot; so down we got and took up our stands some hundred yards or so distant from, and on either side of, the trees which formed the attraction. Within a few minutes we were both hard at work, and in about half an hour, when cartridges gave out, we had each twenty-one birds to our credit.

The shooting was very pretty, and nearly every shot seemed different from the rest. First a few birds would suddenly sweep up into sight, flying low over a belt of bushes in front of us, and going as if the next second would bring them into us; then, at the last moment, with a turn and a twist, they would rise higher into the air and flash by at the rate of sixty miles an hour. The next flock, perhaps, would come into sight far away, and give the impression that they were going to offer easy shots directly overhead, but before coming into range they would suddenly dip in their flight and scurry past us, a few feet from the ground. Then a single bird, or a pair of them, would give a glimpse of themselves as they slipped past between the bigger trees, instead of following the other birds into the more open ground; others, yet again, would come high overhead, but straight on, and offer the most satisfactory rights and lefts possible. Sometimes a bird would flash past from behind us, and skim out of sight before we realized that it had come; but, as a rule, all the birds came from the same direction. My bag of thirty odd couple of Bengal Green Pigeons was made in the same place as these twenty-one couple, but the birds were not quite so numerous, and my shooting lasted from about 4 p.m., when the birds began to come, until sudden dusk made it too dark to see, and the last few birds came and went in peace.

This curious habit of flighting between their feeding-grounds and their roosting or resting-places seems to be common to all Green Pigeons, especially where they are very numerous. Sunrise, as a rule, finds all birds on the wing coming steadily in one direction—towards the jungle or clumps of trees upon which they are intent upon feeding and for an hour or two they will come thick and fast; then the birds, unless they have been too disturbed to feed, begin to work back to the ground where they rest during the heat of the day; but the return journey is never as continuous or as steady as is the first journey in the morning. When the heat of the mid-day sun begins to lessen—any time between three and four—the birds once more flight to their feeding-grounds, not returning in the evening to roost until dusk begins to fall, and then, as far as I have been able to ascertain, always returning by some circuitous route and not by that which they have come by.

The regularity with which, year after year, at exactly the same season, and for exactly the same period, Green Pigeons flight over certain country, is most remarkable. Equally curious is the punctuality displayed as regards their coming and going, and, provided their food-trees are not destroyed, one may count almost to a certainty on seeing each year the first flights in the same week in the same month, at the same time of day, and flying from and to the same direction. Of course, if the trees upon the fruit of which the birds feed are cut down, the following year a few flocks may turn up for a day or two to seek their food, and then the place is deserted for good and all.

One of the prettiest pieces of shooting I have seen with these birds, was one which entailed the dropping of all birds within the narrow area of a high embankment, on which ran a road through swamps covered with dense cane-brakes. On either side of the embankment grew high forest-trees, by which the birds were screened from view until just as they topped them, so that a belated shot, if effective, sent the bird falling straight into the swamp behind, where the dense and prickly canes prevented all attempt to retrieve it. Equally, a hasty shot fired at a bird one had the luck to spot earlier than usual, lost it to the shooter in the swamp in front.

Shooting one day on this embankment my host, the late Mr. F. Holder, brought down sixteen birds in succession, many of these being rights and lefts, and all the birds killed fell, I believe, upon the embankment itself. My own shooting, alas, was rewarded by many splashes in the water behind and by one or two in front, but fall on land these contrary Pigeons would not, and at the end of the afternoon's shoot I had gathered five birds to my companion's thirty or forty. The plumage of all Pigeons, especially perhaps of Green Pigeons, is very dense and close in proportion to their size, and they take a lot of hitting to bring them down clean; more particularly so when the shooter is forced to fire at them coming towards him. The size of shot generally used is No. 7, but many use No. 6 and a few No. 5. This latter is, however, too large, and does not give as good an average as Nos. 6 or 7. Personally I always used the latter, and found this shot, with a full charge of one's favourite powder, whatever that may be, and a choke or semi-choke 16-bore, gave the best all-round results.

The Bengal Green Pigeon does not, as a rule, collect in very large flocks—some eight to a dozen birds form the majority of flocks—but others of twenty or even thirty may occasionally be met with. In their favourite feeding-haunts when the fig trees are in fruit, several flocks often collect on the same tree, and in such circumstances I should think I have seen sixty birds on one tree. These, however, though at the first alarm they all go off together, soon split up into their component parts. Sometimes single birds or pairs may be met with in the non-breeding season, but they are very sociable, and where this particular species is rare, I have often seen it associating with other Green Pigeons and keeping with them as they moved from one spot to another. In spite of their fondness for society they are, all the same, very quarrelsome birds—a characteristic, it is to be feared, of nearly all the "gentle" dove tribe. They are not so bad, however, in this respect as the true Pigeons, and can be kept in some numbers together in a cage, provided it is large enough. I had five or six pairs once in quite a small aviary, about 6 ft. by 8 and about 6 ft. high, and here they lived quite amicably, seldom fighting except over what they conceived to be the finest nesting-places.

Pigeons are greedy drinkers, drinking as everyone knows by burying their bills in the water and taking long draughts without withdrawing them. The hill-tribes firmly believe that Green Pigeons never come on to the ground to drink, but climb down creepers hanging over the water, or down reeds growing in it, until they are close enough over to bend down and drink. It is not correct, however, to say that they never descend to the ground to drink, as I have myself seen them thus drinking, and have shot them as they rose. At the same time I have also often seen them drinking by climbing down overhanging canes and bushes until they were near enough to reach the water, and this latter manner of drinking is, perhaps, that most often resorted to. An interesting experiment with my cage-birds seemed to prove that the birds preferred drinking thus, and did not do so merely because there was no bare ground near to the water convenient to drink from. The birds referred to were supplied with wide shallow pans from which to drink, and when split bamboos, with one end resting in the water and the other slanting up to the perches, were placed in the aviary, it was found that more birds crept down the bamboos to drink than came right down on to the ground for this purpose.

The belief of the hill-tribes in north-eastern India, which has been above referred to, is curiously supplemented by Cripp's note in the seventh volume of *Stray Feathers*, where he writes that the natives of Furredpore in eastern Bengal "say that whenever this bird descends to the water's edge for a drink it holds a twig in its claws; it prides itself on living altogether on trees, and in order that it may not be accused of perching on the ground when it descends to drink, brings down with it a twig to stand on."

They are greatly prized as cage-birds in India, being regularly exposed for sale in the Chiretta Bazaar in Calcutta; but though they whistle freely in captivity, and are not difficult to keep, they soon get rather dishevelled in appearance, especially when, as is generally the case, they are confined in bamboo cages so small that their tails constantly rub against the bars, and get very frayed and dirty. Captive birds are fed principally on plantains and *suttoo*, a mixture of meal and water, but a native bird-fancier told me that he had to vary this diet with dry grain and boiled rice, and also that he gave his birds practically any fruit which happened to be in season. Of fruit, however, the favourite seemed to be the jamans—a kind of wild plum—the fruit of the ber tree, and any kind of fig, such as pepul, banyan, etc.

I never heard of anyone succeeding in getting them to breed in an aviary, or even to nest, though, as in my own case, they always grew very quarrelsome in the breeding-season, and would often spend a long time trying to balance twigs in quite impossible positions. Nesting-sites, such as branches or boards put in convenient positions for them, never seemed to catch their fancy, and they appeared infinitely to prefer trying to make a foundation of twigs on a perch, which, invariably blew or tumbled off before it had advanced far enough to be of any use.

They are great climbers, and if one is fortunate enough to get under a tree upon which they are feeding, without being noticed, he will see them clambering about from branch to branch, and from one twig to another, often leaning over to seize some special tit-bit, until they appear to be standing on their heads. They are not very shy birds, and many a time have I watched them for half an hour until some awkward movement of mine, or a sound of some kind, has startled them. Once frightened they all immediately sink into absolute silence, trusting to the way their green plumage and the green leaves blend to preserve them from molestation. Naturally, when much shot at, they soon become wild, and then the would-be observer must be quiet indeed if he can steal under a tree upon which they are feeding without driving them headlong out of it. Yet sometimes, even when a good deal fired at, they show great persistence in the way they cling to one place, or one set of trees, and it may take several evenings shooting before they finally make up their minds that the place is too hot for them. I remember one tree at which these birds continued to feed for some six or eight evenings and mornings, although they were more or less shot at every evening, and once or twice in the mornings as well. In this case the tree was an enormous single wild-plum standing isolated from all jungle in the middle of a tea-garden, and so lofty that the top of the tree was quite beyond shot. At first the birds fed all over this tree, and flighted into it quite low down, giving excellent shots as they approached; but the last day or two they altered their tactics, and arriving out of shot high overhead plunged into the tree at the very summit, and were off again like a flash when some unwise bird, flying lower than the rest, tempted us to have a shot.

Swift as the flight of these birds undoubtedly is, it is not perhaps as quick as some of its smaller relations, such as *Treron nepalensis* and *Osmotreron phayrei*, but it is decidely faster than either of our Indian species of *Sphenocercus*. I have often noticed that, after firing several consecutive shots at the Bengal Green Pigeon, I was inclined to shoot behind the smaller birds unless I remembered this fact.

All Green Pigeons have the habit of clapping their wings over their backs when first taking to flight, and it may sometimes be heard when the birds dip in their flight and then suddenly rise again. Always, I believe, it is to be heard just as the birds commence to rise and not, as with domestic Pigeons, at other times of their flight; also, in the Green Pigeon, the sound is not so startlingly loud as it is when made by the birds of the genera *Columba* and *Turtur*.

The food of the Bengal Green Pigeon is, of course, entirely vegetarian, and principally frugivorous, and above all it seems to delight in the fruit of the various species of *Ficus*. The gapes of all Pigeons are large for the size of the bird, besides being soft and very elastic, otherwise it would be almost incredible the size of the fruit they can swallow. Plums and similar hard fruit they swallow whole, and often these are as large as the bird's head, only two or three being containable in the crop at the same time. Larger and soft fruit, such as figs, they tear to pieces, pulling off great lumps which they swallow whole. They are very greedy, and their digestion is extremely rapid, so that they are able to indulge their appetite, and the amount these birds will eat is enormous. In confinement they consume almost any sort of grain, and I once shot a pair out of an Indian cornfield whose crops were full of the ripe, but still soft, maize. Whether these birds were feeding on the ground or not, it was impossible to say, but probably they were climbing about on the maize stems and tearing the grains from the growing cobs, though there were at the time a good many of these latter lying on the ground.

My birds in captivity ate plantains greedily and would also eat the inside of oranges, invariably picking out the pips first before eating the fleshy part. Peaches and apricots they also ate, swallowing even the stone—kernel, shell and all, complete. In addition to fruit and grain they also ate a certain amount of green food such as lettuce, and once I saw a bird pulling some green shoots of rice which had just sprouted up in the corner of the aviary. They were also partial to bread and milk.

(2) CROCOPUS PHOENICOPTERUS VIRIDIFRONS (Blyth).

THE BURMESE GREEN PIGEON.

(PLATE 1.)

Treron viridifrons Blyth, J.A.S.B., XIV pt. 2 p. 849 (1845); id. ib., XXIV p. 479; Godw.-Aust., ib., XXXIX p. iii.
Crocopus viridifrons Jerdon, B.I., III p. 449; Hume, Str. Feath., II p. 481; id. ib., III p. 161; Blyth and Wald., B. Burma, p. 143; Godw.-Aust., J.A.S.B., LXIV p. 83; Oates, Str. Feath., V p. 163; Hume and Dav., ib., VI p. 410; Hume, ib., VIII p. 109; Bingh., ib., IX p. 194; Hume and Ing., ib., p. 257; Oates, ib., X p. 235; id., B. Burma, II p. 307; Hume, Str. Feath., XI p. 290; Salvadori, Cat. B.M., XXI p. 28; Sharpe, Hand-List, I p. 153; Stuart Baker, J.B.N.H.S., X p. 363.
Crocopus phoenicopterus (part), Blanf., Avi. Brit. I., IV p. 5; Harington, B. Burma, p. 117; Oates (part), Cat. B.M., I p. 81; Primrose, J.B.N.H.S., XIII p. 78; Macdonald, ib., XVII p. 495; Mears and Oates, ib., XVIII p. 86; Harington, ib., XIX p. 308; id. ib., p. 365.

Vernacular Names. *Ngu Bom-ma-di,* Burmese; *Daorep Gadeba,* Cachari; *Inruigu,* Naga.

Description.—*Adult male.* Differs from *C. ph. phoenicopterus* in having the yellow of the fore-head running back as far as the back of the crown, and generally a good deal brighter than in that bird; the greater part of the cheeks and also the major portion of the ear-coverts are of the same yellowish-green. The upper tail-coverts, on the other hand, are more grey than they are in *phoenicopterus*, and contrast strongly with the yellow band on the tail.

Colours of soft parts are the same as in the western form, and the dimensions are the same.

Adult female. Differs from the male in the same way, and to the same extent as the female of *C. ph. phoenicopterus* differs from its male.

Distribution. The range of this subspecies extends over northern Burma and the hill-ranges of north-east Burma, south-east into Cochin China, and as far south as Moulmein. To the west it extends through Arrakan, Cox's Bazaar into Chittagong and the Chittagong hill-tracts. I have seen no specimens from Comilla, but Sylhet birds and those from the plains of Cachar are intermediate between *phoenicopterus* and *viridifrons*, most birds being nearer the latter, and birds occasionally being obtained which are typical *viridifrons*.

Everywhere north of the Surrma Valley hill-ranges and west of the big rivers running into the Bay of Bengal, only *phoenicopterus* is met with.

In his *Birds of Burma*, Harington says that this Pigeon is common from north to south everywhere except on Mount Victoria, and that it is

THE BURMESE GREEN PIGEON—*CROCOPUS PH. VIRIDIFRONS.*

(¼ Nat. Size.)

PLATE I

the only Pigeon he has met with in the dry zone, where, however, it is certainly plentiful.

Nidification. So far there is nothing on record about the breeding of this bird, except the notes in *Nests and Eggs* by Oates and Bingham. The former writes: "One egg was brought me by my collector with the female bird. It was found in April, and there were two eggs. The nest was reported to have been placed in a bamboo at a good height up one of the branches." Bingham records: "I have only come across this fine Pigeon in the Thaungyeen Valley. It is not uncommon on the banks of the Meplay, where I found a nest as detailed below.

"At the place where the Hteechara-choung flows into the Meplay stands a grand ficus tree, which in March is loaded with fruit, and is the resort of Hornbills, Pigeons, Barbets, and innumerable other birds. On the 16th of the above month I found, in a small ziziphus tree (*Ziziphus jujuba*) growing about twenty yards from this ficus, a nest of this Pigeon containing two pure white eggs slightly set. The nest was the usual careless few twigs laid across and across, and was not more than twelve feet from the ground. I shot the female as she flew off. The eggs measured 1.23 in. by 0.90 and 1.22 by 0.81."

Like most Green Pigeons they are very close sitters, and are hard to drive away from their nests even before the eggs begin to be incubated, and when the eggs are very hard set, or the young recently hatched, they will often sit until almost touched by the intruder. Harington remarks on this *in epistola*: "I have only taken two nests, both at Taunygyi during April. The first was placed about ten feet up a small bushy tree growing on the side of a steep hill, so that one could look into the nest from a very few yards off. The old bird sat very tight, and as she was required for identification I had a shot at her head, knocking it clean off, so that it hit my orderly who was standing below: and for the moment he thought that I had missed the bird and shot him instead. The nest contained one egg, the pair to which was taken from the bird when the orderly was preparing the latter for his dinner."

I have taken a fair number of eggs of this subspecies, and except that I have found several in bamboo-clumps, and one or two in cane-brakes, there is nothing to record about them that would not apply to nests of *ph. phoenicopterus*. The nests in the cane-brakes were about five or six feet from the ground, or rather from the surface of the water over which they hung. The nests in the bamboo-clumps were about the same height up, and well hidden amongst the numerous twigs and branches which then covered the clumps.

Eggs sent me by my native collector from Tennasserim were said to have been taken from small trees or bamboo clumps. The latter were all in fairly thick jungle, and it is possible that *viridifrons*, over part of its range, is rather more consistently a forest-bird than *phoenicopterus* which breeds alike in the open, in forest, or in mango topes, and other clumps of trees.

The eggs cannot be discriminated from those of *C. ph. phoenicopterus*, being of the usual broad oval shape, or broad elliptical, pure, soft white, with smooth surface and close texture. The eggs in my collection average 1.24 by .98 in. (= 31.8 by 24.9 mm).

In habits, flight, voice, etc., this bird does not in any way differ from the other subspecies. Oates says (*Stray Feath.*, Vol. III): "This species is common throughout the plains . . . I have never received it from the Pegu Hills, nor from those of Arracan. It is essentially a bird of the plains, as *Osmotreron phayrei* is of the hills." Davison, in the fifth volume of the same work, records that: "It has all the habits of the other Green Pigeons, and like them, is very noisy and quarrelsome when feeding . . . the note is similar to that of *Treron nepalensis*; it is broader and more rolling."

Harington, describing its occurrence in the dry zone in Upper Burma, writes to me: "Its well-known whistling call can generally be heard round almost every village and *Phonygi Kyoung* during the early morning, so that one can always be sure of bagging one or two of these Green Pigeons when needed for the pot. It is, again, extremely plentiful in the open valleys of the Shan States, at an elevation of some 2,000 ft., being very partial to the ficus and pepul trees which are plentiful near villages and bazaars in these parts.

"I have never noticed them in thick or dense jungle, where their place seems to be taken by *O. phayrei* and *bisincta*, they have, however, been recorded from all parts of Burma.

"When the berries of the ficus and pepul are ripe large numbers congregate, and very fair shooting can be got by finding out their line of flight, as when disturbed at one set of feeding places, they generally take the same route to some other favourite trees."

(3) CROCOPUS PHOENICOPTERUS CHLOROGASTER (Blyth).

THE SOUTHERN GREEN PIGEON.

Vinago chlorogaster Blyth, J.A.S.B., XII, 1st part, p. 167 (1843).
Treron jerdoni Strik., Ann. Mag. N.H., XIII p. 38.
Treron chlorigaster Blyth, J.A.S.B., XIV p. 850; id., Cat. B.M.A.S.B., p. 229.
Crocopus chlorogaster Bp., Con. Av., II p. 12; Adam, Str. Feath., I p. 390; Salvadori, Cat. B.M., XXI p. 30; Blanf., Avi. Brit. I., IV p. 6; Sharpe, Hand-List, I p. 853; Oates, Cat. Eggs B.M., I p. 81; Dewar, J.B.N.H.S., XVI p. 494; Martin Young, ib., p. 514; Moss King, ib., XXI p. 98; Pitman, ib., XXII. p. 194; Aitken, Com. B. Burma, p. 153.
Crocopus chlorigaster Jerdon, B.I., III p. 448; Blanf., J.A.S.B., XXXVIII pt. II p. 187; Ball, Str. Feath., II p. 423; Butler, ib., IV p. 2; Hume, ib.; Fairbank, ib., p. 261; Hume, Nests and Eggs, III p. 492; Fairbank, Str. Feath., V p. 408; Ball, ib., VII p. 224; Murray, ib., p. 113; Hume, Cat. no. 773; id., Str. Feath., VIII., p. 109; Vidal, ib., IX p. 73; Legge, B. Cey., p. 722; Reid, Str. Feath., X p. 58; Davidson, ib., p. 314; Davison, ib., p. 406, Taylor, ib., p. 463; Barnes, B. Bom., 285; id., J.B.N.H.S., V p. 328; Oates, in Nests and Eggs, 2nd ed., II p. 372; Davidson, J.B.N.H.S., XII p. 61.

Vernacular Names. *Harial*, Hin.; *Pacha Gawa*, Tel.; *Pacha pora*, Tam.

Description.—*Adult male.* Differs from *Crocopus ph. phoenicopterus* in having the under-parts practically unicoloured, from chin to vent, yellow; the fore-head shows no green at all, or has this confined merely to the edge of the bill; the lores and the whole of the side of the head are grey unmixed with green and the grey often encroaches on to the sides of the chin and throat; there is no basal band of green on the upper part of the tail, though some birds may have a tinge of this colour upon the outer webs at the base of the central rectrices.

The female differs from the male in the same way as does that of *phoenicopterus* and *viridifrons*.

The size and colour of the soft parts are the same as in the two other subspecies.

Distribution. The Southern Green Pigeon has the widest distribution of the three subspecies, for it is found throughout the whole of southern India and Ceylon, whilst north it extends through Central India and Madras and throughout Orissa, but it is replaced by *C. ph. phoenicopterus* in south Bengal, though here a few birds are intermediate between the two. Further west in Behar, the Southern Green Pigeon is still common in the south, but less so in central Behar, and is entirely replaced by the Bengal form in the north.

Inglis has specimens from Behar which cannot be referred decidedly to either race, and Ball, writing from Lucknow, says: "Most of my specimens belong to the latter species (*chlorogaster*) if it is really a species distinct from *phoenicopterus*, which I am almost tempted to doubt."

Further west and north it extends through Rajputana and the Punjab, except in the extreme west, and through the United Provinces, well into the foot-hills of the Himalayas.

Like the other subspecies this also is more of a plains than a mountain bird, but it has been recorded from the Palnis, Shevaroys, and Neilgherries. Davidson says that it is not common in Kanara, but that it is found there, and that he has taken nests and eggs.

Oates's remarks made in *Nests and Eggs* concerning the three subspecies of *Crocopus* may well be quoted here, though I cannot personally say that my experience, which as regards *chlorogaster* is confined to museum skins, endorses all that he says: "The Bengal Green Pigeon, though found as a straggler in the eastern portions of the Punjab and Rajputana, and somewhat more commonly almost throughout the Central and North-Western Provinces and Oudh, is really *at home* only in Bengal, and the tongue of Bengal-like country that runs up under the Himalayas, westward to the Jumna; everywhere else, the so-called southern species *C. chlorigaster* is much more abundant.

"Following, I suppose, Dr. Jerdon, Mr. Wallace in his article on the 'Pigeons of the Malay Archipelago,' gives *C. phoenicopterus* from northern India and China, and *C. chlorigaster* from Ceylon and the Indian Peninsular. As a matter of fact, *C. chlorigaster* is fully as common in upper India and in most places far more common than *C. phoenicopterus*. In the North-West Provinces both species associate in the same flock, *C. chlorigaster* being, as far as my experience goes, most numerous. Out of sixty odd shot in three days in the Etawah District in March, 1886, only nine belonged to the so-called Northern Indian type, and seven shot near Hansi (Punjab) were all *C. chlorigaster*. Eastwards of Bengal the present species shades into the nearly allied *C. viridifrons*, and throughout Upper India innumerable forms, more or less intermediate between it and *C. chlorigaster*, are to be met with. I have seen specimens of *C. phoenicopterus* from the Malabar coast; and although I have not yet thoroughly examined the question, I suspect that, different as are typical examples of the two races, they as little deserve specific separation as *Aegithina typhia* and *A. zeylonica*."

Nidification. As regards the nidification there is practically nothing to add to the description already given of that of *C. ph. phoenicopterus*. As a rule the birds build a very rough structure of small twigs and sticks with no lining of any kind, and place it on a branch of some small sapling at no great height from the ground, and often in a conspicuous position, though the material of which it is made does not quickly attract attention. Sometimes, however, these Pigeons would appear to line their nests, for Mr. Blewitt thus describes the nests he took at Hansie: "The nests were placed on toon, neem, shishum, and keeker trees, mostly growing on the canal bank, at heights of from fourteen to eighteen feet from the ground.

"They are composed of shishum (*Zizyphus*) and keeker twigs, in some cases slenderly in others densely put together. One or two were absolutely without lining, but they were mostly very scantily lined with leaves, feathers or fine straw. They varied from five to seven inches in diameter, and from 1½ to 3 inches in depth. They contained two eggs in every case, and some taken at the end of May were quite fresh."

Their principal breeding-season is from the end of March to the middle of May, though a good many birds breed as late as the middle of June. Hume says that they have at least two broods yearly, and perhaps more. Their eggs cannot be distinguished from those of *C. ph. phoenicopterus* and *C. ph. viridifrons.*

In habits there is nothing to distinguish the Southern Green Pigeon from the Bengal and Burmese birds. It is curious and should be noted that this subspecies also, like the others, is credited with never coming to the ground to drink. Reid writes in *Stray Feathers*, Vol. X, that " natives believe this bird never descends to the ground, and that when it desires to drink it settles on a reed which bends over with its weight and thus enables it to drink."

Mr. C. S. R. Pitman, l.c., writes that in the Central Provinces he has noticed Green Pigeon (*Crocopus chlorogaster*) drinking both at dawn, and in the evening about 4.30 or 5 p.m.

Jerdon also says that he has seen this bird in Chanda, when it was breeding, " come in large parties, generally about 9 a.m., to certain spots on river banks to drink, and after taking a draught of water, occasionally walk a few steps on the damp sand, appearing to pick up small pebbles, pieces of gravel or sand."

E. H. A. has a charming account of this bird in his *Common Birds of Bombay* which cannot be passed over. He writes : " The Fruit Pigeons are green birds, which try to be parrots, but nature bas stamped them doves ; they live entirely on fruit, which they swallow whole, not having parrot beaks to carve it with. A very wide gape and a most capacious and elastic throat make amends to some extent for this defect ; but still the Fruit Pigeon is obliged to do without mangoes and guavas . . . It finds compensation in the many varieties of wild figs which every forest in India produces in such liberal profusion. When a fig-tree fruits, it fruits all over, and all at once, offering a feast to the whole country, such as a Rajah gives when an heir is born to the throne ; and as mendicant Brahmins gather from distant provinces to the Rajah's feasts, so the Fruit Pigeons from afar flock together to this tree while it lasts ; first about eight in the morning, and again about four in the afternoon. Then is the time to shoot them, for they are excellent eating, especially if their tough skins have been taken off before cooking. It is difficult at first to see them for they are verdant like the foliage among which they sit strangely silent and motionless, but after much peering among the leafy boughs you may catch sight of a tail slowly oscillating like a pendulum. There is a solitary green bird sitting like a wooden figure—you fire and two fall, and a dozen fly off. If you are as other men, you will probably utter loud and naughty words, for if you had known there were so many birds you might easily have had a second shot at them as they flew. But if you are wise, you will rule your spirit and be still, for there may be a score of Pigeons in the tree yet, and others will come in small parties from time to time, so that, with patience, you may make a very respectable bag before the feeding-hour is over. Then remorse will have its turn, perhaps, as you gather up the fallen, and see what loveliness you have destroyed for the sake of your stomach."

It is extremely common in Mysore, where however it appears to be locally migratory, not visiting the hills until after the rains, and presumably breeding lower down and in the plains Taylor says that they were so plentiful that one evening he shot forty-six, and on one occasion got eleven and seven respectively to his first and second barrels, showing that they must have been in very large and densely flying flocks.

Genus OSMOTRERON.

In the British Museum *Catalogue of Birds*, Vol. XXI, Count Salvadori recognizes seventeen species in this genus, but a great number of his accepted species only differ very slightly from one another according to their geographical range, and their differences are certainly not of more than subspecific value.

In the same way Blanford, prior to an acceptance of subspecies and of the consequent trinomial system, admitted seven species of *Osmotreron* as inhabiting the area dealt with in this book. The acceptance, however, of subspecies reduces the number of species within the limits of India, Burma, and Ceylon to four—i.e. *pompadora*, *fulvicollis*, *bisincta*, and *vernans*, whilst the three species *phayrei*, *affinis*, and *chloroptera* are reduced to the rank of subspecies of *pompadora*, and a new subspecies is created for the northern form of *bisincta* under the name of *domvillii*.

The difference between this genus and the last (*Crocopus*) is very slight, and consists mainly in the fact that the latter genus has the first three primaries acuminate whilst *Osmotreron* has them normally shaped. The birds of this genus are also somewhat smaller in size, and the sexes are dissimilar: the males in some cases having maroon on the backs, and in others having highly-coloured breasts, whilst the females have neither.

Key to the Species.

A. Middle tail-feathers green:

- *a.* Head and neck grey and green ... ... *O. pompadora* ♂.
- *b.* Head and neck cinnamon-red ... ... *O. fulvicollis* ♂.
- *c.* Tibial plumes buff or dull yellowish ... ... *O. pompadora* ♀.
- *d.* Tibial plumes bright yellow ... ... *O. fulvicollis* ♀.

B. Middle tail-feathers slaty-grey:

- *a.* Outer tail-feathers with broad grey tips over .5 in. deep *O. bisincta.*
- *b.* With grey tip less than .5 in. deep ... ... *O. vernans.*

OSMOTRERON POMPADORA.

Key to the Subspecies.

A. Lower tail-coverts cinnamon or whitish :
- *a.* Fore-head yellow ... ... *O. p. pompadora.*
- *b.* Fore-head and crown grey :
  - *a′* Grey of head pure, and well defined from surrounding parts ... ... *O. p. phayrei.*
  - *b′* Grey of head dull and ill defined ... ... *O. p. affinis.*

B. Lower tail-coverts largely dark green ... ... *O. p. chloroptera.*

In order to keep this book as uniform as possible with the *Avifauna of British India*, I deal with these subspecies in the same sequence as they are considered in that work.

As regards the specific name which all four subspecies must bear, we find that the earliest name applied to any one of these races of Green Pigeons is that of "*pompadora*," given by Gmelin in 1788 to a Pigeon from Ceylon, called by Brown, in his *Illustrations of Birds* (1766), the "Pompadour Pigeon." In 1840 Jerdon named the female of the race found in the Southern Presidency, *Vinago affinis*; but five years later, in 1845, when describing the male of the same race found in Southern India (*Illus. Orn. Pac. C.*, XXI) he re-names it *malabarica.* As there is no law making the name given subsequently to a male take the place of that given to a female at a previous date, *affinis* certainly has priority over *malabarica*, and must stand for the subspecies. The name *chloroptera* was given by Blyth in 1845 to the race from the Nicobars and finally, in 1862, the same ornithologist named our northern race *phayrei.*

(4) OSMOTRERON POMPADORA PHAYREI (Blyth).

THE ASHY-HEADED GREEN PIGEON.

(FRONTISPIECE.)

Treron malabarica (part) Blyth, J.A.S.B., XIV p. 852 (1845); id., Cat. R.A.S.B., p. 229.

Osmotreron phayrei Blyth, J.A.S.B., XXI p. 344 (1862); Jerdon, B.I., III p. 451; Blyth and Wald., B. Burma, p. 144; Godw.-Aus., J.A.S.B., XXXIX pt. 2 p. iii; id. ib., XLV pt. 2 p. 83; Hume, Str. Feath., III p. 162; Inglis, ib., V p. 39; Hume and Dav., ib., VI p. 412; Hume, Cat. no. 776; id., Str. Feath., VIII p. 109; Bingham, Str. Feath., IX p. 194; Oates, B. Burma, II p. 310; id., Hume's Nests and Eggs, 2nd ed., II., p. 376; Hume, Str. Feath., X p. 235; id. ib., XI p. 291; Salvadori, Cat. B.M., XXI p. 43; Blanf., Avi. Brit. I., IV p. 8; Sharp, Hand-List, I p. 54; Oates, Cat. Eggs B.M., I p. 52; Harington, B. Burma, p. 63; Stuart Baker, J.B.N.H.S., X p. 364; Inglis, ib., XI p. 457; Stuart Baker, ib., XVII p. 970; Mears, ib., XVIII p. 86; Harington, ib., XIX p. 365.

Vernacular Names. *Daorep*, Cachari; *Inruigum*, Naga.; *Vohpolip*, Kuki; *Chota Haitha*, Assamese; *Chota Harial*, Sylheti; *Ngu*, Burmese; *Chota Harial*, Bengali.

Description.—*Adult male.* Whole crown of head and nape ashy-grey, the nape most pale, as a rule, and most pure in colour, the fore-head mixed with green and duller. Neck behind and extreme upper-back green, fairly well defined from the grey of the head and also from the chestnut-maroon of the back, scapulars, and lesser wing-coverts; lower-back, rump, and upper tail-coverts green, rather more yellowish than the neck. Outer tail-feathers black, each succeeding pair becoming more greenish, until the central ones are entirely of this colour and practically unicolorous with their coverts; a broad band of grey at the tips of all but the central feathers.

Lores, sides of head and narrow supercilium green, well defined from the grey of the crown and nape; throat and fore-neck the same, but much more yellow; upper-breast a creamy-orange, occasionally tinged with vinous or pink; lower-breast, abdomen, and flanks greenish, deepening in colour on the lower-flanks and thigh-coverts which are splashed with yellow; feathers of the vent and under tail-coverts cinnamon, the former sometimes a little the paler of the two and with yellowish borders. Median and greater wing-coverts black, fading to grey on the inside of the webs, the former with broad and the latter with narrow borders of yellow on the outer-webs; quills black inclining to grey on the inside of the inner webs, the primaries with narrow yellowish white margins and the secondaries with yellow borders, becoming very broad on the innermost which are also often much suffused with the same tint of maroon as that of the scapulars. Axillaries and under wing-coverts grey, with sometimes a tinge of green.

The amount of orange on the breast is very variable and there are two specimens in the British Museum collection, both from southern Burma, which have none at all, although they appear, otherwise, to be fully adult birds. The grey of the head is also somewhat variable, in some specimens being less sharply defined from the surrounding parts and also more dull and less pure in tint, as well as more restricted in area.

"Length 10.75 to 11.75; expanse 18.46 to 19.5; tail from vent 3.37 to 4.0; wing 6.0 to 6.25; tarsus 0.82 to 0.95; bill from gape 0.82 to 1.0; weight 4.5 to 6 ozs." (Hume).

The huge series of this bird which I have measured shows that this little Green Pigeon varies very considerably in size, wing-measurements ranging from 5.65 in. (= 143.5 mm.) to no less than 6.5 (= 164.7 mm.), the wing-measurement of a specimen from Sylhet. I can trace no geographical connexion with this variation in size: the largest and smallest birds being found in the same areas. The average of over 300 wing-measurements is 6.10 in. (= 154.9 mm.); the measurements of bill and tarsus vary to the same extent in proportion.

Two exceptionally large males shot in the Dibrugarh District of Assam each weighed fully 7 oz., pulling the scale well down at that weight. The great majority of birds do not, however, weigh much over 5 oz.

Colours of soft parts. Bill bluish-white, the base somewhat darker and the lower mandible still paler; legs lake-red, the posterior portion always paler, in old birds the edges of the scales showing white; iris pink with an inner circle of pale blue, orbital-skin bluish or pale slate-grey. In young birds the two rings of colour in the iris are pale and indefinite and the orbital-skin is almost white; nestlings have the iris a pale brown. "Irides usually with an inner ring of bright blue, and an outer ring of salmon or buffy pink, sometimes they are a rosy pink, at others reddish yellow." (Davison.)

Female has the chestnut-maroon of the upper-parts replaced by green; there is no sign of any orange on the breast, which is concolorous with the rest of the plumage, and the under tail-coverts are white or buffy-white with greenish bases and centres. I cannot find that there is any difference between the sexes in size; the biggest birds have been mostly males, but so have the smallest, the range in length of wing for 180 females being between 5.82 in. (= 144.8 mm.) and 6.30 (= 159.10 mm.), and the average of the same number 6.09 in. (= 154.68 mm.).

The young male is like the female, but assumes a certain amount of maroon on the upper-parts, more especially on the lesser wing-coverts, in the autumn moult of the first year.

Birds in their first plumage have the grey of the head duller than in the adult, and the yellow margins to the wing-feathers narrower and paler in colour. The young birds are also very much smaller than adults, and do not attain their full size until they are a year old, that is to say, until the spring of the year succeeding that in which they are hatched.

Distribution. The Ashy-headed Green Pigeon is found in Lower Bengal from about as far south as the latitude of Calcutta, though rare there, becoming more common in the eastern Bengal districts of Maldah, Barisal, Dacca and Mymensingh, and thence north and east extremely plentiful throughout the Assam Valley, Cachar, Sylhet, Chittagong, Comillah, and Noakhali.

In the Khasia Hills, Manipur, Looshai Hills, and the hill-ranges of northern Burma it is equally numerous, and thence it ranges east into Cochin China and south as far as Tenasserim, but not into the Malay States.

Nidification. The breeding-season of the Ashy-headed Green Pigeon commences in the last few days of March or early April and extends through April, May, and June into July and August, but April and early May is the time when most birds lay. In the hills south of the Brahmapootra few birds will be found breeding after May, but in the foot-hills of the Himalayas a good many continue to nest until well into July, whilst in Tavoy, on the other hand, Darling took its eggs as early as the 19th of March.

The nest is the usual platform of carelessly interlaced twigs, with no lining and but very little depression in the centre, though the projection of the twigs prevents the eggs rolling about. Roughly speaking, the nest is anything from 5 to 8 in. across, but they are often far from circular in shape, being much longer one way than the other. In depth they vary between 1 and 3 in., though odd pieces hang about and add to this. They build their nests either in small saplings or in bamboo-clumps as a rule, but now and then one may be taken from quite high up in a biggish tree. Both birds take part in the building, but I think the female does most of the actual work of construction, whilst the male brings the material to her. A pair I watched building their nest in a clump of bamboos quite close to a rest-house I was staying in, were accustomed to work only for about two hours in the morning and again for about the same time in the evening. In spite, however, of the few hours they devoted to work, the nest was completed in three days, and the first egg laid on the fourth day. The nests are not generally well concealed, and as they are more often placed at heights under, than over 8 ft., they are easy to find and get at. Occasionally they are placed in cane-brakes in swampy valleys and then, of course, are far more difficult of access though still easy enough to find, the bird sitting so close that one cannot help but notice her nest as she quits it. The site of it, too, is often given away by the whistling and antics of the cock-bird, which is much given to perambulating up and down a branch close to the nest whilst he croons and whistles to his little mate.

This crooning, a sort of low "coo, coo," very like a dove's but lower and deeper, I have never heard uttered except by the mate to his sitting wife. It is quite a sweet sound, though not so beautiful as the whistling-note.

The eggs are with this, as with nearly all others of the family, two in number, pure white, rather glossy and with a very fine, close texture. In shape they are either broad ellipses or are broad, blunt ovals, but now and then eggs are found with both ends curiously pointed.

The average of 180 eggs is 1.08 in. by .83 (= 27.4 mm. by 21.0), and the greatest length and breadth 1.14 in. (= 28.8 mm.) and .86 (= 21.8 mm.), and the least each way 1.02 in. (= 25.9 mm.) and .80 (= 20.3 mm.) respectively.

They cannot be distinguished from the eggs of *Treron nepalensis* or other Pigeons of the genus *Osmotreron*, though they average a trifle smaller than those of *O. bisincta domvillii*.

I have never yet ascertained exactly how long incubation lasts, but it will probably be found to be from twelve to fourteen days, according to circumstances.

This Pigeon is not a bird of high elevations and though I have shot it as high as 4,000 ft. both in the Khasia and north Cachar Hills, it is found in the greatest numbers in the foot-hills up to 1,500 or 2,000 ft., and thence some way into the more level country adjoining them. In the plains of Dibrugarh, where we have a flora and fauna more like that found elsewhere at an elevation of about 1,000 ft. and upwards, this Pigeon swarms and certainly forms at least two-thirds of the Green Pigeons which annually fall to the guns of the local sportsmen. Twice I have seen bags of over four hundred Pigeons made in one day, and in each case considerably over two-thirds of the birds obtained were of this species. Bingham also records that he "found this the commonest Green Pigeon on Thaungyeen and the higher parts of the Houndraw River."

They are quite first-class little game-birds in every way. Their flight, like that of all Green Pigeons, is wonderfully swift, and they have a most disconcerting habit of coming straight at you over the tree-tops and then swooping down within a few feet of the ground as they approach, only to rise again with equal rapidity just as one is about to fire, and then with a few rapid twists and turns disappear behind you, leaving you with two empty cartridges and an equally empty bag.

As with their larger cousins, the Bengal Green Pigeon and its subspecies, the easiest way to shoot them is to get close to some tree or trees upon which they are feeding, and take them as they come towards you. By this means one meets them as they are slowing down somewhat, and their flight is generally fairly direct; but even under these circumstances, a very few shots put them on the qui vive, and every flock that comes, after one or two birds have been dropped, flies higher and faster than its predecessor, and often after whirling round once or twice in wide circles, departs the way it has come without offering a possible shot.

The most sporting way of shooting them is undoubtedly that practised by the tea-planters of the Panitola and many other tea-districts in Assam. The breeding-season over, the birds collect in very large flocks, and towards the end of July and August frequent certain feeding-grounds in the forests round the tea-gardens. Here and there these forests are traversed by roads, and elsewhere are small patches of cultivation or open spaces beside some stream or forest-pool, and it is in such places the guns are placed when a shoot has been decided upon.

Very early in the morning, whilst the sun is still below the horizon and before the magic dawn of the East leaps into day, the birds commence to arrive at their feeding-ground in ones or twos and small parties, and the first shots at the still unfrightened birds are comparatively easy, so that the sportsman, after a few successful shots, begins to feel on good terms with himself. As the sun begins to peep into sight and climbs slowly up to the tree-tops, the birds come faster and faster and in bigger flocks; but the constant firing that is going on tells them of their enemies' presence, and they put on the pace and dodge, swoop, and turn in a manner that often completely baffles the best shot, so that though cartridges are expended faster than ever, fewer birds fall in proportion, and it is an exceptional shot who can gather on an average one bird for every alternate cartridge. At such times as this I have seen a flock of birds run the gauntlet of seven guns—my own, alas! amongst them—and finally vanish with their number complete and nothing more than a few feathers fluttering slowly to the ground to show that one shot amongst the seven has been more nearly successful than the rest. Up to about 9.30 a.m. the fun is fast and furious, but then by degrees it slackens off until by noon the birds have all retired to the deeper forests, where they take their siestas during the heat of the day, a faint melodious whistle in the distance telling the whereabouts of some belated flock which retires after the others have all gone.

No more shooting can now be expected until about three or four o'clock in the afternoon, so the sportsmen may lunch in comfort, and, if they choose, follow the example of the birds and indulge in forty winks. But an August afternoon in the plains of India is too hot even for sleep out of doors, however thick the shade, so a temporary adjournment is generally made to the nearest planters' bungalow until it is time once more to recommence work at the birds.

As the shadows begin to lengthen the Pigeons again arrive on the feeding-grounds in the forests in numbers that show little diminution in spite of the toll taken from the flocks in the morning. For a couple of hours the birds continue to flight backwards and forwards between the trees on which they are feeding, and until dusk begins to gather there is no cessation to the shooting. As soon, however, as the sun dips behind the distant trees, the flocks commence to wend their way to their roosting-place, and almost before it is too dark to see to shoot, the last of them has left.

The marvellous variety of shots obtained in a shoot of this description is one of its principal charms. If, as is often the case, one is standing in a small open patch in fairly extensive forest, the birds flight backwards and forwards from every direction, and offer every description of shot, and in all four quarters. First a flock may come sailing high overhead from the front, whilst next a single bird may rush past only a few feet from the ground, dodging bushes and trees at a headlong pace. A snap shot between the forest-trees may bring this to bag, and just give the sportsman time to swing round and empty his second barrel at a flock coming up from behind him. Not only is straight shooting required in such cases, but the quickest of eyes and hands, and the man who is prone to dwell over his second barrel will lose nearly, if not quite, a third of his possible shots.

Beating in shoots of this description is not necessary, though often before shooting has become general, men are sent out to the favourite feeding-trees to start the birds. Once the firing has begun in earnest, the Pigeons keep almost constantly on the wing, shifting from one set of trees to another with but few short pauses to feed, whilst on-coming flocks add to their number and replace those frightened away altogether.

Another charm in these shoots is the wonderful variety in the game brought to hand, and in the two big bags of over four hundred birds to which I have referred there were no less than twelve species, including the following: *Crocopus phoenicopterus*, *Osmotreron phayrei*, *O. bisincta*, *Sphenocercus sphenura*, *S. apicauda*, *Treron nepalensis*, *Carpophaga aenea*, *Ducula insignis*, *Chalcophaps indica*, with a few unlucky Doves, generally *Turtur meena*.

A more beautiful bag it would be difficult to imagine and, lovely as are the Sand-Grouse, I think the Green Pigeon are even more so. The marvellous blending of the greens and yellows and soft greys, with here and there the purple sheen of the backs of some of the males and an occasional metallic glint of a Bronze-wing Dove, is a picture difficult to do justice to, either with pen or brush.

Even more difficult shooting than that above described, is sometimes obtained by finding out the birds' line of flight to and from their feeding-grounds and roosting-places, and by stationing oneself at some point of their flighting where the natural advantages are all in favour of the birds. One such place was the crest of a small hill between the Rangagora and Digaltarang Tea-gardens in the Dibrugarh district, where the birds on good days passed in a constant stream every morning and evening for some two hours. Here, if one stood in the open on the top of the rise, the birds came so high and wide that but few shots were obtained; on the other hand, if one stood out of sight of the approaching Pigeon, on the far side of the hill just below the crest, the birds came sweeping up the hill so close to the ground that they were not visible until they cleared the top, not thirty yards in front, and were also protected to a great extent by the scrub-jungle which was scattered about. Behind us, and within a few yards, was heavy tree-forest, and directly the Pigeon came into sight, and also caught sight of us, they scurried through the bushes into this forest like lightening, dodging from one side to another like Jack Snipe, though at four times the pace. I had the pleasure of shooting here once with two other guns when there was a high wind behind the birds, and harder shooting I have never had. We did pick up some sixty birds in the two hours during which we shot, but I am quite sure four cartridges out of every five fired were ineffective.

I think the Ashy-headed Green Pigeon is as fast as any of its tribe, certainly a good deal faster than its bigger cousin, the Bengal Pigeon, and quite as fast as the little *Treron*, whilst the Pin-tailed and Wedge-tailed Green Pigeon are a trifle slower. These latter birds are, moreover, far more direct in their flight, and do not resort to the constant twistings and dodgings which seem habitual to the species we are now dealing with.

Like most other Green Pigeon, they are really rather shy birds, but when feeding in thickly foliaged trees often trust to the effective blending of their colours with the leaves to escape detection. I have known cases in which a bird has been shot out of a tree without the rest of the flock taking to flight, and which, in fact, were not discovered until a second or third shot at other birds approaching the tree frightened them out of it. As a rule, however, the first shot at any one of their number sends them in a hurry from their tree, but always by the side away from the shooter, so that it is but seldom that he can get in another shot as they quit.

They are wonderful climbers, and have great strength of grasp with their feet, wounded birds often seizing a twig or branch and hanging on, head downwards, until they drop off dead, and sometimes even after death the feet retain their hold. They are not, however, quick in their movements about a tree, and are very parrot-like in their actions, especially as they clamber slowly down some hanging branch towards a tempting cluster of fruit or berries.

They are, of course, entirely vegetarian in their diet, but not entirely frugivorous, for they will eat grain of all kinds, and also the tiny new buds of some kinds of trees and bushes. They are very partial to the fruit of the ber tree, and it is incredible the amount and weight of the berries they will cram into their crops, which get so distended and distorted that they look as if they must burst. Naturally, when a shot bird falls to the ground its crop does burst, and as the dense plumage also comes off very easily, birds when gathered often present a very dishevelled appearance. For this reason, also, it is very hard to obtain good specimens for the museum, and not one bird in three shot is any good for this purpose.

Greediness appears not to have any ill effect on Green Pigeons, which are generally in excellent condition, often having regular layers of fat between the skin and the flesh. All Green Pigeons are very good for the table, but they should be skinned and not plucked only, for their skins are very tough and sometimes seem to give a rather rank taste to the flesh. The best way of all to cook them is to jug them in claret, and the next best to roast them in a ball of clay, which keeps in all the juices but takes away skin and feathers complete when the ball is opened.

I have above noted that this little Green Pigeon is entirely vegetarian in its diet, but this is not quite correct, for, like almost every other bird and animal, it will greedily eat white ants. For this purpose it descends to the ground and runs about quite actively, seizing both those termites which drop to the ground on losing their wings and those which are just emerging from their nest-holes.

It will also descend to the ground to eat strawberries or other fruit growing on ground-plants.

This species sometimes assembles in very large flocks, and I think I have seen one or two which must have numbered over two hundred; as a general rule, however, they will be found in flocks of anything from half a dozen to thirty or forty. Even during the breeding-season the birds seem to be more or less gregarious though, perforce, they have to break up into comparatively small flocks. At the same time, I do not remember any month of the year in which I have not seen them in small flocks, as well as singly or in pairs. Nor are these small flocks composed of young birds or unwilling bachelors and spinsters, for birds examined have been proved to be fully adult, whilst both sexes have been seen or shot in the same flocks. The note of the Ashy-headed Green Pigeon has been described as being less musical than that of some of the other Green Pigeons, but I cannot say that I have noted this to be the case. It *may be* somewhat less varied and with a smaller range of notes, but to me it sounds as soft and melodious as any of its cousins, except perhaps *bisincta*, the Orange-breasted Green Pigeon.

When they are quite undisturbed and have no idea that anyone is watching or listening to them, the members of a flock will continue to whistle to one another as they feed, and the volume of sound thus made is very sweet and full. Although, as I have said, naturally shy birds, they very soon become used to being watched, and if not fired at or interfered with in any way, soon lose their shyness and become very tame. In one of the police-stations in the Dibrugarh district some enormous pepul trees grow in the compound, two of their number overhanging the station-building itself. Here the birds are so accustomed to people constantly moving about below them, that they take absolutely no notice and, as they are never fired at in the compound, the birds swarm here, even when the trees are not in fruit, when firing is going on anywhere near.

I do not think that the Ashy-headed Green Pigeon drinks regularly morning or evening, but I have noticed more than once these birds drinking about noon, when they have ceased feeding and were about to take their mid-day rest.

Invariably, when noticed on these occasions, the birds drank by climbing down the cane-brakes or creepers which stood in swamps, until they could reach the water, when they drank their fill, and then clambered back to a more convenient perch. They rest much in the middle of the day in cane-brakes, which form dense masses of jungle in the morasses at the foot of the hills, though they also frequent tall tree-forest for the same purpose.

Like all their relations, I am sorry to say that they are very quarrelsome and pugnacious birds, and it is quite impossible to keep two captive birds in the same cage during the breeding-season, for the males will fight until exhausted or seriously injured, whilst the females are often nearly as bad. I have never myself succeeded in getting them to breed in captivity, but they are such easy birds to tame and do so well in aviaries, that the matter should not be difficult. In the Calcutta Zoological Gardens these Pigeons used to pair freely, and would go as far as partially building nests, but the few eggs they laid were casually dropped about anywhere but in the nests.

(5) OSMOTRERON POMPADORA AFFINIS (Jerdon).

THE GREY-FRONTED GREEN PIGEON.

Vinago aromatica (part) Jerdon, Madr. J.L.S., XII p. 13 (1840), nec *Columba aromatica* Gm.
Vinago affinis Jerdon, l.c. ♀.
Vinago malabarica Jerdon, Ill. Orn., III, letterpress pl. XXIV (1845); Blyth, Cat. B.M.A.S.B. p. 229; id., J.A.S.B., XXI p. 56.
Treron malabarica Blyth, J.A.S.B., XIV p. 852; id., Cat., p. 229.
Osmotreron malabarica Bp., Con. Av., II p. 13; Jerdon, B.I., p. 450; Hume, Nests and Eggs, p. 493; Fairbank, Str. Feath., IV p. 261; Hume and Bourd, ib., p. 403; Hume, ib., p. 424; id., Cat. no. 775; Fairbank Str. Feath., V p. 408; Vidal, ib., IX p. 74; Butler, ib., p. 419; Davidson, ib., X p. 406; Barnes, B. Bom., p. 286; Oates, in Hume's Nests and Eggs, 2nd ed., II p. 375; Salvadori, Cat. B.M., XXI p. 45; Sharpe, Hand-List, I p. 54; Oates, Cat. Eggs B.M., I p. 82; Barnes J.B.N.H.S., V p. 329; Davidson, ib., XII p. 61.
Osmotreron affinis Wal., Trans. Z.S., IX p. 212; Blanf., Avi. Brit. I., IV p. 8; Fergusson J.B.N.H.S., XVI p. 1.

Vernacular Name. *Poda-putsa Guwa*, Tel.

Description.—*Adult male.* Similar to *O. p. phayrei*, but the upper-parts in this subspecies are considerably deeper in colour, in fact, more a purple- than a chestnut-maroon; there is never any orange on the breast, and in both males and females the grey of the head is duller and darker, and ill defined from the surrounding green. In addition to this, the male has the shoulder of the wing very much blacker and not mixed with grey.

Adult female. The female *affinis* differs from the male in the same way as that of *phayrei* differs from the male of that subspecies.

As I have already pointed out, all the differences between this subspecies and the others is one of degree only. Thus, there are some otherwise typical specimens of *phayrei* which have the heads dull and the grey ill defined; here and there are some with no orange on the breast and, whilst in some males of *phayrei* the back is nearly as dark as the typical *affinis*, in this latter subspecies there are a few which have their backs and scapulars quite as pale as the normal *phayrei*.

Colours of the soft parts are the same as in *phayrei*.

Measurements. "Length about 10.75; tail 3.6; wing 5.75; tarsus .8; bill from gape .9" (Blanford).

This is a decidedly smaller bird, on an average, than the last, though the measurements overlap and birds from Khandesh seem a good deal bigger than the smallest *phayrei*, but all over the area they inhabit there is a considerable range in their extremes of size.

The wings of males I have measured vary from 5.44 in. (= 138.2 mm.) to 5.92 (= 150.3 mm.) in length, the average of sixty birds being 5.61 in. (= 142.5 mm.).

The females do not appear to be any smaller than the males, and the biggest male in the British Museum series is no bigger than the largest female.

Colours of soft parts of both sexes. "The soft basal part of the bill is glaucus green, but the tips of both mandibles are ashy. The iris is blue with an outer ring of pink or lake red." (Fairbank.)

"Legs and feet lake pink; claws bluish white" (Davison).

Distribution. Blanford thus notes on the distribution of this Green Pigeon: "Forests of the Malabar Coast from the neighbourhood of Bombay to Cape Cormorin. Jerdon states that he also obtained this bird in Central India and in the Eastern Ghats; but neither the late Doctor V. Ball, nor I, met with this species in the area specified; the name does not occur in either of the lists of Shevaroy birds (for which I am indebted to Mr. Daly and Mr. Worth), and no one, as far as I know, has obtained this bird away from the Malabar Coast since Jerdon's time."

Davidson (l.c.) says that it is very common in Kanara, and extends as far east as Birchia, but is rare beyond Sirsi, and that he had not noticed it either in Musyodi or Halzae. Bourdillon reports it as common in suitable localities in Travancore, but Davison did not find it abundant either in the Wynaad or in Mysore. It also occurs in the Lacadives.

Nidification. The Grey-fronted Green Pigeon breeds throughout its range, principally in February and early March, but its eggs may be taken at any time between the beginning of January and the end of April.

Barnes records that this "is much the commonest Green Pigeon in Kanara . . . both above and below the Ghata. I have taken numbers of the nests, which are generally slight structures placed from 8 to 15 ft. from the ground, and mostly in small trees. The male is quite as commonly seen incubating the eggs as the female."

Mr. J. Darling's account agrees with Barnes, and he describes the nest as "a slight ragged, shapeless thing composed of thin dry twigs laid together in a very disreputable fashion, with a circular central depression lined with a few grass stalks. The nests were 5 or 6 in. in diameter; the depression hardly more than ½ in. in depth. The eggs measured 1.12 in. by 0.8."

Normally, this Pigeon, like others of the genus, undoubtedly prefers scrub-jungle and small trees or saplings as a site for its nest, but Mr. F. W. Bourdillon found its nest in the Assamboo Hills built on the bough of a tree at 40 ft. from the ground.

In colour the eggs are, as usual, a pure white. The shape and texture does not differ from that of other Green Pigeons' eggs. They vary in length between 1.08 in. (= 27.6 mm.) and 1.17 (= 29.7 mm.), and average 1.12 by .86 (= 28.4 by 21.8 mm.). In breadth they only vary between .84 in. (= 21.3 mm.) and .88 (= 22.3 mm.).

I have only seen a very small series of these eggs and a larger number would probably show a greater difference between extremes of size.

In habits there seems to be nothing peculiar to this species of Green Pigeon calling for remark. It is, perhaps, more strictly a forest-bird than is the case with some, but like the others of this genus wherever found, it is resident, merely moving higher up the hills in the hot weather and rains. Bourdillion says that it ascends as high as 3,000 ft. in Travancore, but Davison, possibly referring to other months, says that it does not ascend the hills at all. Though common enough in some parts of its distribution, the Grey-fronted Green Pigeon seems nowhere to be found in as vast numbers as is the Ashy-headed Green Pigeon. It collects also in rather smaller flocks, generally of half a dozen or so, and there appear to be no record of flocks much over twenty. Mr. F. W. Bourdillion says that it "may be found in great numbers in the neighbourhood of the hill-men's clearings, but in February and March they ascend the hills to over 2,000 ft. Their note is a low chuckling whistle."

This description of their call would, however, apply only to some of their notes, as other writers describe their whistle as a most beautiful and melodious sound, apparently much like that made by the other birds of this genus.

(6) OSMOTRERON POMPADORA POMPADORA (Gm.).

THE POMPADOUR GREEN PIGEON.

Columba pompadora Gm., Syst. Nat., I p. 775 (1788); Blyth, J.A.S.B., XIV p. 852.
Treron pompadora Blyth, J.A.S.B., XXI p. 356.
Vinago aromatica Jerdon, Madr. J.L.S., XII p. 13.
Treron malabarica (part) Blyth, Cat. B.M.A.S.B., p. 229.
Treron flavogularis id., J.A.S.B., XXVI p. 225.
Osmotreron flavogularis id. ib., XXXI p. 344.
Osmotreron pompadora Hume, Str. Feath., III p. 162; id. ib., VI p. 414; id., Cat. no. 777; Legge, B. Cey., p. 728; Parker, Str. Feath., IX p. 481; Salvadori, Cat. B.M., XXI p. 51; Blanf., Avi. Brit. I., IV p. 9; Sharpe, Hand-List, I p. 54; Butler, J.B.N.H.S., X p. 311.
Osmotreron pompadoura Jerdon, B.I., III p. 452.

Vernacular Names. *Batta-goya*, Cing.; *Patcha-praa*, *Alam-praa*, Tamil in Ceylon.

Description. *Adult male.*—The colour of the upper-parts where red, agrees in tint with the same parts in *O. p. affinis*. It differs from that subspecies in having the fore-head, lores, and sides of the head more yellowish and the chin and throat a pure, almost lemon-yellow. The grey of the crown is generally entirely replaced with green, though a few specimens have a fairly distinct patch of grey in the centre. The lower tail-coverts are a pale, buffy-white instead of cinnamon.

Adult female. Differs from the male in the same way as they do in the other subspecies.

Colours of soft parts. "Bill glaucous green, paling to bluish in the apical portion; irides carmine red with a cobalt inner circle; eyelids glaucous green; legs and feet purple-red" (Legge).

Measurements. Length about 10.5 in; tail 3.6; wing 5.6; tarsus .8 bill from gape .9 in. (Blanford).

There is only a small series of these birds in the British Museum, but enough to show that the sexes do not differ materially, if at all, in size. The wings vary from 5.45 in. (= 138.4 mm.) to 5.76 (= 146.2 mm.) and average 5.63 (= 142.8 mm.), the extremes in size being, in each case, the measurement of the wing of a female.

Distribution. Ceylon.—Jerdon gives the habitat of this bird as Southern India also, but this is probably due to some mistake. Since Blanford wrote the *Avifauna of British India*, several field-ornithologists have worked Southern India well (amongst others who might be mentioned are Cardew, Fairbank, Bell, Dewar, Major Smith, Bourdillon, and others), but none have ever come across it.

Mr. J. Stuart has also worked Travancore for the last ten years or so with great thoroughness, employing an army of observers in the location of birds and nests, but has failed altogether to ever come across, or to obtain a specimen, of the Pompadour Green Pigeon.

Nidification. There is practically nothing on record regarding the nidification of this Green Pigeon. Butler found a nest being built in June, but the bird did not lay, and no description is given of the nest. Parker, in *Stray Feathers*, merely states that the average of eight eggs is 1.15 in. by 0.88, and observes that "this bird deserts its nests on the least possible provocation." One pair of Parker's eggs sent to me was taken on 24.5.88, and is said to have come from "a small roughly-made nest of sticks placed in a sapling."

I have a fair series of these eggs taken by W. Jenkins, chiefly at or about Welgampola. They are, of course, pure white, and of the usual smooth but not very close texture, and in shape broad ellipses, with the exception of one pair, which are somewhat lengthened. They vary in length between 1.10 in. (= 27.9 mm.) by 1.21 (= 30.7 mm.) and in breadth between .91 in. (= 23.1 mm.) and .96 (= 24.4 mm.).

No nests were sent me with the eggs, but they were described as rough platforms of twigs interlaced with one another with the slightest of depressions in the centre, and measuring about 6 in. across. In no case was there any lining, and all the nests were either on high bushes or small trees in forests.

This is a bird of both hill and plains country, being found at certain seasons at the level of the sea, and at others as high as 4,000 ft., whilst it is resident practically over the greater part of this area. The one essential is that the country should be well wooded, and it is seldom, if ever, to be found outside forest-land, or at least land that is well timbered, though it may wander into the open country, or short distances away from forest when tempted by plentiful feeding.

It appears to be entirely frugivorous in its diet, though it would doubtless soon take to grain in captivity. A pair I saw in a cage in Slave Island, Ceylon, were fed entirely on bread and milk and plantains, and they seemed to be in a very good condition.

There is very little on record about this Green Pigeon except as recorded by Legge in his *Birds of Ceylon*. He there writes: "This Pigeon is an inhabitant of woods, forests, and open timbered country: it collects together in the fine Banyan, Bo, and Palu trees, which are scattered through the low jungles of the eastern and northern Districts, and also in the magnificent outspreading Mee trees which line the borders of the jungle tanks, and in such resorts feeds in flocks on the luscious berries which these large trees provide. Its flesh is at all times delicious; but when killed during the fruiting time of the Banyan and ironwood, there is nothing which surpasses this Pigeon in flavour in the Island. It is a shy bird and difficult to kill, except when feeding; it may then be easily shot out of large forest trees, provided the sportsman be concealed, as it feeds so greedily that many do not take flight on the discharge of a gun. They collect in groups of a dozen or more, in the early morning or after feeding, and sit motionless on the tops of trees. On being alarmed one or two dart off, and are followed by their companions, one after another, till the whole have taken flight. They are very strong on the wing, and fly with a steady straight course. Their note is a melodious, soft, modulated whistle, which can be precisely imitated, and by doing which many are enticed by 'Eurasians' in the North of Ceylon, into uttering it, and are thus more easily descried in the green foliage and then shot. There is something peculiarly charming in their human-like notes when heard in the tops of lofty trees, overshadowing the mighty bunds by which the ancient Kings of Ceylon dammed up valleys, and skilfully formed vast reservoirs for the support of their subjects in the wild forests of the Vanni. In the Wellaway Korale, where the Pigeon is abundant, I have seen, as in the case of the two preceding species, large flocks in scattered company returning in the evening from their feeding ground, or from the widely dispersed waterholes of that district, and by remaining in wait for them in the same position I have had excellent shooting. Both this, and the Orange-breasted Pigeon, however, are very strong birds, and take more killing to bring them down, especially when perched, than almost any bird of the same size in Ceylon."

(7) OSMOTRERON POMPADORA CHLOROPTERA (Blyth).

THE ANDAMANESE GREEN PIGEON.

Treron chloroptera Blyth, J.A.S.B., XIV p. 852 (1845); id., Cat., p. 229.

Osmotreron chloroptera Jerdon, B.I., IV p. 451; Ball, J.A.S.B., XLI pt. II. p. 286; id., Str. Feath., I p. 78; Hume, ib., II p. 258; id. ib., III p. 162; id. ib., VI p. 414; id., Cat. no. 777, bis; Salvadori, Cat. B.M., XXI p. 49; Blanf., Avi. Brit. I., IV p. 10; Sharpe Hand-List, I p. 54; Butler, J.B.N.H.S., XII p. 687; Osmaston, ib., XVII p. 488; Richmond, Proc. N.M.U.S., XXV p. 308.

Osmotreron chloroptera andamanensis Butler, ib.

Vernacular Names. None known.

Description.—*Adult male.* Differs from the male of *phayrei* in having the lower wing-coverts green, of a darker, less yellow tinge than the neck, and the green of the upper-parts is more yellow except on the central rectrices. The maroon on the back is darker than it is in *phayrei*, and as dark as it is in *affinis*. There is no orange on the breast and the lower tail-coverts are dark, rather dull green, with broad yellowish-white borders. The grey of the head is lighter and unmixed with green on the fore-head, fading into the green of the lower half of the lores and also merging into the green of the neck, from which it is never sharply defined.

Legs and feet pale carnation-pink or purplish-pink, claws horny or plumbeous tinged with pink; bill a whitish-blue or leaden-blue tinged with green near the base, and with plumbeous cere. Iris, first ring pale blue, second ring darker blue, and third ring fleshy-buff. Orbital skin plumbeous, yellowish next the eye (from W. Davison's notes). "Feet dull purple" (Butler).

Dimensions. "Length about 12.5; tail 4; wing 6.75; tarsus 1, bill from gape 1.05" (Blanford).

The wing-measurements of the series in the British Museum vary between 6.75 in. (= 171.4 mm.) and 7.2 (= 182.9 mm.) and average 6.91 in. (= 175.5 mm.). Davison gives the weight of a big male as being .75 lb.

Adult female. Similar to the male, but wanting the maroon on the upper-parts. The cap of grey is perhaps even less well-defined and duller in colour.

Colours of soft parts, as in male. Davison says that the iris is "pale blue blending into puce."

"Bill leaden greenish at base and on cere" (Butler).

Dimensions much the same as in the male. The females in the British Museum series have an average wing-measurement of 6.93 in. (= 176.0 mm.).

Young male of the year is always smaller than the adult, and has the purple-maroon of the upper-parts imperfectly developed.

Dr. Richmond (l.c.) separates the birds inhabiting the Andamans from those inhabiting the Nicobars on account of their smaller size and general darker colour both above and below. He says that "the pigeon from the Andamans is similar to *O. chloroptera* from the Nicobars, but rather smaller, colour somewhat darker below; breast and sides deeper yellowish-green, and under tail-coverts more yellowish. The throat is yellower than in *O. chloroptera*."

Dr. Richmond appears to have obtained only three females of the Andaman form, and a very careful examination of a larger series than that examined by him shows that the grounds upon which he creates his new subspecies do not hold good.

The biggest male in the British Museum collection is a bird with a wing of 182.9 mm. from the Nicobars, whilst the biggest female is a bird from the Andamans. On the other hand, the smallest male birds in the collection are two with wings of 171.4 mm., of which one comes from the Nicobars and the other from the Andamans.

As regards coloration, I can see no differences that are not individual only, and dark and light coloured birds are found equally often in either group of islands. I think therefore the subspecies *Osmotreron chloroptera andamanensis* must be suppressed.

Distribution. The Andamans and Nicobar Islands.

Nidification. Beyond the facts noted below, which would lead one to infer that May and June are probably two of its breeding-months, we know nothing about its nidification, and its nest and eggs have yet to be discovered.

There is practically nothing on record about the habits of this form of Green Pigeon. Davison, in *Stray Feathers*, has the following short note: "This Hurrial is exceedingly abundant, both at the Andamans and Nichobars, more so at the former than at the latter place. It is always in flocks, keeping generally to the larger forest trees during the heat of the day, but coming into gardens and clearings, or wherever there may be trees with fruit, in the morning and evening. Its fine clear whistling note (very like, but more powerful than that of *O. malabarica*) is one of those most frequently heard in the jungles about Port Blair. A few days before leaving Port Blair for Calcutta I noticed one of these Pigeons with a twig in its bill fly into the top of a tall slender tree standing just on the outskirts of the forest. This was in May, so it is probable that these birds breed during that and the following month." Messrs. B. B. Osmaston and A. L. Butler both record the bird as being abundant in the Andamans, and the latter adds that a bird he shot in the month of May was apparently breeding.

The above exhausts all that has hitherto been written about this Pigeon, and I have not been able to elicit anything further about its habits.

(8) OSMOTRERON FULVICOLLIS (Wagl.).

THE CINNAMON-HEADED GREEN PIGEON.

(PLATE 2.)

Columba fulvicollis Wagl., Sys. Av. sp. 8 (1827).
Osmotreron fulvicollis Hume, Str. Feath., IV p. 224; id., Cat. no. 776, bis; Hume and Dav., Str. Feath., VI p. 413; Oates, B. Burma, II p. 311; Hume, Str. Feath., VIII pp. 67 and 109; Salvadori, Cat. B.M., XXI p. 52; Blanf., Avi. Brit. I., IV p. 10; Sharpe, Hand-List, I p. 53; Butler, J.B.N.H.S., XII p. 772; Harington, B. Burma, p. 117.
Treron fulvicollis Blyth, Cat. B.M.A.S.B., p. 339; Everett, J.S.B.A.S., p. 196 (part).

Vernacular Names. None recorded.

Description.—*Adult male.* Head, neck, and upper-breast cinnamon; above darker and tinged with purple, below paler and more yellow, changing gradually to orange-ochre on the lower-breast. Interscapulars, scapulars, back, and lesser wing-coverts purple-maroon; rump slate changing into olive-green on the upper tail-coverts. Central tail-feathers above dull olive-green, the others olive-grey with a pure grey terminal band and a subterminal black one. Abdomen mixed yellowish-green and grey, varying very greatly in their proportions in different individuals; flanks dark dove-grey, becoming deep slate-grey posteriorly; tibial plumes and vent bright yellow, much mixed with slate; under tail-coverts dull cinnamon, the longer often with green centres. Under aspect of tail black with grey tip. Primaries black, very narrowly margined on the outer webs and on the terminal quarter of the inner webs with yellowish-white; winglet, secondaries, greater and median coverts black with yellow margins, broadest on the inner secondaries; innermost secondaries glossed with olive-green; under wing-coverts and axillaries french-grey.

Colours of soft parts. "Legs and feet purplish pink, claws white, lower mandible to angle of gonys and upper mandible to just beyond nostril deep red, rest of bill dead white, strongly tinged with greenish blue. Iris buffy pink; naked space round eye plumbeous green" (Davison). The edges of the iris are orange.

Measurements. "Length about 10.5; tail 3.6; wing 6; tarsus .8; bill from gape .8" (Blanford).

The series I have examined have wings varying between 5.85 in. (= 148.5 mm.) and 5.40 (= 136.2 mm.), and average 5.65 in. (= 143.5 mm.).

Adult female. Has the cinnamon and maroon of the upper-parts replaced by dull olive-green and below by pale yellowish-green, more or less mixed with grey on the abdomen. The crown from the fore-head to the nape is grey, showing in good contrast to the greenish supercilia. The chin in some

THE CINNAMON-HEADED GREEN PIGEON—*OSMOTRERON FULVICOLLIS.*
(½ Nat. Size—Male on left, female on right.)

PLATE 2

specimens has a very faint rufescent tinge. Under tail-coverts pale buff, the centres and bases more or less marked with green.

Colours of soft parts. "Iris with an outer ring of pink and an inner ring of ultramarine. The legs and feet are paler and pinker than in the male." (Davison.)

Measurements. "Females are rather smaller than the males" (Blanford). The series in the British Museum do not show that there is much difference in size between the two sexes. The average wing-measurement is 5.62 in. (= 142.5 mm.), and there are several adult males with wings smaller than any of the females.

Young male. Young males are like the females, but assume the adult plumage, to some extent, at the first autumn moult, completing it in the spring. The maroon and cinnamon of the upper-parts are only partially assumed in the autumn, giving the young bird in its first winter-plumage a very patchy appearance.

Distribution. Blanford records this as only a winter-visitor to Tenasserim, where Davison obtained it at Bankasoon in December and January. It is, however, most probably a resident in Tenasserim, for my collectors found it there in March, when they obtained nests and eggs, though they reported it as very rare.

Outside our Indian limits it is found in Cochin China, the Federated Malay States, and Malay Archipeligo to Celebes and the Phillipines.

Nidification. The only note I can find on the breeding of this Green Pigeon is that by A. L. Butler in the *Journal* of the Bombay Natural History Society. He there records: "I took a pair of eggs of this handsome Pigeon in Pahang in May. The nidification, which is, of course, exactly similar to that of other Green Pigeons of the genus, is not described in Vol. IV of the Birds in the *Fauna of British India*, so perhaps it may be worth while to record the dimensions of the eggs. They are rather short and broad, both measuring 1.1 to 1.32 by 27/32, the shell of the usual *Osmotreron* texture and gloss.

"The nest was placed in a low tree in a little sandy Island in the Pahang River, on which I landed to try for a jungle fowl. The male bird flew out of the tree close to the nest, and I shot him before I noticed it."

The first pair of eggs I ever received of this bird was taken by Mr. W. A. T. Kellow in Simpang, Federated Malay States, who kindly sent me two pairs, together with portions of the skin of the parent birds. The nests were taken on the 11th May and 14th June respectively, and each contained two eggs, the former hard-set and the latter fresh. The nests were said to be the usual doves' platform of sticks and twigs placed in a small sapling, low enough down to be reached by hand, and situated in heavy forest near the banks of a stream.

Other nests and eggs received after these appear to be similar in all respects, but were taken in the months of January and February, and, *in epistola*, Mr. Kellow writes that he believes these two are the principal breeding-months in that part of the Malay Peninsula.

My series of eggs vary in length between 1.06 in (= 26.8 mm.) and 1.16 (= 29.3 mm.), and in breadth between .80 in. (= 20.3 mm.) and .90 (= 22.8 mm.), averaging 1.12 in. (= 28.4 mm.) by .86 (= 21.7 mm.).

They are, of course, pure white and of the usual short ellipse shape, and do not differ in grain or texture from those of other Green Pigeons.

My collectors found this bird very rare in the south of Tenasserim, but sent me thence several specimens both of birds and their eggs. During the months of November to February the birds kept much to the outskirts of jungle and the more open country, assembling in very large numbers, together with other Pigeons and fruit-eating birds, wherever there were trees in fruit; but although the total numbers so collected may have been large, the flocks are said to have always been small, numbering some half dozen or so only. Their flight, voice, and general habits were said to be like those of *Treron nepalensis*, a bird very well known to the collectors.

Davison seems to think that the birds worked south in spring, but this was probable merely because they retired into deeper forest during the breeding-season, and so escaped observation. He says of this Pigeon: "This species only makes it appearance in Tenasserim for a couple of months, in December and January. It occurs in small flocks about the borders of the forest. Its note is very similar to that of *O. vernans*. It is apparently rare and very local, as I only met with it in two places near Bankasoon, though I was always on the look out for it.

"It appeared to have come solely to eat the berries, much resembling red currants, of a thick bushy shrub about two feet in height which, near the Pakchem, grows about the clearings."

OSMOTRERON BISINCTA.

Key to the Subspecies.

A. Wing under 6 in. ... ... *O. b. bisincta.*
B. Wing over 6 in. ... ... *O. b. domvillii.*

(9) OSMOTRERON BISINCTA DOMVILLII (Blyth).

THE ORANGE-BREASTED GREEN PIGEON.

Vinago bisincta (part) Jerdon, Madr. J.L.S., p. 13 (1840); (part) id., Ill. I. Orn., pl. 21.
Vinago unicolor (part) id., Madr. J.L.S., XII p. 14 (1840).
Treron bisincta Blyth, J.A.S.B., XIV p. 851; id., Cat., p. 229.
Osmotreron bisincta Bp., Con. Av., II p. 12; Jerdon, B.I., III p. 449; Godw.-Aus., J.A.S.B., XXXIX pt. II p. 272; Ball, Str. Feath., II p. 423; Hume, Nests and Eggs, p. 493; id., Str. Feath., III p. 162; Blyth and Wal., B. Burma, p. 144; Armstrong, Str. Feath., IV p. 337; Oates, ib., V p. 163; Hume and Dav., ib., VI p. 411; Hume, ib., VI p. 414; Ball, ib., VII p. 224; Hume, ib., VIII p. 109; id., Cat. no. 774; Hume and Inglis, Str. Feath., IX p. 257; Oates, ib., X p. 235; Dav., ib., p. 406; Oates, B. Burma, II p. 308; id., Hume, Nests and Eggs, 2nd ed., II p. 374; id., Str. Feath., XI p. 291; Salvadori, Cat. B.M., XXI p. 57; Blanf., Avi. Brit. I., IV p. 11; Sharpe, Hand-List, I p. 54; Oates, Cat. Eggs B.M., I p. 82; Barnes, J.B.N.H.S., V p. 328; Davidson, ib., IX p. 489; Stuart Baker, ib., X p. 363; Inglis, ib., XI p. 475; Davidson, ib., XII p. 61; Macdonald, ib., XVII p. 495; Stuart Baker, ib., p. 971; Harington, ib., XIX p. 308.
Osmotreron domvillei Blyth, B. Burma, p. 144.
Osmotreron domvillii Swinh., Ibis 1870.

Vernacular Names. *Chitta putsa guwa,* Tel.; *Gnu,* Burmese; *Daorep kashiba,* Cachari; *Inrui-gahergu,* Naga; *Harial,* Hindi; *Haitha,* Assamese.

Description.—*Adult male.* Fore-head, lores, and crown as far back as the back of the eye, dull yellowish-green, changing into a beautiful blue-grey on the nape, hind-neck, and upper-back where it in turn changes into the brownish-green of the back, scapulars, rump, and upper tail-coverts and smaller wing-coverts; these last and the rump are rather less brown, and the upper tail-coverts somewhat more brown than that of the other parts. Tail dark ashy-grey with a broad terminal band of pale grey, and a dark, almost black subterminal band, very broad and dark on the outermost feathers, and less distinct and narrower on the central ones. Chin, throat, and fore-neck green, more yellow on the chin and the centre of the throat; a broad band of lilac across the breast and bending backwards towards the shoulders of the wing so as to nearly enclose a second broad band of orange; lower-breast pale yellowish-green, changing into bright king's yellow on the abdomen; tibial plumes yellow, splashed with dark green and grey; under tail-coverts cinnamon, the outermost feathers with pale yellowish edges. Quills nearly black, the outer primaries narrowly edged with bright pale

E

yellow; the inner-secondaries the same, but gradually changing to the same colour as the back on the innermost, which are also broadly edged with yellow on the outer webs; greater-coverts black with broad margins of pale king's yellow, median-coverts green with the same border on a few of the largest and outermost feathers. Winglet black; lower surface of wing, flanks, and axillaries grey.

Colours of soft parts. "The legs and feet vary from purplish pink to lake red, the irides have an inner ring, at times not very apparent, of deep blue, and an outer one of salmon pink, the eyelids bluish or pale plumbeous. The bill is pale bluish, the basal portion darker." (Hume.)

The legs and feet are often almost a coral-red with paler soles, and claws a pale horny-brown. The inner ring of the iris varies from bright pale ultramarine to a deep blue, and the outer part from vivid salmon-pink to a deep crimson-pink. The bill is very often more of a pale green than a pale blue, more especially in the central portion. The eyelids and bare orbital skin are a bright lavender-blue.

Adult female. Differs from the male in having no lilac and orange bands across the breast; in having the blue-grey of the upper parts duller, darker and less in extent, and in having the under tail-coverts pale dull cinnamon, much mottled with dull greenish on the inner webs, and with the whitish-yellow on the outer webs still wider. The amount of green on the vent and tibial plumes also, is perhaps greater. I cannot see that the back, as is sometimes alleged, is either more or less green in the female than it is in the male.

Colours of soft parts. Similar to the same parts in the male, but the eyelids and orbital skin are somewhat more livid and less bright in tint.

Young birds of both sexes in this, as in other Green Pigeons, have the eyes a watery pale brown, but acquire the double-coloured iris in the first autumn-moult, though it is not even then quite so vivid in colour as in the adult. The feet also are duller coloured and with less lake, and the eyelids and orbital-skin are of a livid colour.

Measurements. Length about 11.5 in., tail 3.75, wing 6.25, tarsus .85, bill from gape .95. Females rather less " (Blanford).

The huge series of this Pigeon in the British Museum Collection (excluding birds from Ceylon and Madras) give wing-measurements which range from 6.08 in. (= 154.4 mm.) to 6.70 (= 170.2 mm.) This latter, however, is an extraordinarily large bird, and the next biggest is only 6.55 in. (= 166.2 mm.). The difference between the sexes is not much, and the biggest females far exceed in size the smallest males, but on an average the female has a wing not quite .25 in. (= 6.35 mm.) shorter than that of the male.

Assam and Burmese birds are, on the whole, larger than those from Bengal and China, but they well overlap one another and cannot be divided as can the Ceylon and Southern Indian birds.

A very careful examination of the series of this Green Pigeon in the British Museum Collection shows, as has already been noted by Blanford and others, that in the extreme south of India and Ceylon there is a much smaller race which appears to be well worthy of subspecific rank. Unfortunately, amongst the birds I have been able to examine, though there are a fair number from Ceylon there are very few from Madras; but from the material available it would appear that the drop in size between the northern and southern races is very sudden.

The following table shows the comparative size in wing-measurements of the Orange-breasted Green Pigeon in the various countries it inhabits :—

Burma ...	... 6.29 in. (= 159.6 mm.)	Average 158.5 mm.
Assam and North-east India	6.25 „ (= 158.7 „)	
Bengal ...	... 6.22 „ (= 158.0 „)	
China ...	... 6.13 „ (= 155.7 „)	
Madras ...	... 5.68 „ (= 144.2 „)	Average 144 mm.
Ceylon ...	... 5.65 „ (= 143.5 „)	

The biggest male bird from Madras or Ceylon has a wing of 5.72 in. (= 145.3 mm.) whilst the smallest female from anywhere else has one of 6.08 in. (= 154.4 mm.) ; thus, whilst the average bird in Ceylon and Madras has a wing more than ½ in. smaller than the average northern birds, the biggest from the former area is still more than ¼ in. smaller than the smallest from the latter.

The type-birds ♂ and ♀ of *bisincta* are the two described by Jerdon from Madras, so that the northern species must bear another name, and the earliest available appears to be that of *domvillii*, given to a Hainan bird by Swinhoe in 1870.

Distribution. Orissa, the whole of Bengal in suitable localities, Assam, through Chittagong into northern Burma, and thence through the whole of that country into Hainan and Cochin China, and south into the Malay Peninsula. Beavan recorded it as common in parts of Chutia Nagpur, but no one else has found it there since his time, and it seems to be restricted to the wooded parts of Manbhum and Purulia. I once saw a small flock of them in Hazaribagh of which one was shot, but this is the only time they have been seen in that district, and it is probable that throughout the dry zone in east-central India they only occur as very occasional stragglers from the more humid countries adjoining, and do not enter at all into the western dry country. Harington reports it from the dry zone in Burma, but apparently even there it is more rare than in the wetter climate north and south.

Oates, in Hume's *Nests and Eggs*, writes : "It is entirely unknown in Khandesh, Goozerat, Kattywar, Sind, the Punjab, Rajputana, and the North-West Provinces, and is only known in the Sub-Himalayan Terais of Behar and Oudh, and the Eastern forest-regions of the Central Provinces. It is a purely Indo-Burmese type, not to be found, I think, in India out of the 60 in. rainfall regions."

Nidification. Throughout its area of habitation, the Orange-breasted Green Pigeon is resident and breeds, though it may move locally with the seasons ; and it also appears to move higher into the hills and further into the plains in July and August, at the end of the breeding-season.

In the hills north and south of the Brahmapootra Valley it breeds regularly up to an elevation of about 4,000 ft., and occasionally up to some 2,000 ft. higher than this. On the other hand, it also breeds throughout the plains where there is a sufficient forest and rainfall, and is quite common during the breeding-season even in the low-lying Sunderbunds, where the daily tides actually surround with salt water the trees on which they build.

It is now over forty years since Blyth first discovered this bird breeding, and took its nest in the Botanical Gardens, Calcutta ; but when I was there two years ago, in 1911, we were attracted, by the whistling of Green Pigeons, to the huge banyan tree which forms one of the well-known sights of the gardens, and there we saw a male bird "bowing and scraping" to his little mate: so evidently the spread of buildings for miles in all directions round these gardens has not yet driven it away.

The actions of the male Orange-breasted Green Pigeon when courting, are those of the genus generally. The bird puffs out its feathers and waddles up and down a bough, to and from the female, solemnly bobbing its head at regular intervals all the time—sometimes whistling its beautiful notes, sometimes croaking and crooning in an undertone which it considers even more seductive and musical. The female is content, as a rule, to feed whilst her consort shows off, but she, too, will now and then indulge in a clumsy step-dance, and bow and whistle in response to her mate's protestations of love.

Over most of its habitat this Green Pigeon is an early breeder: Oates found it breeding in Pegu from March to May; from the Malay States I have received eggs laid in January, February, and March; in Lower Burma it appears to breed principally in February and March; Irwin took eggs in Hill Tipperah in April, and Hodgson records its breeding-season in Nepal as being from April to June; in Dacca I found it breeding in March, and throughout the plains districts of Bengal. I think March and April are the principal breeding-months, but in the hill-ranges the favourite breeding-season is from early April to late May. It must, however, be remembered that all Green Pigeons are very irregular in their breeding-time, and doubtless many have two broods, for though I have often taken eggs of this species in early March, I have equally often taken fresh eggs in late August.

The nest is a typical Green Pigeon's nest, but is even more flimsy than most. Writing long ago in the *Bombay Natural History Journal* about this bird, I recorded: "The nest of this species seems to be about the most primitive of all Pigeons' nests. I have seen some which it would appear ridiculous to suppose capable of holding a young brood, and how they *do* succeed in so doing I cannot understand. I took one nest in 1893, in which I do not think there were more than about a score of twigs used, and gaps showed through the nest fully half an inch in diameter, only just small enough not to allow of the eggs falling through."

They do not seem at all particular where they make their nests, but generally select a site either inside fairly thick jungle or forest of some kind, or else just on the outskirts of it. It is quite exceptional for the nest to be placed in an isolated tree or clump of trees, though it may now and then be taken in the large mango-orchards in Bengal, especially if these have been somewhat neglected, and have a good deal of undergrowth in them.

I have seen these nests placed well up in big trees twenty, twenty-five, and even thirty feet from the ground. Others have been placed in small saplings, thick high bushes, and in bamboo-clumps hardly beyond the reach of a tall man; whilst yet a few others have been built in cane-brakes in swamps, in bushes and dwarf bamboos not four feet above the land or the water of the swamps in which the cane-brakes grow.

The nest takes but very few days to construct, both birds joining in the work, the male doing most of the carrying of the twigs and the female placing them in position. They work for a few hours only morning and evening, and during the rest of the day feed and doze. The nest made, the two eggs are generally laid with an interval of one day between, but sometimes, on consecutive days; and from this time onwards the male bird accepts all the responsibilities of his position, taking half the duties of incubation, feeding his wife with occasional dainties, and cheering her with his whistling when she is sitting.

Incubation takes, I think, twelve or fourteen days; but I have never made quite sure of this, and it may be a day more or less according to the weather, which affects incubation to a great extent.

The eggs are, of course, the same soft smooth white like those of the rest of the family, and the average size of 100 eggs is 1.1 in. (= 27.9 mm.) by .89 (= 22.6 mm.).

This beautiful Green Pigeon is extremely abundant throughout the Province of Assam, alike in the plains and in the hills up to about 2,500 ft., thence becoming more scarce up to about 4,000 ft., above which it is rare. It does however sometimes occur up to at least 6,000 ft. for I have shot one of a pair seen at the Peak, near Shillong in the Khasia Hills, in heavy rhododendron and oak forest, and have occasionally also seen it in the highest ranges to the east of the North Cachar Hills round and about Hungrum.

It is principally a bird of forest-country and prefers above all the vast stretches of forest-land running along the foot of the Himalayas, and for some few miles into the adjoining plains, especially frequenting such places as are broken up by a certain amount of cultivation and scattered villages. At the same time, wherever there are trees bearing fruit for them to eat, these birds will also be found, except in the most open of plains, and occasionally they may be met with even in clumps of fruit-trees and village orchards—or topes, as they are called—far from any forest.

Around villages and in the more open parts of their habitat they will be found resorting to their feeding-places from daybreak until 8 or 10 a.m., and again in the cool of the evening; but in forest-country and about villages standing in heavily wooded tracts they will feed more or less throughout the day, except for two to four hours of the hottest time, when they retire to the densest foliaged forest-trees for their siesta. In Gunjong, North Cachar Hills, these birds came into my garden more frequently than any other Green Pigeon, and used to feed greedily on a kind of fig of which there were two or three trees bearing fruit nearly all the year round. They were also very partial to the guava-fruit which, when ripe and soft, they tore to pieces with their bills, swallowing huge bits as big, if not bigger, than their own heads. A more objectionable habit they had was that of getting into the orange-groves and pulling off the tiny oranges when about the size of small marbles. I don't think they ate many of these, for after a flock had visited and been frightened away from a grove, a large number of these little oranges were to be found lying under the trees; and it really looked as if, after they had tasted the fruit and found it unpalatable, they had then set to work to mischievously destroy what they did not care to eat.

They are rather shy birds, and if seated in scantily covered trees generally take to flight before one gets close enough for a shot, but if in very densely covered ones they often trust to the foliage screening their green bodies from view, and will remain where they are, absolutely still and silent, until the intruder departs, or curiosity gets the better of their nervousness, and they commence to move about in the endeavour to get a better view of him. Beavan found them in Manbhum, feeding on the fruit of the nux vomica in company with other Pigeons.

Their movements when feeding are very slow and methodical, and though they will occasionally fly from one part of a big tree to another, they usually make their way by climbing hand over hand—or I suppose one should say foot over foot—along the boughs and branches. They are quarrelsome birds, of course—all Pigeons and Doves are—and resent any other bird, Pigeon or other kind, coming too close to them as they feed. If thus disturbed they open their mouths wide and emit a sort of hissing croak; and if this awe-inspiring sound is not sufficient to induce the other bird to go, they clamber up to within a foot or two of him, and then launch themselves at him, endeavouring to beat him over the head with their wings. They also peck one another freely, and will try to get a firm hold of the feathers of the other bird's head; and this once obtained, will shake and pull until the feathers come out, or the opponent gets in a smack with his wing hard enough to make the other leave go. I have often seen males in the early spring, when most of the fighting goes on, with their heads quite raw and bleeding; but at the same time the most serious injuries are probably caused by blows with the shoulder of the wing, which are given with quite sufficient force to stun.

They have quite a large range of conversational notes, covering much bad language, and not a little which we may hope to be good; but their ordinary notes are the sweet whistling ones common to all the Green Pigeons. Possibly the whistling of the Orange-headed Green Pigeon is not quite so melodious as that of some others, such as the Pin-tailed and Wedge-tailed Green Pigeon, but it is very sweet and mellow—now rising, now falling, but never anything but soft and full: never shrill, and never out of tune. Davison says that it has a lower and more jerky note than *C. viridifrons* and a less-soft one than *vernans* and *fulvicollis*.

I don't think they assemble in such large flocks as do some of their nearest relations, and even where most common, small flocks numbering from half a dozen to a dozen are most often seen, whilst flocks of over a score are quite exceptional. It is not unusual, also, to see a single bird of this species, or indeed two or three of them, consorting with a flock of *Treron nepalensis* (the Thick-billed Green Pigeon), or with one of the forms of the Grey-headed Green Pigeons, for although quarrelsome, it is very sociable, and it would always rather fight with a pal than be left by itself in peace.

Its flight is much like that of the two Pigeons just mentioned, perhaps not quite so fast or strong as either, but the difference, if any, is so slight that it makes it no easier to kill, and as a sporting-bird it is practically on a par with the others, whilst in beauty it ranks even higher than they do. In Assam it always forms a considerable proportion of the general bag at large shoots, being outnumbered invariably only by the Grey-headed Pigeon, equalling in number the Thick-billed, and generally more numerous than the rest.

(10) OSMOTRERON BISINCTA BISINCTA (Jerdon).

THE LESSER ORANGE-BREASTED GREEN PIGEON.

(PLATE 3.)

Vinago bisincta Jerdon, Madr. J.L.S., XII p. 13 (1840); id., Ill. I. Orn., p. 21.
Vinago unicolor id., Madr. J.L.S., XI p. 14.
Osmotreron bisincta id., B.I., III p. 449; Legge, B. Cey., II p. 725, III p. 1218; Butler, J.B.N.H.S., X p. 311; Taylor, Str. Feath., X p. 463; Ferguson, J.B.N.H.S., XVI p. 1.

Vernacular Names. *Chitta putsa guwa*, Tel.; *Patcha-praa*, Tamil in Ceylon; *Batta-goya*, Singhalese.

Description. This subspecies only differs from the last in being very decidedly smaller, with a wing of only 5.65 in. (or 143.5 mm. against 158.5 mm. in the northern and eastern form). The male and female differ from one another in exactly the same way as do those of the Common Orange-breasted Pigeon.

"Bill greenish glaucus; legs pinkish-red; irides red, surmounted by a blue circle" (Jerdon).

"Iris carmine outwardly and beautifully cobalt blue inwardly; divided by a narrow dark ring, eyelid glaucus green; bill with the soft basal half glaucus green, and the terminal half pale blue; legs and feet coral red or pink red; claws bluish brown" (Legge).

Distribution. Ceylon, Malabar, and the Bombay Presidency as far north as Kanara, the south of Madras to about latitude 14°; and it has also been recorded by Jerdon from the Carnatic and east of Nellore.

Although so very closely allied to the last bird this subspecies appears to have a very well-defined habitat, and there seems to be a very wide stretch of country in north Madras, the extreme south of Orissa, and the Central Provinces, where no form of Orange-breasted Green Pigeon is to be found, or if it does occur at all, only with extreme rarity. Consequent on this definitive gap in their distribution, we have a very well-defined difference in the measurements of the two subspecies, as already shown.

This appears to be one of those interesting cases in which a race of birds has established itself, and thriven at some distance from its parent stock whilst the intermediate area has proved unsuitable, so that the intervening form inhabiting it has, or will very shortly have, died out. Legge went into the question of the racial difference of this Pigeon from the Indian form, but only compared his Ceylon specimens with those from south India, from which, as he says, they cannot be divided.

Nidification. The breeding-season of this bird is variously reported by different collectors. Layard took its nest in May, but Legge says that it also breeds in August. Sykes took its eggs, which he very kindly sent me, near Kandy in February and March, and Jenkins collected three clutches for me in January and February.

THE LESSER ORANGE-BREASTED GREEN PIGEON—*OSMOTRERON B. BICINCTA*

(½ Nat. Size—Male on left, female on right.) PLATE 3

It is probably a very irregular breeder, generally building its nest during the months from January to March, but sometimes not until April or even May, and having a second brood in the months of July and September.

Layard describes its nest as formed of sticks, with a slight lining of roots, etc., placed in the fork of a tree.

My own correspondents describe the nest as being of the usual character, built of small twigs, roughly interlaced, and with no lining whatsoever.

It should be noted that all the gentlemen who have sent me eggs, or notes upon the nidification of this Pigeon, agree that it is very partial to big forest-trees as sites for its nest, and that it commonly builds them on a large horizontal bough at a very considerable height from the ground.

The eggs in my collection only differ from those of *Osmotreron bisincta domvillii* in being decidedly smaller. Eight eggs average 1.04 in. (= 26.3 mm.) by .85 (= 21.6 mm.). The largest 1.10 in. (= 28.0 mm.) by .88 (= 22.35 mm.) and the smallest 1.0 in. (= 25.4 mm.) by .83 (= 21 mm.).

There is nothing to record about this bird's habits which differ from those of the Common Orange-breasted Pigeon.

It is very common in parts of Ceylon, Travancore, and in Malabar, but outside these districts seems to be very rare, wandering into south-east Madras only as an occasional straggler. The species, both this and *domvillii*, seems to require forest or extremely well wooded country of considerable humidity, and is rare or absent in the more dry zones. Legge records about the bird: "The Orange-breasted Green Pigeon affects the low jungle, the outskirts of the forest, detached rows of trees in open country, and sundry other localities where its favourite fruit abounds. It associates in small parties as a rule, but collects in large flocks in trees which are in heavy fruit. Its favourite fruit consists of the berries of the Bo, Banyan, Pala and Poppalille trees; on them it feeds with such avidity that it will return to the trees very shortly after being shot at. Its flight is swift, and when returning from its feeding-grounds in a continuous stream at evening time, affords good shooting as it crosses the roads in the northern and eastern jungles. This and the next species are much shot by the natives who possess guns. They take up their position beneath some fruit-bearing monarch of the forest, and shoot the Pigeon as they fly to feed in the mornings. It has a regular time, like other Fruit-Pigeons and Doves, for drinking, which is about seven in the morning and four in the afternoon. The flesh of this species is succulent and well-flavoured, but is not so delicate as that of the next bird [*pompadora*].

"Its note is a hoarse croak, repeated at intervals, but it is usually a silent bird.

"In the South of Ceylon I found they fed much on wild dates; an example I shot near Galle had its crops almost extended to bursting with the fruit. They are fond of frequenting hedges of fruit-bearing trees on open land, and I have often seen them frequenting rows of the common 'Cadaru' tree, although there can be nothing, of course, in the large nauseous fruit of that tree to tempt them."

Layard says that vast numbers are killed in the southern and western Provinces, as these birds swarm to the tree for the time being in fruit. They appear, according to him, to be always shot in the trees rather than in the more sporting manner carried out in Assam and India where, as already narrated, a perching bird is practically never shot, all being killed as they flight to and from their feeding-places. How numerous they are may be realized from what Layard says of his own shooting—when firing at one bird in the tree he "brought down seven or eight others which he could not see."

(11) OSMOTRERON VERNANS (Linn.).

THE PINK-NECKED GREEN PIGEON.

Columba vernans Linn., Mant., p. 526 (1771); Lath., I. Orn., II p. 599.
Columba purpurea id. ib., p. 599.
Treron vernans Blyth, J.A.S.B., XIV pt. II p. 851; Everett, J.S.B.A.S., p. 196.
Osmotreron vernans Bp., Con. Av., II p. 12; Hume, Str. Feath., III p. 323; Wald, in Blyth's B. Burma, p. 144; Hume and Dav., Str. Feath., VI pp. 411 and 414; Hume, Cat. no. 774, bis; id., Str. Feath., VIII pp. 67 and 109; Oates, B. Burma, II p. 309; id., in Hume's Nests and Eggs, 2nd ed., II p. 375; Salvadori, Cat. B.M., XXI p. 60; Blanf., Avi. Brit. I., IV p. 13; Sharpe, Hand-list, I p. 54; Oates, Cat. Eggs B.M., I p. 83; H. R. Baker, J.B.N.H.S., XVII p. 760.
Osmotreron viridis Hume, Str. Feath., I p. 461; id. ib., III p. 162; Blyth, B. Burma, p. 144.

Vernacular Name. *Ngu*, Burmese.

Description.—*Adult male.* Head and throat grey, in some cases with a tinge of green on the fore-head and throat; neck all round as far as the upper-breast below and extending on the sides and back as far as the shoulder purple-lilac, somewhat mixed with grey where the purple adjoins the back; back, scapulars, lesser and median wing-coverts and innermost secondaries green, the median wing-coverts broadly edged with pale lemon-yellow; rump green, changing to a bronze-tan on the upper tail-coverts; tail grey with a broad subterminal band of black, widest on the outer rectrices, narrowest on the central ones. Primaries and outer secondaries black, the first three or four primaries with narrow pale yellow margins. The greater coverts are the same colour as the back, but have broad yellow margins to the outer webs. Winglets and outer primary-coverts black. A broad circular patch of orange covering the whole breast; abdomen yellow-green, faintly splashed with grey at the sides; tibial plumes and feathers about vent darker green with wide yellow borders. Under wing-coverts and axillaries grey, and the flanks mingled grey and green. Under tail-coverts deep chestnut, sometimes with a blackish patch near the ends of the longest. Under aspect of the tail black with a narrow grey tip.

Colours of soft parts. "Iris pink; feet light lake; bill plumbeous, nail whitish, cere and edge of gape green; weight about 6 oz." (Davison).

"Irides with three rings, the outer buff or pink, the next prussian blue, the inner ultramarine" (Davison).

Measurements. "Length about 11; tail 4.0; wing 5.8; tarsus .8; bill from gape .8" (Blanford).

The large series of this Pigeon in the British Museum shows a very wide range of measurements, the largest wing being no less than 6.10 in. (= 154.9 mm.) and the smallest only 5.30 (= 134.6 mm.), whilst the average is a little over 5.55 (= 141.0 mm.).

Adult female. Has the grey and lilac-purple of the male replaced with olive-green, varying a good deal in shade in different individuals, the head generally rather paler and brighter, and the fore-head suffused with yellow. There is no orange on the breast, which is olive-green and shades gradually into the yellow of the abdomen. The under tail-coverts are pale yellowish-buff, more or less suffused with cinnamon, especially on the basal half of the inner webs, and with the shortest ones freckled with dull brownish-green.

The colours of the soft parts are the same as in the male, though some females seem to have the legs and feet duller and paler.

Measurements. The females are very little, if at all smaller than the males. The series I have measured have an average wing of 5.52 in. (= 140.21 mm.), and the greatest and least length is 6.02 (= 152.9 mm.) and 5.25 (= 133.3 mm.) respectively. The tail of both sexes varies very greatly. A female from Manilla has a tail of 4.2 in. (= 106.7 mm.) whilst another from the same place has one of only 3.4 (= 86.3 mm.).

Young male. Resembles the female but assumes the adult plumage in patches after the first autumn-moult. The rufous on the upper tail-coverts is not developed, and the central rectrices are more green.

Young female "has the rufescent colour of the upper tail coverts scarcely visible and the central tail-feathers are more or less tinged with green" (Salvadori).

Young birds of both sexes have the iris much duller, and until the first autumn-moult it is generally a dull fleshy-brown.

Despite the great difference in the size of individuals of this species, and the considerable variations in the depths of colouring, and the extent of yellow on the head, I can trace no correlation between this and the differences in their geographical limits. The biggest birds, undoubtedly, do come from Manilla, but overlapping these in size, specimens occur even amongst those obtained furthest away from this place.

As regards the females from Manilla, it does appear to me that these have the grey tips to the tail-feathers somewhat broader and paler on the whole, and perhaps, also, the fore-head more yellow; but I do not consider the differences sufficient or sufficiently constant to warrant birds from these islands being separated as another subspecies.

Salvadori records that he has "seen in the Paris Museum a variety entirely of a canary-yellow."

Distribution. Salvadori gives the range of the Pink-necked Green Pigeon as "Siam and Cochin China, South of Tenasserim, Malay Peninsula and also Sumatra, Nias, Bangha, Billiton, Java, Sambawa, Borneo, the Phillipines, Sulu Islands, and Celebes."

Within our limits it is found as far North as Mergui in Tenasserim.

Davidson records it as very common in Tenasserim in the southern part of that province, and it appears to be equally common in suitable localities, throughout the Malay Peninsula and into Singapore.

Nidification. At present I know of but one note on this bird's breeding other than those recorded in Hume's *Nests and Eggs.* In this note Major Baker merely says that in Singapore it breeds "from March to May or June; the usual nest and eggs."

Davison, in southern Tenasserim, "on the 12th June found a nest of this Pigeon in a small very dense, thorny bush. The nest was of the usual Pigeon and Dove type, consisting merely of a few dry twigs. It was placed about five feet from the ground." The eggs found by Davison measured 1.15 in. in length by .81 and .82 in breadth respectively. Two other eggs found in Kussoom in the Malay Peninsula measured 1.11 in. by .86 and 1.05 by .85 in breadth.

I have had a fair series of these eggs sent me: a few from southern Tenasserim taken in June and July after the rainy season had well set in and a number from the Malay Peninsula which were all taken in the months January to March. It seems probable, therefore, that the majority breed during the first three months of the year, though others—these may be second broods—continue to breed until well on into July.

My eggs are decidedly small in comparison with the bird's size, sixteen only averaging 1.08 in. by .85 (= 27.4 by 21.6 mm.). The longest and broadest eggs are 1.14 (= 28.8 mm.) by .88 (= 22.3 mm.) respectively, and the shortest and most narrow 1.03 (= 26.2 mm.) and .80 (= 20.3 mm.).

The six eggs in the British Museum Catalogue vary from 1.08 in. to 1.12 in length and from .8 to .88 in breadth.

According to Davidson, this beautiful little Pigeon is an inhabitant of the denser forests only, being seldom found in thin jungle or in close proximity to villages and gardens. They appear to go about in small parties, as a rule of only six or eight members, though in some places they collect in enormous numbers to feed or roost.

Major H. R. Baker notes that "these birds roost in enormous numbers on the small mangrove-covered islands which are dotted about the North of the Johore river. Here sportsmen betake themselves in July and August, and stationing guns round an island await the flighting in the early morning and evening; in this way bags of several hundreds of birds are sometimes made."

In a letter to me Major Baker gives the following interesting account of one of these shoots: "The Pink-necked Green Pigeon is extremely common in Johore, Singapore and other parts of the Malay Peninsula, and forms a very favourite object of shooting from July to September, and one of these battues, though not a successful one, I will try to describe to you.

"We had received word that the Pigeons had commenced to flight, a sure indication that the breeding-season had finished, and that the young ones had joined the old birds in the morning and evening flight to and from the feeding-ground. It was with pleasurable anticipation, therefore, that C. and I hurried down one morning to the wharf at Singapore, with beds, kits, guns and food, at the invitation of our friend the doctor who had offered to take us in his launch to one of the roosting-places, a mud island in the Johore river, thickly covered with mangrove trees. We started early for the sea.

was rough, and we had some thirty miles to go, first along the coast and then up the river, and as we were delayed by having to rescue two Chinamen from a nearly swamped sampan, it was mid-day before we reached the mouth of the river. Tiffin taken on board and with no further delay, we arrived at our destination about 4 p.m., pulling up at a tangled mass of mangrove trees, about six acres in extent standing out of the water almost in mid-stream, and the river, even here, was almost a mile wide.

"This was our shooting ground, and most uninviting it looked with the tide half out and the gaunt finger-like roots of the trees exposed, to say nothing of the stench arising from the filthy black mud which was becoming more and more visible every minute. But there was no time to waste, for the Pigeons might begin to arrive at any moment. The only question to settle was whether to stand in the mud and water near the trees, in which case one was liable to sink in deeper than would be pleasant, or to squat in a tiny dug-out canoe which rocked dangerously at the slightest move; choosing the lesser of two evils we each cautiously crept into a canoe—they had been ordered beforehand, and were waiting for us—and proceeded to take up our positions around the island. I can well remember my feelings as time kept slipping away and the sun sunk lower and lower, and the mosquitoes became more and more attentive, and could not help thinking the whole affair was going to turn out a farce, when from across the river I saw a small sort of cloud which increased rapidly in size and was evidently coming towards me. Could it be the Pigeons? A very few moments settled the question, for with a swish and whirl of wings they were down, not on us, but on the trees. Talk about a hot corner at a pheasant battue or partridge drive! Child's play to this! And I was soon firing as fast as I could load, but alas! with poor results; then a rest of a few minutes and a similar burst of fire round the other sides told me that my companions were hotly engaged. But there was no time to speak now, scarcely time to think, for on came the Pigeons, battalion after battalion, mass after mass, from all quarters of the globe; a truly marvellous sight, and one would have imagined that the slaughter would have been correspondingly great, and that one would only have to fire at one bird to bring down half a dozen—as is actually the case at the beginning of the season before the birds have been much shot at and frightened and rendered cunning, and

I have seen parties bring in over two hundred birds. Our luck was out, however, on this occasion for it afterwards transpired that another party had, unknown to us, visited this same spot a couple of days before; the result was that instead of approaching the island fairly low over the water the Pigeons flew high up, mostly out of range, till exactly over the trees, when they seemed to close their wings and dive headlong into the trees. On reading this some may ask why we did not land and stand under the trees or in a clearing? The obvious retort would be that such people had never seen a mangrove swamp at close quarters—there is not an inch of dry land, nothing but slimy mud of unknown depth, and a tangled mass of roots which nothing but a snake or mongoose could get through! By this time it was getting dusk, and the flight ceased as abruptly as it had begun, and as we could not induce any Pigeons to come out and fly around (no amount of shooting or firing into the air will make them quit the trees) we picked up the slain—only some two dozen—and made for the launch where baths, dinner, pipes and beds awaited us."

Davison says that they have "a soft, low whistle, ending in a sort of 'coo,' very unlike that of *O. chloroptera*, *malabarica*, etc." And again he says that its note is much like that of *Treron nepalensis*, though much softer, and he adds that in habits also it closely resembles that bird.

Genus BUTRERON.

The genus *Butreron* consists of a single species, which forms a connecting link between *Osmotreron* and *Treron*, for whereas the former has a soft cere covering well over one-third of the basal portion of the bill, and the latter has the whole of the culmen clear of the cere, *Butreron* has the horny part or ramphotheca including more than two-thirds, and the cere less than one-third of the culmen. It also has a narrow orbital space bare, though this is not so extensive or vividily coloured as in *Treron*.

The bill is stout and high; the third primary is sinuate on the inner web, but less so than in *Crocopus* and *Osmotreron*; the lower tail-coverts are very long.

(12) BUTRERON CAPELLII.

THE LARGE THICK-BILLED GREEN PIGEON.

(Plate 4.)

Columba capellii Temm., Pl. Coll. 143 (1823).
Treron capellii Blyth, J.A.S.B., XIV p. 848; id., Cat. B.M.A.S.B., p. 228; Hume, Str. Feath., VIII p. 67; Everett, J.S.B.A.S. 1889, p. 196.
Butreron capellii Bp., Con. Av., II p. 9; Blanf., Avi. Brit. I., p. 13; Finn, J.B.N.H.S., XIV., p. 577.
Butreron capellei Salvadori, Cat. B.M., XXI p. 32.

Vernacular Names. Not recorded.

Description.—*Adult male.* Whole upper-plumage an olive-grey green, the fore-head paler and more grey, and the back of the neck more yellowish; upper tail-coverts still more yellow, especially on the longest which are practically the same in tint as the centre tail-feathers. These are greenish-yellow with pale brown shafts, the outermost feathers are dark slate-grey, with a broad pale grey tip, and the intermediate feathers gradually change in coloration between the two extremes. Lesser and median wing-coverts like the back; greater coverts, shoulder of wing, bastard-wing, and quills deep slate-grey, a few of the outer median and all the greater coverts narrowly margined bright king's-yellow; innermost secondaries paler than the other quills, and becoming green like the back on the smallest—broadly margined on the outer webs with king's-yellow. Throat and neck pale greenish-yellow, changing on the sides of the neck and face to the colours of the upper-parts; breast bright deep orange, the sides washed with a tinge of chestnut, remainder

THE LARGE THICK-BILLED GREEN PIGEON—*BUTRERON CAPELLII.*

(½ Nat. Size—Male below, female above.) PLATE 4

of lower plumage oil-green, the back of the tibia and feathers about the vent buff; under tail-coverts deep chestnut-maroon, except a few of the shortest lateral ones, which are buff; under surface of wing dove-grey, the coverts more or less mixed with green, axillaries and flanks greenish-grey.

Colours of soft parts. "Iris deep brown or deep reddish brown; bill very pale whitish green, cere and gape bice green; legs, feet, and eyelids bright yellow, claws horny blue" (Davison).

"Iris dark ash or golden yellow" (Hartert).

"Orbits slightly bare, tinged yellow; feet chrome yellow" (Wallace). "Iris dull red; eyelids, orbital skin, and feet yellow" (Butler).

Weight 15 to 17 oz., according to Davison's notes.

Measurements. Wing 7.65 in. to 8.2 (= 194.3 to 208.2 mm.), tail 5 in. to 5.75 (= 127.0 to 146.0 mm.), tarsus .8 in. to .9 (= 20.3 to 22.8 mm.); bill at front .85 in. to .95 (= 21.5 to 24.1 mm.), and from gape about 1.3 in. (about 33 mm.).

Blanford gives the tarsus as 1.1 in. (about 28 mm.). Length in the flesh 387-400 mm. (Butler).

Adult female. Has the orange of the breast replaced by green strongly suffused with golden-yellow, and showing up brightly against the adjoining parts. The posterior feathers of the flanks and of the tibia are a darker grey-green and more mixed with buff, and the under tail-coverts are buff with dull brownish-green bases and centres.

Colours of soft parts. "Legs and feet pale yellow, claws pale blue; hard part of bill greenish white, soft part plumbeous, irides deep brown and edges of eyelids pale yellow. Weight about 13 oz." (Davison.)

The measurements of the series of females in the British Museum do not show any definite difference between the male and female, but the latter is the slighter, lighter bird, and seems to have, on the whole, a somewhat more slender bill.

Distribution. The only instance of this Pigeon being found within the limits of the area dealt with in this work, is that of a single bird obtained by Dr. Anderson in Elphinstone Island near Mergui. Outside our limits it is found in the Mergui Archipelago, Malay Peninsula, Sumatra, Borneo, and Java.

Nidification. Nothing yet known.

There is practically nothing on record about this bird, but it appears to differ in no way in its habits from the other Fruit-Pigeons.

Genus TRERON.

The genus *Treron* is very closely allied to *Osmotreron*, and our sole Indian species of the genus, *T. nipalensis*, is extremely like *Osmotreron phayrei* in coloration. The former can, however, be distinguished at once by the fact that the soft cere does not cover the top of the culmen next the fore-head, the horny portion, or ramphotheca, extending over the whole of the culmen. There is also a wide naked space round the eye.

In the Indian species the vivid green of this orbital skin and the equally vivid red of the base of the upper mandible, distinguishes at a glance this species from all our other Green Pigeons.

There are only two species of *Treron*—our Indian bird *nipalensis*, and *nasica*, which is found in Sumatra, Engano, Bangka, and possibly southern Borneo. But our bird is, as a matter of fact, only a subspecies of *Treron curvirostra* of Borneo, Sumatra, etc., as I show when dealing with the distribution of the two forms; though, having but the one subspecies within Indian limits, we need not, in this instance, adopt the trinomial system.

(13) TRERON NIPALENSIS (Hodg.).

THE THICK-BILLED GREEN PIGEON.

(Plate 5.)

Toria nipalensis Hodg., As. Nes., XIX p. 164 pl. IX (head and foot) 1836; Blyth and Wald., B. Burma, p. 143.
Treron nipalensis Blyth, J.A.S.B., XIV p. 847; id., Cat. B.M.A.S.B., p. 228; Jerdon, B.I., III p. 245; Godw.-Aus., J.A.S.B., XLIII pt. 2 p. 171; Hume and Oates, Str. Feath., III p. 160, Wald., B. Burma, p. 145; Hume and Dav., Str. Feath., VI p. 410; Hume, ib., VIII p. 100; id., Cat. no. 771; Bingh., Str. Feath., IX p. 193; Hume and Inglis, ib., p. 257; Oates, B. Burma, II p. 306; id., Str. Feath., X p. 235; Hume, ib., XI p. 289; Salvadori, Cat. B.M., XXI p. 34; Sharpe, Hand-List, I p. 54; Oates, Cat. Eggs B.M., I p. 83; Stuart Baker, J.B.N.H.S., X 363; Inglis, ib., XI p. 475; H. R. Baker, ib., XVII p. 764; Stuart Baker, ib., XVII p. 971; Harington, ib., XIX p. 308.
Treron nepalensis Oates, in Hume's Nests and Eggs, 2nd ed., II p. 370; Blanf., Avi. Brit. I., IV p. 14.
Hook-billed Pigeon Lath., Syn., II p. 632 (1783).
Columba curvirostra Gm., Sys. Nat., I p. 777 (1788).

THE THICK-BILLED GREEN PIGEON—*TRERON NIPALENSIS*

(½ Nat. Size Male on right, female on left.)

PLATE 5

Vernacular Names. *Thoria*, Nepalese; *Gnu*, Burmese; *Harial*, Bengali and Sylheti; *Lali Haintha*, Assamese; *Daorep buku-gajao*, Cachari; *Inruigu gaherba*, Naga.; *Angee Koll Hurrial*, Sylheti.

Description.—*Adult male.* Fore-head and lores grey, deepening in colour on the crown and thence changing to olive-green on the nape and neck; scapulars, interscapulars, back and lesser wing-coverts chestnut-maroon, palest on the back where it meets the green neck, where also it is often suffused with grey; rump and upper tail-coverts olive-green, brightest and tinged with golden-yellow on the latter; central rectrices the same, outer rectrices grey with a band of black across the middle, widest on the outermost; the two pairs of feathers next the centre pair are also more or less suffused with green, and the others when in perfect condition have a very narrow terminal margin of the same. Quills black, the two outer primaries very narrowly margined with yellowish-white at the centre of the outer webs; innermost secondaries next the scapulars green, and the shoulder of the wing and a few coverts next the maroon also green; remaining wing-coverts black, with broad yellow edges to the outer webs; outer secondaries black with fine yellow borders. Cheeks, ear-coverts and sides of neck and lower-surface olive-green, more yellowish than on the upper-neck, and with the chin and throat still more yellow. In some specimens there is the faintest tinge of fulvous on the breast; feathers of the posterior flanks, tibial plumes, and about vent darker green mixed with white; under tail-coverts cinnamon, the outer ones mixed green and white.

Colours of soft parts. Irides with two rings, the inner and narrower of deep blue, the outer and broader varying from golden-yellow to orange-red; orbital skin a vivid verdigris-green; legs and feet deep lake-pink to coral-red, generally the latter; bill pale yellowish, or greenish, or less often a leaden-white with a deeper and more distinctly green tip, the base of upper mandible and round gape a bright coral-red.

Measurements. "Total length about 10.4 in., wing 5.62 to 5.76; tail 3.46 to 3.35; bill 0.6; tarsus 0.75 to 0.9" (Salvadori).

The series in the British Museum cover a far greater range of variation than is shown in the above. In wing-measurements the males vary from 4.90 in. (= 124.4 mm.) to 5.75 (= 146 mm.), but from these must be eliminated a large number of individuals which belong to a very well-marked subspecies from the south-eastern portion of its range. The average of the northern form is about 5.5 in. (= 139.7 mm.).

Adult female. Differs from the male in having no trace of maroon on the upper-plumage and in having the under tail-coverts pale buff with dull olive-green bars on the longest and olive-green bases to the shorter feathers.

Colours of soft parts. Similar to the same in the male, but the verdigris blue-green of the bare orbital skin is not so bright.

Measurements. The series of skins in the collection of the British Museum show that the female is, on an average, no smaller than the male, the wing being about, or a trifle over 5.5 in. (= 139.7 mm.).

Young male. Similar to the female, but getting a small amount of maroon on the upper-plumage in the first autumn-moult.

Nestling. Like the adult female, but everywhere more grey and duller and with the lower-parts an oily grey-green. The iris is pale grey-brown, the skin of the face a livid-grey, and the bill whitish with the terminal third bluish, and the basal portion a livid-pink.

Distribution. The Thick-billed Green Pigeon is found throughout the Himalayas from Nepal in the west, through Sikhim, in all the hill-ranges north and south of the Brahmapootra River, the better wooded parts of eastern Bengal, throughout Burma, the Chin Hills, Shan States into the extreme south of Tenasserim, Annam, Siam, and Cochin China into the north of the Malay States. In the south of the Malay States, Borneo, Sumatra, and the Phillipines it is replaced by the true *curvirostra*.

The earliest notice of this form of Green Pigeon is the plate in Latham's *Synopsis of Birds*, a figure which agrees quite well with the Sumatran Thick-billed—or, as he calls it, Hook-billed—Pigeon, except that it does not show the grey of the head. On this plate was founded the description of *Columba curvirostra* in Gmelin (*Systema Naturae*, I p. 777) in which again the grey of the head is not mentioned. There cannot, I consider, be the slightest doubt that the present bird is the one depicted by Latham and described by Gmelin, and the specific name for the Thick-billed Pigeon must therefore be *Treron curvirostra*. Our Indian form, however, is quite easily distinguished from the Sumatran bird, the latter being separable at a glance by its generally darker hue both above and below. In addition to this the grey of the crown is distinctly darker and more dull, and often considerably restricted in area; the upper-plumage is of a duller darker green, and the under-parts, instead of being a comparatively bright greenish-yellow, are a dull oily yellow-green.

In size the southern bird is also very much smaller, the wing running from 4.90 in. (= 124.4 mm.) to 5.12 (= 130.0 mm.).

Nidification. Wherever found the Thick-billed Pigeon is resident and breeds, and in Cachar and the Khasia Hills I have taken great numbers of their nests. They commence breeding very early and some few eggs may be taken in the end of March, but April is the month in which most may be taken, and they continue to lay throughout May and June, whilst in July and August there is a fresh increase in the numbers breeding, so that it is probable that most birds have two broods in the year.

I do not think either nest or eggs can be distinguished from those of *Osmotreron phayrii*, and like that bird the Thick-billed Pigeon is a very speedy builder. A nest built in an orange-grove outside my house took only four days to build, though for some few days previously the pair of birds were constantly placing a few twigs in position, either in the same tree as that in which they eventually built, or in one of the other orange-trees in the same grove.

Incubation, I believe, took fourteen days, but I cannot be sure as I was afraid of disturbing the birds by too close inspection. They were not timid, and did not mind my moving about in the orchard, although the nest with the sitting bird on it was quite visible from one or two points of view.

When nesting in the jungle they place their nests either in a sapling, quite unconcealed, in a high bush or in a bamboo-clump, and very often two or three nests are placed in close vicinity to one another. The male bird takes at least an equal share in the duties of incubation, and also helps in the building of the nest and the care of the young.

The eggs are, as usual, two in number, pure white with a fine close grain, very smooth, but not highly glossed. The average of 100 eggs is 1.10 in. by .82 (= 27.9 by 20.8. mm.), and the greatest length and breadth is 1.15 in. by .86 (= 29.1 and 21.8 mm.) respectively, and the least 1.07 in. and .79 (= 27.1 and 20 mm.).

All round the north-east frontier of India from the extreme west of Nepal through Bhutan, the Miri, Dafla, Abor Hills, Assam and north-west Burma, the Thick-billed Green Pigeon is very common, and always forms a prominent feature in any large miscellaneous bag of Pigeons.

As a rule it does not collect in very large flocks, anything from ten or twelve to a score of birds being most often met with, but sometimes it is found in much bigger numbers, and I have seen several flocks of over fifty and more than once one of over a hundred.

Of course, upon the larger fruit-trees very great numbers of these and other Pigeons gather together for the feeding; but though these may become very intermixed as they scramble about from one branch to another in their search for berries and fruit, when frightened away they at once separate up into their smaller companies.

Quarrelsome as are all Pigeons and Doves, this small member of the family is even more so than most; at the same time it is given, like the rest of its relations, more to the uttering of bad language than to the giving of actual blows. These, however, are quite often enough indulged in, and result in feathers flying freely accompanied with loud clappings and beatings of the wings and guttural notes of anger. The row usually commences when two males, perhaps of different flocks, approach the same tempting cluster of figs or other dainty. The two birds will clamber slowly along the branch towards one another until they are a foot or two apart, when both will stop abruptly and bob energetically up and down uttering a few cuss "words" at the same time. If neither of the warriors are rendered nervous by the appearance of the other, they again approach one another with mouth wide open, and uttering a constant half hiss and half guttural note the bowings and bobbings increase in violence, and the birds dance about with wings semi-lifted. Then, suddenly, there is a clap of wings, and the two birds launch themselves at each other, attempting to strike with their wings, or to seize the feathers of their opponent's head with their bills. If either can accomplish this he then proceeds to drag his victim along the branch until the feathers come out, when the fight is again renewed after an interval of more posturing, or the wounded bird finds he has had enough of it, and retires to another part of the tree.

The guttural note of the Thick-billed Pigeon has been alluded to by some writers as peculiar to this particular species, but this is not so. All the Green Pigeon—some half dozen—well known to me in life, have this, or a very similar note, though I do not think any of them employ it quite so freely as this bird does. It is an argumentative or angry note, I think, and the ordinary conversational notes, though somewhat the same, are much softer and very low, so low indeed, that one must be very close to the utterer to overhear them. The whistling-notes, to me, seem much the same as those of the other species, but most observers say they are not so sweet and melodious, as well as being less sustained and more jerky.

It consorts freely with other species when feeding, and though so much smaller than most of them, allows no bullying and can hold its own well, even with the bigger birds. Its flight is very strong and swift, and owing to its exceptionally tough skin and very dense feathers it requires a very straight, hard-hitting gun to deal with it effectively. As far as I can remember I have seen no big bag made exclusively of this Green Pigeon, but I have several times seen forty or fifty shot—amongst others—in an afternoon, and now and then small bags of twenty to forty couple will be found to be made up almost entirely of them.

They sometimes ascend the hills to at least as high as 4,000 ft., and are common enough up to 3,000, but they are also equally at home right away in the plains at long distances from any mountains.

Like all Green Pigeons it is essential that the country they inhabit should be well wooded, but they are by no means exclusively forest-birds, and are frequently seen in more or less open plains and extensive clearings, feeding on the fruit of the few trees which have been left standing.

Just as they share the family failing of bad temper so, also, they share the family trait of greediness, and these small birds will continue to swallow huge plums and other fruit until their crops almost burst, and when they are shot and fall to the ground their crops are so full that they generally do give way, whilst their breasts, lined with thick yellow fat, also often burst open. Undoubtedly these birds in a wild state eat grain as well as fruit, for though I have never seen them in a grain-field, I have more than once shot birds with rice in their crops, and once one with some tiny millet in it. In captivity they take to grain freely, but at the same time they prefer soft fruit or boiled rice, and are especially greedy over plantains, often making their breast and head-feathers in a very dirty state in their anxiety to get as much as possible inside, in the shortest time on record.

They drink fairly regularly, morning and evening in captivity, and probably also in a state of nature, for this is one of the Green Pigeons I have frequently seen on the ground by hill-streams, walking about quite freely on the sandy bank or in amongst the " dhup " grass which grows so freely in such places. I have also seen this Pigeon on the ground feeding on wild-strawberries and the berry of a plant which runs along the ground beside jungle-tracks.

At night they seem to prefer roosting in high trees, but sometimes also frequent cane-brakes for the same purpose, and I once found them frequenting a dense bed of reeds in the Diyung River in north Cachar. Day was only just breaking and the birds were fluttering about the reeds as if they had been there all night, and I do not think they had merely just come down to drink.

They do well in captivity, and are very handsome little Pigeons, the brilliant red of their bill and the vivid green of the orbital skin considerably enhancing the general beauty of their lovely plumage. If the birds get ill the green of the orbital skin becomes very dull and more of a livid than a verdigris green.

In the plate of this Pigeon the artist has well shown the attitude adopted by the male bird when commencing to posture before the female during the courting-period.

GENUS—SPHENOCERCUS.

The genus *Sphenocercus* is very closely allied to *Osmotreron* in its general outward characteristics, but it differs from that genus, and from all other genera of the subfamily *Treroninae*, in having no sinuation on the inner web of the third primary, and in having the tail-feathers somewhat lengthened and graduated. In regard to its bill it is nearest to *Osmotreron*, the soft basal part or cere covering even a greater portion of the bill than it does in that bird, occupying about two-thirds of its total length.

The under tail-coverts in our two Indian species are very long, exceeding in length the outermost rectrices.

Both our species are, for Green Pigeon, rather big birds, with a wing exceeding 7 in.

Salvadori recognizes eight species of Green Pigeon in this genus, but of these at least three, and probably four—*sieboldi*, *sororius*, *formosae*, and *permagnus*—must be relegated to the rank of subspecies of our Indian *sphenurus*, or if the first-named can be considered a good species, then the three latter will be subspecies of *sieboldi*.

Key to the Species.

A. Central tail-feathers acuminate and extending two or three inches beyond the next pair ... ... *S. apicauda*.

B. Central tail-feathers not acuminate, and only a little longer than the next pair ... ... *S. sphenura*.

(14) SPHENOCERCUS APICAUDA (Hodg.).

THE PIN-TAILED GREEN PIGEON.

(PLATE 6.)

Treron apicauda (Hodg.), Blyth, J.A.S.B., XIV p. 854 (1845).
Sphenocercus apicaudus id., Cat. B.M.A.S.B., p. 230; Jerdon, B.I., III p. 454; Godw.-Aus., J.A.S.B., XXIX pt. 2 p. 3; Wald., in Blyth's B. Burma, p. 144; Hume and Davison, Str. Feath., VI p. 415; Hume, Cat. no. 779; id., Str. Feath., VIII p. 109; id. ib., XI p. 292; Stuart Baker, Ibis 1896, p. 356; Harington, B. Burma, p. 64; Stuart Baker, J.B.N.H.S., X p. 364; Inglis, ib., XI p. 475; Stuart Baker, ib., XVII p. 971; Harington, ib., XIX p. 308; id. ib., XX p. 1010; Cook, ib., XXI. p. 674.

THE PIN-TAILED GREEN PIGEON—*SPHENOCERCUS APICAUDA.*

(½ Nat. Size—Male on left, female on right.)

PLATE 6

Sphenocercus apiciauda Oates, B. Burma, II p. 305; Salvadori, Cat. B.M. XXI p. 5; Blanf., Avi. Brit. I., IV p. 16; Sharpe, Hand-List, I p. 55.

Vernacular Names. *Sang-pong*, Lepcha; *Daorep-galou*, Cachari; *Lumba-dum Kohhila*, Hin.; *Bor Haitha*, Assamese; *Harial*, Bengal Terai; *Ngu*, Burmese.

The vernacular names generally used for this Pigeon are the same as those used for the Bengal Green Pigeon or for the Wedge-tailed Green Pigeon, some adjective to designate its long tail being added.

Description.—*Adult male.* Whole head and neck bright yellowish grass-green, paling on the nape and changing to olive-green washed with french-grey, which forms a broad collar at the base of the hind-neck; back, scapulars, and wing-coverts grass-green, the feathers of these parts when examined very closely showing very fine, but faint, vermiculations of a darker grey shade which, however, are too indefinite to affect the general tone of coloration; rump and upper tail-coverts bright greenish-yellow; quills, bastard-wing, and greater-coverts black, three outermost primaries with very narrow yellow edging, secondaries rather more broadly edged with yellow on their terminal halves, and the innermost secondaries the same green as that of the back with broad lemon-yellow margins, forming, together with the yellow borders of the greater coverts, an oblique wing-bar. Under-surface greenish-yellow, the breast washed with orange-pink which merges into the surrounding colours; flanks, lower-abdomen, and vent much darker and with pale yellow-buff edging to the feathers varying in extent in different individuals. Under tail-coverts cinnamon, the outer webs with broad buffish-white margins. Whole under-wing surface dove-grey, axillaries mixed green and grey. Tail grey, dark above and pale below, the long central rectrices often becoming green on the greater part of the long narrowed ends; shafts of rectrices dark brown above, almost white below.

Colour of soft parts. Iris with an outer ring varying from rather pale but bright salmon-pink, through brick and terracotta-red to an intense carmine-red; the inner ring is a bright pale blue. Bill pale bluish-horny, often with a green tinge, the cere and basal portion more bright and blue in tint, and the edges of the lids more leaden. Legs and feet bright red, sometimes coral-red, often with a touch of crimson, and more rarely a crimson-red. Claws horny-brown. Orbital skin a pale livid-blue to clear blue.

"Iris blue, surrounded by a rim of pinkish brick-colour; bill a delicate pale blue or glaucous blue, feet deep lake" (Wardlaw Ramsay).

"Irides, outer ring salmon pink, inner bright ultramarine blue, bill and orbital skin bright blue or pale blue, corneous portion of the bill whitish blue; legs and feet crimson" (Davison).

"Legs and feet bright coral red" (Davison).

Normally the legs are a coral-red with only the faintest sign of crimson, but in very old birds they become a deep lake-colour, showing by the rough edges of the scales and the state of the feet generally the age of the birds. In these birds, also, the outer ring of the iris is usually rather deep in tint, and doubtless the coloration of the iris becomes deeper and richer as the birds increase in age.

Measurements. Length about 16 or 17 in. (= 406 to 431 mm.); wing 6.3 in. (= 160 mm.) to 6.9 (= 175 mm.) and averaging over 6.6 (= 168 mm.); tail generally between 8 or 9 in., but running up to over 10 in. (=254 mm.) in exceptional cases; bill from gape about .95 in. (= 24.1 mm.) and from front about .6 (= 15.24 mm.); tarsus about .95 in. (= 24.1 mm.).

Weight from 6½ to 7½ or 8 oz. Cripps gives their weight as up to 9½ oz., but these must be exceptionally fat, big birds.

Throughout its great range there is no constant variation in the size of this bird, and specimens I have received from the extreme south have had wings above the general average, although this, the average, in southern Burma may be a little less than it is in Nepal and the Himalayan Terai. The largest bird measured comes from Darjeeling, and the smallest from Manipur.

Adult female, and male in first plumage. Differs from the adult male generally in being duller everywhere, but more especially about the head. The grey of the hind-neck is either absent or very faintly indicated, and there is never any orange-pink on the breast; the under tail-coverts are duller and paler, the outer webs being almost entirely white, with the centres marked with dull sage-green.

Colours of soft parts. "Legs and feet deep coral red, claws pale brown; corneous tips of the mandible pale horny green, rest of the mandible and bare lores bright, pale smalt blue, skin of eyes duller and more leaden, irides —inner ring blue, outer coral red" (Davison).

Davison seems to distinguish two points of difference between the male and female in coloration of the soft parts, i.e. in the bill and outer ring of the iris. As regards these two points however, after examination of a very large number of birds alive and freshly killed, I can detect no differences that are not individual rather than sexual. The green tint of the bill is often present in both sexes, and the bill of the female is often as clear a smalt or lavender-blue as that of the male. The outer ring of the iris seems also to vary to exactly the same extent. It is possible, however, that the lavender-blue of the orbital-skin is brighter in the male than in the female in most cases.

Measurements. The females average a trifle smaller than the males, the length of wing varying between 6.15 in. (= 156.2 mm.) and 6.75 (= 171.5 mm.), the average being about 6.5 (= 164.7 mm.); the tail is generally much shorter, being but little over 6 in. (= 152.4 mm.), though a specimen from Manipur in the British Museum collection has a tail measuring 6.9 in. (= 175 mm.). Davison gives the weight as about 7 oz.

The young male resembles the adult female, but partially acquires the grey on the hind-neck and the pink breast at the first autumn-moult, but not the dark under tail-coverts until the following spring. The long tail-feathers are not obtained until the bird is a year old, and these probably increase in length at each subsequent moult until the bird is three years old.

Measurements. The wings of both young males and females in the autumn of the first year average little over 6 in. in length, and such birds, even if very fat, seldom exceed 6 oz. in weight.

Distribution. Throughout the Himalayas and the broken country at their bases, from Kumaon in the west to Sadiya in the east, the mountain ranges of Assam south of the Brahmapootra, thence throughout the hill-ranges of Burma, Chin Hills, Shan States into the Malay States, whence I have a skin of a bird shot on the nest. A straggler only in the plains-districts of eastern Bengal, but not rare in the plains of the Brahmapootra and Surrma Valleys.

Nidification. The breeding-season of this Fruit-Pigeon begins early in the lower elevations of its habitat, but not until April at all heights from 2,500 ft. upwards. They continue to breed throughout April, May, and to some extent in June, whilst many birds have second broods in July and August. Like all the members of this family, however, their breeding-season is a very lengthy and very irregular one, and there is practically no month in the year in which one may not come across their nests containing both eggs and young of all ages. They breed most commonly between 2,000 and 3,000 ft., but Dr. A. N. Coltart took numerous nests in the plains of Dibrugarh, and I have also taken nests in the foot-hills of Cachar and Sylhet. On the other hand it certainly breeds as high as 6,000 ft., and possibly still higher in Nepal and Sikhim.

During the breeding-season the male bird indulges in the usual demonstrations of love performed by all Green Pigeons, including the general puffing out of the feathers, drooping of the wings, and constant bowings and bobbings. As usual, also, the interest of the female in such displays is of the slightest, though occasionally she too indulges in a minor display of pirouettes.

The nest is the normal platform of small twigs, and these may be either dry or green and torn from the tree by the birds themselves. Roughly speaking the nest may be anything from 5 to 8 in. in diameter and from one-half to 2 in. deep, according to its situation; the depression, if any, is very slight, and the eggs are often prevented from rolling out only by the projections of the interlacing twigs. They do not take long to construct, although the work of building is only carried out in the cool of the morning and evening, and whilst some nests are completed in three or four days, most take about a week. Incubation lasts about fifteen or sixteen days, and both birds take part in this labour, the cock also taking upon himself to feed the hen-bird whilst she sits.

The nest is nearly always placed upon a number of twigs or small branches of a sapling, generally between ten and fifteen feet above the ground, but I have also taken it from thick bushes at anything between five and twelve feet, and less often from large boughs of forest-trees. Bamboo-clumps, which form such favourite nesting-sites for many Green Pigeons, are very seldom made use of by this species, and I have never seen their nests placed in cane-brakes.

As a rule, the kind of country selected for nesting purposes is evergreen-forest, a tree being chosen either on the outskirts of this, or else in an opening near a stream, a patch of cultivation, or some natural glade of grass and fern.

The eggs are, as usual, two in number, pure white and elliptical in shape, though often one, and sometimes both ends are somewhat pointed. The texture is the same as that of the eggs of the genus *Osmotreron*, perhaps a trifle more coarse and porous, as they seem to get discoloured and stained more easily.

The average of one hundred eggs is 1.25 by .98 in. (= 31.7 by 24.8 mm.) and they vary in length between 1.09 and 1.37 (= 27.6 and 35 mm.) and in breadth between .87 and 1.03 (= 22.1 and 26.1 mm.).

The Pin-tailed Green Pigeon is essentially a bird of the hills and mountains, ascending them throughout its range to over 6,000 ft., and being more common above 2,000 ft. than below this height. At the same time it is also found quite down into the plains near the hills, and is by no means rare in Cachar, Sylhet, Tipperah, and Chittagong in the flat country below the hill-ranges.

Personally I have not noticed much, if any, variation in the elevation of their habitat connected with the seasons, and the birds seemed quite as common at 6,000 ft. in the North Cachar and the Khasia Hills in December and January as they were in the hot weather months, April to August. So, also, they are just as common in the foot-hills and the broken country round about in the hottest weather as in the coldest. The actual plains they probably do desert, during the breeding-season, for the forests of the foot-hills, but even this is doubtful, for one of my collectors told me that he found several pairs breeding in the forests and swamps of the Hylakandy district, and Inglis also obtained birds in the same place during the rains. In Burma, however, Harington and other observers have only recorded this beautiful Pigeon from the hills, and it does not appear to be found in the dry zone in central Upper Burma at any time of the year.

This Pigeon is certainly not as gregarious as some of its nearest relations. Many flocks consist of only some half-dozen birds, and whilst often they are to be seen in twos or threes, they are very seldom found in groups exceeding a score. At the same time very large numbers of these birds collect together at any place where there is attraction in the way of food, and on one occasion at Laisung, in North Cachar, at some 4,000 ft. elevation, I think there must have been literally thousands of these Pin-tailed Pigeon and the Wedge-tailed Pigeon collected to feed on a species of *ficus* which was then, in the month of May, in full fruit. It being the breeding-season a few birds only were shot for the pot, but for a distance of some three miles above and below my camp and on either side of the Laisung stream, the birds simply swarmed, and the numbers one could have bagged need only have been limited by the powers of the shooter to tramp up and down and fire off his gun.

Once the kind of fig in season had been eaten, the birds all dispersed —and ten days later, when I returned over the same route, no Pigeons were to be seen beyond the few who habitually resided in that particular spot, and the trees which had been brick red with the masses of small ripe figs, were stripped of the very last and most unripe berry.

I have already remarked on the curious similarity in the actions of the Green Pigeons and the Paroquets when climbing about a tree. In this particular Pigeon the likeness is further heightened by the long tail, and really it is often, for a few moments, difficult to tell which kind of bird one is watching until the discordant scream of the Parrot or the mellow whistling of the Pigeon gives away their identity.

The Pigeon climbs about the branches with head tucked in close to the branch, and his long tail also held close to it, just as a *Palaeornis* holds his and, in the same way, if the Pigeon reaches over to clutch at some tempting morsel a few inches away, up goes his tail to balance him, and is then held rigid and somewhat erect until the balance is restored. His foot-work, too, is quite similar to that of the Parrot, a slow and rather stolid manner of working up and down the branches, step by step, without hurry or flutter of wing. One point of difference, however, always exists, and that is the Parrot never proceeds far without using his bill to assist his legs, whereas never, as far as I have been able to make out, does the Pigeon use his bill for the purpose. But even this requires close watching to detect, for the Pigeon holds his head tucked in so close to the branch that it often looks as if he too was employing his bill as an additional "hand." Harington seems to have been deceived by the attitudes assumed by the Pin-tailed Pigeon in climbing, for he says: "It also has the regular parrot-like habit of using its bill for climbing up branches." Personally, however, I have never seen the bill so used, either by wild birds or by those in captivity, nor is the Pigeon's bill formed for such work, and it is possible that this accurate and close observer has on this point been mistaken.

The notes of the Pin-tailed Green Pigeon run through much the same range of sounds as the rest of the tribe; in anger the guttural notes are used, whilst its beautiful whistling-notes to me seem as mellow and sweet as those even of the Orange-breasted bird. It has, however, some additional notes not often, if ever, uttered by any other Green Pigeon, except its first cousin *sphenurus*, the Wedge-tailed Green Pigeon. Harington describes these notes as "something like the subdued chattering of monkeys."

Its flight is quite typical of the family, but is, perhaps, the least swift of all the Green Pigeons, and at the same time rather more direct and steady even when the bird has been fired at and frightened.

I have never personally made a big bag solely of these Green

Pigeon, nor have I ever heard of such, but they always form a certain percentage of any bag of Green Pigeon made in Assam and, in the hills above 4,000 ft., this and the Wedge-tailed bird are far the most common forms to be met with.

In North Cachar at a place below Hungrum, at about 5,000 ft. elevation, I once had an evening's very pretty shooting at these two species, getting eighteen couple of these, a few Grey-headed Pigeon and a single *Treron.* The birds were feeding on two clumps of trees divided by a shallow dip in which hill-rice had been grown, and where still stood a few of the creeping beans always grown by the Nagas beside the pathways intersecting these plots of rice. Hiding by a clump of these creepers in the middle of the dip, I sent some Naga youngsters to either group of trees to keep the birds on the move, and thus had very sporting shots as the startled birds swept down the slopes towards me and made for the trees on the far side. For a couple of hours the birds continued to flight backwards and forwards until dusk fell with the usual startling rapidity of the East; the birds disappeared, and gathering the spoils we made our way home to camp.

Hume found this species very common in Manipur, and has recorded the following interesting notes upon its habits: "They are rather stupid birds. You mark a flock on to a tree; you get under it and walk round, peering up into the green depths. You know that there are at least twenty large birds above you, and you know by falling berries and twigs that they are hard at work feeding, but they keep quite quiet, and it is often quite impossible, even with binoculars, to see a single bird, embowered as they sit in leaves coloured precisely like themselves. Then you shout, and kick the trunk of the tree, and stand eager for a shot, but 'they sit beside the nectar' careless of the bolts below, and at last you adopt the only feasible plan, and that is to get someone to fire into the tree at a bird, if he has chanced to spy one, otherwise by guess, and take a brace as they fly off. These guess shots are by no means always thrown away, one such one day brought down four birds. Notwithstanding the firing of these barrels one or two are generally sure to return to the tree and settle on it before your eyes in less than a minute, when, of course, seeing them alight, it is easy to pot them. But in from ten minutes to half an hour the whole of the rest of the flock is sure to return, and though you drop a couple of them as they pass to the tree, the rest alight as if nothing had happened, and so *da capo*. One afternoon at Matchi I bagged thirteen without moving, sitting in the shade under a stockade that commanded a fair shot at all birds crossing to and leaving a tree which happened for the day to be the object of their devotions. Their flight is smooth but not very rapid."

As already described this Green Pigeon and all others of the sub-family resort very regularly to certain fruit-bearing trees, and it is most probable that although Hume continued to get shots at them time after time, it was not the same flock at which he fired on each occasion. All the birds within a certain area, often a very large one, resort to the tree or clump of trees which, as Hume says, for the time being is the object of their devotions, and my own experience has certainly not shown me that these birds are as anxious to court destruction as Hume makes out to be the case.

(15) SPHENOCERCUS SPHENURA.

THE WEDGE-TAILED GREEN PIGEON.

Vinago sphenura Vig., P.Z.S. (1831), p. 173.
Vinago cantillans Blyth, J.A.S.B., p. 166 (1843).
Treron sphenura id. ib., XIV pt. 2 p. 853; Seebohm, B. Jap. Emp., p. 163.
Treron cantillans Blyth, J.A.S.B., XIV pt. 2 p. 854.
Sphenocercus cantillans id., Cat. B.M.A.S.B., p. 230.
Sphenocercus sphenurus Jerdon, B.I., III p. 453; Stoliczka, J.A.S.B., XXVII pt. 2 p. 65; Godw.-Aus., ib., XXXIX pt. 2 p. 3; id. ib., XLV pt. 2 p. 203; Hume and Hen., Lah. to Yark., p. 270; Hume, Nests and Eggs, p. 494; Hume and Oates, Str. Feath., III p. 163; Wald., in Blyth's B. Burma, p. 144; Hume and Dav., Str. Feath., VI p. 415; Hume, ib., VIII p. 109; id., Cat. no. 778; Scully, Str. Feath., VIII p. 339; Oates, B. Burma, II p. 304; Hume, Str. Feath., XI p. 292; Oates, in Hume's Nests and Eggs, II p. 377; Salvadori, Cat. B.M., XXI p. 8; Blanf., Avi. Brit. I., III p. 17; Sharpe, Hand-List, p. 52; Oates, Cat. Eggs B.M., I p. 80; Stuart Baker, J.B.N.H.S., X p. 364; Finn, ib., XIV p. 577; Rattray, ib., XVI p. 663; Ward, ib., XVII p. 943; Stuart Baker, ib., p. 971; Magrath, ib., XIX p. 155; Cook, ib., XXI p. 674; Venning, ib., p. 631.
Sphenocercus minor Brooks, Str. Feath., III p. 255.

Vernacular Names. *Kokla, Kokila,* Hin.; *Kaku,* Lepcha; *Gnu,* Burmese; *Haintha, Bor Haintha,* Assamese; *Daorep gadeba,* Cachari; *Kainal,* Paharee (Simla).

Description.—*Adult male.* Head and neck yellowish-green, the crown tinged with orange-rufous; the green of the hind-neck passing into olive-grey on the upper-back, and from that again into maroon on the scapulars, interscapulars, back, and lesser wing-coverts; lower-back, rump, upper tail-coverts and remaining wing-coverts and innermost secondaries olive-green, the median wing-coverts in old birds often more or less maroon or else edged with this colour, and the greater coverts narrowly edged with yellow on the outer webs; quills black, or dark blackish-grey, the 2nd, 3rd, and 4th primaries very finely margined yellow, the secondaries changing from black to green until the innermost are all of this colour; the outer ones with fine yellow margins to the outer webs on their terminal halves. Central rectrices the same green as the back, the outermost dark grey washed with green and with a broad subterminal band of very dark grey, whilst the intermediate feathers grade from the green of the central ones to the grey of the outermost. Chin and throat yellow, breast washed with orange-pink; lower-breast and abdomen greenish-yellow; the flanks and tibial plumes dark green with broad yellow margins; vent pale yellow; short outer tail-coverts yellow and green, the longer pale dull cinnamon with dull narrow green centres and shafts. Under wing-coverts, quills, and axillaries dark dove-grey, the latter more or less mixed with green.

In a great many males, which appear to be fully adult birds, the maroon on the back and interscapulars is very slight in extent, and it is always paler there than on the shoulders of the wing.

Colours of soft parts. "Legs, feet and claws, crimson pink; bill dull smalt blue; horny portion pale skim milk blue; orbital skin smalt blue; irides with an inner ring of pale bright blue and an outer ring of buffy pink" (Davison).

I have known the colours of the feet to vary from coral-red, with only a faint tinge of crimson, to an almost pure deep crimson; the soles are almost invariably paler and the claws are horny, or horny-brown, in exceptional cases only suffused with pink. The bill has the cere and the terminal portion dull smalt-blue, the central hard portion duller and paler, and, in a few specimens, there is a very faint tinge of green here. The orbital skin is pale lavender or smalt-blue. The irides have two rings, the inner bright pale ultramarine, the outer ranging from a buffy-pink to a very bright crimson-pink, the colour being brightest and most intense in old birds.

Measurements. Total length in life about 13 in. Length of wing from 6.8 in. to 7.3 (= 172.7 to 185.4 mm.); tail from 4.5 in. to 5.5 (= 114.3 mm. to 139.7); tarsus .65 to .75 (= 16.5 mm. to 19); bill from front the same and from gape .95 in. to 1.05 (= 24.1 to 26.6 mm.).

Throughout its range the variations in size seems to be much the same and I cannot find that northern birds are any larger than southern ones.

Adult female. There is no rufous on the head or maroon on the upper-plumage, and the under tail-coverts are pale ochre with green centres and white shafts.

Colours of soft parts. The same as in the male, the colour of the iris being, perhaps, not so brilliant as it is in very old males.

Measurements. There is practically no difference between the male and female, and in the very large series in the British Museum the average wing-measurement of both males and females works out at about 6.95 in. (= 176.5 mm.).

Young male. The young male is like the female in general coloration, but still duller and rather darker. The quills are of a very dull tint of brown, and often a rather greenish-brown, whilst all the quills are very narrowly edged with yellow.

The maroon on the upper-parts appears at the first autumn-moult as small patches on the wing, but is not acquired to its full extent together with the rufous crown until the subsequent spring-moult. Also, it is not until the first moult, or even after a still later one, that the birds grow to their full size.

"The base of the bill and orbital skin cobalt blue; tip of bill pale blue; irides brownish grey" (Scully).

In very young birds the bill is almost white, and the orbital skin and cere are pale dull lavender. The irides, composed of one ring only, are a pale, rather watery-looking grey.

The wing of the young male in the first year averages under rather than over 6 in. (= 152.4 mm.), and the tail about 4.5 in. (= 114.3 mm.).

The two specimens of *Sphenocercus cantillans* referred to by Mr. P. L. Dodsworth in a recent number of the *Avicultural Magazine*, and by myself in a subsequent number, are merely cage-birds which have lost their green pigment. When Mr. Dodsworth and I wrote about these birds we, neither of us, had the specimens to examine or a full library to refer to.

In the *Ibis* for 1868, p. 45, Blyth thus refers to these specimens: "*Sphenocercus cantillans*, nobis, (*passim*) figured also by the late Prince of Canino, is merely *S. sphenura* the common Kokhela of the Himalayas, after moulting in captivity, when the green of the plumage is more or less completely replaced by delicate pearl grey, as was long ago remarked by my friend Captain Thomas Hutton of Masuri."

These two specimens are now in the Gould collection in the British Museum, and on examination they show not only that they have practically lost all the green and yellow pigment in their plumage, but in one case also a few of the quills of the left wing are pure white, showing a further development towards accidental albinoism. As already remarked the yellow pigment has practically disappeared both above and below, leaving the reds and greys dominant, though the red is also showing signs of exhaustion. The breast is a dull pink with no trace of orange, and the maroon of the back is as usual in area, but is dull and pale.

It seems quite probable that in time these two birds would have become practically white, either from ill health, bad or unsuitable feeding, or some other cause. Captivity does not, though Blyth would seem to imply the contrary, normally cause Green Pigeons to lose their yellow or other pigment. I have now seen a good many, both of this and allied species, in captivity, but have so far come across no similar instance of discoloration. At the same time yellow pigment is undoubtedly the most volatile of all colouring matter in birds' plumage, and in other species of green birds, such as the *Cissas*, the green, in captivity or in ill health, often becomes a blue through the yellow pigment evaporating and not being re-supplied.

Distribution. The Wedge-tailed Green Pigeon is found from Kashmir in the west, through Nepal, Sikhim, Bhutan, the Dafla and Abor Hills, north of the Brahmapootra, and all the Assam hill-ranges south of that river, into the Chin Hills, Shan States and Burmese hill-ranges into Tenasserim.

Nidification. The Wedge-tailed Green Pigeon, as far as I personally know, and in so far as anything has yet been recorded, breeds only in evergreen forests, or in forest which is in full leaf during their breeding-season. This commences in early April and extends through May and into June, but the great majority of young birds are well on the wing by the beginning of August or end of July.

As usual with Green Pigeon both parents share the labour of making the nest, and of incubation when the eggs are laid. The nest is exactly like that of the Pin-tailed Green Pigeon, but is often placed at much greater heights from the ground. Mr. Dodsworth records one placed on a bough of a large tree about forty ft. up, and Hume says that they build their nests in trees at any height from six to fifty feet. Hume also says that they make their nests of coarse grass and twigs, but though I have seen a very large number of nests certainly not one in ten has had any grass in it, and they are usually made of dry dead twigs, more or less mixed and interlaced with live ones torn from the tree in which the bird is building.

Most of the nests taken by myself were at heights between fifteen and twenty-five feet from the ground, but they were far more often placed above than below twenty feet, and more often than not on fairly large branches and boughs rather than on clusters of twigs and small branches.

Though generally laying two eggs both these and the Pin-tailed Green Pigeon seem occasionally to lay but a single egg. I have found such hard-set, and nothing to show that a second egg had fallen from the nest.

In the article in the *Avicultural Magazine* attention is drawn to the habit this Pigeon has of placing its nest under the protection of some bird more capably pugnacious than itself. Mr. Dodsworth remarks: "Another curious feature about these birds is that, as their eggs and young suffer largely from the depredation of Jungle-Crows (*Corvus macrorhynchus*), they sometimes show considerable intelligence in availing themselves during the breeding season, of the protection afforded them by the more quarrelsome and powerful species. Now the *Dicruri* are notoriously pugnacious during the breeding season, never allowing Crows, Kites *et hoc genus omne*, ever to approach within their 'spheres of influence,' and it is, therefore, not at all unusual to find nests of the Kokla in close proximity to those of Drongos. The former belonging to the nests are always allowed free access and regress to the tree, but it is very different when a stranger shows himself in the vicinity."

This habit is, however, by no means confined to the Kokla, for it is recorded of many Doves and Pigeons that they have built their nests and reared their young in the same tree, or in close proximity to one in which is also the nest of a bird of prey which under normal every-day circumstances would at once make a meal of the Pigeons, parents and young.

Mr. Dodsworth, in the article quoted, gives the incubation of the Koklas' eggs as taking eighteen or nineteen days; this seems to me an extraordinary long period for such small eggs, and I fancy it will be eventually found to be some two to four days less in anything but abnormally cold weather.

The eggs cannot be distinguished from the Pin-tailed Green Pigeon either in shape, size or texture. The average of a hundred eggs measured by myself is 1.24 in. by .90 (= 31.5 by 22.8 mm.), the range of variation in length and breadth is practically the same as in those of the Pin-tail.

This Green Pigeon is, more exclusively than most, a bird of evergreen-forests, and will seldom, if ever, be found at any distance therefrom. It is also essentially a hill and mountain bird, though found throughout the plains of eastern Assam, more especially close to the mountain-ranges. In Cachar, Sylhet, Tipperah, and Chittagong it is practically confined to the mountain-ranges running to the north of these districts, and to the foot-hills and broken ground immediately adjoining them; though stragglers now and then may be shot in the cold weather some distance therefrom.

Hume, Jerdon, Blanford, and others consider the bird to be locally migratory, and this appears to be correct in so far as its western habitat is concerned, but to the east, that is to say from and including Nepal to its extreme south-eastern limit in Burma, the bird is resident throughout the year, perhaps in parts moving to some extent vertically with the change in seasons.

In Simla and the extreme west it ascends as high as 8,000 ft. at least, in the hot weather, but it appears to visit this portion of its range only during the breeding-season, and there is nothing on record as to whether or not it is found during the winter months in the adjacent valleys and lower hills.

Hume, in "*Lahore to Yarkand*," drew attention to the fact that vast multitudes "of this species were found during the summer in a zone of hills ranging from twenty to one hundred miles in width, and stretching, at any rate, from the borders of Afghanistan to the banks of the Ganges at Hardwar," but, that during the winter they disappeared altogether. Hume suggests that these birds migrate to Assam, Cachar, Tipperah, and Burma, but I feel sure that there are no grounds for this belief, for twenty-five years' residence in these parts have shown that there is no influx of birds into them during the cold weather. In Nepal there is nothing to show whether it ever moves up and down the mountains at the advent and departure of the hot weather, and in the Assam ranges I have been unable to ascertain that there is any movement of this nature. In North Cachar it was common up to about 6,000 ft. throughout the year, and equally so at all heights down to about 2,000 ft., below which it was somewhat less common though still plentiful right down to the level of the plains.

In the *Avicultural Magazine* for March, 1912, Mr. P. T. L. Dodsworth refers to local migration in the following notes on the habits of this Green Pigeon: "The Kokla, or Wedge-tailed Green Pigeon is a common summer visitant to the North-west Himalayas, south of the first snowy ranges, arriving from Nepal and farther eastwards about the last week in April, or the beginning of May, to breed, and then returning to their old haunts about September, or as autumn sets in. During their summer sojourn in these mountains they are generally to be found along the outer ranges, at elevations of 4,000 to 7,000 ft., but are most common about 5,000 ft. They principally affect well wooded and shady dales, hill-sides, valleys, and glens, and are not so gregarious as the Green Pigeons mentioned by Mr. Dewar, which are to be found in large flocks, sometimes numbering as many as thirty to forty individuals, and even more. Our birds are to be seen either singly or in pairs, or in small parties of three or four. They are strictly arboreal, and are exclusively frugivorous. They are very partial to the ripe berries of the *Kaiphul* (*Myrica sapuida*). When hunting for fruit, they are continually gliding about the branches, like squirrels; and, from their strong feet, they can hang over to seize a fruit, and recover their position at once by the strong muscles of their legs. When perfectly quiet they are very difficult to observe from the similarity of their tints to that of leaves. They are heavy feeders, and generally seek their meals early in the mornings and late in the afternoons. To avoid the heat they retire during the middle of the day to some shady trees, where, hidden amongst the foliage they sit motionless, and spend the time dozing; occasionally one wakes up and utters its soft plaintive whistle, and it is by these alone that the birds betray their presence. Their flight is rapid and strong."

In the above note Mr. Dodsworth mentions the fact of its being found only in small family parties, pairs or single birds, but it must be remembered that he writes only of their habits during the breeding-season, and in the cold weather they will be found in flocks just as all the other Green Pigeons are. Even, however, during this season the flocks seldom run to any great size, being more often under than over a dozen, whilst single birds and pairs may frequently be met with consorting with other species.

On account of their beautiful notes, which are fuller, richer and more sweet than those of any other Green Pigeon, these birds are specially sought after as cage-birds. Beautiful, however, as they are, both as to plumage and song, they are on the whole uninteresting pets. In a cage they are slow, lethargic and, indeed, stupid birds, and the two bad traits of greediness and quarrelsomeness which they share with the rest of their tribe, do not add to their attractions.

In the article just referred to, Mr. Dodsworth gives a long description of a pair of these birds, which he reared by hand, which describes well their habits and manners in captivity. He writes: "On the 1st July, 1910, one of my egg-hunters brought me a pair of these birds, about a fortnight or three weeks old, from a nest which he had found in the neighbourhood of Simla (North-west Himalayas), placed on one of the outer branches of a large oak, at an elevation of about 6,300 ft. The young Koklas were immediately taken in hand by my wife, and rearing operations commenced. On being handled at first they would slightly raise the wing, nearest to their supposed enemy. They were kept in a small wooden box, lined with some straw and grass, and were fed about five or six times a day exclusively on small pieces of ripe plantains, which had to be thrust down into their mouths. A little water used occasionally to be poured down their throats after the last meal in the evenings. When they were almost fledged, they were transferred to a cage containing two Doves (Turtur ferrago), which had also been taken from a nest, and were being reared by the hand.

"By about the end of September the Koklas appeared to be full-grown; and their irides, which were hitherto brown or greyish brown, now assumed the characteristic coloration of the adult bird, viz., a pale blue ring followed by an outer ring of red. As far as I can now recollect, the birds had, up to this, uttered no note of any kind. As the migratory period of this species had now arrived, I was anxious to see whether my birds would exhibit those symptoms which are usually displayed by roving birds when in confinement, but no such indications were observed. The Koklas were as dull and inactive as ever, and seemed quite reconciled to their home.

"Towards the latter end of the following November, the cock began uttering his notes, but these were incomplete, or, in the language of bird-fanciers, he was only 'recording.' These 'half' notes were generally uttered late in the evenings between seven and eight p.m.

"During the winter the birds throve excellently. Their diet still consisted of pieces of plantains, which they would accept *sitting on their perches*, and only from the hand of their mistress. If the fruit was placed in the cage it was never touched. They were fed about four or five times a day. They always drank water from a cup, which, like their food, had to be held up to their mouths. When hungry, the birds always became very active, hopping about from perch to perch and peering anxiously at their mistress, if she happened to be standing near their cage. If no notice was taken of them, or she walked away from their cage without feeding them, they would settle down into their usual lethargic condition, but immediately renewed their activities on catching sight of her; the presence of strangers or of others in the house was entirely ignored by the birds.

"Spring had now come, and the Koklas which were still sharing their cage with the Doves, began to get unusually active. The cock kept chasing the hen from perch to perch, and constantly uttered his melodious notes, which were now complete.

"Remembering the old adage that 'two is company,' and hoping that under such a condition the Koklas might be induced to form a matrimonial alliance, they were separated from the Doves and put into another cage to the mutual advantage of both couples, and shortly afterwards we witnessed the courtship of the male bird. He would utter his notes, puff out his throat, expand his tail feathers, spread out his wings, and hop from perch to perch with bowed head, uttering a low 'coo' the whole time. The hen did not seem to relish these attentions, for she would drop down on to the floor of the cage, as if to avoid her mate, who immediately followed her, and with a low 'coo-coo' called her into a corner of the cage. Both birds would then pretend to pick up something from the ground, and after a short time fly back to their perches. This was constantly repeated during the day, and the proceeding on the part of the male struck me as being very similar to that of a cock in the poultry yard calling his hens round him when a dainty morsel has been found. During the breeding season here I have often heard the male Kokla in the wild state utter the low 'coo-coo' note after his usual song, but have never up to this had the good fortune actually to witness the courtship.

"Just when matters were reaching a most interesting stage with my birds, the hen suddenly sickened and died, and it is almost impossible to describe in words the intense grief which was displayed by her mate. For a long time he walked round and round her body, singing and calling her, and would not allow any one to touch her. When the dead bird was eventually removed and placed on the ground outside the cage, he still kept walking round and round, singing and calling her. For the whole of that day, and for several days after the death of the hen, he was perpetually whistling at short intervals and going through the form of courtship already described, and there seemed no doubt whatever that he was greatly distressed at the domestic calamity that had befallen him.

"Three months have now passed since the death of the hen, and the cock seems to be somewhat reconciled to his loneliness. The courtship proceedings are still occasionally indulged in, but as there is now no fair one to whom he can pay his attentions, he eliminates the final act of dropping in the corner of his cage, and calling to his mate. He seems at times to get tired of his plantain diet, and for two or three days at a time will eat nothing else but grain—a habit no doubt acquired from his quondam companions, the Doves: he also occasionally eats large quantities of mud, apparently as an aid to digestion. The sound of a bugle or the striking of a clock sets him off singing at once. His powers of discernment appear to be highly developed. I have three dogs in the house, and these appear to be on the most friendly terms with him: he does not mind their presence in the least, and sometimes when he gets a chance even pecks at their noses, when the animals come too close to his cage. But when a stray dog happens to come close to him the bird recognises the difference at once, and begins fluttering and dashing himself against the bars of his cage."

The flight of this bird is similar to that of *Sphenocercus apicaudus*, direct and about as swift, but it is a less difficult bird to shoot than any of its smaller cousins in that it is not nearly so disconcerting in its manner of flight. Indeed, when feeding on trees scattered about in forest and not frightened by previous firing, it is an easy bird to knock over as it leisurely flaps its way from one tree to another.

SUBFAMILY CARPOPHAGINAE.

This subfamily contains a number of very large Pigeons which closely approach the Green Pigeons in their habits generally, but in their anatomy are nearer the *Columbinae*. Like the *Treroninae* they have no caeca, but unlike that subfamily and like the *Columbinae* they possess both ambiens muscle and an oil-gland. They are essentially arboreal Pigeons, but are not such constant or such powerful climbers as are the smaller Green Pigeon. They are all birds of great size, bigger than the common Pigeon, and are generally known as " Imperial Pigeon " amongst sportsmen and field-naturalists.

According to Blanford's classification the subfamily contains three genera and six species, but in the present work, whilst admitting the three genera, I reduce three of the species to the rank of subspecies, i.e. *Carpophaga insularis*, and *Ducula griseicapilla* and *D. cuprea*.

Key to the Genera.

A. Head, neck and lower-parts grey :

a. Mantle green with metallic-green or bronze ... ... *Carpophaga.*

b. Mantle not green and with no metallic-green gloss ... *Ducula.*

B. Whole plumage black and white ... ... *Myristicivora.*

GENUS CARPOPHAGA.

The birds of this genus are very large birds with the upper-plumage very highly glossed with metallic-green or bronze. The feet are stout and strong with broad soles and a short stout tarsus, feathered on its upper half. The bill is rather slender and long with a long cere and short horny tip. The primaries are normal.

According to Sharpe the genus contains twenty-four species, which are distributed from India to New Guinea and throughout the Malayan Archipelago and intervening islands. Many of these so-called species are, however, only geographical races, and in a revision of the genus some of these species would have to be reduced to subspecies and others, perhaps, added to them. In his genus *Carpophaga*, Sharpe also includes *Ducula* and four other genera. Within Indian limits we have but one species of the genus as now restricted, with a subspecies in the Nicobars.

SPECIES (one only) AENEA.

Key to the Subspecies.

A. Under tail-coverts deep dull maroon ... ... *C. a. aenea.*
B. Under tail-coverts dull rufous-brown ... ...*C. a. insularis.*

THE GREEN IMPERIAL PIGEON—*CARPOPHAGA O. OENEA*

($\frac{1}{3}$ Nat. Size.)

PLATE 7

(16) CARPOPHAGA AENEA AENEA (Linn.).

THE GREEN IMPERIAL PIGEON.

(PLATE 7.)

Columba aenea Linn., Syst. Nat., I p. 283 (1766); Lath., Ind. Orn., II p. 602.
Columba sylvatica Tickell, J.A.S.B., II p. 581 (1833).
Carpophaga aenea Jerdon, Madr. J.L.S., XII p. 11; Hume, Str. Feath., II p. 260; Ball, ib., p. 424; Hume, ib., III p. 163; Blyth and Wald., B. Burma, p. 144; Hume, Nests and Eggs, p. 496; Ball, Str. Feath., IV p. 235; Armstrong, ib., p. 337; Inglis, ib., V p. 57; Ball, ib., p. 418; Hume and Dav., ib., VI p. 416; Hume, Cat. no. 780; Ball, Str. Feath., VII p. 224; Hume, ib., VIII pp. 67, 109; Bingh., ib., IX p. 194; Parker, ib., p. 481; Oates, ib., p. 235; Legge, B. Cey., p. 718; Oates, B. Burma, II p. 301; Hume, Str. Feath., XI p. 294; Barnes, B. Bom. p. 286; Oates, in Hume's Nests and Eggs, 2nd ed., II p. 366; Salvadori, Cat. B.M., XXI p. 190; Blanf., Avi. Brit. I., IV p. 19; Sharpe, Hand-List, I p. 64; Oates, Cat. Eggs B.M., I p. 85; Davidson, J.B.N.H.S., V p. 329; id. ib., IX p. 489; Butler, ib., X p. 310; Stuart Baker, ib., p. 360; Inglis, ib., XI. p. 475; Davison, ib., XII p. 62; Sinclair, ib., p. 185; Butler, ib., p. 687; Finn, ib., XIV p. 577; Bourdillon, ib., XVI p. 2; Osmaston, ib., XVII p. 488; Macdonald, ib., p. 495; H. R. Baker, ib., p. 760; Stuart Baker, ib., p. 970; Mears, ib., XVIII p. 86; Harington, ib., XIX pp. 308, 365; Hopwood, ib., XXI p. 1214; Harington, B. Burma, p. 65.
Carpophaga sylvatica Blyth, J.A.S.B., XIV p. 856; id. ib., XXVII p. 270; id., Cat. B.M.A.S.B., p. 231; id., J.A.S.B., XXX p. 97; Jerdon, B. of I., III p. 455; Blanford, J.A.S.B., XXXVIII, pt. 2 p. 188.
Carpophaga pusilla Blyth, J.A.S.B., XVIII p. 816; Hume, Str. Feath., II p. 260; id. ib., VII p. 424; id. ib., VIII p. 109; id., Cat no. 780 ter.

Vernacular Names. *Dunhal or Dumkal, Sona Kabutra, Barra Harial*, Hin.; *Pogonna*, Mal.; *Kukurani guwa*, Tel.; *Maratham praa*, Tam. Ceylon; *Maha nila goya, Mata Bata goya*, Cing.; *Ghurti*, Kolaba; *Hunget-ma nwa* and *Bom-madi*, Burmese; *Paguma*, Assamese; *Daohukuruma*, Cachari; *Inruikuru*, Naga.

Description.—*Adult male.* Head, neck, and the whole of the lower-parts except the tail-coverts, a beautiful pale dove-grey, varying very much in tint in different individuals: in some the whole of these parts are a vinous-pink more than grey, the abdomen having even more pink than elsewhere; in other specimens the vinous tint is practically absent or else is confined to certain parts of the plumage such as the abdomen or the breast; occasionally it is confined to the head and nape, or only to the sides of those parts. The feathers next the bill, both above and below, are often a pure white and, in a few birds, there is a distinct semi-ring of white feathers round the lower half of the eye.

The whole of the back, rump, upper tail-coverts and exposed portion of the wing except the primaries dark, but bright metallic-green. This again varies as much in tint as the lower-plumage; in the majority of birds there is a faint bronze gloss over the green, more or less mixed with patches of deep blue or purple; but in some birds the whole of these parts are a brilliant, almost fiery copper-bronze and between these two extremes every possible tint and combination of tints may be found.

The tail is the same colour as the back, but less metallic and often a much deeper blue than elsewhere. Under tail-coverts a rather dark, rich liver-colour, or brownish-maroon; under surface of the tail a dull pale brown. Primaries dark blue-grey changing to pale brown on the inside of the inner webs, and becoming more and more green on each succeeding feather until the innermost secondaries are exactly like the back; under aspect of the wings dove-grey, varying a good deal in tint and brownish on the quills.

Colours of soft parts. Irides deep red, maroon-red, or almost lake-red; legs and feet dull purple-red, lake-red or deep coral-red, very rarely the latter; claws horny-brown tinged lake; bill white at the extreme tip, bluish or greyish-white, grey or blue-grey in the centre and dull lake-red or purplish-red on the basal half and cere. Edges of the eyelid purple-red.

Measurements. Length from 15 to 18 in. (= 381 to 457 mm.); wing 7.90 to 9.75 in. (= 200.6 to 247.6 mm.); bill at front about 1.0 in. (= 25.4 mm.) and from gape 1.4 (= 35.5 mm.); tarsus 1.0 (= 25.4) to about 1.2 in. (= 30.5 mm.); tail from 5.5 to 6.5 in. (= 139.7 to 165.1 mm.).

Adult female. Does not differ from the male, and averages much the same in size. The colours of the soft parts are the same in both sexes.

Nestling. "Similar to the adult and just as brightly glossed on the back, wings and tail, but was, of course, very much smaller, wanting the vinacious tinge below, and still having quantities of pale rufous threadlike down attached to the tips of the feathers" (Hume).

The extent of the vinacious tinge, as I have shown, is individual, and allowing for this, the nestling is exactly like the adult. The irides are dull brown and legs and feet paler and duller than in the adult.

Nestling, in down. Covered with a dark rufous down above and pale dull rufous-brown below.

It is with some hesitation that I have decided not to divide the small Ceylon and southern Indian form, which has been described as *pusilla*, from the larger northern and eastern form. I find, however, that it is quite impossible to draw any definite geographical line between the two forms. It is true that Ceylon birds average very small, with a wing of little if anything over 8 in. (= 203 mm.) and with a maximum of 8.5 (= 216 mm.); southern Indian birds are but little bigger, whilst those from Orissa and Bengal average over 8.6 in. (= 218.2 mm.) and those from upper Assam, the Dooars, and the Indo-Chinese countries well over 9 in. (= 228.6 mm.). At the same time, in all these different geographical ranges small birds are common and even from Assam and northern Burma birds with wings of under 8 in. (= 203 mm.) are constantly met with, whilst in Hainan we again find a bird which has *on the average* a wing no longer than that of the Ceylon bird.

Again, there is no difference in the coloration of this species which coincides with the variation in size, and, given a sufficient series from each place, one finds exactly the same gradations of colouring existing in the tints of the head, neck, and breast, and exactly the same extent of variation in the bronze or green glossing of the upper-plumage. The under tail-coverts do not vary, except very slightly, in individuals, and the depth of the blue on the rump, lower-back, and upper surface of the tail does not show any constant geographical variation. Thus, all that can be said is that in the extreme south and north-east of its range, this Pigeon *averages* a good deal smaller than those in the more central portions, but that the size is so variable in individuals throughout both, that no geographical race can be established.

Hume has dealt with the alleged differences between the geographical races in Vol. II. of *Stray Feathers*, and there he thus sums up the differences between the Andamanese birds and others: "Taking a very large series, the fully adult birds have the frontal band and chin purer white, and the lower tail coverts a deeper maroon chestnut than in any Continental birds I have yet seen. As a race it is of the largest size, greener, with deeper coloured under tail coverts and whiter forehead and throat than any Continental race taken as a whole."

As a matter of fact, an examination of the huge series in the British Museum will show that of these characteristics the green or bronze of the upper-parts is purely an individual matter, and that all the other points are shown even more strongly in many birds from the north-east frontier of India than they are in the Andamanese birds. Thus it is as impossible to separate the Andamanese form as it is to separate that of Ceylon.

Of the Hainan birds there is but a small series available for comparison, but there is no doubt that these are very deeply coloured as a whole, and are, as I have already shown, very small. Until, however, a much larger series have been examined I shall not attempt to differentiate them.

Distribution. Salvadori gives the habitat of this Imperial Pigeon as being "India, Ceylon, Andamans, Indo-Burmese Countries, Cochin-China, Hainan, Sunda Islands with Lombok and Flores, The Philippines and Zula Islands." Within Indian limits its distribution is rather curious, but may be said generally to follow the line of combined ample rainfall and heavy forest. It is common in Ceylon and thence up the north-west of India, through Travancore and Malabar as far north in the Bombay Presidency as the north of Kanara, where Davidson reports it as common in the Karwar district. Jerdon remarks that he found it breeding in the forests of Central India, but since his time no one else seems to have found it there. On the east it extends up the coast and through the forested parts of Madras, Orissa, Bengal, and Assam into the Indo-Burmese countries and back west along the Bhutan and Sikhim Dooars and the Nepal Terai, whence I have received specimens. It is found throughout the Chin Hills, Shan States and Burma generally wherever the rainfall is sufficient and evergreen-forest grows, but appears to be very rare in the north-central dry zone, though it is recorded as occurring there by Harington. It is common in the Andamans, but is replaced in the Nicobars by the next subspecies.

Nidification. Throughout the north-eastern portion of its range, April and May are the two principal months of the breeding-season, and according to Legge and Jerdon the same would appear to be the case in the south of India and Ceylon, but Davidson took an egg from a nest as early as February in Kanara, though he also shot a female with an egg ready for expulsion on the 30th April. Wimberley and Osmaston record their breeding in the Andamans in April and May, though the former also took eggs near Mt. Harriet in July, whilst in Burma, Harington, Hopwood, Bingham, and others record their breeding-season as from February to May. Inglis states that they breed in Cachar principally during the rains, but I have taken very many eggs in that district, where April is certainly the month in which most are laid, and I have seen very few laid after June; at the same time it must be remembered Inglis took his eggs in the plains whilst I took mine in the hills.

The nest is the usual Pigeon's nest of twigs, more or less interlaced so as to form a platform with a rough and extremely shallow depression in the centre. In size the nest may be anything from eight inches to a foot across, and in depth one to three inches according to the site in which it is built. I have never seen any lining to these nests, but Colonel Bingham, writing about a nest found in Thoungyeen, notes: "On the 19th March, on the road from the village of Podresakai to Meplay, I found a nest of the above Pigeon with the usual solitary egg, which proved to be hard set. It was easily seen from below through the flimsy nest of a few sticks and straws laid across and across a horizontally growing bamboo, where a smaller shoot had forked out from it."

Inglis also mentions a nest consisting "of a very few sticks and a few stiff grasses"; but this admixture of grass with the twigs must be very exceptional, for in some forty or fifty nests which have come under my observation I can remember but one such, and Bingham, describing four other nests found by him, says that they were mere platforms of twigs without a semblance of lining.

The great majority of nests are built upon small saplings at a height of ten to twenty-five feet from the ground, but I have taken them occasionally from high, heavily-foliaged trees, such as the banyan and pepul, at a height of over forty feet. Occasionally, also, they may be placed in bamboo-clumps, but though two or three such nests have been reported to me, I have never *seen* any so placed.

The tree selected is one generally placed in fairly thick forest, but close to, or on the borders of some opening, either natural, such as a river-bed or open glade, or artificial, such as caused by a road or a piece of cultivated ground. On the other hand they are sometimes placed on a tree well in the interior of evergreen-forest and far removed from all civilization.

I have not found it breeding over 3,500 ft., and very seldom over 2,500 ft., its usual breeding-grounds being from the level of the plains up to some 1,500 or 2,000 ft.

Invariably but one egg is laid, white, of course, and elliptical in shape, a few specimens being met with which have one or both ends a little pointed. The texture is very close and fine with a hard compact surface and sometimes a slight gloss. In size they average 1.78 in. by 1.28 (= 45.2 by 32.4 mm.), and the greatest length and breadth is respectively 2.03 in. (= 51.5 mm.) by 1.48 in. (= 37.6 mm.), and the least both ways 1.68 in. (= 42.6 mm.) by 1.23 (= 31.2 mm.).

The four eggs in the British Museum vary in length from 1.6 in. to 1.85 and in breadth from 1.25 in. to 1.32, but the smallest of these must be quite abnormally small.

This is a bird of hills and plains alike, being found throughout the latter wherever there is forest, in Madras, Bengal, Assam, and Burma, and ascending the former up to at least 6,000 ft. It is perhaps most common in the foot-hills of mountain-ranges and the broken grounds and plains immediately adjoining them up to some 3,000 ft. in the mountains themselves, though many observers do not give them credit for going higher up than 1,000 or 1,500 ft.

They are not very gregarious birds, though, of course, they collect in large numbers when attracted by the fruit of any special tree or trees.

Jerdon says that they collect in small parties, now and then uniting in flocks of twenty or more, but I have found flocks of anything over five or six to be very exceptional, and single birds and pairs are seen quite as often as flocks.

Harington, *in epistola*, writes: "It is very common in Chindwin, both upper and lower, especially the latter, where at certain seasons it may be seen in hundreds, nearly always singly, or in pairs."

Legge remarks that "though very shy when feeding it may easily be shot when wending its way across country in flights to drink in the morning or to roost in the afternoon. At such times a regular stream of these birds will continue to cross a road in the Eastern Province for perhaps half an hour together, and they afford very good shooting. It is well styled, together with all its genus, Imperial Pigeon. On the wing when dashing into a forest glade in the Pasdun Korale or Saffragam, or sweeping across an opening in the dense jungle of the Park country, it is a splendid bird."

In eastern Bengal, Assam, and Burma it is seldom that opportunities arise for obtaining a bag of these birds alone, but when shooting Pigeon flighting to and from their feeding-grounds, a few generally go to form a portion of the bag. Colonel Bingham records having bagged over thirty of these birds one day in July on the Salwin River, driving them backwards and forwards between a few ficus trees.

Their flight is very swift though, unless the birds have been frightened, the wing-beats are slow and thus give the impression of leisurely flight. As a rule, also, they flight higher than the smaller Green Pigeons do, so that often very few come within shot, though a number may pass within sight. When starting from a tree or suddenly frightened into diverting their course, the wings beat loudly against one another and make a sound audible at a great distance.

They are entirely frugivorous in their diet, and in the eastern and northern portion of their habitat resort in large numbers to any species of *ficus* which may be in fruit for the time being. They are also extremely partial to all wild-plums, the berries of the ber tree, etc. In Ceylon, Legge says that it is "perhaps fonder of the berries of the Bo tree (*Urostigma religiosum*) and of the Palu or 'Iron-wood' (*Mimusops indica*) than those of any other trees. In the south-east of Ceylon both these trees are to be found growing by themselves among small scrubby jungle and towering far above it; and when in fruit Pigeon flock to them from all sides, until the branches are literally laden with them. In Suffragam I found them feeding on the wild Cinnamon fruit, and also on wild nutmegs which their enormous gape enables them to swallow with ease. The nutmeg is, of course, as in the case of the Myna, voided after the mace has been digested."

It is credited with being a regular drinker. As already quoted, Legge infers that it drinks regularly in the morning, and Jerdon also says that " like the Green Pigeons, it betakes itself to river banks to drink, about 8 or 9 a.m. and again, I believe, in the afternoon." Blanford also says that it drinks morning and afternoon, and that he has seen it drinking at the latter hour. I have myself, more than once, put them up from sand-banks on river-sides where they were drinking, and on one occasion watched a pair for some minutes as they were drinking from a forest-stream in the early morning. These two birds moved about quite freely on the flat, sandy bank, walking much like the birds of the genus *Columba*, but not so fast. Every now and then they returned to the water's edge, and thrusting their bills deep in, after the manner of all Doves and Pigeons, took long draughts of water.

They are occasionally caged by the natives of India, and I have seen one or two birds in captivity; but they are uninteresting pets when kept in small cages, for they become very lethargic and slow in their movements, and in their intense greediness make themselves in a terrible state when gorging on plantains, or *suttoo*, a kind of porridge which forms their principal article of diet when caged. Nor have they the beautiful whistling-notes of the Green Pigeon, their note being a very deep guttural "coo" of the same character as that of the Wood-Pigeon, but very deep, and consisting of two notes well syllabified as " wuck-woor," the second syllable the deeper and prolonged with a rolling sound. Jerdon describes its call as a "low, deep, plaintive moan." Tichell as "deep and ventriloquous," and another writer as not unlike the croaking of a bull-frog.

If kept in a big aviary it might possibly form a more interesting pet to keep than it does when in a small cage, for, undoubtedly, it is a very handsome bird, and as it is not quarrelsome, it could be kept in the same aviary with other birds.

It is an excellent bird for the table, though it varies a good deal in flavour according to what it has been feeding on. It should always be skinned, not only plucked, prior to cooking, as the skin is often loaded with a dense coating of yellow fat, not always pleasant to the taste.

(17) CARPOPHAGA AENEA INSULARIS (Blyth).

THE NICOBAR IMPERIAL PIGEON.

Carpophaga sylvatica (var.) Blyth, J.A.S.B., XV p. 371; id., Cat. B.M.A.S.B., p. 231.

Carpophaga insularis Blyth, J.A.S.B., XXVII p. 270 (1858); Ball, ib., XXXIX pt. 2 p. 32; id., Str. Feath., I p. 79; Hume, ib., II p. 262; id. ib., IV p. 291; id., Nests and Eggs, 496; id., Cat. no. 780, bis; id., Str. Feath., VIII p. 109; Legge, B. Cey., p. 719; Oates, in Hume's Nests and Eggs, 2nd ed., II p. 367; Salvadori, Cat. B.M., XXI p. 185; Blanf., Avi. Brit. I., IV p. 20; Sharpe, Hand-List, I p. 64; Oates, Cat. Eggs B.M., I p. 85; Butler, J.B.N.H.S., XII p. 687.

Vernacular Names. None recorded.

Description.—*Adult male.* Differs principally from *aenea aenea* in having the under tail-coverts a dull reddish-brown, in no case approaching the liver-brown of that bird. The grey of the head and under-parts is purer, very seldom having the slightest tinge of pink or vinous, and the fore-head is generally distinctly paler than the rest of the head. The green of the upper-parts is darker and more mixed with blue, and appears never to have any copper reflections upon it; the upper-surface of the tail is also darker and more blue, and the under-surface is a much darker brown.

Colours of soft parts. "Legs and feet dull deep pink, pinkish red or livid purple, the bill is pale plumbeous, paler on tip and darker on cere and base; the irides vary a good deal, sometimes they are pale ruby red; the eyelids are pale lavender" (Hume).

Measurements. Length 17 to 20 in. (= 431 to 508 mm.); wing 8.75 to 10.25 in. (= 222.3 to 260 mm.); tail about 6 to 7 in. (= 152 to 177 mm.); bill at front 1 to 1.25 in. (= 25.4 to 31.7 mm.), and from gape about 1.45 to 1.8 in. (= 36.8 to 45.4 mm.); tarsus about 1 (= 25.4 mm.) to 1.2 in. (= 30.4 mm.) or rather more.

"Weight 1 lb. to 1 lb. 12 oz." (Hume).

"Weight 1½ lbs." (Richmond).

Adult female. Does not differ from the male in coloration, size, or in the colour of the soft parts.

Nestling, in first plumage. Like the adult, with dull brown irides and paler, duller feet and legs.

Distribution. Nicobar Islands.

Nidification. As regards its nidification Davison, in *Stray Feathers*, says that: "They breed in February and March; on the 17th February I found a nest on the Island of Trinkut; it was built on a cocoanut palm, and was about 20 feet from the ground. As usual with pigeons and doves it was simply a platform of dry twigs very loosely put together, and was built on a dried up fruit branch, which is itself merely a mass of dry twigs. It contained one large white egg."

The birds must sometimes commence breeding as early as December, as Mr. de Roepstoeff shot a young bird on the 20th February full fledged, and nearly full sized.

The egg taken by Davison in Trinkut Island is now in the British Museum: it is elliptical in shape, smooth and fine in texture with a faint gloss, and it measures 1.9 in. by 1.37 (= 48.2 by 34.8 mm.).

The habits do not appear to differ in any way from those of *aenea aenea*, though the bird, probably from being less harassed, is said to be very tame. Kloss records that they are "Common on all these Islands [Nicobars]. On Tilanchong and Trinkut they were remarkably tame; we easily shot them with the 32 cal. auxiliary barrels. They, with the Megapodes, formed our staple diet in the Nicobars until we loathed the sight of them."

Davison, in the notes above referred to, records that: "The Nicobar Imperial Pigeon is very numerous all over the Nicobars, much more so than its congener is at the Andamans. In habits it is much the same, being found singly, in pairs, or in small parties; its deep low coo may be heard resounding through the forest all day."

Genus DUCULA.

The genus *Ducula* differs from the last (*Carpophaga*) in having no green or bronze on the upper-plumage, in having a comparatively longer tail, and in having the inner primaries obliquely truncated at their ends, so that the outer webs project beyond the shaft. The two genera are not divided by either Salvadori or Sharpe, but the characteristics relied on, consisting as they do not only of striking differences in type of coloration, but also of differences in external structure, seem good grounds for keeping the genera distinct.

This genus contains but one species, *Ducula insignis*, with two subspecies, *griseicapilla* and *cuprea*, which form geographical races to the north-east and south respectively of the general range.

Key to the Subspecies.

A. Breast and abdomen pale ashy grey:
 a. Crown and hind-neck both lilac ... ... *D. i. insignis.*
 b. Crown grey contrasting with lilac hind-neck ... ...*D. i. griseicapilla.*

B. Breast and abdomen lilac ... ... *D. i. cuprea.*

(18) DUCULA INSIGNIS INSIGNIS (Hodg.).

HODGSON'S IMPERIAL PIGEON.

Ducula insignis Hodg., As. Res., XIX p. 162 (1836); Blanf., Avi. Brit. I., IV p. 21; Stuart Baker, J.B.N.H.S., X p. 360; Sharpe, Hand-List, p. 66.

Carpophaga insignis Blyth, J.A.S.B., XIV p. 855; id., Cat. B.M.A.S.B., p. 232; Jerdon, B.I., III p. 458; Godw.-Aus., J.A.S.B., XLIII pt. 2 p. 171; id. ib., XLV pt. 2 p. 83; Hume, Nests and Eggs, p. 496; id., Str. Feath., III p. 328; id. ib., VIII p. 109; id., Cat. no. 781; Oates, in Hume's Nests and Eggs, 2nd ed. II p. 368; Salvadori, Cat. B.M., XXI p. 216; Harington, B. Burma, p. 65.

Vernacular Names. *Dukul,* H. in Nepal; *Fomok,* Lepcha; *Lal Pagoma,* Assamese; *Daohukuruma gajao,* Cachari; *Inruikuru gaherba,* Naga.; *Hgnet-nga-nwa,* Burmese.

Description.—*Adult male.* Whole upper part of the head, nape, neck, and shoulders a vinous or lilac-grey, changing gradually into copper-brown on the mantle, back, scapulars, lesser and median wing-coverts; lower-back, rump, and upper tail-coverts dark grey, the first named more or less suffused with copper-brown. Upper aspect of tail black on the basal two-thirds, the extreme base being rather paler and the terminal third brownish-grey. Chin, throat, and lower half of cheeks white, changing gradually into ashy or vinous-grey on the breast and rest of the lower-parts except the under tail-coverts, which are pale buff; the abdomen is often paler than the breast; flanks and axillaries a purer grey; under-surface of the wings dark grey, the primaries and secondaries above being black except on the inner secondaries which, with the greater coverts, are olive-brown. Under aspect of the tail the same in pattern as above, but much paler in colour.

Colours of soft parts. Iris pale grey, grey or bluish-grey; bill whitish at the extreme tip, pale brown on the succeeding portion, and deep purplish-fleshy or dull carmine on the cere and basal portion; legs and feet deep purple-lake, or rather dull coral-red much suffused with carmine, soles paler and pinker, the claws pale brown, darker at the tip; orbital skin purple-grey, purer grey immediately round the eye.

Measurements. Length 18 to 20 in. (= 457 to 508 mm.); wing 9 to 10.2 in. (= 228.6 to 259 mm.); tail 7 to 8.5 in. (= 177.8 to 216.0 mm.); bill at front about 1 in. (= 25.4 mm.) and from gape about 1.5 in. (= 39 mm.); tarsus 1 to 1.25 in. (= 25.4 to 32.2 mm.).

Adult female. Does not differ from the male.

The series I have measured shows that the female is on an average a trifle smaller than the male, the wing measuring 9.2 in. (= 233.6 mm.) against 9.45 in. (= 239.5 mm.).

Young. "Duller; scarcely any purple tinge on the back and wing coverts; the latter edged with rufous chestnut; the head greyish with scarcely any vinous tinge" (Salvadori).

Distribution. From the extreme west of Nepal, Sikhim, Bhutan, the whole of the Dooars, and the broken ground at their feet, the Assam Valley and the hills north of it, the Miri, Dafla, Abor Hills as far east as Sadiya. The Garo and Naga Hills running east on the south of the Brahmapootra. In the Surma Valley, North Cachar Hills and Tipperah Hills the birds are intermediate, most however in the first-named place being nearer the true *insignis* whilst the Tipperah birds are nearer *griseicapilla*.

Nidification. The breeding-season of this Pigeon on the north-east frontier of India, from Nepal to Sadiya and the hills south of the Brahmapootra, appears to commence when the rains break, and to last through July and August, but I have seen its nest containing a young bird in March, and it is possible they have two broods, the first from February to March and the second during the rains.

The nest is of the usual description—a rough platform of sticks with practically no depression in the middle, and measuring anything between nine inches and a foot in diameter by some two to four inches thick. There is no lining of any description whatever, though some of the smaller, more pliant twigs seem to form the uppermost part of the centre of the nest. The majority of the twigs and sticks of which the nest is composed appear to have been torn living from the tree, but many also are pieces of twig and stick dead long before the bird made use of them.

As a rule the nest is placed at no great height from the ground—some twenty to twenty-five feet—in small saplings, but I have seen nests as low down as twelve feet, and one or two at heights of over forty feet. No attempt is made to place the nest in a concealed position, and this with the sitting bird can usually be seen at some distance. All the nests I have taken have been in the interior of evergreen-forest, but often the site selected is one near some natural clearing or opening, and occasionally is one beside some village track.

The number of eggs is never more than one, and though, on one occasion I took two from the same nest, it is probable that they were laid by two hens.

The average of twenty-two eggs is 1.82 by 1.32 in. (= 46.2 by 33.5 mm.), the greatest and least long being 1.93 in. (= 49.0 mm.) and 1.69 in. (= 42.9 mm.) respectively, and the same extremes in breadth 1.42 in. (= 36.1 mm.) and 1.26 in. (= 32 mm.).

The shape is generally a fairly regular ellipse, but some eggs are decidedly pointed at one end and, more rarely, one end is somewhat compressed. The texture is hard and close, with considerably more gloss than in any of the Green Pigeon's eggs.

There is very little on record about this fine Pigeon, Jerdon's interesting notes all referring to its subspecies, *insignis cuprea*—Jerdon's Imperial Pigeon. It is an extremely common bird at all elevations between 1,000 and 4,000 ft. in the hill-ranges, and thence it is less common up to about 6,000 feet, above which it is rare. It extends into the plains adjacent to the hills during the cold weather, but will only be found in places which are well forested, and have an ample rainfall. It is essentially a forest Pigeon, and will not be found in open country or round about cultivation. In North Cachar it was extremely common, often collecting in very large numbers in forest-trees when they were fruiting, and I have seen literally hundreds collected on a single pepul tree, feeding on the berries which were just ripe. On another occasion, also, when shooting in a forest in the Mahor Valley, at an elevation of some 1,000 ft., I was attracted to some jaman, or wild-plum, trees by the continuous loud and very deep call of " wuck-wurrr " made by these Pigeons, and when I went close up, I could see these birds moving about all over the higher branches, feeding greedily on the ripe plums. As it was impossible to shoot them on the wing owing to the very dense forest all round, I contented myself with watching their movements, which were most interesting. They were not half so clever with their feet as the Green Pigeon are, and often after clambering up or down a branch to get to some choice morsel would, in craning over to catch hold of it, lose their balance, and to save themselves take to wing. Once overbalanced they did not seem able to pull themselves up again, yet their feet and legs must be pretty powerful, for when shot and not killed outright they will often hang, head downwards, clinging on to a branch until a second shot dislodges them.

They do not appear to be very quarrelsome birds, though a certain amount of squabbling and sparring goes on from time to time. On the occasion above referred to I was watching the birds for fully two hours, but I saw no actual fights, though now and then one bird would try to push another away from a bunch of plums.

A very noticeable thing about them was the fact that they constantly uttered their very deep note during the time they were feeding, whilst their cousin, the Green Imperial Pigeon, is a very silent bird when so employed. The birds in this tree seemed very tame, perhaps because of the extreme denseness of the foliage and because I was so completely screened by the undergrowth, but even when I shot a couple of birds for the pot the majority of the others, numbering some two or three hundred, just flew round a few times and again settled to their feast. As a rule I think they are rather shy birds, and are difficult to get near if the trees they are in are not dense enough to hide them effectually.

It has only once fallen to my lot to make a respectable bag of these fine Pigeons. On this particular occasion I was lucky enough to come across a gigantic pepul tree standing in bamboo-jungle which had seeded and was therefore very thin and bare. Consequently the tree stood well in view, and by selecting a comparatively bare place amongst the bamboo-clumps which was well under their line of flight, I enjoyed a couple of hours shooting which resulted in the gathering in of thirty-two of these birds, besides a few other Green Pigeon. I have said above that Hodgson's Imperial Pigeon is less quarrelsome than most of the family, but at the same time it should be noted that it is very exceptional to find other Pigeon feeding in the same trees with it, so that it looks as if they stood rather in awe of these big relations. Although, however, I have never seen the smaller members of the Pigeon-tribe feeding in the same tree with Hodgson's bird, the Barbets, Hornbills, and other fruit-eaters seem to stand in no fear of them and will be found feeding in security, often on the same branch.

The flight of Hodgson's Pigeon is much like that of the Green Imperial Pigeon, rather stately and regular, with slow beats of the wing, yet travelling at a very great pace, and when frightened, dashing along in splendid style. When startled out of a tree, or when rising higher into the air, the wings often clash over their backs, making a clapping noise almost as loud as that made by a tame Tumbler Pigeon when performing his somersaults.

Jerdon has remarked on the curious fact of *Ducula cuprea* being in the habit of visiting "salt-licks." This habit, however, seems common to all the Imperial Pigeon and, to a less extent, to all the other members of the family. Often and often, when visiting such places to pick up the tracks of big game, or when sitting up over one to watch for tiger or leopard, I have seen both this bird and the last fly down to the salt-lick and walk about thereon, picking up scraps of the earth from time to time, or drinking the brackish water and mud that oozed up from the ground. They walk well and at a good pace, though not as actively as the Doves and true Wood-Pigeons.

(19) DUCULA INSIGNIS GRISEICAPILLA (Blyth).

THE GREY-HEADED IMPERIAL PIGEON.

(PLATE 8.)

Carpophaga insignis (part) Blyth, Cat. B.M.A.S.B., p. 232 (1849); id., J.A.S.B., XXVIII p. 416; Blyth and Wald., B. Burma, p. 144.

Ducula griseicapilla Wald., Ann. Mag. N.H., XVI p. 228; Hume, Str. Feath., III p. 402; Blanf., Avi. Brit. I., IV p. 22; Sharpe, Hand-List, I p. 66; Oates, Cat. Eggs B.M., I p. 86; Stuart Baker, J.B.N.H.S., XVII p. 970; Harington, ib., XIX p. 309; Cook, ib., XXI p. 674; Harington, B. Burma, p. 65.

Carpophaga griseicapilla Davis, Str. Feath., V p. 460; Hume and Dav. ib., VI p. 418; Hume, ib., VIII p. 109; id., Cat. no. 781, bis; Oates, B. Burma, II p. 302; id., Hume's Nests and Eggs, 2nd ed., II p. 369; Hume, Str. Feath., XI p. 295; Salvadori, Cat. B.M., XXI p. 217; Stuart Baker, J.B.N.H.S., X p. 360.

Vernacular Names. *Hgnet-nga*, Burmese; *Daohukuruma gajao*, Cachari; *Inruikuru gaherba*, Naga.

Description.—*Adult male.* Differs from *insignis* in having the crown, fore-head, and nape grey, in some specimens quite sharply defined from the vinous or lilac-grey of the hind-neck; the rump and upper tail-coverts are often more brown and less grey than in *insignis*, but I can trace no constant difference in the plumage of the upper-back, scapulars, and wing-coverts.

Colours of soft parts. "Feet a rich purplish lake red, claws brown, paling at base; soles whity brown; corneous tip of bill pale brown, rest of bill and gape the same colour as the feet" (Davison). The irides are greyish-white.

Measurements. The same as in *insignis*. Davison gives the weight of two males as 1 lb. 7 oz., and 1 lb. 4 oz. respectively. The females do not differ from the males either in coloration or size, but average about 1 lb. 3 oz. as against an average of about 1 lb. 6 oz. in the male.

Distribution. This bird is found practically throughout Burma, north and south, though absent from the dry zone of plains in north-central Burma. Harington records it from the Shan States, Hopwood reports it from the Chin Hills, and it extends thence north into the Chittagong hill-tracts, Hill Tipperah, and Manipur. In Sylhet and Cachar a few birds are intermediate between this and typical *insignis* but the majority are nearer that bird. In the hill-ranges of the Assam Valley typical *insignis* is found and not *griseicapilla* as recorded by Blanford—possibly a slip.

Nidification. The nest and eggs are exactly like that of Hodgson's Imperial Pigeon.

THE GREY-HEADED IMPERIAL PIGEON—*DUCULA INSIGNIS GRISEICAPILLA.*

(½ Nat. Size.) PLATE 8

Davison was the first to obtain its nest which he took in Tenasserim. He writes: "While ascending the North West slope of Muleyet on the 27th January I flushed a Pigeon (which I shot) off her nest in a small sapling growing close to the path, but in very heavy virgin forest. The nest was the usual Pigeon type of nest, a mere apology, of a few dry twigs loosely put together. There was only one egg fresh, but the female, on dissection, showed no signs of being about to lay another, so it is probable that one egg only is laid by this species. The egg is, of course, pure white and glossy, nearly the same thickness at both ends, but a little pointed towards the smaller end. It measures 1.61 in length by 1.15 in width."

I have taken two or three nests of this fine Pigeon in North Cachar, taking also one of the parent birds, so that there was no doubt as to their identification. These nests were all slight structures of twigs and sticks, mostly torn from trees and still quite pliant and soft, interlaced into platforms about 10 in. across, and some 2 or 3 in. deep. There was no lining of any kind, and the depression was of the shallowest.

In each case the nest was placed in a small tree in evergreen-forest at about 12 to 20 ft. from the ground.

Of the three nests of which I have personal records, one was taken at Laisung, North Cachar, over 4,000 ft.; one at Guilang, a little lower, and one in the Mahar Valley at about 2,000 ft. Each contained a single fresh egg and they were taken in May and June.

Hopwood, in a letter to me, says that he has taken the eggs in the Chin Hills this year, apparently in the end of April.

Six eggs in my collection vary between 1.72 in. (= 43.6 mm.) and 1.94. (= 49.1 mm.) in length, and between 1.26 in. (= 32 mm.) and 1.44 (= 35.4 mm.) in breadth.

They are of the usual regular elliptical shape, in one or two cases a trifle more pointed at one end. The surface is highly glossy and the texture soft and smooth.

In its habits this bird differs in no way from the last. Harington says that it is entirely a hill-bird, keeping to the higher hills.

(20) DUCULA INSIGNIS CUPREA.

JERDON'S IMPERIAL PIGEON.

Columba cuprea Jerdon, Mad. J.L.S., XII p. 12 (1840).

Carpophaga badia id. ib., XIII p. 164.

Carpophaga insignis Blyth, J.A.S.B., XIV p. 855; Jerdon, B.I., III p. 457; Barnes, J.B.N.H.S., V p. 329; Davison, ib., XII p. 62.

Carpophaga cuprea Hume, Str. Feath., III p. 328; Hume and Bourd., ib., IV p. 403; Hume, ib., VIII p. 109; id., Cat. no. 781, bis; Bourd., Str. Feath., IX p. 300; Davison, ib., X p. 407; Taylor, ib., p. 464; Salvadori, Cat. B.M., XXI p. 215; Davison, J.B.N.H.S., VI p. 340, ib., XII p. 62.

Ducula cuprea Blanf., Avi. Brit. I., IV p. 22; Sharpe, Hand-List, I p. 66; Oates, Cat. Eggs B.M., I p. 86; Sinclair, J.B.N.H.S., XII p. 185; Bourd., ib., XVI p. 2.

Vernacular Names. None recorded.

Description.—*Adult male.* Differs from *insignis* in having the back and wings an olive-brown with little or no gloss, and no tint of copper; in having the rump darker and sometimes tinged with olive; in having the terminal pale band on the tail much narrower, hardly one-quarter of the total length of the tail, and in having the under-surface darker and more vinous, and much mixed with ochre on the abdomen and posterior flanks. The under tail-coverts are often more or less faintly freckled with dusky, and the axillaries and under aspect of the wing are much darker than in either *insignis* or *griseicapilla*. As a rule, also, the white of the chin and throat is much more restricted in area.

Colours of soft parts. "Bill dull lake-red at the base, slaty at the tip; orbits lake-red, irides red-brown; legs dull lake-red" (Jerdon).

Measurements. Length 16 to 18 in. (= 396.4 to 447 mm.); wing 8.3 to 9.2 in. (= 210.8 to 233.6 mm.); tail about 7 in. (= 177 mm.); bill at front about .98 (= 24.9 mm.), and from gape about 1.4 in. (= 26.5 mm.); tarsus about 1 in. (= 25.4 mm.).

Adult female. Does not differ from the male, except in being very slightly smaller on an average, with a wing of about 8.5 in. (= 215.9 mm.).

Distribution. Southern India as far north as the Kanara district in the Bombay Presidency on the west, where Davison records it as common. Throughout the mountainous regions of Koorg, Wynaad, and Neilgherries, but apparently not in the east of the Madras Presidency. It has been recorded from the hills east of Mysore which run southwards from Bangalore to the Neilgherries, but has not yet been recorded from further east than this.

Mr. J. Stewart also obtained this bird, together with its egg, at Ratnapura in Ceylon.

Nidification. Bourdillon states that Jerdon's Imperial Pigeon "has two broods in the year, but only lays one egg at a time. These two breeding-seasons are in April and again in November. I have seen a bird building in the latter month, and have had the young bird brought to me in January. The nest is a loose structure of twigs without any lining, and exactly resembling an English Wood-Pigeon's. I was so fortunate as to find a nest at an elevation of 4,000 ft. above sea-level and 20 ft. from the ground, placed in a mass of tangled scrub (*Beesha travancoria*). The bird was sitting and returned to look at the nest, so we had a full view of her. Besides this I have had an egg sent me which had been taken at an equally high elevation. The egg is white and rather glossy; it is small for the size of the bird, being only 1.38 by 1 in."

Davison, *vide* Barnes, took its egg and nest in Kanara in February, but does not give details of the former, and elsewhere he merely remarks that it resembles that of *aenea*. Mr. J. Stewart has taken numerous nests of the Pigeon in Travancore, where he found it breeding in January, March, and April, and has been so good as to send me a series of its eggs taken in that district, together with an egg obtained by him in Ceylon in October.

The series sent me range in length from 1.64 in. (= 41.6 mm.) to 1.88 (= 47.7 mm.), and in breadth between 1.21 in. (= 30.7 mm.) and 1.36 (= 34.4 mm.).

They are of the usual ellipse shape, but a little smaller at one end than the other, have a considerable gloss and a close fine texture, though not of the fineness and hardness of those of the genus *Columba*.

Jerdon's notes, written fifty years ago, are still the fullest account we have of this Pigeon's habits in southern India. He writes: "It associates in general in small parties, or in pairs, frequenting the loftiest trees and feeding on various fruits. Its note is somewhat similar to that of the last [*C. aenea*], but still deeper, louder and more groaning. Tickell calls it a deep, short and repeated groan, *woo woo woo*.

"During the hot weather, from the middle of April to the first week in June, when the rains almost invariably commence on the Malabar coast, large numbers of this Pigeon descend from the neighbouring mountainous regions of Coorg and Wynadd to a large salt swamp in the neighbourhood of Cannanore, and there not only eat the buds of *Aricennia* and other shrubs and plants that affect salt and brackish swamps, but also (as I was credibly informed by several native Shikarees, to whom I was first indebted for the information of these Pigeons roosting there) pick up the salt earth on the edge of the swamp, and of the various creeks and backwaters that intersect the ground. I visited this place towards the end of May 1849, when many of the Pigeons had gone, as I was informed, but even then saw considerable numbers flying about and feeding on the buds of *Aricennia*, and then retiring a short distance to some lofty trees to rest. Although the day was unfavourable and rainy, I killed about a dozen of these fine Pigeons, and several natives who were there with guns for the purpose of shooting them, assured me they often killed from one to two dozen daily, simply remaining in one spot. Had I not secured the birds myself in this locality, I confess I would barely have credited the account I received of these mountain residents descending to the Plains during the hottest season of the year."

Bourdillon, quoted by Hume in *Stray Feathers*, says that in Travancore it is an abundant species, "occurring at all elevations from the base to the very summit of the hills, wherever there is heavy forest. As the generic name implies, their food consists entirely of the larger jungle-fruits, and they appear to be very greedy feeders, stuffing themselves to repletion with any favourite fruit. Their note is a peculiar deep moaning coo, but in addition to this they utter a low guttural croak of suspicion while seated motionless on some bough, should anything unusual attract their attention. They take some time getting under weigh, but once well started their flight is rapid, and they can carry off a large quantity of shot."

Major H. R. Baker writes to me: "I once shot one of these fine Pigeon which had been feeding on some wild nuts the size of a walnut, and of which I found four in the bird's crop. It surprised me at first to find that the bird had ever been able to swallow so large a nut, but on trying I found that I could easily place one inside its mouth and push it down its throat. Its deep booming notes sounding something like who-who-o, who-who-o, reminded me rather of the sounds uttered by monkeys."

Genus MYRISTICIVORA.

The genus *Myristicivora* contains, according to both Salvadori and Sharpe, five species, some of which, however, would only rank as subspecies with those who adopt the trinomial system. Of these five species, only one is to be found within Indian limits, and this is easily distinguished from all other nearly allied Pigeons by its peculiar creamy-white and black coloration. The genus differs from *Carpophaga* in having a comparatively shorter tail.

(21) MYRISTICIVORA BICOLOR (Scop.).

THE PIED IMPERIAL PIGEON.

(PLATE 9.)

Columba bicolor Scop., Del. Flor. et Faun. Insub., II p. 94 (1786).

Carpophaga myristicivora Blyth, J.A.S.B., XV p. 371; Ball, ib., XXXIX pt. 2 p. 32.

Carpophaga bicolor Blyth, Cat. B.M.A.S.B., p. 232 no. 1436; Hall, J.A.S.B., XXXIX pt. 2 p. 32; id., Str. Feath., I p. 79; Hume, Nests and Eggs, p. 496; id., Str. Feath., II pp. 80, 84, 96, 103, 114, 119, 264; Blyth, B. Burma, p. 145; Hume and Dav., Str. Feath., VI p. 418; Hume, ib., VIII p. 109; id., Cat. no. 781, quint.; Oates, B. Burma, II p. 303; Everett, J.S.B.A.S.; id., Hume's Nests and Eggs, 2nd ed., II p. 369.

Myristicivora bicolor Bp., Con. Av., II p. 30; Walden, Trans. Z.S. Ins., p. 217; Salvadori, Cat. B.M., XXI p. 227; Blanf., Avi. Brit. I., IV p. 23; Sharpe, Hand-List, I p. 671; Oates, Cat. Eggs B.M., I p. 86; Butler, J.B.N.H.S., XII p. 688; Osmaston, ib., XVII p. 489; H. R. Baker, ib., p. 761; Osmaston, ib., XVIII pp. 201-2; id. ib., p. 359; Kinnear, ib., XX p. 453; Hopwood, ib., XXI p. 1214.

Vernacular Name. *Kaluia*, Car Nicobarese.

Description.—*Adult male.* Whole plumage, with the exceptions noted, white, tinted with the faintest and most delicate cream, generally more pronounced on the head than elsewhere and varying greatly in extent and distribution in different individuals. Bastard-wing, primaries, and outer secondaries deep slaty, almost black; central tail-feathers with a terminal band of black nearly two inches wide, this band decreasing in width on each succeeding pair of feathers until on the penultimate pair it is only about half an inch wide, and on the outermost is seldom more than a quarter of an inch, and often much less; on the outermost pair also, the outer web on its central portion is margined with black. The under tail-coverts are sometimes pure white, sometimes narrowly margined with black on the longer feathers, whilst in a few cases the black assumes the proportion of a broad band at the tip of these feathers. Though the bastard-wing itself is black, the shoulder of the wing is white.

Colours of soft parts. "Legs and feet pale smalt blue; the bill is leaden blue, the tip darkish horny or dark plumbeous; irides dark brown" (Davison).

Measurements. "Length 16 to 17 in.; expanse 27.5 to 30; wing 8.82 to 9; tail from vent 5.12 to 5.5; tarsus 1.10 to 1.3; bill from gape 1.4 to 1.5; bill at front 0.9 to 1.05; wings when closed reach to within from 1.5 to 1.75 of end of tail; weight from 12 oz. to 1 lb." (Hume).

Adult female. Similar to the male.

It is extremely doubtful whether the creamy tint on this fine Pigeon is not due principally to stains from the fruit upon which they live. It is very irregularly disposed over the plumage, in one bird being most pronounced on the back and rump, and in another all round the vent and abdomen; but

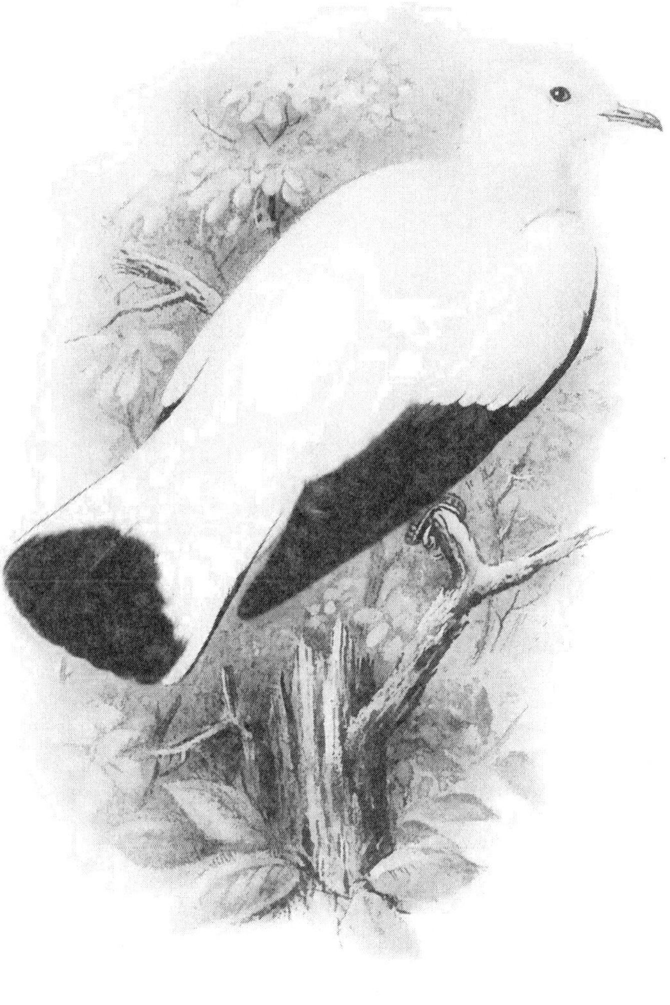

THE PIED IMPERIAL PIGEON—*MYRISTICIVORA BICOLOR.*

(½ Nat. Size.)

PLATE 9

in nearly all cases, as I have already said, it is most highly developed about the head, especially round the gape. If, as I think, this tint is merely nutmeg or some other vegetable stain, we should expect to find, as is the case, that normally the head, which comes in constant contact with the fruit, most deeply stained, and the abdomen and rump which the bird constantly preens with its dye-covered bill, next most deeply marked. The tint fades considerably after death, though persisting in regular patches here and there on the body, and nearly always to some extent on the head.

Distribution. Blanford thus defines the range of this beautiful Pigeon, "From the Andamans and Nicobars through the Malay Archipelago to New Guinea and Australia where a local form (*M. spilorrhoa*) occurs. This Pigeon breeds in the Nicobars, and is a seasonal visitant to the Andamans, Cocos, Narcondam, Barren Island, according to Blyth to the Mergui Archipelago, but not, so far as is known, to the mainland of Tenasserim. According to Dr. Mainjay, this species also visits the Islands only on the coast of the Malay Peninsula." Since this was written it has been procured by Mr. C. Hopwood's collectors a little south of Sandoway in Arakan, Burma (1910), and long prior to that Dr. A. L. Butler recorded them as occurring at Kuala Selangor on the mainland of the Malay Peninsula, and it would therefore appear that this bird regularly, if in no great numbers, is found on the mainland of Burma from the latitude of Sandoway all down the Malay Peninsula. Mr. Hopwood's men, moreover, it should be noted, knew the bird well, and said that they were numerous, breeding on the islands off the coast, and visiting the mainland during the winter months.

Nidification. Davison failed to actually take the nest, but writes: "Although I did not obtain the nests or eggs of this bird myself, from all I could ascertain from the convicts, etc., these birds breed in January, February, and March, building their nests, which, like those of other Pigeons, are merely platforms of sticks, by preference in the mangroves, and laying usually only one white egg."

Captain Wimberley took its egg on Trinkut Island during the first week of February, and describes its nest as being similar to that of an English Wood-Pigeon, placed in an old mangrove tree overhanging a river. It contained one addled egg measuring 1.78 in. by 1.25, of the usual shape and description. I have a nice series of these eggs in my collection taken by Mr. B. B. Osmaston at South Sentinel Island on the 17th March, 1907, and kindly given by him to me. In shape these eggs are rather long ovals, almost ellipses, and in one or two cases distinctly pointed at both ends. The texture is very fine and close with a smooth surface, in some cases decidedly glossy. They vary in length between 1.73 (= 43.9 mm.) and 1.90 in. (= 48.2 mm.), and in breadth between 1.24 (= 31.4 mm.) and 1.30 in. (= 33 mm.), the average being 1.8 (= 46.2 mm.) by 1.26 in. (= 32 mm.).

Mr. Osmaston describes the taking of these eggs in the *Bombay Natural History Journal* as follows: "We found the Island simply swarming with the Pied Imperial Pigeon, and it was not long before we discovered a nest containing a single fresh egg, followed by many others. Altogether we found some 50 nests containing each a single egg, some fresh, some more or less incubated.

"The nests were not, as a rule, close together. They were placed near the tops of small trees, or on the lower branches of big ones, usually about 25 ft. from the ground. One nest I found was only 10 ft. from the ground, but this was exceptional.

"The nest is the usual flimsy platform of sticks through which the egg is usually visible from below.

"The eggs are, of course, pure white, generally rather elongated ovals with a fair amount of gloss. The measurements are as follows :—

"Longest egg 1.91 by 1.26 in.
"Shortest egg 1.67 by 1.20 in.
"Mean of 28 eggs 1.80 by 1.24 in."

Butler has the following interesting notes on this Pigeon in the *Journal* of the Bombay Natural History Society : "A strikingly handsome bird, it associates in large flocks, and fifty or sixty dashing with a clatter of wings out of a tall tree, their black and white plumage showing up vividly against the background of green foliage, are a sight to gladden the eyes of a naturalist wandering in these steamy jungles. Though one would hardly think it, their boldly pied colouring of jetty black and cream colour is more or less protective. On the wing they are, of course, conspicuous, but among the shifting lights and shadows of a thickly-leafed tree on which the sunlight is falling, they are extremely hard to make out. I have known a flock were in the branches above me, and yet perhaps only one bird on the outside of the tree with the light shining on its bright breast would be visible. Their note is a chuckling hu-hu-hu.

"In his paragraph on its distribution, I see Mr. Blanford quotes Dr. Maingay as stating that this Pigeon only occurs on the Islands down the coast of the Malay Peninsula. This is incorrect, it certainly keeps principally to the small islets of the coast, but only this week I shot three, and saw several more at Kuala Selangor on the mainland of the Peninsula."

On the islands it frequents, this Pigeon seems to be extraordinarily plentiful, and as tame as numerous, so that where it is not feeding on trees more than usually high, it is very easy to kill. Hume speaks of killing fifty of them in a very short time, and the limit obtainable seems to have been only restricted by cartridges and the anxiety to get other species. Davison speaks of the islands being "simply alive with them," whilst so little did this and the next species fear the presence of man that one of the latter allowed him to get close enough to shoot it with a walking-stick gun.

The food of this Pigeon seems to be entirely frugivorous and, when in season, the favourite diet is a species of wild nutmeg (*myristica* sp.), "conspicuous with their blood red orillas, fruits that no one could believe that even this large Pigeon could swallow, but two or three of which we took out of the crops of every bird we killed."

Subfamily CALAENADINAE.

This is a very small family consisting of a single genus (*Calaenas*) and that genus of a single species, which again is divided into two subspecies, one of which inhabits the Indian region.

The subfamily differs from those already dealt with in having a tail of only twelve feathers, but it agrees with the genus *Carpophaga* in having an ambiens muscle and an oil-gland, but no intestinal caeca. The legs are long, and both legs and feet strong and well adapted for walking, and the bill has a fleshy protuberance at the base, more highly developed in the male than in the female. The most striking external characteristic, however, consists in the long metallic green hackles of the neck, which at once distinguishes it from all other Pigeons.

Genus CALAENAS.

Characteristics those of the subfamily.

(22) CALAENAS NICOBARICA (Linn.).

THE NICOBAR PIGEON.

(PLATE 10.)

Columba nicombariensis Briss., Orn., I p. 154 (1760).

Columba nicobarica Linn., Syst. Nat., I p. 283, no. 27 (1766); Lath., Ind. Orn., II p. 605.

Columba gouldiae Gray and Hardw., Ill. I. Zool., II pl. 57.

Geophilus nicobaricus Blyth, Cal. J.N.H., I p. 605.

Caloenas nicobarica Gray, List Gen. B., p. 59 (1840); Ball, J.A.S.B., XXXIX pt. 2 p. 32; id., Str. Feath., I p. 81; Hume, ib., II pp. 133, 271, 481; Hume and Dav., ib., VI p. 425; Hume, Cat. no. 798, bis; Oates, B. Burma, II p. 299; id., in Hume's Nests and Eggs, 2nd ed., II p. 365; Salvadori, Cat. B.M., XXI p. 615; Blanf., Avi. Brit. I., IV p. 24; Sharpe, Hand-List, I p. 91; Oates, Cat. Eggs B.M., I p. 106; Butler, J.B.N.H.S., XII p. 690; Osmaston, ib., XVII p. 489; id. ib., XVIII pp. 201, 202, 359.

Calaenas nicobarica Blyth, J.A.S.B., XV p. 371; id., Cat. B.M.A.S.B., p. 238.

Calaenas nicobaricus Jerdon, B.I., III p. 480; Hume, Str. Feath., II p. 70.

Vernacular Name. *Lo-ung*, Nicobarese.

Description.—*Adult male.* Head, neck, and upper-breast deep slaty-black, in perfect specimens having a beautiful purple-blue sheen; shorter neck-hackles the same, but glossed with metallic green near the tips; longer hackles metallic blue or copper-bronze, but nearly all with narrow margins of deep blue-black and dark green shaft-stripes. Upper-plumage from shoulders to upper tail-coverts, lesser and median wing-coverts, and innermost secondaries brilliant metallic-green, but varying greatly in individuals. In some the greater portion is a copper-bronze, in a few specimens becoming almost a flaming copper-colour, whilst in a few others the copper tint is almost absent; shoulder of wing, greater coverts, and outer secondaries deep prussian-blue with more or less of a metallic sheen and a varying amount of green gloss; primaries blue-black on the visible portions and brown-black on the inner webs and concealed portions of outer webs; tail with a few of the longest upper coverts and all the lower coverts white. Lower-plumage from breast to vent, flanks, and under aspect of wings metallic green, more or less marked with prussian-blue.

Colours of soft parts. "Legs and feet dull purplish lilac, bill greyish black; irides hazel nut brown" (Davison).
"Irides white" (Sir J. Ingram).
"Irides buff" (Layard).

THE NICOBAR PIGEON—*CALAENAS NICOBARICA.*

(½ Nat. Size.)

PLATE 10

Weight 1 lb. 4 oz. to 1 lb. 12 oz. These weights include the extremes recorded for adult males by Davison, Hume, and others.

Measurements. "Length 15.25 to 16.5; expanse 30 to 32.5; wing 9.8 to 10.6; tail from vent 3.1 to 3.82; tarsus 1.55 to 1.85; bill from gape 1.4 to 1.6; bill at front in adult 0.95 to 1.1; in the nestling and quite young birds the frontal feathers do not advance nearly so far forward, and in these the bill varies from 1.2 to 1.4; weight 1.25 to 1.75 lb." (Hume).

Adult female. Similar to the male, but the head, neck, upper-breast, and hackles are generally decidedly more grey and no females in the Museum Collection have the deep blue sheen visible in some of the males. The neck-hackles are always shorter.

Colours of soft parts. As in the male but the irides appear never to become pure white as they do in old birds of that sex.

Measurements. The same as in the male.

Young male. Like the adult but having no hackles and the tail concolorous with the rest of the upper-plumage and glossed above with the same tint of green or copper.

The white tail is assumed at the first autumn-moult and the neck-hackles also then make their appearance, though they probably do not assume their greatest length until the following year. The irides are a dull hazel-brown.

Distribution. Extends from the Cocos and Andaman Islands, Nicobars and islands of the Malay Archipelago as far as the Solomon Islands. It has not yet been found on the Timor group. In the Nicobars it is extraordinarily numerous and probably far more common in the Andamans and Cocos than has hitherto been held to be the case.

Nidification. Davison thus records the breeding of this magnificent Pigeon: "*Calaenas nicobarica* builds a regular Pigeon's nest and always on trees; on Battye Malve where we found this bird in thousands, almost every thick bushy tree contained several nests. I counted thirteen on one tree, and I must have examined a couple of dozens of these nests; we visited the Island rather late: nearly all the occupied nests contained young and hundreds of young had left the nests. I only succeeded in finding two eggs, one partially incubated, the other ready to hatch off; the former of these unfortunately got broken on the Island, the latter I succeeded in preserving by cutting a hole in one side and placing the egg in a small paper tray near an ants' nest. The nests were, as I have mentioned above, regular Pigeons' nests, merely a platform of twigs, very loosely and carelessly put together and without lining of any kind, and in no single case contained more than the one young or one egg. Many of the nests I examined contained young ones only a day or two old, perfectly devoid of even down, and with closed eyes; in fact, exactly like the young of the domestic pigeon when first hatched. Other nests contained young that flew from the nests on our climbing the tree. One nest I found was only about ten feet, but the others ranged from twenty to thirty feet from the ground and were always placed in thick bushy trees.

"The egg which measures 1.84 in., is pure white and spotless; the shell, though compact is very finely pitted all over, and it has scarcely a trace of gloss."

Osmaston also found the bird breeding in South Sentinal Island, but only in small numbers and on the first occasion he only succeeded in obtaining two nests, which he describes as being exactly like those of the Pied Imperial

Pigeon breeding on the same island. Each of the two nests contained a single egg, quite fresh and only differing from those of the bird just mentioned in being a trifle larger, 1.92 by 1.32 in.

Osmaston states that "the fresh egg of *Calaenas* may, moreover, be recognised from that of *Myristicivora* by the colour of the membrane underlying the shell, which imparts a delicate purple tinge to the egg of the former, that of the latter being pure white or faintly yellow."

Later on Osmaston got a fine series of these eggs from Battye Malve in the end of March, 1907, and was good enough to send me a considerable number. These eggs are rather long, regular ovals like those of the Pied Imperial Pigeon, and like those of that bird, are often curiously pointed at one end. In texture they cannot be distinguished from the eggs of *Myristicivora*, but it is very curious that even in eggs some five years old the difference in the colour of the membrane is still quite distinct, for, whereas, that of the egg of the Pied Pigeon is a pale lemon-yellow, that of the egg of the Nicobar bird is almost an orange-yellow.

My eggs vary from 1.82 to 2.15 in. (= 46.2 to 55.1 mm.) in length, and from 1.30 to 1.36 in. (= 33 to 34.5 mm.) in breadth, the average being 1.95 by 1.34 in. (= 49.6 by 33.9 mm.).

It breeds freely in captivity, and both this bird and the last have frequently reared their single young ones in the Calcutta Zoo. They feed the young, of course, in the same manner as do all other Pigeons and Doves, that is to say, on regurgitated and partially digested food. The late Mr. Sanyal, Keeper of the Calcutta Zoological Gardens, told me that they were excellent parents, both male and female sharing in the incubation of the egg and the care of the young bird.

Davison's full and interesting notes on this Pigeon contain so much information, that I quote them here in full. He writes as follows in the second volume of *Stray Feathers :* "On Katchall Island I first observed these birds 'at home' if I may use the expression ; I met with them in the vicinity of some caves situated in the forest about a mile from the shore, sometimes singly, at other times a pair together, and occasionally in small parties about half a dozen to a dozen. I went several times to Katchall to study the habits of these birds.

"I always found them on the ground ; when disturbed they fly some distance, almost always beyond range of shot, and then perch, usually high up, but sometimes low down, invariably on the thicker lower branches, along which I have often seen them walk. On Battye Malve I had the best opportunities of observing them. I had wandered some distance from the rest of our party and got into a part of the jungle where the birds had not been disturbed. Feeling very tired when forcing my way through the tangled underwood, I seated myself at the foot of a large tree ; after remaining here for some little time, several of these birds flew down from the adjacent trees and settled on the ground within ten yards of me, they were soon joined by others, till there must have been at least thirty, old and young, all round me. I remained perfectly still (hardly daring to breathe) and watched them for some time.

"Their gait is quite Pigeon-like. Every now and then one would stop, and tossing the leaves aside, dig into the ground with its bill. They did not move in any regular manner but walked hither and thither, and if two adults, or two young ones met they generally made a peck or two at one another before separating. I did not observe them use their feet to scratch aside the leaves, like gallinaceous birds, nor did I see any of the adults run, they kept up a steady but sprightly walk the whole time. Occasionally one would rush up with wide spread wings to one of its neighbours, and then stand with open mouth flapping its wing until it was either beaten off, or the other beat a retreat; but I did not see any of the young fed by their parents. They are very silent birds, and the only note I heard was a somewhat hoarse, guttural kind of croak, not unlike that sometimes made by the domestic Pigeon when taken in the hand.

"The stomachs of those I shot on Katchall contained seeds very similar to a prune stone, more or less broken up, but on Battye Malve they seem to have eaten a whitish seed about the size of the head of a blanket-pin. The gizzard of this bird is very peculiar, being composed of two discs of cartilage as hard as, and of the same texture as bone, slightly convex on the inner surface, between which is a pebble, usually a white quartz a little larger than a fresh pea.

"Many of these birds are caught on the western coast of Nancowry and Camorta with horse-hair nooses placed on the ground in places they frequent, the bait used being wild fruits. They sell at Camorta for three rupees or six shillings per pair, and a good many find their way to Calcutta."

Butler adds a good deal of interesting matter to these notes in his article in the *Bombay Journal* (l.c.), where he writes: "I found it very shy and difficult to shoot. It is quite silent so that you have no means of knowing its whereabouts; creeping through the jungle you are startled by a tremendous flutter of wings overhead, and get just a glimpse of a large dark bird with a short white tail disappearing on the wrong side of at least two trees. You may have time to get in the snappiest of snap shots, and it may be effective; mine generally were not, though occasionally the report would be followed by a cheery thud. Fortunately one does sometimes get easy sitting shots and opportunities of observing the birds fairly closely, but they are not often.

"I usually came across them singly or in parties of three or four to a dozen or so. When feeding on the ground the *Caloenas* walks about much like a large Emerald Dove, but carries its wings much lower, often indeed dropping them so much as to give one the idea of their being injured at the shoulder.

"When not feeding they sit silent and alert on some bare horizontal bough, about thirty or forty feet from the ground; seen thus they look very dark in colour, almost blackish, as, indeed, they generally do when seen in the shade.

"Their flight is swift and very strong, though heavy looking; the flutter they make in leaving a tree is peculiarly loud and characteristic, so that I could always tell by ear whether a bird flying out over my head was a *Caloenas* or one of the common Imperial Pigeons."

Butler found that birds killed on Car Nicobar had been eating the same kind of food as that described by Davison. They are said to be very good to eat, and to get, like most Pigeons, very fat when their favourite foods are plentiful.

This bird is a very favourite cage-bird throughout Asia, and in most other countries also, as it is extremely hardy and not nearly so quarrelsome as are most Pigeons, provided it is accommodated with a large enough aviary. As might be expected from its terrestrial habits it is largely a grain-feeder, and in captivity its diet generally consists more of rice, corn, maize, etc., than fruit, though it greedily eats almost any fruit that is given to it.

Some of the individuals in the Zoological Gardens in Calcutta have got so used to visitors and so tame that they fly down to the wires of the aviaries and follow people round in quest of dainties. These birds eat scraps of bread and biscuit freely, and, I am informed, with no bad effects. They seem very tolerant in their disposition towards other birds sharing their captivity, and I have never noticed them fighting with one another in the manner described by Davison, even during the breeding-season.

Mr. Sanyal describes their "display" as being very beautiful; the cock-bird bowing and scraping just as all other Pigeon do, but during these antics the gorgeous metallic feathers are all puffed out and glitter and shine in the most wonderful way with each bob of the bird or each strut he makes along the ground. Needless to say perhaps, but the female appears to be quite unmoved, uninterested even, in all the show got up on her behalf, and if there is any food about pays much more attention to that than to her lover's antics.

Subfamily PHABINAE.

The present subfamily contains a group of twelve genera and twenty-two species of small Doves, very terrestrial in their habits and very closely allied with *Calaenas*, with which they agree in anatomy and also in having twelve tail-feathers, but they differ in their smaller size and in having no lengthy neck-hackles. They are to be found in Africa and in Asia, in India and the Malay Archipelago, and Australia.

Genus CHALCOPHAPS.

This genus contains six species of very beautiful small Pigeons or Doves, which are found in India, through Burma and the Malay Archipelago to Australia, but of which only one species is found within our limits. The upper-plumage of our bird is metallic like that of *Calaenas*, the tail is of twelve feathers, wings moderate with second and third primaries subequal in length, feet and tarsus bare and the former with slender toes well adapted for running about on the ground.

THE BRONZE-WINGED DOVE—*CHALCOPHAPS INDICA.*

(½ Nat. Size—Male on left, female on right.)

PLATE 11

(23) CHALCOPHAPS INDICA (Linn.).

THE BRONZE-WINGED OR EMERALD DOVE.

(PLATE 11.)

Columba indica Linn., Syst. Nat., I p. 284 (1766); Penn, Faun. I., p. 41; Lath., I. Orn., II p. 598.

Columba albicapilla id. ib., p. 597.

Columba coeruleocephala id. ib., II p. 610.

Chalcophaps indica Gray, List Gall. B.M., p. 18 (1844); Blyth, J.A.S.B., XIV pt. 2 p. 589; Jerdon, B.I., III p. 484; Godw.-Aus., J.A.S.B., XXXIX pt. 2 p. 112; Ball, Str. Feath., I p. 80; Hume, Nests and Eggs, p. 509; id., Str. Feath., II p. 269; id. ib., p. 481; id. ib., III p. 165; Blyth and Wald., B. Burma, p. 147; Hume and Bourd., Str. Feath., IV p. 404; Inglis, ib., V p. 40; Fairbank, ib., p. 409; Butler, ib., p. 503; Hume and Dav., ib., VI p. 424; Ball, ib., VII p. 225; Cripps, ib., p. 298; Hume., ib., VIII p. 110; id., Cat. no. 798; Legge, B. Cey., p. 719; Vidal, Str. Feath., IX p. 75; Bing., ib., p. 195; Butler, ib., p. 421; Reid, ib., p. 500; Davison, ib., X p. 408; Taylor, ib., p. 464; Oates, B. Burma, II p. 297; Barnes, B. Bom., p. 293; Hume, Str. Feath., XI p. 300; Oates, in Hume's Nests and Eggs, 2nd ed., II p. 263; Salvadori, Cat. B.M., XXI p. 514; Blanf., Avi. Brit. I., IV p. 26; Sharpe, Hand-List, I p. 84; Oates, Cat. Eggs B.M., I p. 108; Sarat Chandra Mittra, J.B.N.H.S., III p. 266; Blanf., ib., IX p. 186; Butler, ib., X p. 310; Stuart Baker, ib., p. 361; Inglis, ib., XI p. 475; Butler, ib., XII p. 690; Osmaston, ib., XVII p. 489; Mears, ib., XVIII p. 86; Osmaston, ib., p. 359; Harington, ib., XIX pp. 309, 365; Cook, ib., XXI p. 675; Hopwood, ib., p. 1214; Harington, B. Burma, p. 66.

Chalcophaps augusta Bp., Con. Av., II p. 92 (1854); Ball, Str. Feath., I p. 81; Hume, ib., II p. 270.

Vernacular Names. *Ram-ghugu, Raj-ghugu,* Beng.; *Andi-bellaguwa,* Tel.; *Pathaki-prau,* Tam. Ceylon; *Nila Robeya,* Cing.; *Ka-er,* Lepcha; *Muti-Ropuha,* Assamese; *Gyo-sane, Gyo-sein,* Burmese; *Daotualai,* Cachari.

Description.—*Adult male.* Fore-head and broad supercilia white, changing to dark blue-grey on the crown and nape; sides of the head, neck, shoulders, and upper-breast a deep vinous-red gradually paling on the lower-breast and abdomen; back, scapulars, wing-coverts and inner secondaries metallic emerald-green with a varying amount of bronze reflections, in a few individuals this bronze tint practically replacing the green; edge of wing, bastard-wing, primaries and greater primary-coverts dark brown; secondaries the same, those next the green innermost ones with bronze reflections. Smallest wing-coverts and shoulder of wing vinous-red like the neck, sometimes more grey, bordered by a fringe of white feathers. Lower-back deep copper-bronze with a band across of feathers fringed with white or greyish-white; rump grey next the lower-back deepening in colour to the upper tail-coverts which are dark grey edged deep brown; tail brown, the outermost two or three pairs grey with a broad black band. Under aspect of wing bright brick or copper red; under tail-coverts dark slaty-grey.

Occasionally a very old male has a few spots of metallic bronze, like the eyes on a peafowl's plumage, on the lower-breast and abdomen.

Colours of soft parts. Bill red, the cere deeper and somewhat sanguine, the tip paler and more a coral-red; iris hazel or dark brown; the eyelids leaden-grey; legs coral-red, the soles paler and the claws pale horny-brown.

Measurements. Total length 10 to 11 in. (= 254 to 279 mm.); wing 5.5 to 5.95 in. (= 149.7 to 151.0 mm.), tail about 3.75 in. (= 95.2 mm.), tarsus rather less than 1 in. (= 25.4 mm.), bill at front .6 in. (= 15.2 mm.) and from gape .9 in. (= 22.8 mm.).

Adult female. Differs from the male in having the white fore-head and supercilia much less in extent and sometimes hardly visible; the slate-grey of the crown and nape is replaced with the vinous-red of the neck, which is, as a rule, less bright in tint than it is in the male. The white wing-patch is not present, and the bars of white or grey across the lower-back are *generally* less pronounced. The tail has the central two pairs dark reddish-brown, the succeeding pairs more red still but tipped darker, and the outermost pair as in the male.

Colours of soft parts. The same as in the male.

Measurements. On the whole the female appears to differ little, if at all, from the male in size and the biggest and smallest specimens in the British Museum Collection are both females.

Young male. Like the female but still duller and with the bronze-green much less in extent and freely barred with copper-red. There is a broad rufous bar across the wing, often plainly visible when the bird is a year or more old; the feathers of the winglet and the inner secondaries are boldly tipped with rufous-red and the whole under-surface is barred dull brown and rufous.

Over its very wide range this little bird is remarkably constant in coloration, although individuals vary considerably *inter se.* Attempts have frequently been made to subdivide this species on the following grounds:—

1. Difference in the extent of the white fore-head and supercilia.
2. Extent and purity of the white bars on the rump and lower-back.
3. Depth of the vinous-red colouring of back, neck, and breast.
4. Presence or absence of grey line running down from the nape to the interscapulars.

All these points are *entirely* individual, and may all be seen in their extremes in a series from Sikhim in the British Museum. Thus a few birds have the fore-head white almost as far back as the centre of the eye, whilst others have the white confined to the edge of the bill. The nuchal line in some birds forms a broad streak dividing the red of the neck in two; in some it is weak and broken, and in one or two not perceptible. The bars on the rump vary to the same extent, and the depth of the red colouring is equally an individual and not a subspecific character.

Distribution. The Emerald Dove is found throughout the greater part of India in forest-country where there is a sufficient rainfall. It extends down the west coast of India from the south of Bombay, through Malabar, Travancore, and thence into Ceylon. On the east coast it is found south nearly to the latitude of the mouths of the Kistna or Krishna River, as I have seen the skin of a bird shot inland from Masulipatam, but it is undoubtedly rare south of latitude 18. It is found in Orissa and throughout the whole of Bengal in the forested parts, Kashmir, Nepal, Bhutan, Assam, and the hill-ranges north and south of the Brahmapootra River up to at least 6,000 ft. It is very common in Manipur, Looshai Hills and throughout Burma, the Malay Peninsula and Archipelago into New Guinea, and again through southern China into the Phillipines. In Burma it appears to be absent from the dry central zone.

Nidification. It is resident throughout the whole of its range, and breeds wherever found. I have had its eggs sent to me from Nepal taken at an elevation of over 4,000 ft., and have personally taken them at elevations higher than this both in the Khasia and North Cachar Hills. As a rule, however, it breeds below 3,000 ft., and is common from this elevation down to the plains.

The nest is the usual Dove's nest of small twigs and sticks, but is better put together than most, and the depression in the centre is often well formed and nearly an inch in depth at the deepest point. The twigs of which it is composed are both those which are picked up dry and such small living twigs as it is able to tear from the tree, and on a few occasions I have seen twigs used with a leaf or two still attached to them. Most nests will be found placed on high bushes or small saplings some five to ten feet from the ground but a few may be taken from bamboo-clumps and, in the Nicobars, Davison found them sometimes placed on the fronds of young coconut palms about six feet from the ground.

I think the Bronze-winged Dove is more particular in seeing that its nest is concealed than are the Green Pigeons and other Doves which make their nests in similar places, and frequently I have taken nests so well hidden in thick bushes, brambles, and cane-brakes that it was with no little difficulty they were discovered.

Incubation is carried on impartially by both sexes and takes about twelve days. The young are fed as usual by the parent-birds regurgitating food in a nearly digested state.

The eggs, always two in number, are not white but a pale cream, café-au-lait, or fawn colour, sometimes so pale that the egg appears white unless placed alongside a really white egg, at other times quite a distinct buff or fawn of the shade of dark wet sand.

In shape they are long elliptical, a few more or less drawn out and pointed at one end, and a few others very broad ellipses.

In length the eggs vary from .95 in. (24.1 mm.) to 1.12 in. (= 28.4 mm.) and in breadth from .78 in. (= 19.8 mm.) to .86 (= 21.8mm.), and the average of 100 eggs is 1.08 in. (= 26.1 mm.) by .82 in. (= 21.0 mm.).

The breeding-season varies according to locality; in southern India and Ceylon January and February appear to be the two principal breeding-months and the same in the Andamans and Nicobars. In Burma and the north-eastern countries of India, March to May are the three months in which most eggs may be taken, but in southern Burma and the adjacent districts, January and February again seem to be the favourite months. In all parts of its range, however, the Emerald Dove breeds more or less over a great portion of the year, and the majority of birds undoubtedly have two broods and many probably have three.

This charming little Dove is essentially a forest-bird and, moreover, one confined almost entirely to damp evergreen-forests and their vicinity, though it may be met with less often in deciduous forest and bamboo-jungle. It is extremely partial to the banks of the smaller forest-streams and to mossy tracks through heavy forest. Working along the former, the fisherman will often see it running along the bank in front of him, finally making off as he gets too close, but seldom flying far and often pitching again within a couple of hundred yards or so. In the same way the traveller along the forest-tracks may see a little dark bird, or perhaps a pair, get up almost at his feet as he rounds some corner, and flit away down the path with incredible speed—dark and sombre-looking unless a flash of sunlight catches it, when it gleams like a jewel until once more the shadows embrace it and it vanishes from sight. Probably, however, once out of sight it has again dropped to earth, and the same procedure may go on for some half a dozen times within the next half mile before at last it dashes aside into the forest and makes its way back to its original haunts. It is a very conservative little bird, and day after day a pair or a single bird may be put up at the same spot if visited at the same hour, and in spite of its powers of flight it does not seem to range over much country. Almost any place where there is a "salt-lick," by a river-bed or in fairly thick evergreen-forest, is sure to be much frequented by these Doves, and the *Cacharies* have a saying to the effect that: elephants and deer *like* salt-licks, buffalo and gour *must* resort to them at times, but that the Emerald Dove *dies* if kept away from them more than a day.

They are very active on the ground, and though normally they move about in a rather sedate and graceful manner, they are capable of great speed when disturbed or when roused to extra exertions by a flight of white ants. Naturally, like all their family, they are entirely vegetarian except for this one lapse, but they catch and eat termites greedily, and I have watched them so feeding until I have wondered where they could possibly put all they had caught. But the termite is food for everything—mammalian, avian, or reptilian, and any Pigeon or Dove will eat them as readily as do squirrels, dormice, and other vegetarian mammals.

The Emerald Dove is very fond of wild strawberries, and I often used to see them eating these on the village-paths in the North Cachar

Hills, and less often would also sometimes see them eating raspberries and blackberries from the bushes which grew in profusion in almost any open glade or roadway.

Their flight, as already noted, is extremely swift, and at the same time wonderfully silent, and it is often quite startling the way these birds flit into sight and then disappear without a sound, twisting and turning so as to avoid bushes and other obstacles in their flight. Invariably they keep low down, and it is rare to see them rise twenty feet from the ground even when they dash across some opening in the forest or are hustled across a wide roadway from one patch of forest to another.

Their note is a soft but very deep and rather plaintive coo, and during the breeding-season they may often be heard calling to one another for some minutes together. They are not gregarious, and except when actually nesting single birds seem to be more often seen even than pairs, but in some favourite spots half a dozen or more may sometimes gather together. In spite however of its solitary habits it is not, I think, for a member of this family, at all a quarrelsome bird, and it can be kept quite safely as a rule with other birds, either of its own or other species.

It thrives in captivity, but does not seem often to be caged in India, though one may meet with such specimens occasionally in the Calcutta and other big bazaars.

It has a curious habit of entering and passing through buildings, which, doubtless, it hopes will afford refuge from the glare of the sun; but finding the interior so different from what it expects, it passes straight through instead of resting. Two or three writers have commented on this curious habit of entering buildings, and it will sometimes even dash through a tea-factory in which many people are working and where the noise of machinery is continuous and loud.

SUBFAMILY COLUMBINAE.

In his family *Columbidae* Salvadori includes but three subfamilies —*Columbinae, Macropygiinae,* and *Ectopistinae.* The last of these three has no representative in Asia, and consists of a single genus and species— *Ectopistes migratorius*, the Passenger-Pigeon of North America.

Of the other two subfamilies, the *Macropygiinae* will be dealt with in detail later on. Here it will suffice to say that, agreeing with Blanford that the birds of the genus are nearer the true Doves than the Pigeons, I place them after these latter birds in order of classification, though uniting them all under the one subfamily *Columbinae* together with the former.

The difference between the Pigeons and Doves of this group are, as pointed out by Blanford, only superficial, and there are no structural characteristics by which they can be divided : they all have twelve tail-feathers, and all have the ambiens muscle, intestinal caeca, and oil-gland.

The feet and legs are more adapted for walking about on the earth than are the arboreal Pigeons hitherto dealt with, but there is a considerable amount of difference in this respect between the various genera of the *Columbinae*, some being far more terrestrial in their habits than others.

The subfamily, according to the classification adopted, contains seven genera of Pigeons and Doves. The former includes the genera *Columba* (Rock-Pigeons), *Dendrotreron*, *Palumbus*, and *Alsocomus* (Wood-Pigeons), and the latter includes *Streptopelia* and *Oenopopelia* (True Doves) and *Macropygia* (Cuckoo-Doves).

Blanford's key to the genera of this subfamily, given in the *Avifauna of British India*, is very simple, and founded on characteristics very easy for the sportsman and field-naturalist to follow, and I therefore adopt it as it stands.

Key to the Genera.

A. Tail less than two-thirds of wing in length :

- *a.* Neck-feathers not acuminate ; dark bars on secondaries ... *Columba.*
- *b.* Neck-feathers acuminate ; no dark bars on secondaries ... *Dendrotreron.*

B. Tail exceeding two-thirds of, but not longer than, wing :

- *c.* Larger, wing 7.5 in. or over ; no white tips to tail-feathers ; tarsus shorter than middle toe without claw :
  - *a′* A white bar, conspicuous beneath, across tail ... *Palumbus.*
  - *b′* No white bar across tail ... ... *Alsocomus.*
- *d.* Smaller, wing 7.4 in. or under ; white or grey tips to tail ; tarsus longer than middle toe without claw :
  - *c′* Sexes alike ; second and third quills longest ... *Streptopelia.*
  - *d′* Sexes different ; first and second quills longest ... *Oenopopelia.*

C. Tail longer than wing, and much graduated ... ... *Macropygia.*

GENUS COLUMBA.

Salvadori includes in the genus *Columba* all our Indian Rock-Pigeons and Wood-Pigeons of the first four genera given above, but even he adds in a footnote: "I feel quite sure that the numerous species of the genus *Columba* ought to be arranged in several sub-genera, but as only some of them can be easily defined . . . I have thought it best to leave them all, as a whole, in one genus."

As regards our Indian birds, they are not difficult to divide into genera; the typical Rock-Pigeons with their grey plumage and the Snow-Pigeon with a similar type of plumage, only snow-white instead of grey, are conveniently placed together in the genus *Columba.* The Speckled Wood-Pigeon with its curious lanceolate plumage and coloration, different from all other Rock- or Wood-Pigeons, at once singles itself out from the rest and thus comes alone in the genus *Dendrotreron.* Of the true Wood-Pigeons, *Palumbus*, we have but one—a very near relative of the English Stock-Dove; and, finally, we have a number of Wood-Pigeons similar in structure to *Palumbus*, but varying considerably in coloration, which are placed together in the genus *Alsocomus.*

The genus *Columba,* as restricted according to this classification, contains four species of Pigeon, one of which is again divided into two subspecies.

With the exception of the Snow-Pigeon, which is mostly white to suit its snow-clad habitat, they are birds of grey plumage of different shades, with a certain amount of metallic lustre about the neck. In habits they are more terrestrial than arboreal, though perching freely and sometimes roosting on trees.

The tails are short, the tips of the closed wings reaching almost to the end of the tail; the tarsi and feet are longer and formed for walking, the former being unfeathered; the nostrils are narrow and obliquely set in the swollen cere, and the wings are long and pointed, the first or second primary being the longest.

Key to the Species.

A. Plumage principally grey:
  a. Bill blackish; legs red:
    a' No white band across tail ... ... *C. livia.*
    b'. A white band across tail ... ... *C. rupestris.*
  b. Bill and legs yellowish ... ... *C. eversmanni.*
B. Plumage principally white ... ... *C. leuconota.*

COLUMBA LIVIA.

Key to the Subspecies.

A. Lower-back white ... ... *C. l. livia.*
B. Lower-back grey ... ... *C. l. intermedia.*

(24) COLUMBA LIVIA LIVIA (Bonn.).

THE BLUE ROCK-PIGEON.

Columba livia Briss., Orn., I p. 82 (1760).

Columba oenas Linn. (part), Syst. Nat., I p. 279.

Columba domestica Lath., Ind. Orn., II p. 589.

Columba domestica livia id. ib., p. 590.

Columba livia Bonn., Encycl. Méth., I p. 227 (1790); Blyth, Cat. B.M.A.S.B., no. 233 (part); id., J.A.S.B., XIV p. 861; Hume, Str. Feath., I p. 218; Blanf., East Persia, II p. 268; Cripps, Str. Feath., VII p. 296; Hume, ib., VIII p. 109; id., Cat. no. 788, bis; Barnes, Str. Feath., IX p. 457; id., B. Bom., p. 289; Salvadori, Cat. B.M., XXI p. 252; Blanf., Avi. Brit. I., IV p. 30; Sharpe, Hand-List Birds, I p. 69; Oates, Cat. Eggs B.M., I p. 87; Barnes, J.B.N.H.S., V p. 330; Rattray, ib., XII p. 344; Inglis, ib., XIV; p. 561; Marshall, ib., XV p. 352; Nicol Cumming, ib., XVI p. 691; Ward, ib., XVII p. 943; Perreau, ib., XIX p. 919; Whitehead, ib., XX p. 966.

Columba affinis Blyth, J.A.S.B., XIV p. 862.

Columba neglecta Hume, Lah. to Yark., p. 272 (1873); id., Str. Feath., I p. 218; Severtz, ib., III p. 430.

Columba spelaea Hume, Lah. to Yark., p. 273.

Vernacular Names. *Kabutar*, Hin.; *Konturam*, Pushtu.

Description.—*Adult male.* Head dark purple-grey; nape, neck all round, upper-breast and the extreme upper part of the interscapulary region dark grey glossed with brilliant metallic purple and green, according to the light in which it is held. Upper-back ashy-grey grading gradually into white on the lower-back, where the white forms a broad band, about 2 in. deep; rump and upper tail-coverts dark grey, generally a little darker than the upper-back; tail dark grey like the rump with a broad black band across the end leaving only a narrow final tip of grey. The outermost rectrices with a broad border of white on the outer web between the base and the black band. Wing-coverts and innermost secondaries grey, of the same shade as the back, with two broad bars of black, the first formed by the black bases of the greater coverts and a second by the innermost secondaries which are mostly black or blackish-brown, though with the concealed bases and the tips grey; primaries brownish-grey, paler on the inner webs except at the tips. Lower-parts slaty-grey, darkest on the breast; under wing-coverts and axillaries white, the former more or less suffused with very pale grey.

Colour of soft parts. "Iris orange red; bill vinous slate colour, inclining to white on the cere; legs red" (Salvadori).

Measurements. "Total length 11 in., wing 8.7 in., tail 4.6 in., bill .79 in., tarsus 1.2 in." (Salvadori).

According to Hume, who measured a very big series of British birds, the wing varied from 8.3 in. to 9.7 in. The series in the British Museum, a singularly poor one as regards typical birds, varies between 8.2 in. (= 208.2 mm.) and 9.05 in. (229.8 mm.). Weight 8 to 12 oz.

Adult female. Similar to the male.

Colours of soft parts. As in the male.

Measurements. The female is a rather smaller bird than the male, with a wing-measurement averaging about .3 in. (7.6 mm.) less. It is also a good deal more slender and lighter in weight. Weight 7 to 9½ oz.

Young male. "Duller in coloration, and having the black bands on the wing less clearly defined and with but little of the green gloss on the neck" (Salvadori).

Nestling, in the downy stage, is covered with a yellow, or pale yellow-buff down.

Distribution. "The Western Palaearctic region, with Afghanistan, Baluchistan, Sind, the Punjab, Kashmir, and occasionally other parts of India" (Blanford).

A careful examination of such data as we have on record, together with the skins available in the British Museum and elsewhere, induce me to make rather a drastic curtailment in the above definition of the area of the western form of the Blue Rock-Pigeon in the East.

In the collection in the British Museum, including Hume's collection, there are but two specimens which could be held to be true *livia*: these are two birds collected in Ladak, the one by Henderson on the 18th of October, 1890, and the second by Strachey on the 1st of January, 1880, and even in these two birds the white band is narrower than is normal in western birds and in one also it is slightly, though faintly, suffused with grey. Nearest to these is a third bird collected by Hume in Sind: in this the white is less than an inch broad and as the collection contains eight birds from the same locality, all typical *intermedia*, it looks as if this bird was individually aberrant or a reversion to the original white-rumped stock of the West. Another specimen labelled *livia* from Jhelam is really intermediate between *livia* and *intermedia* and nearer the latter than the former. Cripps's specimen from Furredpore is almost a typical *livia* though the normal bird of this district is quite as typically true *intermedia*, and here again I look upon this as an individual aberration or reversion. Specimens from Mesopotamia are inclined to *livia*, and one such is almost a typical bird of that subspecies, though others are quite typical *intermedia*.

When we work through northern Africa, from Tunis eastwards to Egypt, and thence through Palestine, north Arabia and Persia, we find a form very closely allied to *intermedia*, if not identical with it, which has been named *gymnocyclus* by G. R. Gray, *schimperi* by Bonaparte (1854), and lately (1912) *palestinae* by Graf Zedlitz, and before that (in 1874), *neglecta* by Hume, and *spelaea* by Hutton (1873) (in a letter to Hume). Salvadori describes this species, or subspecies (*schimperi*) as similar to *C. livia*, but lighter, and with the rump light grey like the back, not white; the area of habitat he gives as Egypt, Nubia, and Palestine. Birds, however, from Tunis in the west and Arabia in the east are identical, and these, again, I find it difficult to separate from our north-west Indian *livia intermedia*. Throughout Europe and north-west Asia and Asia Minor, all the specimens I have seen are typical *livia*.

From the material available, therefore, I think it would be difficult to prove that typical *C. livia livia* ever comes within our Indian limits, except perhaps as the rarest of stragglers into the extreme north-east, as with the two Ladak birds, and possibly also into Kashmir.

When, however, we examine the *written* records of its appearance in India the case is very different, and at first sight it would appear to be overwhelmingly conclusive that *C. livia livia* is an exceedingly common bird in many parts of the north-west of India and the adjoining countries. First, we have Hume who records that Dr. Day shot a typical specimen of *livia* in the Rooree district, and that he himself obtained one in the Gaj, whilst Dr. Day reported the bird as common at Durgalo, all these being places in Sind. Rattray found both the European and Indian Blue Rocks very common during the winter in Thull, but apparently did not collect any specimens or examine them very closely. In Chitral, Perreau identified a great number of skins, and states that from December to March he obtained only *intermedia*, whereas in March he only procured specimens of *livia*; and Whitehead, writing of the Kurram Valley, records the former as only occurring in amongst flocks of the latter and never collecting in separate flocks. Inglis obtained a single specimen in Behar as did Cripps in Furredpore. Ward, whilst recording the European Rock-Pigeon as occurring in Kashmir, says that the Indian bird is the common form, but gives no details.

Now, in considering this evidence it has always to be borne in mind that the wild and domestic pigeon interbreed with the greatest freedom, and also that domesticated birds wander away with flocks of wild ones. All over India and the surrounding countries the natives keep domestic pigeons, and there is therefore hardly a place where the possible taint of a cross with a tame bird could be ruled out of consideration.

The evidence which it is hardest to get over is undoubtedly that of Perreau, who obtained Indian birds in the cold weather and then the European bird in March—a reversion of what we should have expected, yet proving that the typical English bird, or one very much like it, does come into, or close to, India in large flocks at certain times of the year. But it may well be that Perreau whilst correctly identifying the March Pigeon as a bird quite different to our Indian Blue Rock, did not see that it differed somewhat from the European bird also, and the bird he saw was possibly the intermediate form, *schimperi*, vel *neglecta*, vel *palestinae*.

The conclusions I have arrived at are that our Indian Blue Rock-Pigeon, *C. livia intermedia*, is found in India and extends into Afghanistan, Baluchistan, Persia, Arabia, and through Egypt and northern Africa as far west as Tunis, whilst the European Blue Rock-Pigeon is found throughout Europe, Asia Minor, north-west and Central Asia, and possibly northern Persia.

Owing, however, to their enormous power of flight, their constant interbreeding with domestic Pigeons, and the tendency of this family, domestic or wild, to *throw back*, aberrant birds are constantly occurring: so that even where *livia* is the dominant bird, we everywhere find, except in the extreme west of its habitat, specimens which are nearer *intermedia*, and vice versa specimens which are nearer *livia* in the normal habitat of *intermedia*.

This will be the case whether we are content to recognize only the two self-evident subspecies, *livia* and *intermedia*, as dominant respectively over the greater part of their eastern and western ranges, or whether we again divide the intermediate birds in the intervening range into one or more subspecies.

Before leaving the subject, however, it should be noted that in his *Hand-List* Sharpe recognizes the following species, *livia*, *intermedia*, *schimperi*, and *neglecta*. The last species he gives as confined to Persia and north-west India, but he also gives south Persia and central Asia as part of the normal habitat of *intermedia*, whilst he only recognizes *schimperi* as occurring in Palestine, Egypt, Nubia, and Madeira.

Nidification. Of its breeding in Great Britain, Seebohm writes: "The Rock-Dove breeds on the coasts of Great Britain, Ireland, and all the adjacent islands, even including the district of St. Kilda, wherever the rocks are precipitous enough to give it protection and provide suitable breeding-places for it in their recesses. The range of this species is much wider than that of any other British Dove, extending from the Atlantic to the Pacific, and its exact limits are very difficult to determine, in consequence of the impossibility of discriminating between wild birds and those which have been or are in a semi-domesticated state.

"It is a very early breeder, its eggs being often laid by the middle of March, and as it rears two, if not three or four broods in a season, fresh eggs may be obtained from that month till August or September. April and May are the principal breeding months. A few Rock-Pigeons build their nests in the crevices of the cliffs, but the greater majority resort to caves for breeding purposes. The eggs are only two in number, pure white in colour, oval and rather elongated in form; they vary from 1.5 to 1.38 inch in length, and from 1.2 to 1.1 inch in breadth. As a rule the eggs of this bird are rather more rotund in shape than that of the Ring-Dove, and they are always smaller than the normal eggs of that bird."

The nest is a rough platform of sticks and twigs without any lining, and very carelessly put together on some ledge of rocks. Whether the twigs employed for the purpose are picked up as dry twigs or are torn from trees there is nothing recorded, but from recollections of nests seen when I was a boy the former seemed invariably to be the case. This is what might be expected from a Pigeon that does not haunt trees, whereas the arboreal Pigeons certainly tear some of the material they use from the living tree.

The eggs in the British Museum Collection are all within the measurements given by Seebohm. The texture is fine and close with a considerable gloss, and the most frequent shape is a rather long ellipse, truly oval eggs being most rare.

The European Rock-Dove or Rock-Pigeon lives in very large colonies all the year round, living and roosting in the same caves as those they breed in. Generally speaking in western Europe and Great Britain these caves are situated on the more rocky cliffs on the coasts, but where there are inland cliffs sufficiently high and precipitous to afford them shelter, they may also sometimes be found frequenting these. In Eastern Europe and in Asia they are found haunting cliffs many hundreds of miles from the sea, and indeed seem equally common in the mountain-ranges as on the coasts. They certainly ascend to at least 12,000 ft. in the higher ranges which they frequent, and possibly ascend even higher than this during the hottest months of summer.

Their note is a bubbling "coo," too well-known to need description, and their flight, to those who have never seen the lightning speed of some of the larger Spine-tailed Swifts, has always been held up as the acme of speed achieved by a bird's wings. Certainly the speed at which they fly is very great and whilst they can cover sixty miles an hour in ordinary flight they must be able to nearly double this when frightened. Ussher, in his "Birds of Ireland," gives an interesting instance of the speed of this bird's flight. He writes : "I was leaning on the cliff fence looking out to sea, when I suddenly heard something cleaving the air ; three birds glanced past me, and darted downwards to the rocks below. In an instant a rock that ran into the sea was reached, and one of the birds shot, as it were, into the heart of the stone ; the other two skimmed the rock and rose into the air ; then I recognised these two birds were Peregrines. Wishing to know what the third bird was, and what had befallen it, I went down to the rock ; in the centre was a fissure which terminated in a crab hole, and in this was a Rock-Pigeon panting heavily, and with its eyeballs starting from their sockets."

Their diet consists principally of grain and seeds, but they will also eat berries, fruit, and shoots of young plants and certain trees. In the coast counties of England and Wales they are said often to do considerable damage to the crops adjacent to their colonies, and the farmers are very keen on their numbers being kept in check, though these birds are certainly less mischievous than their cousins, the Wood-Pigeons.

(25) COLUMBA LIVIA INTERMEDIA (Strick.).

THE INDIAN BLUE ROCK-PIGEON.

Columba oenas Jerdon, Madr. J.L.S., XII p. 14; Bingh., Sport. Rev. 1845, pl. IV.

Columba intermedia Strick., Ann. and Mag. N.N., XIII p. 39 (1844); Blyth, J.A.S.B., XIV p. 861; Layard, Ann. and Mag. N.H., XIV p. 59; Stoliczka, J.A.S.B., XXXVII 2nd pt. p. 66; id. ib., XLI 2nd pt. p. 248; Jerdon, B.I., III p. 469; Hume, Str. Feath., I p. 217; Adam, ib., p. 390; Ball, ib., II p. 425; id. ib., III p. 208; Hume, Nests and Eggs, III p. 499; Butler, Str. Feath., IV p. 3; Fairbank, ib., p. 262; Blanf., E. Persia, II p. 268; Hume, Str. Feath., VI p. 419; Dav. and Wen., ib., VII p. 86; Ball, ib., p. 224; Cripps, ib., p. 296; Hume, ib., VIII p. 109; id., Cat. no. 788; Legge, B. Cey., p. 608; Scully, Str. Feath., VIII p. 339; Doig, ib., p. 371; Vidal, ib., IX p. 74; Biddulph, ib., p. 357; Butler, ib. p. 419; Barnes, ib., p. 457; Reid, ib., p. 59; Oates, B. Burma, II p. 288; Barnes, B. Bom., p. 289; Hume, Str. Feath., XI p. 297; Oates, in Hume's Nests and Eggs, 2nd ed., II p. 344; Salvadori, Cat. B.M., XXI p. 259; Sharpe, Hand-List, I p. 69; Oates, Cat. Eggs B.M., I p. 87; Harington, B. Burma, p. 67; Barnes, J.B.N.H.S., V p. 330; Davidson, ib., XII p. 62; Rattray, ib., p. 344; Primrose, ib., XIII p. 708; Inglis, ib., XIV p. 561; Marshall, ib., XV p. 352; Wall., ib., p. 722; Bourdillon, ib., XVI p. 2; Fulton, ib., p. 60; Dewar, ib., p. 495; Martin Young, ib., p. 515; Nicol Cuming, ib., p. 691; Macdonald, ib., XVII p. 496; Ward, ib., p. 943; Harington, ib., XIX p. 309; Perreau, ib., p. 919; Whitehead, ib., XX p. 966; Moss-King, ib., XXI p. 99; Whitehead, ib., p. 167.

Columba livia (part) Blyth., Cat. B.M.A.S.B., p. 233; Blyth, B. Burma, p. 145.

Columba livia, var. *cyanotus*, Severtz, Str. Feath., III p. 430.

Vernacular Names. *Kabutar*, Hin.; *Páraivá*, Mahr.; *Gudi pourai*, Tel.; *Kovilpura*, Tamil; *Mada-praa*, Tam. Ceylon; *Kabtretar*, Behari; *Nōni Daotu*, Cachari; *Kóntióram*, Pushtu; *Kho*, Burmese; *Kapoth*, Baluchi; *Kaftar*, Persian.

Description.—*Adult male.* Similar to the last bird, but, typically, the colour of the plumage generally is darker than it is in true *livia*, and the lower-back is concolorous with, or only very little paler than, the upper, though contrasting with the still darker rump; the primaries and outer secondaries are also darker, and have the grey on the inner webs less pale and less in extent, and the grey on the inner quills less well defined.

Colours of soft parts. Irides orange-yellow to orange-red; bill black, the cere livid-grey or whitish, and the base of the lower mandible paler; eyelids livid-white, or greyish-white; legs generally a deep crimson-red, sometimes paler and sometimes a rather light coral-red, the soles paler and the claws horny.

"Bill black, with a white mealiness at the humid base of its upper-mandible; irides brownish-orange; lids bluish-white, and legs reddish-pink" (Blyth).

Measurements. Much the same as those of *Columba livia livia*, its European cousin. The series in the British Museum, a very complete one, from the Hume Collection principally, has wing-measurements varying from 8.3 in. (= 209.8 mm.) to 9.35 in. (= 237.4 mm.), with an average of almost exactly 9 in. (= 228.6 mm.). The weight runs up to about 12 oz., but averages somewhere about 10 oz. or a little over; "10 to 11.5 oz." (Scully).

Adult female. Similar to the male.

Colours of soft parts. Similar to the same parts in the male, but the iris possibly never assumes as bright a golden-red tint as it sometimes does in old males.

Measurements. The female is a decidedly smaller bird than the male, with a wing-measurement averaging very little, if anything, over 8.70 in. (= 220 mm.) and varying between 8.02 in. (= 202.7 mm.) and 8.80 in. (= 222.4 mm.). The other measurements differ from those of the male in corresponding degree.

Weight from 8½ oz. to 11 oz., and averaging about 9½ oz.

Young male. Similar to the adult, but rather browner, and with the wing-bars less distinct and the iridescent colours of the neck not so well developed.

The feathers of the back, wing-coverts, and more rarely of the head and breast, are fringed with pale dull brown.

Colours of soft parts. The iris is at first a dull glaucous-brown, then a pale reddish-brown, from which it gradually changes to the orange-red of the adult. The legs are a less brilliant red in tint and often paler.

Nestling, in down. Pale yellow-buff.

Nestlings just prior to leaving the nest are often so fat that they weigh as much as, and sometimes even more than, the adult birds.

Distribution. Throughout India from Ceylon over the whole peninsula of India to the extreme north-west, throughout the Himalayas to a considerable elevation, Kashmir, Nepal, Sikhim, and Tibet. It occurs in south Sylhet, but I never came across it in the North Cachar Hills or in Cachar itself except in Hylakandy, where it was very rare. It is not found in the eastern Assam Valley, but is occasionally seen in Goalpara and north-east of Mymensingh, and is again fairly common in Noakhali and Chittagong. In Burma it is common in the central dry zone, and is recorded as common in the Myingyan district by Macdonald, but is apparently absent from most of the wet and well forested parts, and is *not* common all over Burma, as stated by Blyth.

As it is certain that future systematists will examine this Pigeon very carefully, with a view to splitting it up into various geographical subspecies, it may be as well for me to record here the result of my own investigations into the subject.

In the first place it is undoubtedly the fact that birds from the Himalayan regions, from Afghanistan and Baluchistan, and those from the more desert countries and parts of the Deccan, are on the whole paler than are birds from southern India, Ceylon, north-east India, and Burma; that is to say, birds from high elevations and desert-country average somewhat lighter than those from forested and more humid places.

When dealing with the European Rock-Pigeon I have already said that I cannot differentiate between Bonaparte's *schimperi*, Hume's *neglecta*, Hutton's *spelaea*, and Graf Zedlitz's *palestinae*; and again, that I cannot discriminate between these forms and the paler form of our Indian Rock-Pigeon, *intermedia*. At the same time there is a distinct difference between pale, light-backed specimens from all the other regions mentioned and a typical dark grey specimen from Ceylon, Madras, or Behar. Unfortunately there is no difference which is constant or which is sufficiently constant for the trinomialist to be able to say here at this end of the range of the species is a dark race and here at the other end we always have a pale race with, as might be expected, an intermediate form in the intermediate area. We can say this of the two forms *livia* and *intermedia*, but we cannot lay down any such definite rules for our Indian birds. Thus amongst the pale Himalayan and desert-form, dark birds are quite common, and on the other hand, amongst the dark birds of southern and eastern India, we get such specimens as Cripp's so-called *livia* from Furredpore and other birds which are almost as pale as this particular individual.

Under the above circumstances I have preferred not to create any more races than the two well-defined forms, *livia* and *intermedia*.

When, however, we come to consider the Chinese birds, and when we can get a *big* series from which to draw conclusions, it may be found desirable to divide this race from *intermedia*. There are, unfortunately, only three specimens in the British Museum Collection, but these all differ from typical *intermedia* in their relatively dark heads and pale backs, in the breasts being much darker and contrasting with the pale abdomens, and also in the metallic coloured plumage of the hind-neck being extended well into the interscapulary region, where it is sharply defined from the pale grey of the back.

Nidification. The breeding-season of the Indian Rock-Pigeon might almost be said to commence on the 1st of January and to end on the 31st of December. In Behar, Inglis reports that he found them breeding in large numbers in an old temple at Laheria Seria and adds that he took eggs in every month of the year with the exception of February. In some districts in Eastern Bengal, where they breed principally in the roofs of masonry houses and also in the walls of deserted factories and other buildings, they certainly breed throughout the year though, perhaps, fewer have eggs during the height of the rains, say August and early September, than in the other months.

According to Hume, in upper India the breeding-season lasts from Christmas to May Day, and Barnes considered the breeding-season in the Bombay Presidency to last from November to May. In the Doab, Colonel Marshall found them breeding in April, May and June, and in Ceylon Legge gives May and June as the two principal breeding-months.

Practically wherever found, the Indian Blue Rock-Pigeon is resident and breeds, whether at the level of the plains or 10,000 ft. up in the hills, as found by Fulton, Ward, Whitehead, and others.

The natural site for this bird's nest is undoubtedly holes and caves in steep cliffs, or in the sides of rocky ravines, but as the bird itself has gradually spread across the Continent and has left places where such natural sites are obtainable, it has adapted itself without difficulty to the requirements of civilization, and now breeds regularly in masonry wells, old temples, ruined buildings of all kinds, and even in occupied brick and stone buildings. Marshall found them breeding in the *kurezas*, or underground water-channels, peculiar to the country round Quetta; and another curious place I found some birds breeding in was a collection of deep borrow-pits beside the main road leading into the town of Krishnagar, and this was the more strange in that there was an abundance of masonry buildings of all kinds, old and new, within a very few hundred yards of where they were nesting.

They breed in colonies, often very large ones, and I know of no instance of single nests being found. The nest itself is the usual untidy platform of dry twigs, but much mixed with a good deal of rubbish, such as straw from cattle-bedding, grass, and the accumulation of feathers from countless generations of birds. They make use of the same nest for several broods, and I think, almost certainly, for many consecutive years, so that as might be expected, they get into a filthy state, and are full of vermin.

Many years ago, when I was stationed in Nadia, some two hundred pairs of these Pigeons bred in the roof of a very old police-station in that district. This roof consisted of an upper stone-slab one, and a lower false one of bricks with a gap between the two of some four feet, in which the birds placed their nests, finding entry by the holes left for ventilation. As this was a part of India where the birds were not held sacred, I forced an entry into the roof and inspected the nests, the owners of which had left in a panic-stricken crowd prior to the commencement of my housebreaking operations. There must have been from fifty to sixty nests in this place, some in groups of five or six all huddled together, others a few feet apart from any other, but all alike were in a filthy condition, and the material looked as if it must have been collected there by many generations previously, each generation merely adding its quota of feathers and insects and a little dirty straw collected from a cattle-byre a few yards away.

In spite of the close proximity of their nests to one another, in none did I find more than two eggs or squabs, nor have I personally ever seen more than two such, but Fergusson, Inglis, and others have taken three eggs from the same nest, so it may be that this Pigeon does occasionally lay three eggs, or, and this is more likely, two birds may lay their eggs in the same nest.

As far as I can ascertain, there is as yet no recorded instance of this Pigeon ever making its nest on a tree: invariably they place the nest in a hole of some kind in masonry, or cave or crevice in a cliff, in a hole in an earthen wall or bank, or in some underground tunnel or cutting, but never have they, previous to this, been known to make their nest in a tree. The finding, therefore, of two such nests is a most interesting fact.

Captain C. R. S. Pitman, the finder of these two nests, writes to me about them, *in epistola*, as follows: "On 16th July, 1913, I found this Pigeon still breeding amongst the precipitous cliffs and craggs of the Girni Sar (5,880 ft.), a ridge of hills in independent territory across the administrative border to the north of the Derajat District. I found a lot of egg shells lying about in the nullahs below the cliffs where the 'Blue Rocks' swarmed and on one occasion I saw a Pigeon fly into the cliff and a few minutes afterwards she came out again and threw down the egg shells from which her nestlings had apparently just hatched out. I also found two nests placed in wild-fig trees in a nullah full of rushes and grass.

"Both nests were quite massive constructions of sticks and twigs lined with finer material and dead grass. One was placed among the thin top branches about 18 ft. from the ground and contained two smooth white glossy eggs on the point of hatching. The other was placed in a stout branch 12 ft. from the ground and contained two young ones about ten days old; these latter had seeds and small bits of grain in their crops ! ! "

Both sexes share equally in the labour of constructing the nest, incubating the eggs, and feeding the young. The latter process is carried out in the same manner as by the domestic pigeon, the parent birds semi-digesting the food and regurgitating it for the benefit of the young. In feeding, the young bird thrusts its head nearly into the mouth of the parent engaged in looking after it, the whole bill and face disappearing from view. The young grow with great rapidity, and are nearly as big as their parents in about three weeks.

The eggs cannot in any way be discriminated from those of the European Rock-Pigeon, or Rock-Dove, though they would seem to average a little bigger. Hume's measurements of a series of sixty eggs gave an average of 1.45 in. (= 35.7 mm.) by 1.12 in. (= 28.4 mm.), and the extremes in length as 1.20 in. (= 30.4 mm.) to 1.65 in. (= 41.4 mm.) and in breadth 1.02 in. (= 25.9 mm.) to 1.25 in. (= 32.7 mm.). All the eggs I have measured come within the range of variation of the above eggs, and the average is exactly the same as Hume's.

The normal shape is a long ellipse, oval or pointed eggs being very exceptional. The texture is close and smooth, but not very fine, though the surface is often highly glossed.

The Indian Blue Rock-Pigeon is, like its European cousin, more a bird of open country than of dense forest, but it is found practically anywhere where there are suitable sites or buildings for it to build in, and as it is a bird which easily adapts itself to circumstances, there are not many districts from which it is altogether excluded.

In all probability its original haunts were cliffs on rocky coasts, and ravines and precipices in mountainous regions, from which it spread gradually to quarries and ruined buildings deserted by man, and from these again it in time ventured into the actual towns, villages, and forts occupied by human beings.

Jerdon says: "They are most partial to large buildings, such as Churches, Pagodas, Mosques, Tombs, and the like; frequently entering the verandas of inhabited houses and breeding in the cornices. Holes in walls of cities or towns, too, are favourite places, and, in some parts of the country, they prefer holes in wells, especially, I think, in the west of India, the Deccan, etc. In default of such spots, they will breed in crevices and cavities of rocks, caverns and sea-side cliffs, and I have often noticed that they are particularly partial to rocky cliffs by water-falls."

Wherever found it congregates in colonies as great as the breeding accommodation will permit of, and in some places it collects literally in many thousands. A specially favoured place, and one referred to by Jerdon, is the Gaissoppa Falls in southern India, which they frequent in myriads in company with the Alpine Swift. Here the sound of a gun being fired, or any unaccustomed noise, brings the birds out in such numbers that they have been likened to locusts or to a swarm of bees or white ants.

If the Gaissoppa Falls however forms a good specimen of one of their wilder haunts, free from the presence and influence of man, on the other hand they will be found in almost equal numbers breeding in the walls and buildings of great cities and famous forts. Over a great portion of north-west India they are considered more or less sacred, and scrupulously looked after and protected, and in many other places where they are not actually held to be sacred, they are considered birds of good omen, and all shooting of them is strictly prohibited. In reference to this protection afforded to the Rock-Pigeon, Adam writes: "As the killing of the common Blue Pigeon is strictly prohibited, all through Rajputana, this species is very abundant. The native Governments allow a certain quantity of grain to be given to the Pigeons each morning, and pay a man to feed them. Every morning at break of day flocks of Pigeons may be seen hurrying into Sambhar from the surrounding villages, and when the grain is thrown out to them the fluttering and fighting of the thousands of birds is a sight well worth seeing. When the grain has been consumed, each flock starts off for home."

Owing to the veneration in which they are held, many an unwary or unthinking shooter has got into trouble over these birds, and has unwittingly brought down on his head physical blows from the Hindu inhabitants, and moral ones from the benign Government who looks after the superstitions and prejudices of its Indian subjects with far greater eagerness than it pays to the safety and well-being of its European ones.

Where the Pigeons are not considered sacred, and no European *sportsman* worthy of the name would *intentionally* hurt the religious feelings of any Indian, they afford splendid sport, for the Indian Blue Rock-Pigeon is not one wit behind his European cousin in power of flight and speed of movement. Away in the Himalayas, and in the wild and mountainous country across the borders, the sportsman can pursue his shooting amidst the finest of scenery, or the most desolate and forbidding of country, perhaps with the chance thrown in of being potted by wily trans-frontier tribesmen, on the look out for bigger Pigeons than Blue Rocks.

My own shooting has, however, been restricted to the vicinity of civilization, where the birds were frequenting deserted factories or the like, or else to the shooting of birds wending their way to and from the towns they frequent. Even under such circumstances, though the surroundings were unromantic, the sport was excellent, and on more than one occasion in a couple of hours, during the mornings and evenings, I have got thirty or forty couple to my own gun, and have finished with the comforting feeling that the toll taken of the flock left it *apparently* undiminished in numbers.

One of our favourite places for these shoots was an old deserted indigo factory in the district of Nadia: the house and factory still stood upright, though ruinous, and all around were the remains of village-houses, fragmentary, yet each still affording shelter for a few pairs of Pigeons, the great bulk of which, many hundreds in number, dwelt in the bigger buildings. About a quarter of a mile from these buildings, or perhaps rather less, we used to stand with our guns, and shoot the Pigeons as they left in the early morning to feed, or returned in the evening to roost. Generally the birds came flying rather low, only some six to twelve feet from the ground, so that they were well screened from our view by the mongo topes, bushes, plantain trees, and clumps of bamboos which grow in luxuriance all round. Dodging in and out between these trees the birds would come swooping down upon us either singly or in twos or threes, affording only the quickest of shots in front of us, or rather easier shots as they rose in the air to avoid us and hurried away in the opposite direction. Now and then, of course, a bird would come sailing home well over the trees and give a simple chance, and, still less often, a flock of a dozen or so would come scurrying along so closely packed that a bad shot might miss the bird aimed at yet get another one, or, with luck, kill the bird aimed at and one or even two others as well.

Taking one with another, however, we always considered one bird to every two cartridges quite fair shooting, whilst two birds to three was above the average.

Shooting the birds as they fed all round about in the fields after the rice was cut, was much simpler, and a good shot should get three birds out of four fired at unless the birds had been much worried, when they naturally got very wild, and it was difficult to get anywhere near them.

Over the greater part of its range, the Blue Rock-Pigeon is resident, breeding, as already stated, in practically every month of the year; but in some places it would seem as if they were partially migratory, or as if they resorted to one kind of country to roost and breed in, and quite another kind in which to feed. Thus Rattray found them "breeding in hundreds in a cliff near the fort [Thull] about the middle of April they all disappeared." Whitehead, in his notes on the birds of Kohat and the Kurram Valley, says that he found them in large flocks from August to April. Perreau also seems to have found them in Chitral only from December to March. Other observers in Kanara have noted that, though it retires to the hill-ranges for the night, it feeds during certain seasons of the year in the low coast country.

It is principally a grain feeder, but will also eat many kinds of fruits and berries, and also young shoots of certain plants and crops. I found that it was very partial to very young shoots of the mustard-plant, and villagers have told me that where the birds are numerous they often do considerable damage to the mustard crops, and in the wheat-growing countries they are an unmitigated nuisance, the more so that, in being sacred it is not permitted to do anything more than attempt to drive them away—an attempt which is very seldom effective, for the birds soon learn that they have nothing really to fear from the beating of drums and banging of bamboos on the earth.

Wherever they are protected they become incredibly tame and have, literally, often to be pushed to one side by the native passer-by, though they will not allow of so near approach by the strangely-clad European. When they are much shot at, however, they become very wary, and it is then almost impossible to get within gunshot of them when feeding in the open, and even in flight-shooting the shooter must be suitably dressed, or more or less hidden by grass or bushes, if he wishes for a successful shot.

Their notes are exactly the same as those of the European form, and need no description. They are not noisy birds individually, but when they are in great numbers the rise and swell of the constant cooing that goes on is indescribable—more like a distant rumbling of thunder than anything else I can think of, though it is always a soft and rather melodious rumbling.

They are, of course, excellent eating, but the wise man will take the full-grown squabs from the nests when he can get them and leave the parent birds. The young birds get enormously fat before they leave the nest, and must sometimes weigh more than their parents, being coated with a dense layer of yellow fat. This skin and coating of fat, however, should be removed before the birds are cooked, as it is sometimes rather rank and coarse to the taste. When in camp our favourite way of cooking them was to roll them up, feathers and all, into a ball of clay, and throw them into a fire of glowing wood-ashes. All the gross fat melted into the clay, and when this was broken open, skin and feathers came away with the clay and the juicy young bird inside was ready for the table.

(26) COLUMBA RUPESTRIS Pall.

THE BLUE HILL-PIGEON.

(PLATE 12.)

Columba oenas, var. *C. rupestris*, Pall., Zoogr. Rosso-Asiat., I p. 560, t. 35 (1811).

Columba rupestris Bp., Con. Av., II p. 48; Jerdon, B.I., III p. 420; Stoliczka, J.A.S.B., XXXVII pt. 2 p. 66; Hume, Str. Feath., VIII p. 110; id., Cat. no. 789; Sharpe, Yarkand Miscel. Av., p. 116; Salvadori, Cat. B.M., XXI p. 250; Blanf., Avi. Brit. I., IV p. 30; Sharpe, Hand-List, I p. 68; Ward, J.B.N.H.S., XVII p. 943; Perreau, ib., XIX p. 919; Bailey, ib., XXI pp. 182-3.

Columba livia Adams, P.Z.S. 1858, p. 497; id. ib. 1859, p. 187.

Columba rupicola Pall., Zoogr. Rosso-Asiat., I p. 562; Hume and Hend., Lah. to Yark., p. 273; Scully, Str. Feath., IV p. 176.

Vernacular Names.—*Yáivá Kabtar*, Turki.; *Angoa*, *Oron*, Tibetan.

Description.—*Adult male*. Whole head, chin, throat, and nape dark dove-grey; hind-neck and shoulders still darker grey, glossed with green, and to a much less extent with purple, though the comparative amount of the two varies in different lights. Upper-back, scapulars, wing-coverts, and innermost secondaries pure dove-grey, much lighter than that of the head; quills grey, tinged with brown on the outer webs and the tips and edge of the inner webs; shafts dark hair-brown.

Lower-back white, rump and upper tail-coverts dark plumbeous-grey like the head, but often still darker; tail dark slate-grey, the tip darker than the base and a broad white band across the middle, outermost pair of feathers white on the base and middle of the other web; breast vinous-grey tinged with purple lustre next the neck, and changing gradually to a lighter dove-grey on the lower-breast, flanks, abdomen, and lower tail-coverts; under wing-coverts white except on the edge of the wing, which is grey; axillaries white.

Colours of soft parts. Iris orange-red, golden-red, or deep orange-yellow; bill almost black with a tinge of plumbeous or livid flesh-colour on cere; legs and feet coral or lobster-red, rather darker in front than behind, with the soles paler and the claws horny-black or horny-brown. "Irides blood-red, straw colour at pupillary margin" (Scully).

Measurements. Total length 13 to 14 in. (= 330 to 355 mm.). The average wing-measurement of sixty-three birds is exactly 9 in. (= 228.6 mm.), and the greatest length is 9.60 in. (= 243.6 mm.) in a bird from Tibet, unsexed, and the least is 8.50 in. (= 215.9 mm.) in a bird, also unsexed, from China.

The average length of wing in birds which have been sexed as males is 9.25 in. (= 235.9 mm.), and the greatest and least length are the same as those already given.

BLUE HILL-PIGEON—*COLUMBA RUPESTRIS.*

($\frac{1}{3}$ Nat. Size.)

PLATE 12

Bill .60 in. to .66 in. (= 15.2 mm. to 16.7 mm.) at front, and about .95 in. (= 24.1 mm.) from gape; tarsus 1.0 in. to 1.1 in. (= 25.4 to 27.9 mm.). Weight 8.8 oz. to 9.75 oz. (Scully).

Adult female. Similar to the male.

Colours of soft parts. The same as in the male. "Irides brick-red, dark straw colour at pupillary margin." (Scully.)

Measurements. The female would seem to average decidedly smaller than the male, the average wing-measurement being only 8.73 in. (=221.7 mm.) although the biggest females have a wing up to 9.2 in. (= 233.6 mm.).

Weight 9.2 oz. (Scully).

Young bird of the year. Generally the whole head, neck, and shoulders are a dark slate-grey with no gloss of any kind, the breast is a dark grey-brown with narrow rufous-brown edging to the feathers, but the depth of the colour varies a good deal in individuals. The upper-parts are almost invariably a less pure grey, being tinged with vinous, and the wing-coverts and scapulars are the same, with narrow pale edges to the feathers. The feathers of the rump are also browner than in the adult bird and have very narrow borders of white.

Colours of soft parts. Irides pale watery-brown, feet dull red, and the bill horny-brown.

In very young birds the pale margins to the feathers of the wing extend to the feathers of the back also.

Nestling, in down. Dull, pale buffish-yellow.

Distribution. Blanford thus records the range of the Blue Hill Pigeon: "Central Asia from Gilgit to south Siberia and Corea; common in Tibet and some of the drier valleys of the higher Himalayas. This Pigeon has been recorded from Gilgit, Dras, Leh, and the upper Indus Valley generally, Lahaul, Upper Kumaon and Tibet north of Sikhim, but specimens labelled Kashmir, Sikhim and Darjiling in the British Museum Collection probably come from more northern localities." Ward, however, reports them as common in Kashmir, and says that it is "plentiful on the Ladak road, at high altitudes of the side valleys of Kashmir, and in most of the northern parts." It undoubtedly also occurs not uncommonly in the higher, barer parts of Sikhim, and might therefore possibly straggle into Darjiling. It has also been found in Nepal on the high bare uplands which are beyond the forest line and are very rocky.

In 1893 Rothchild and Hartert divided this Hill-Pigeon into two subspecies (R. and H., *Orn. Monatsb.* 1893, I. p. 41) i.e. *Columba rupestris rupestris* from the Amur region, type from Dauria, and *Columba rupestris pallida* from the Altai Mountains. Dr. Hartert, in *epistola* to me, writes: "The two forms are quite distinct and there can be no doubt whatever about them. *C. r. pallida* is generally lighter, especially on the abdomen and under tail-coverts, and the middle of the abdomen is almost pure white, not slaty-blue as in *C. r. rupestris.*" Since then Zarudny has again divided a third subspecies from south Russia, and Swinhoe long ago gave the Chinese form the name of *leucozonura*.

Nidification. There is very little on record about the nesting of the Blue Hill-Pigeon; Marshall mentions, in the *Ibis* for 1884, having found them breeding in the high cliffs in the Panji Valley, Upper Pherab, but gives no details of nests or eggs. Bailey likewise gives no description of these but says that he found it breeding both at Gyantse (13,100 ft.) and at Kangmar (14,000 ft.), in ruined houses, during the months April to July.

I have received a few of their eggs from Gyantse, and the nests in which these were found are reported as being typical domestic Pigeons' nests, composed of all sorts of rubbish and placed on the tops of walls close to the roofs of deserted and broken down houses. One nest, placed in a hollow from which part of the material of the wall—my informant does not say whether it was brick or stone—had fallen out, was made of scraps of a scraggy tough weed, a few sticks, some straw, and a good many feathers. The materials were not wound together much, but had been trampled into a very dirty mass which fell to pieces as it was pulled out of the hole.

Another of my correspondents in Tibet apparently overlooked their breeding in houses when he first went there, and in writing remarked that it was difficult to get these eggs for me, as though the birds were very plentiful they all made their nests in crevices and holes in exceedingly high and precipitous cliffs, quite ungetable, except by letting men over the edge with ropes.

In these cliffs the birds apparently breed in vast colonies, placing their nests in any crevice or hollow which they deem suitable, in some of the larger several birds breeding in company, and in the smaller a single pair, or perhaps two having their nests. I have also had eggs sent me from the Altai, where they would appear to breed in places similar to these last described.

The eggs are exactly like those of *Columba livia*, though smaller; they are white, smooth, and close in texture and highly glossed, and the shape is a broad, very regular oval: in one case only was the egg slightly smaller at one end than at the other.

The average of my eggs is 1.46 in. by 1.12 in. (= 37.1 by 28.4 mm.). My eggs from the Altai were taken in May, and those from Gyantse in the end of May and in June.

In its general habits, this Pigeon seems to be very similar to *Columba livia intermedia*, the common Rock-Pigeon, with which and with the Snow-Pigeon, it often consorts. It is a bird of cliffs, rocks, and open country, not of forests, but, as Bailey shows, it is not afraid of comparative civilization, and enters the more deserted parts of villages in Tibet much as the Blue Rock-Pigeon does the villages in the plains. Scully says that "This Pigeon was common in the hills on the south side of Eastern Turkestan during the months of August and September, at elevations of from 8,000 ft. to 16,000 ft. The birds seemed to be very fond of rocky cliffs, and usually flew about in small flocks or parties."

In powers of flight they are equal to the Rock-Pigeon or Stock-Doves and therefore form a very sporting bird for the gun, and they carry off a good lot of shot as well as flying fast, so that the man who "tinkers" his birds and fires that wee bit too much behind, is sure to lose a large percentage of his birds. Bailey, in his list of game killed in Tibet for the years 1906-9, gives the total of Pigeon killed as 351, but in a letter to me written about that time, says that they seldom troubled to kill them unless they wanted a few for the pot.

They are well-flavoured birds, just like the ordinary wild Pigeon, that is to say, like a tame one, but drier and less fat.

They are grain, seed, and berry eaters, like the true Rock-Pigeons, and not fruit-eaters.

Their notes are said to be indistinguishable from those of the Blue Rock.

(27) COLUMBA OENAS EVERSMANNI Bp.

THE EASTERN STOCK-PIGEON.

(PLATE 13.)

Columba eversmanni Bp., Compt. Rend., XLIII p. 838 (1856); Scully, J.A.S.B., LVI p. 86; Sharpe, Yarkand Miscel. Av., p. 116; Salvadori, Cat. B.M., XXI p. 264; Blanf., Avi. Brit. I., IV p. 31; Sharpe, Hand-List, p. 69; Inglis, J.B.N.H.S., XII p. 429; id. ib., XIV p. 561; Nicol Cumming, ib., XVI p. 691; Ward, ib., XVII p. 943; Whitehead, ib., XX p. 966.

Palumboena eversmanni Bp., Compt. Rend., XLIII pp. 838, 948 (1856); Jerdon, B.I., III p. 467; Hume, Str. Feath., I p. 217; id., Lah. to Yark., p. 271; Scully, Str. Feath., IV p. 175; Hume, ib., VIII p. 109; id., Cat. no. 787; Barnes, B. Bom., p. 288; Reid, Str. Feath., X p. 59.

Palumboena oenicapilla Blyth, J.A.S.B., XXVI p. 219.

Columba fusca Severtz, Str. Feath., III p. 431.

Vernacular Names. *Kamar-Kular*, Hin.; *Ban Parawa, Bagar*, Behari; *Pahari Kabutar*, Hin. Lucknow; *Kapoth, Chah-i-kapoth*, Baluchi; *Kaftar*, Persian.

Description.—*Adult male.* Upper part of the head and neck ashy-grey, tinged with vinous or lilac; cheeks, ear-coverts, lores, chin, and throat dove-grey, the three first sometimes tinted with the same colour; hind-neck and interscapulars ashy-grey, glossed with green and a little lilac-red; sides of neck the same but with a very well marked red patch of glossy purple-red, visible as a distinct patch in the living bird or in well-made skins; back and scapulars greyish-ashy; lower-back pure white, rump and upper tail-coverts slaty-grey, the feathers margined with dark brown; tail brownish-black at the tip, slate-grey at the base with a dark band, fairly well marked except on the central rectrices, about one and a half inches from the tip; outer webs of outermost rectrices white below the black tip. Wing-coverts dove-grey, all except the primary-coverts margined with ashy-grey like the back; bases of outer row of median and greater secondary-coverts black and showing as two bars across the wing; primaries and outer secondaries ash-grey, the base of the inner web of the first primary white; inner secondaries like the back, but with a broad bar of black.

Breast dark dove-grey, strongly tinged with lilac or vinous-pink, abdomen and under tail-coverts dove-grey, darkest on the latter; under wing-coverts and axillaries white, edge of the wing grey, and under aspect of quills very pale grey-brown.

Colours of soft parts. Irides light yellow, golden-yellow, yellowish-brown, or light brown; bill pale greenish, slaty at the base and amber-green at the tip; legs and feet pale fleshy-pink, purplish, or yellowish-fleshy, nails horny-brown.

"Skin round the eye yellow; irides buff" (Jerdon).

Measurements 11 to 12 in. (about 280 to 305 mm.); wing, greatest length 8.25 in. (= 209.5 mm.), least 7.5 in. (= 190.5 mm.), and average of twenty-five birds 7.78 in. (= 197.6 mm.); bill at front, .68 in. to 73 in. (= 15.4 to 18.5 mm.) and from gape about .95 in. (= 24.1 mm.); tarsus, about .95 in. (= 24.1 mm.).

With the exception of one bird from Turkestan with a wing of

THE EASTERN STOCK-PIGEON—*COLUMBA OENAS EVERSMANNI*

(½ Nat. Size.)

PLATE 13

8.25 in. (= 209.5 mm.), there is no other bird with a wing of over 8.05 in. (= 204.4 mm.), and this Turkestan bird in size somewhat approaches typical *oenas oenas*.

Adult female. Similar to the male; perhaps a trifle duller in general tint.

Colours of soft parts, as in adult male.

Measurements. The female is generally supposed to be rather smaller than the male, but curiously enough, in the very small series of sexed females in the British Museum, only six in number, the opposite is the case, and the average wing-measurement is 8.07 in. (= 205 mm.). It is probable, however, that in a large series the female would prove to be smaller than the male, as it is in the European Stock-Dove.

Young male has not yet been described but will certainly be found to differ from the adult in the same way that the young of its European cousin does, in wanting the black markings on the wing, and being duller and browner in tone.

Distribution. According to nearly all authors, the Eastern Stock-Pigeon is a migratory bird, summering in Central Asia and visiting India only in the cold weather, and in this country only coming into the Punjab, Sind, the North-West Provinces, and United Provinces and the Himalayas as far east as Tibet. It has also been recorded as far east as Behar where " it puts in an appearance every cold weather."

The Eastern Stock-Pigeon, or Stock-Dove as it is more usually called in England, is only a geographical race of *Columba oenas oenas*, the European bird. It differs in the first place in being very much smaller, but in colour also there are many differences. The head in the Eastern form is vinous, in the Western a pure grey, and whilst the neck-patch in the former is very conspicuous and purple, in the latter it is less conspicuous and green instead of purple; the lower-back also is white instead of grey in our Indian bird. Perhaps the most important difference, however, though it is one which seems to have escaped notice, is that shown by the under wing-coverts and axillaries, which are white in the Eastern bird and dark grey in the Western.

The grey of *C. eversmanni* is generally ashy above, whilst in *oenas* it is a pure dove-grey, and the grey band on the tail is much more conspicuous in the Indian than in the European bird.

Intermediate forms between the two are naturally sometimes met with, even if they are not common like the intermediate forms between the Eastern and Western Rock-Pigeons. The Afghan Commission obtained four such birds, three male and one female, all of which differ from typical *eversmanni* in having the lower-back a pale grey instead of white, and the under wing-coverts also not a pure white. The same Commission, it should be noted, also obtained a quite typical specimen of the Western bird. I do not propose to give the Afghan bird any distinguishing name, looking upon it merely as the connecting link residing in an area where the two forms meet.

Nidification. At present there is no record of this bird breeding within Indian limits, but it seems more than possible that a certain number of birds may stay and breed in Ladak and the higher ranges of the extreme north-western Himalayas. Reid, writing of the birds of the Lucknow Division, speaks of them staying there in these hottest of Indian plains until May, and if they stay as late as this in the plains of India, it would seem certain that they must breed somewhere close by. In the Altai, if indeed it is *eversmanni* we get there, they lay as early as the first half of May, at a time when they are said to have only just left the plains of India, for I have eggs from Kobdo taken on the 5th of May, 1906.

In the Altai and in Turkestan, they are reported to build nests of the regular Stock-Dove type in trees, mere platforms of twigs, many of which must have been torn from the living tree. These are well twisted, not merely laid criss-cross as is the case with the Rock-Doves' nests, which are built on a firm foundation of rock or wall. On the other hand there is no lining.

As far as my correspondents' information goes, the nests are generally placed, quite unconcealed, upon clusters of twigs or a stout branch of some tree, poplars appearing to be the favourite one, and they are not tucked away amongst creepers or ivy, as the European Stock-Dove's nest so often is.

The eggs are, of course, pure white as usual, and only differ from those of the European bird in being a great deal smaller. The eggs in my collection from Altai average 1.50 in. by 1.16 in. (= 38.1 by 29.4 mm.) and are probably not eggs of the real Eastern form; a single egg from Afghanistan, taken by the late Lieut. H. E. Barnes, measures only 1.35 in. by 1.03 in. (= 34.3 by 26.1 mm.)—this, an undoubted egg of the smaller Eastern bird, is probably typical of what the egg should be in size.

Throughout the greater part of India visited by the Eastern Stock-Dove, the bird is only a winter-visitor. In its extreme eastern limit, Behar, Inglis tells me that it is a visitor only during late December, January and February, but that it turns up regularly every year, and the natives know it well, having a distinct name for it. Reid does not appear to have noticed this Pigeon in the Lucknow district until March and April, when he says they appear "in vast flocks when the spring crops are ripening and being cut, and disappear in the beginning of May." Hume says that he only once came across them in Sind, but unfortunately does not mention the month; he adds that at some periods they are much more numerous than they were at the time he saw them.

But even in the mountains they are to some extent migratory, for Ward records them as only passing migrants in Kashmir, and Whitehead says that "they migrate through Kohat in the latter half of April in small flocks."

Their habits probably do not differ in any way from that of the European bird. They are strictly arboreal normally, but descend freely enough to the ground when tempted thereto by ripe crops, and the wheat-growers in parts of the United Provinces declare them to be a pest which, if they are to be believed, is even worse than what our farmers at home complain of in connexion with the Stock-Dove or Wood-Pigeon of our own isles.

Jerdon writes of this bird: "It flies in pretty large flocks and affects trees. A correspondent of the Bengal *Sporting Review* states that he saw them in hundreds at Hansi in March, but they soon disappeared. They feed in the fields, morning and evening, and roost in the day (and I suppose in the night also) in trees, generally in the common pepul trees. To Europeans here (in Hansi) they are known as the Hill-Pigeons. They are probably migratory in India, breeding in Central Asia. Buchanan Hamilton, however, states that a wild Blue-Pigeon breeds in Goruckpore in plantations, and is a great consumer of grain. He however considered it the 'same as one that breeds on rocks on the banks of the Jumna and other places,' i.e. the Common Blue Rock-Pigeon."

They are grain, seed, berry and fruit-eaters, under normal circumstances living principally on the latter and various seeds and nuts of trees, but greedily attacking ripe and ripening crops when in the vicinity of civilization. Whitehead found them when in Kohat in the latter half of April feeding principally on the mulberries which were ripening. He also states that he found them less wary than other members of the same family. In the Kurram Valley he found it scarce, and only passing through on migration. A specimen shot by him on the 2nd of May, at an elevation of 6,500 ft., was killed in Ilex-scrub.

Reid found that they roosted during the heat of the day, and also at night, in the mango groves, and if they were not molested would keep to the same grove for days and even weeks together.

Major J. Lindsay-Smith informs me that he has noticed that the bird has a curious predilection for roosting near water. At Lyallpur, during the cold weather, he found them roosting in very great numbers—often hundreds—in the dead trees by the two great canal reservoirs, the Rodo-koru and the Sonari. Here, where the overflow water periodically escapes from the canal over a considerable area, the trees stand, withered skeletons, in a waste of water some four feet deep, and Major Lindsay Smith informs me that he has seen some of these trees black with the birds roosting on them. At and about Mooltan he also noticed that the birds always seemed to select trees along the banks of the Chenab for roosting purposes, both by night and during the heat of the day.

The number in which these birds collect in these roosting-trees may be imagined when one shot is capable of bringing down fourteen birds, an experience which happened to a Mr. E. P. Ussher, when shooting on the banks of the same Chenab above referred to.

Mr. Ussher informs me that he found them very confiding birds on their first arrival into the country, but they soon became very wary and wild after they had been shot at for a day or two.

In flight and voice they resemble exactly the eastern Stock-Dove, and for the table they are equally good.

(28) COLUMBA LEUCONOTA Vigors.

THE SNOW-PIGEON.

(PLATE 14.)

Columba leuconota Vigors, P.Z.S. 1831, p. 23; Gould, Cen. Him. B., pl. 59; Blyth, J.A.S.B., XIV p. 864; id., Cat. B.M.A.S.B., p. 234; Jerdon, B.I., III p. 471; Stoliczka, J.A.S.B., XXXVII pt. 2, p. 66; Blanf., ib., XLI pt. 2 p. 70; Hume and Hen., Lah. to Yark., p. 274; Brookes, Str. Feath., III p. 256; Hume, ib., VIII pp. 110 and 340; id., Cat. no. 790; Salvadori, Cat. B.M., XXI p. 249; Blanf., Avi. Brit. I., IV p. 32; Sharpe, Hand-List, I p. 68; Finn., J.B.N.H.S., XIV p. 577; Fulton, ib., XVI p. 60; Ward, ib., XVII p. 943; Perreau, ib., XIX p. 919; Bailey, ib., XXI p. 182; Magrath, ib., p. 1312.

Vernacular Names. *Bujul*, Chamba; *Lho-peu-rintiep*, Lepcha, *Bya-den*, Bhot.

Description.—*Adult male.* Whole head and neck very dark slaty-grey, darkest on the nape and practically black where it adjoins a white nuchal collar. In turn this white collar gradually changes into a light brown on the upper-back, scapulars, and the innermost lesser wing-coverts and secondaries. Lower-back white; rump and upper tail-coverts black; tail slaty-black at base, followed by a broad white band across the middle, and broadly tipped black, this black band narrower on the outermost tail-feathers. Wings grey, with three visible broad bands of brown running across the median and greater coverts and the secondaries; a fourth band, concealed by the tips of the overlying feathers, on the bases of the innermost median coverts. Primaries grey, browner at the tips, and with a very narrow edge of silver-grey on the outer webs when these feathers are fresh and in perfect condition; outer secondaries grey at the base and brown on their terminal halves; all quill-shafts dark brown.

Below, breast pure white, changing to pale dove-grey on the posterior flanks and abdomen; under-tail-coverts very pale dove-grey; under aspect of the wing the same, with the edges of the shoulders a darker grey.

Colours of soft parts. Bill black; irides golden-yellow; legs and feet bright scarlet-red, the soles paler, and the claws black; "mouth bright fleshy-red" (Hume).

Measurements. Length 12.5 in. to 13.5 in. (= 317.5 to 342.7 mm.); wing 8.5 in. to 9.6 in. (= 215.9 to 243.8 mm.); tail about 5 in. (127 mm); tarsus 1.2 in. (= 30.4 mm.); bill from gape about 1 in. (= 25.4 mm.) and at front about .65 in. (16.5 mm.).

"Weight 10 oz." (Hume).

Adult female. I cannot see that there is any constant difference between the sexes, but Salvadori says that the grey colour of the back and wings in the female is somewhat duller.

Colours of soft parts. As in the male.

Measurements. With the exception that the female is a more slender built and lighter bird, the measurements are the same as in the male.

THE SNOW-PIGEON—*COLUMBA LEUCONOTA.*
(½ Nat. Size.)

PLATE 14

Young. The feathers of the upper-parts and wings have narrow margins of pale buff, and the under-parts are a pale dull buff rather than white.

Distribution. Throughout the higher Himalayas from about the 70° long. (Chitral) through Kashmir, Ladak, Tibet, Nepal, Bhutan, and the highest ranges of the Dafla and Mishmi Hills. It undoubtedly spreads even further west, however, than this, into the higher ranges of Afghanistan, and it has been recorded as breeding in the Altai ranges in Persia.

Nidification. The Snow-Pigeon breeds in colonies at high altitudes in the Himalayas, above 10,000 ft.—everywhere, practically, where there are suitable rocky cliffs with crevices or caves in which they can place their nests. Ward found it breeding in many places in Kashmir, and Magrath found it breeding in company with a small colony of Kashmir House-Martins.

The nests are, of course, always placed in holes, clefts, or crevices in rocky cliffs and precipices, or in caves such as that mentioned by Colonel Magrath. Often they are quite inaccessible, and in Tibet I have had several colonies reported as being well-known, though the nests were said to be quite unobtainable except with ropes and an amount of trouble out of proportion to the object to be attained. Also they are frequently placed so far inside the crevices and holes that even when the men have been let down to a position from which they can see into the holes, they cannot get at either nests or eggs. The nests themselves are the usual platforms of sticks, but as they rest upon the ledge of rock or limestone they are even less compactly put together and intertwined than are the materials of most Pigeons' nests. They are said to get into a very filthy state and to be full of vermin, in spite of the cold, before the young leave the nest.

The number of eggs is invariably two, and they are generally laid late in May, throughout June, and well into July; in the earlier part of the season when the birds breed at a comparatively low elevation, in the later portion where they breed at 14,000 ft. upwards.

I have a fair series of these birds's egg from Sonamerg, in Kashmir, which were given to me by Colonel R. H. Rattray, Colonel A. E. Ward, and Mr. J. Davidson, C.S., and a few others taken in the Chambi Valley and near Gyantse in Tibet.

They cannot be in any way distinguished from those of *Columba livia* and *intermedia*; in shape they are broad ellipses, or broad ovals, practically the same at either end, and the surface is close and smooth, but not very glossy.

My biggest egg measures 1.62 in. by 1.22 in. (= 41.1 by 31 mm.), and the smallest 1.4 in. by 1.02 in. (= 34.5 by 25.9 mm.). The average of 24 eggs is 1.55 in. by 1.15 in. (= 39.3 by 29.2 mm.).

The Snow-Pigeon is essentially a bird of the more lofty mountains, breeding, as already noted, at elevations from 10,000 ft. up to 15,000 ft. In the winter months it descends to lower hills, but even then it is apparently never seen below 5,000 ft., at which height Perreau found it in the Chitral Hills in winter. In Kashmir, however, Ward says that it only comes down to about 7,000 ft., and that only in severe winters, retiring again to greater heights directly the weather breaks. In the Abor and Mishmi Hills, the natives, who brought me a couple of skins, said that it never came lower than some peaks of about 9,000 ft., which formed the usual snow-line from December to March. They reported the bird as very common above this range wherever there was no forest and the hill-tops were bleak and rugged.

Throughout its range it is entirely a Rock-Pigeon in its habits, and only very severe stress of weather will drive it into forested country. It collects in very large flocks, haunting the faces of steep cliffs, precipitous hill-sides, and rocky ravines, and is said, generally speaking, to be a less shy bird than most Pigeons, and not difficult, if the ground be possible, to get within easy shot of. Bailey, however, in his record of the game shot at Gyantse during the years 1906-9, notes only eight Snow-Pigeons as having been shot, though during the same period no less than three hundred and seventy one Rock-Pigeons were brought to bag. This however may have been because the bird is rare close to Gyantse though common further away in Chambi.

It is sometimes trapped in Nepal and sent down to Calcutta for sale, and although a bird of such cold climates in its wild state, stands heat in captivity very well.

Its note has been described as the usual "purring coo" of the Common Rock-Pigeon, but Finn says: "As its note had apparently not been recorded, I may mention that it is not a coo, but a repeated croak, not unlike a hiccough, and," he continues, "much as the bird sometimes resembles the domestic Pigeon, I have never seen it sweep the ground with its tail when courting, but rather raise it."

Its flight resembles that of the Common Rock-Pigeon, and a flock of these Pigeons sweeping down a hill-side with the sun glistening on them is said to be a wonderful sight.

It is a berry and grain, rather than a fruit eater, but there is very little on record about its food.

Where the two birds' habitat overlaps, both this and the Rock-Pigeon (*Columba rupestris*) may be seen consorting together in the same flock.

GENUS DENDROTRERON.

The Genus *Dendrotreron* contains two species of Pigeon, which both Sharpe and Salvadori include in the genus *Columba*: but it forms, as a matter of fact, a sort of connecting link between the Wood-Pigeons of the genera *Palumbus* and *Alsocomus*, and the Rock-Pigeons of the genus *Columba*, and is really quite as close, both in structure and habits, to *Palumbus* as it is to the last-mentioned. I therefore, in agreement with Blanford, retain the genus as a convenient one.

In type of coloration, *Dendrotreron* is *sui generis*; for although it has not the barred wings of the Rock-Pigeons, neither has it the barred tail of the Wood-Pigeons. In length also this member is intermediate between the short tail of the former and the longer tail of the latter birds. So also the feet and legs are intermediate between the two, the feet being broader and more suited to its arboreal habits, whilst the tarsi are partially feathered.

Our Indian bird, *Dendrotreron hodgsoni*, is curiously like an African form, *Dendrotreron arquatrix*, which differs principally in having a purple fore-head, but which is in the rest of its coloration very close indeed to *hodgsoni*.

(29) DENDROTRERON HODGSONI (Vigors).

THE SPECKLED WOOD-PIGEON.

(PLATE 15.)

Columba hodgsoni Vigors, P.Z.S. 1832, p. 16; Blyth, J.A.S.B., XIV p. 867; Salvadori, Cat. B.M., XXI p. 274; Sharpe, Hand-List, I p. 70.

Columba nepalensis Hodg., J.A.S.B., V p. 122.

Dendrotreron hodgsoni Hodg., in Gray's Zool. Miscel., p. 85; Hume, Nests and Eggs, p. 497; Blanf., Avi. Brit. I., IV p. 33; Ward, J.B.N.H.S., XVII p. 943; Harington, B. Burma, p. 67.

Alsocomus hodgsonii Blyth, Cat. B.M.A.S.B., p. 233; Jerdon, B.I., III p. 463; Stoliczka, J.A.S.B., XXXVII pt. II p. 65; Blanf., ib., XLI pt. 2, p. 70; Hume, Str. Freath., VIII p. 109; id., Cat. no. 783; Scully, Str. Feath., VIII p. 399; Oates, in Hume's Nests and Eggs, 2nd ed., II p. 346.

Vernacular Names. *Hagrani Daohukuruma*, Cachari; *Pahari Pagooma*, Assamese.

Description.—*Adult male.* Whole head, chin, throat and upper-neck ashy-grey, the chin generally paler and sometimes the centre of the throat also; lower-neck and upper-breast the same as the head, the bases of the feathers blackish-grey, this blackish colour gradually increasing in extent and becoming a claret-red until on the upper-back the grey edges to the feathers have disappeared, and the back, shorter scapulars, and lesser wing-coverts are a claret-red or claret-maroon; longer scapulars, lower-back, and rump slaty-brown, rump darker than the other parts and contrasting with the dark dove-grey upper tail-coverts, the longest of which and the rectrices themselves are a dark brown. Median wing-coverts claret-red, speckled with white gradually changing to very dark dove-grey or slaty-grey on the outer-most and greater coverts; primary-coverts and quills dark brown, but not quite as dark as the tail. Below, the feathers of the breast are centred dark claret-red bordered with grey, as the abdomen is approached the grey becomes less and less in extent and more suffused with pink until on the abdomen itself the grey only consists of spots, disappearing altogether on the posterior flanks; tibial plumes, region of the vent, and under tail-coverts dark slaty-grey, this merging into and not contrasting with the red of the abdomen. Under aspect of wings tinged with grey on the smaller coverts.

Colours of soft parts. Bill black, purplish in the high lights and sometimes livid-black on the cere. Irides white or hoary-white, the surrounding orbital skin livid-grey or slate-colour; legs and feet dark dull green, almost black in front of the tarsus and paler and more yellow behind; claws pale bright yellow.

Measurements. Length 14 in. to 16 in. (= 355.6 to 406.4 mm.); wing 9 in. to 9.5 in. (= 228.6 to 243.3 mm.); tail about 5.5 in. to 6.0 in. (= 139.7

THE SPECKLED WOOD-PIGEON—*DENDROTRERON HODGSONI.*

(½ Nat Size—Male above, female below.) PLATE 15

to 152.4 mm.); tarsus under 1 in. (25.0 mm.); bill at front .6 in. to .7 in. (= 15.2 to 17.7 mm.) and from gape about 1 in. (25.4 mm.).

Adult female. In the female the whole of the grey is tinged with brown, and there is no pink on the grey margins to the feathers of the breast and abdomen. The claret, or maroon-red, on the upper-parts of the male is replaced with dark brown, in some individuals more or less suffused with slaty-grey. The red of the under-parts is replaced by dark grey-brown, but a few specimens, probably very old females, show a slight tint of claret-colour in small patches on the flanks and abdomen.

Colours of soft parts. As in the male, but the iris is often a brownish-white.

Measurements. The female is a slightly smaller bird than the male with a wing between 8.5 in. (= 215.9 mm.) and 9.0 in. (= 228.6 mm.), and the other dimensions in proportion.

Young male. Like the female, but the smaller wing-coverts all edged with rufous-brown and with practically no white spotting. The under-surface of the body is also more or less barred with grey and rufous, and the abdomen is nearly entirely of this latter colour.

Distribution. From the extreme west of Kashmir, where however it is not common, throughout Nepal, Sikhim, Tibet, the hill-ranges north and south of the Brahmapootra, Manipur and the Looshai Hills into the Chin Hills and Shan States in northern Burma.

Nidification. The only note hitherto recorded about these Pigeons' breeding is contained in Captain Irby's remarks in the *Ibis* for 1861, where he notes that "some nested in inaccessible cliffs, near Monsheyaree, about seventy miles from Almorah." In this Captain Irby was probably mistaken, as I have taken their nests myself in trees, and Mr. H. Stevens, though he failed to actually take their nests, shot birds which were breeding in the well-forested parts of Nepal and not in the higher rocky parts above the forest.

The only two nests taken by myself were both found in a lofty hill-range, running to over 6,000 ft., an offshoot of the Barail Range in north Cachar. Here in winter this Pigeon was not very uncommon, but it must have been quite exceptional for it to stay and breed as for many years I failed to obtain a nest, or indeed to find the bird after April, nor did I ever again meet with it breeding after this one year.

Both nests were of the usual type of Wood-Pigeon's nest, a rough platform of twigs, green and dry, interwoven with one another, with but little depression for the eggs, and no lining of any kind. Both were placed in small stunted oaks, which here were almost the only kind of tree to be met with, and were built on horizontal boughs some 15 to 20 ft. from the ground. In one case the nest half-rested on a clump of that sweet-scented white orchid, *Celogyne odorissima,* and in the other case, half on the bough and half on a cluster of twigs.

Each nest contained a single fresh egg and the dates on which they were found were on the 28th May and 1st June, 1896.

Last year, 1912, I was fortunate enough to obtain six of these eggs from Nepal, all taken at elevations between eight and ten thousand feet and on dates between the 22nd May and the 18th June; each nest contained but a single egg, and it would therefore appear as if this was the normal number laid, and not two as laid by most Wood-Pigeons. All the nests were said to have been, like those found by myself, built on small trees growing in stunted forest-growth.

My eggs vary in length between 1.34 in. (= 33.9 mm.) and 1.64 in. (= 41.5 mm.) and in width between 1.02 in. (= 25.9 mm.) and 1.16 in. (= 29.4 mm.).

In shape, texture, and surface they are typical Wood-Pigeon's eggs, but in one egg the shape is somewhat elongated and pointed at one end.

This Pigeon has always been considered a bird of very high elevations, i.e. as Blanford says, from 10,000 to 13,000 ft. in summer, and from 6,000 to 9,000 ft. in winter. Doubtless it does often range up to these heights, but probably it is also resident at much lower altitudes. Ward says that it is fairly common in Kishtwar in Kashmir, and that it breeds in that district at about 8,000 ft. In the Naga Hills it certainly breeds as low down as this, and perhaps lower; Stephens found it at 8,000 ft. during the breeding-season in Nepal, and I have had it from about the same elevation in native Sikhim.

In habits, as far as these are known, it is more of a Wood-Pigeon than a Rock-Pigeon, being very arboreal, though it will also descend to the ground to feed when there is anything to entice it there. It assembles in very small flocks as a rule and in north Cachar more than four or five were never seen together; very often it went about in pairs only, and occasionally a single bird might be met with.

Its note is easily distinguishable from that of any other Pigeon I have ever heard; it begins with a coughing, jerked-out note, and then continues with a deep double rolling-note which might be syllablized as "whock-whrroo-w h r r o o," the third note more prolonged than the second. It is a very deep resonant note, and can be heard at a great distance.

It is said to be fairly common in some of the pine-forests of Nepal and Sikhim, but on the north-eastern frontier of India it is found almost always in the stunted oak-forest which grows above 5,000 ft., and I have never met with it in the pine-woods of either the Khasia Hills or north Cachar.

It feeds on berries, acorns, small wild-plums, grain, and blackberries, raspberries, and strawberries. I have also shot them out of stubble in patches of rice-cultivation, but they appear only to frequent these when they are well surrounded by the oak-forest. The crops of those shot in such places were always full of rice, often mixed with tiny pebbles and a little earth.

Their flight is very powerful and swift, and even birds rising from the ground, though they did this with the clatter and noise made by all Pigeons when thus rising, seemed to get the pace up extraordinarily quickly.

For the table they seemed to me much the same as the native domestic Pigeon, perhaps a little drier and more closely grained in the meat. As, however, the birds I shot were wanted as specimens, all those eaten were skinned first, and the coating of fat being missing from the dish may have affected the flavour one way or the other.

Genus PALUMBUS.

The genus *Palumbus*, which contains the true Wood-Pigeons, differs from *Dendrotreron* in external structure much as that genus itself differs from *Columba*. The tail is still longer, proportionately, than in *Dendrotreron*, being about two-thirds the length of the wing, and the wing itself is more rounded than in either of the other two genera, having the first quill about equal to the fourth. The tarsus, also, is shorter and more feathered, and the feet are broader and more arboreal in their character than in *Columba*.

Outwardly the Wood-Pigeons differ somewhat in type of coloration from the Rock-Pigeons, having no wing-bars, though they have a bar on the outer feathers of the tail.

Salvadori, as already noted, placed Blanford's genera—*Columba*, *Dendrotreron*, *Palumbus*, and *Alsocomus*—in the one genus *Columba*, but the divisions as made by Blanford seem both reasonable and convenient, and divisions in classification being primarily made for convenience in working, I retain Blanford's genera.

In India we have but one species as here restricted, and that in fact is but a subspecies of *Palumbus palumbus*, the European Wood-Pigeon.

(30) PALUMBUS PALUMBUS CASIOTIS Bp.

THE EASTERN WOOD-PIGEON, RING-DOVE, OR CUSHAT.

(PLATE 16.)

Columba palumbus (part) Blyth, J.A.S.B., XIV p. 866.

Palumbus torquatus var.? Blyth, Cat. B.M.A.S.B., p. 233.

Palumbus casiotis Bp., Con. Av., II p. 42; Jerdon, B.I., III p. 464; Stoliczka, J.A.S.B., XXXVII pt. 2 p. 66; Cock and Marsh, Str. Feath., I p. 358; Hume, Nests and Eggs, p. 497; id., Str. Feath., VIII p. 109; id., Cat. no. 784; Butler, Str. Feath., VIII pp. 386, 500; id. ib., IX p. 298; Barnes, ib., pp. 218, 457; Swinhoe, ib., p. 237; Oates, in Hume's Nests and Eggs, 2nd ed., p. 346; Blanf., Avi. Brit. I., IV p. 34; Marshall, J.B.N.H.S., XV p. 352; Ward, ib., p. 943; Magrath, ib., XIX p. 142; Perreau, ib., XIX p. 919; Whitehead, ib., XX p. 967.

Columba casiotis Salvadori, Cat. B.M., XXI p. 302; Sharpe, Hand-List, I p. 70; Oates, Cat. Eggs B.M., I p. 91.

Vernacular Name. *Dahnud*, Hin., Chamba.

Description.—*Adult male.* Whole head and neck dark grey, the chin and throat sometimes slightly paler than the rest, the lower hind-neck glossed with green- or purple-copper according to the light in which the bird is seen; a broad buff semi-collar on the lower hind-neck and shoulders, interrupted in the middle with grey, glossed as in the neck; below the buff collar there is a broad expanse all round the shoulders glossed with green and purple; but the green is the dominant sheen next the collar, and the copper-purple more strong below this next the back, so that in the same light the green and purple reflections are both visible at the same time on these two portions. Upper-back, scapulars, quills, smaller and median coverts, light earth-brown, changing to grey on the outer median coverts; outermost secondary-coverts pure white on the outer web, and those next them with a white border forming two oblique bands of white across the wing; edge of shoulder of wing and primary-coverts dark brown, the inner ones grey on the outer webs and edged white; the primaries are also edged white on the outer webs. Back, rump, and upper tail-coverts dark ashy-grey; tail brownish-black with a broad grey band across the middle, lighter and broader on the outermost feathers. Breast vinous-pink, darkest next to the neck and gradually becoming paler and changing to pale dove-grey on the flanks, abdomen, and under tail-coverts. Tail below black with a broad white band across the middle corresponding to the grey band above.

Colours of soft parts. Irides pale yellow, yellowish-white, or almost white; cere of bill almost white, base of bill carmine-orange or orange-red, whitish-livid in the centre and orange at the tip; legs and feet coral-red, not very bright.

THE EASTERN WOOD-PIGEON OR RING-DOVE—*PALUMBUS P. CASIOTIS.*

($\frac{2}{5}$ Nat. Size.) PLATE 16

Measurements. Length about 16 to 17 inches (= 406.4 to 431.8 mm.); wing from 9.6 to 10.35 in. (= 243.8 to 262.8 mm.); tail from 5.5 to 6 in. (= 139.7 to 152.4 mm.); bill at front about .7 in. (17.7 mm.) and from gape about 1.1 in. (= about 28 mm.); tarsus a little over 1 in. (= 25.4 mm.).

Adult female. The female of *Palumbus palumbus* is said to be somewhat duller in the colouring than the male, but I can see no difference between the male and female of *casiotis*.

Colours of soft parts. As in the male with the exception that the irides are never a bright yellow.

Measurements. As in the male, but in life the two sexes can generally be discriminated, the female being a lighter built, more slender bird, and perhaps on an average a trifle smaller.

Young of both sexes. Paler and more dull in coloration than the adult, the purple and green gloss being practically absent and the neck-patches entirely so until after the first autumn-moult. The edging to the feathers of the wing is more pronounced and often buffish in tint in the bird in its first plumage. The irides are very pale blue-brown.

Distribution. The present bird replaces the European Wood-Pigeon in south Persia and Turkestan; in Afghanistan, Baluchistan at comparatively low elevations, and the whole of the north-west Himalayas as far east as Sikhim, extending into the Punjab and rarely into Sind in winter. It is common in Kashmir, but is rare in Tibet, though I have records of its occurrence from the better wooded parts about Gyantse and further north. In the extreme north of Persia our Indian form is replaced by the European Wood-Pigeon which is the resident form.

Nidification. The Eastern Wood-Pigeon breeds throughout the greater part of its range in the Himalayas from an elevation of some 2,500 to 12,000 ft. or over, but there are certain areas in which it would seem never to nest. Hume says that about Simla, Mussoorie, and Almorah they appear about the beginning of November and stay until the middle of April, when they depart for other quarters. Hutton and Wilson, Colonel Ward and others all confirm this curious local migration, which is probably governed by its food supply. In Chitral it must be a resident breeding species as Perreau found it there in November, May, and again in July. In Kashmir it undoubtedly breeds in suitable localities and Whitehead records that "Mr. Douglas tells me that it nests freely near the Zera Kotal, above Shinauri and north of the Samana. It also occurs in the Kurram Valley and probably breeds there."

Marshall, Cock, and later collectors have taken its eggs at and about Murree; Barnes and Wardlaw Ramsay took them in Afghanistan, where it breeds in great numbers, and Colonel Unwin took its nest with two fresh eggs in the Agrore Valley at an elevation of only 2,500 ft.

It is a late breeder not commencing to lay until the end of May, and most eggs will be found in the month of June and some well on into early July.

The nest is exactly like that of the English Wood-Pigeon, a mere platform of sticks placed on a thick bush or small sapling and seldom if ever on big trees. Marshall found them in the valley of the Jhelam breeding in dense thorny jungles, but does not describe the actual sites of the two nests obtained.

The eggs are invariably two in number and similar to those of the

European Wood-Pigeon, but average a trifle smaller. Oates, in Hume's *Nests and Eggs*, says that they vary in length between 1.53 in. and 1.65 in., and in breadth from 1.06 in. to 1.2 in.

There seems to be nothing in this bird's habits calling for special remark, these being exactly the same as those of its European relation.

It collects in very large flocks during the autumn, as soon as the breeding-season is over. Whitehead, writing of Kohat and the Kurrum Valley, says that in the autumn he found them in large flocks "in the scrub jungle above Marai, about Shinauri and in the wooded nullahs of the northern slopes of the Samana." It is however, on the whole, a bird of well-wooded country, and it is probably exceptional for it to frequent scrub-jungle except at intervals when food is plentiful in such.

It is quite active on the ground, though generally rather slow and deliberate in its movements. It feeds on grain, berries, shoots of trees, acorns, etc., and takes these as found, high up in a tree or on the ground itself. Its note is the same deep, soft "coo" as that of its European congener.

Like the latter bird, also, it is not difficult to domesticate. Barnes remarked of a bird in his possession which he obtained in Chaman: "One that I have reared from the nest, and which I have brought with me to India, is wonderfully tame, answers when called, is fond of perching on my shoulders, and never attempts to fly away, although as usual I allow it full liberty."

GENUS ALSOCOMUS.

The genus *Alsocomus* is included by Salvadori in the genus *Columba*, but there are several differences from typical *Columba* in the group separated by Blanford and placed in the present genus, both structural and in habits, which would seem reasonably to render the division desirable.

All the species are birds of dark coloration, having a metallic lustre over the greater part of the plumage, formed by iridescent borders to the feathers, varying in depth and brilliance. Neither wings nor tail have any bars upon them, and the latter is decidedly longer in proportion than it is in either *Columba* or *Dendrotreron.* In habits the birds of this genus are nearer *Palumbus* than *Columba*, being very arboreal in their habits, and like *Carpophaga*, with which they have sometimes been included, they are to a great extent fruit-eaters.

The Pigeons of this genus are represented by species extending from India through the Malay Archipelago to Japan and Oceana.

Within Indian limits we have five species, two of which are very closely allied and possibly should only rank as subspecies, i.e. *elphinstonii* and *torringtoniae.*

Key to the Species.

A. A *patch* of black feathers with white tips on either side of base of neck :

a. Head above and lower-parts grey ... ... *A. elphinstonii.*

b. Head above and lower-parts lilac ... ... *A. torringtoniae.*

B. A *collar* of black feathers tipped with glossy buff ... *A. pulchricollis.*

C. No patch or collar of white or buff-tipped feathers :

c. Upper-parts chestnut-purple ... ... *A. puniceus.*

d. Upper-parts blackish ... ... *A. palumboides.*

(31) ALSOCOMUS ELPHINSTONII (Sykes).

THE NILGIRI WOOD-PIGEON.

Ptilinopus elphinstonii Sykes, P.Z.S. 1832, p. 149; Jerdon, Madr. J.L.S., XII p. 11.

Columba elphinstonii Blyth, J.A.S.B., XIV p. 866; Jerdon, Ill. I. Orn., pl. 48; Salvadori, Cat. B.M., XXI p. 304; Sharpe, Hand-List, I p. 71; Oates, Cat. Eggs B.M., I p. 91.

Carpophaga elphinstonii Gray, Gen. B., II p. 469.

Palumbus elphinstonii Blyth, Cat. B.M.A.S.B., p. 233; Gould, B. Asia, VI pl. 57; Jerdon, B.I., III p. 465; Hume, Nests and Eggs, III p. 498; Fairbank, Str. Feath., IV p. 262; Bourdillon, ib., IV p. 404; Fairbank, ib., V p. 408; Ball, ib., p. 418; Hume, ib., VIII p. 109; id., Cat. no. 786; Vidal, Str. Feath., IX p. 74; Butler, ib., p. 419; Davison, ib., X p. 407; Macgregor, ib., p. 440; Terry, ib., p. 479; Barnes, B. Bom., p. 288; Oates, in Hume's Nests and Eggs, 2nd ed., II p. 347; Davidson, J.B.N.H.S., XII p. 62.

Alsocomus elphinstonii Blanf., Av. Brit. I., IV p. 36; Betham, J.B.N.H.S., XIV p. 620.

Vernacular Names. None recorded.

Description.—*Adult male.* Head above, nape, and sides of neck dove-grey, faintly glossed with iridescent emerald-green; fore-head, sides of head, and lores the same, but paler and tinged with pink; hind-neck with a large patch of black feathers tipped white and with tiny metallic edging below these tips, the lowermost feathers of this black-and-white patch glossed with green; back brick-red brown, gradually getting more brown and less red towards the rump; the upper-back, and base of hind-neck brilliantly glossed with metallic copper-purple, showing green in places in some lights; the purple gloss extends down the back in a lesser degree, but not on to the scapulars. Rump, upper tail-coverts and tail blackish-brown, the feathers of the rump obsoletely edged with metallic green. Wings dark brown, in very fine specimens the whole of the visible portions of the smaller wing-coverts are the same colour as the back and the other wing-coverts, except the greater primary-coverts, are edged with the same. In some specimens also the scapulars and innermost secondaries are powdered with this colour, giving them a general reddish hue.

Chin and centre of throat whitish, neck below and breast ashy-grey or grey tinted with vinous, and with all the feathers edged with metallic emerald-green, pale and sometimes scarcely visible; on the abdomen the grey becomes paler and more ashy or vinous, and on the flanks, axillaries and under aspect of the wing a good deal darker; under tail-coverts brownish-ashy.

Colours of soft parts. "Corneous part of bill and claws horny-white;

fleshy part of bill, eyelids, legs and feet pink; irides pale yellowish-red to red-brown" (Davison). "Eyelids, legs and feet lake-red" (Davison).

"Bill brick-red at base, yellowish tip, legs and feet pinkish with white marks" (Miss Cockburn).

Measurements. Total length 15 in. to 17 in. (= 381 to 431.8 mm.); wing from 8.05 in. to 8.80 in. (= 204.4 to 223.5 mm.); tail 6 in. to 7 in. (= 152.4 to 177.8 mm.); bill at front .65 in. (= 16.4 mm.), and from gape about 1.15 in. (= 29.1 mm.); tarsus about 1 in. (= 25.4 mm.). The average length of wings is about 8.40 in. (= 212.3 mm.).

"Weight 10 to 12 oz." (Davison).

Davison gives the wing-measurements as 8.3 to 9 in., and the tarsus as 1.08 to 1.15 in. These measurements are, of course, taken from fresh skins or living birds.

Adult female. This has hitherto been described as similar to the male, but it would seem as if it never became quite so brick-red on the wings and lower-back as old males do, and the amount of metallic gloss is also, perhaps, rather less.

Colours of soft parts are the same as in the male.

Measurements. Females are decidedly smaller than males, the length of wing in the series in the British Museum Collection varying in length between 7.7 in. (= 195.5 mm.) and 8.20 in. (= 208.2 mm.), with an average of 7.85 in. (= 199.9 mm.) exactly. Tail 5.75 in. (= 146 mm.) to 6.5 in. (= 155.1 mm.) and other measurements in proportion.

With the exception of one bird from the Nilgherries, sexed by Miss Cockburn, there is no other female over 8.05 in. (= 204.4 mm.), and this is therefore quite an abnormally big bird.

Young male. Like the adult, but browner and less red above and with the metallic colours undeveloped. The patch at the back of the neck is also less black than in the old bird. The wing-coverts, scapulars and innermost secondaries have dull narrow fringes of rufous, quite different in colour to the red of the adult bird.

Distribution. Confined to the Hill tracts of western southern India, from Kanara south to Cape Cormorin, the Nilgherries, Palni Hills, Brahmagerries, and Wynaad. Colonel Sykes found it, though rare there, in the Deccan Ghâts. Captain Blaxland also informed Ball that he had met with this Pigeon on the Mahanadi and Godavery Rivers, but his identification has never been confirmed.

Nidification. Hume, in *Nests and Eggs*, says that the Nilgiri Wood-Pigeon breeds in many of the better wooded localities of the Blue Mountains (the Nilgherries) at elevations of 5,000 ft. and upwards, and both Miss Cockburn and Davison took nests at and above this height, and they have been taken in the same hills by Messrs. Cardew, Rhodes, W. Morgan, Howard Campbell, and others. In the Palni Hills their nests have been found by the last mentioned gentleman, Macgregor and Captain Horace Terry, and I have received an egg from the Shevaroys. Mr. J. Stewart informs me that he has found them breeding in the higher ranges of hills in Travancore, and that he has taken an egg there.

Miss Cockburn describes the nest as resembling "that of all Pigeons and Doves in the careless manner in which a few sticks are put together. On high trees in dense woods this bird prepares the abode for her young, and chooses a projecting bough, as if she had some thought for the safety of the egg she lays. (I say *egg*, for I have seen four nests of the Nilgiri Wood-Pigeon; two had one egg in each, and the other two contained one young one in each). I have also remarked that only one Pigeon is noticed near the nests."

Other observers agree with Miss Cockburn in her description of the nest and the number of eggs laid, but all disagree with her description of the site, and doubtless her nests were somewhat abnormal in this respect, as these Wood-Pigeons generally make their nests either in tall, thickly-foliaged bushes or in small saplings more often under than over 15 ft. from the ground.

Hume would appear to have received a fair number of their eggs from different collectors, but in the British Museum Collection there are only three of them left. They are, of course, pure white as usual, and are fairly glossy, but the texture is not so fine and close as in some Pigeons' eggs. In shape they are rather broad ovals, practically the same at either end.

The Museum eggs, my own, and three others I have been enabled to measure vary between 1.42 in. (= 36 mm.) and 1.53 in. (= 38.8 mm.) in length, and between 1.05 in. (= 26.6 mm.) and 1.18 in. (= 30 mm.) in breadth.

The breeding-season appears to commence in March, as Miss Cockburn took her nests with young in April, and Mr. Morgan reports finding nests in that month also. Cardew, Howard Campbell and Captain Terry took their eggs in May, and on the other hand Davison did not take its eggs until June.

All writers agree that they only make their nests in the interior of very thick forests and are consequently difficult to find, nor does the parent bird seem to render any assistance in disclosing the place in which its nest is located.

This species is essentially a Wood-Pigeon in its habits. Jerdon says that "on the Nilgherries, it frequents sholas or dense woods, singly, or in small parties of five or six, feeding on various fruits and buds, and occasionally on small snails, to procure which it descends to the mossy banks, and I have now and then seen it on the ground outside a wood. I frequently found some small *Bulimi* in the crops of those I examined. Colonel Sykes says it is a rare bird in the Deccan, and only found in the dense woods of the Ghâts."

It has been stated that the genus *Alsocomus* differs from *Palumbus*, the true Wood-Pigeon, in that it is more frugivorous, but as a matter of fact even the European Wood-Pigeon is very fond of fruit; admittedly its food in the main consists of beech-mast, acorns and grain, but it will on the other hand greedily eat almost any soft fruit it can get at.

In London, where the Wood-Pigeon is now very common, it enters gardens freely and any gooseberry or currant bush which is not carefully netted is soon stripped of all the ripe fruit, the unripe being left by this discriminating bird for a future meal. I have also seen them feeding on crab-apples, cherries, and plums, swallowing the latter whole when possible, and when not possible tearing them to pieces, their apparently fragile bills being amply strong enough for this purpose.

Davison records of the Nilgiri Wood-Pigeon that it is not uncommon in the woods and slopes of the Nilgherries, though he did not meet with it either in the Wynnad or Mysore. He adds: "It moves about a good deal, and a shola that may be full of them one week, will not contain a single specimen of them the following week; this is due, I fancy, to the prevalence or otherwise of berries. I too have noticed the fact mentioned by Jerdon of their feeding on the ground outside the forests. I found them very numerous in March in the forests about Meddivuttam, and procured a good number of specimens."

It is said to be a shy, wary bird, and where it is much shot at it soon becomes impossible to get near enough with a gun.

The flight is much the same as that of the European Wood-Pigeon, very powerful and fast, and they are also said to generally fly at a good height when passing from one feeding-ground to another.

During the cold weather they are nearly always found in flocks —rarely singly or in pairs; but all field-naturalists who have watched these Pigeons agree that the flocks are invariably small, and a party of a dozen birds seems quite exceptional.

The only note I have concerning its call is one contained in a letter from a friend, in reply to a query, who stated that "it is on the whole a very quiet bird, and I cannot distinguish its coo in any way from that of its European cousin. Its soft, sweet notes may sometimes be heard in the sholas very early in the morning, as the birds call to one another before flighting to their feeding-grounds, and again in the evenings, when the birds carry on a soft murmuring conversation amongst themselves before settling off to sleep."

(32) ALSOCOMUS TORRINGTONII (Kelaart).

THE CEYLON WOOD-PIGEON.

Palumbus elphinstonii var. Blyth, J.A.S.B., XX p. 178 (1851).

Palumbus torringtonii Kelaart, Pro. Faun. Zey., p. 107 (1852), *descr. nulla*; Bp., Con. Av., II p. 42; Jerdon, B.I., III p. 466; Hume, Nests and Eggs, p. 499; id., Str. Feath., VII p. 424; id. ib., VIII p. 109; id., Cat. no. 786, bis; Oates, in Hume's Nests and Eggs, 2nd ed., II p. 348.

Palumbus torringtoniae Houldsworth, P.Z.S. 1872, p. 466; Legge, B. Cey., p. 693; Butler, J.B.N.H.S., IX p. 310.

Columba torringtoniae Salvadori, Cat. B.M., XXI p. 303; Sharpe, Hand-List I p. 71.

Alsocomus torringtoniae Blanf., Avi. Brit. I., IV p. 96.

Vernacular Names. *Mila-goya*, Cing. in central provinces, Ceylon; *Mahavilla goya*, Cing., *apud* Layard.

Description.—*Adult male.* General type of coloration like that of the Nilgiri Wood-Pigeon. The upper part of the head and nape lilac-grey glossed with lilac, a faint green gloss also showing in certain lights; patch on back and sides of neck black, broadly tipped white, the patch being much smaller than in the last bird and with fewer green edgings, which are often altogether absent; upper-back and sides of neck below patch, lilac-brown glossed with the most brilliant copper-purple; back, rump, upper tail-coverts, and wing-coverts deep slaty, almost blackish-grey, most of the feathers of the back, rump and inner coverts narrowly edged with black; quills dark brown with very narrow pale edges to the tips and outer webs; tail blackish-brown; sides of head, lores, and sides of throat pale vinous-grey; the chin and centre of throat albescent; lower-neck and whole breast reddish-grey or reddish-ashy and glossed with a purple sheen somewhat less intense than the purple lustre on the back; remainder of lower-parts dull reddish-ashy, palest on centre of abdomen and darkest on under tail-coverts; under wing-coverts, axillaries, and flanks very dark ashy-grey or slaty-brown.

Colours of soft parts. "Iris pale red, orbital skin dull pink; bill plumbeous, apical half bluish; legs and feet pinkish fleshy, toes and soles red; legs sometimes white with the front of the tarsus and tops of the toes reddish" (Legge).

Measurements. Length 13 or 14 in. (= 330.2 to 355.6 mm.); wing 7.20 in. (= 182.8 mm.) to 8.20 (= 208.6 mm.) with an average of 7.63 in. (= 193.8 mm.); bill at front barely .6 in. (= 15.2 mm.) and from gape about 1 in. (= 25.4 mm.); tarsus about .9 in. (= 22.8 mm.).

"Length 13.5 to 14.3 in.; wing 7.7 to 8.0 in.; tail 5.25 in.; tarsus 1.1 in.; middle toe 1.72; its claw (straight) 0.4 in.; bill to gape 1.1 in." (Legge).

Adult female. Like the male. "Head, chest, and under-surface more ruddy than in the male, and the cupreous hue of the lower hind neck deeper; under tail-coverts and flanks redder" (Legge).

"Length 13.2 in.; wing 7.2 in.; tail 5.0 in.; bill to gape 1.0 in." (Legge).

Colours of soft parts are also similar to the same parts in the male. "Legs and feet not so red, with the posterior part of tarsus and sides of toes fleshy-white" (Legge).

Measurements. Unfortunately, very few of the specimens in the British Museum collection are sexed and it is impossible to say from these whether there is any difference in size between the sexes though it is probable the female will be found to average smaller.

Young male. Similar to the adult male but less highly glossed and with the grey parts more brown and less slate coloured. The grey of the head is also browner and not at all glossed.

A young bird is thus described by Legge: "Upper surface ashy plumbeous; forehead and face slightly ruddy; neck patch not developed; the feathers of the nuchal patch being blackish, with ashy whitish tips, not pure white; the metallic hues of the hind neck faintly developed; chest ruddy plumbeous; the under surface vinaceous slaty, washed with fulvous brown on the breast. Some examples have the wing-coverts edged with rusty and the chin and gorge more albescent than in the adult.

"Birds of the year have the iris yellowish-grey, with generally an outer ring of pale red (the normal colour of the adult); bill dusky at the tip; legs and feet dull red anteriorly, dusky fleshy behind."

Birds on first leaving the nest have the wing-coverts and some of the feathers of the back edged with rusty-rufous, but all these markings seem to be lost in the first autumn moult.

Distribution. Ceylon only. Within the limits of Ceylon, Legge thus describes the places it frequents: "Essentially a bird of the mountain forests, this splendid Pigeon is well known to all Europeans in the Central Provinces. It is very abundant in the Newara Eliya plateau forests and on all the surrounding wooded slopes down to an elevation of about 3,000 ft.; below this it is not numerous; Kelaart speaks of examples being obtained at Gampola; but this was in the days of forest; now that the whole country round that district is denuded, the visits of the Torrington Pigeon to it must be few and far between. I met with it at Newara Eliya in May, and found it plentiful on the Horton Plains in January; it seemed then to prefer the singular isolated groves on the plains to the surrounding forest, no doubt owing to a greater abundance of food obtaining at that time in the former. It is very numerous in the Peak forests, where I procured it under 3,000 ft.; and I have no doubt these vast jungles stretching along the high mountain chain up to the Horton Plains now forms its chief stronghold. In the Morowah Korale I have killed it at Aning Kanda Estate as low as about 2,400 ft., and between these and the Kukul Korale it is, I understand, almost abundant at times.

"Mr. Holdsworth remarks that it 'changes its locality according to the season and the time at which the fruit of particular trees ripen.' He found it numerous at Newera Eliya at the end and beginning of the year. Mr. Bligh has noticed that a migratory movement takes place just previous to the 'bursting' of each monsoon; which, together with its wanderings in search of fruit, will probably account for its somewhat periodical appearance in many districts."

Nidification. There is not much on record about the breeding of this fine Wood-Pigeon. Kelaart records that: "It comes to Newera Eliya to breed and I have seen a nest with only one egg as large as that of the domestic Pigeon."

Legge never found the nest himself, but Bligh wrote him: "I have seen their nests both in Spring and Autumn as late as October; they generally build in lofty forest trees, but I once frightened a large young one from a nest on a small tree some 15 ft. above the ground." Butler says, in reference to the Ceylon Wood-Pigeon breeding: "I have one egg, taken by my brother, Mr. C. E. Butler, in Uda Pusselawa, on November 11th, 1894. He described the nest as placed in a small tree in jungle about 25 ft. from the ground. The egg is similar to, but smaller than, an English Wood-Pigeon's, $1\frac{3}{4}$ in. by $1\frac{1}{8}$ in. At the present minute I know of a nest being built near here (September 24th). I believe it lays only one egg, as the one my brother took was hard set, and Mr. Bligh mentions frightening a single young one from a nest; but Natives tell me it lays two eggs."

Beyond Legge's notes there is practically nothing on record about the habits of this fine Pigeon, and I must therefore again indent upon him. In his *Birds of Ceylon*, he writes: "Frequenting, for the most part, lofty trees in the primeval forest of the mountains, and being of a very shy and wary disposition, this fine Pigeon is generally a difficult bird to procure; but notwithstanding, it is much sought after on account of its excellent flesh, and frequently falls to the planter's gun. It is entirely a fruit-eating species, and feeds more on the wild cinnamon fruit than any other kind; on this it gorges itself to such an extent that I have found its crop burst wide open with the shock of falling to the ground. When thus satiated, it is not so watchful as usual, and may sometimes be approached without the crackling of a twig or the noise of leaves crushed underfoot frightening it off. It comes very early to roost; and I found that it resorted to the same tree night after night, coming home from its forest wanderings about 4 p.m., and settling down either in or somewhere near its intended roosting-place. It then commences its 'coo' (which is a fine deep note, but not so guttural or resounding as that of the Imperial Pigeon), and now and then moving about in the adjacent trees, but not flying away to any distance.

"By waiting in such places it may be more easily shot than in any other manner. About 10 o'clock in the morning after feeding, I have found it resting on the under branches of moderately sized trees in the Newara Eliya District; but as a rule it selected the loftiest branches to perch on. Its flight is very strong and swift, and it takes a good shot to bring it down as it darts out of some lofty tree in its forest haunts; Kelaart says that 'it flies high and in long sweeps.' In common with other Pigeons, it drinks in the morning, and I have found it in mountain-streams as late as 9 p.m. Mr. Bligh informs me that it is unusual to find many together while feeding, but I imagine this depends on the quantity of fruit there may be on any given tree ; he tells me he once saw thirty or forty on a large tree in the Dambetenne gorge, but never observed so many together on any other occasion."

Butler describes its note as " far more like the hoot of an owl than the ooo of a Wood-Pigeon, a deep guttural 'hoom' repeated at intervals."

(33) ALSOCOMUS PULCHRICOLLIS (Hodg.).

THE ASHY WOOD-PIGEON.

(PLATE 17.)

Columba pulchricollis Hodg., in Gray's Zool. Miscel., p. 85 (1844): *descr. nulla*; Blyth, J.A.S.B., XIV p. 866; Salvadori, Cat. B.M., XXI p. 305; Stuart Baker, Ibis 1896, p. 355; Sharpe, Hand-List, I p. 71.

Palumbus pulchricollis Blyth, Cat. B.M.A.S.B., p. 233; Gould, B. Asia, VI pl. 58; Jerdon, B.I., III p. 405; Hume, Str. Feath., VIII p. 119; id., Cat. no. 785; Stuart Baker, J.B.N.H.S., X p. 360.

Alsocomus pulchricollis Blanf., Avi. Brit. I., IV p. 37; Thompson and Craddock, J.B.N.H.S., XIV p. 600; Osmaston, ib., XV p. 515; Harington, B. Burma, p. 67.

Vernacular Names. *Hko*, Burmese; *Ka-o*, Lepcha; *Daohukuruma majungbi*, Cachari.

Description.—*Adult male*. Head and nape dove-grey, paler on the sides of the head, and faintly glossed with grey-green; chin and centre of throat white: a patch on the neck black, the feathers broadly tipped buff, paling to whitish on the extreme margin—this patch is produced round the neck as a very narrow collar, the black hardly showing on the neck below the throat and the buff being almost entirely replaced by white. Next to this collar, above and below, blackish-brown, the feathers all highly glossed with metallic green and purple, extending above into the interscapulars; lower-back and rump slaty-black becoming slaty-grey on the shorter upper tail-coverts; longest tail-coverts and tail blackish-brown; wing-coverts plumbeous-brown, darkest next to the back, and most pale on the outer greater coverts; quills dark brown, the second to fifth edged narrowly with pale rufous. Below changing from the slaty-brown of the breast to dull buffish on the vent and abdomen, the sides of the latter more or less lilac-slate; under tail-coverts buff and under aspect of wings and axillaries blackish-brown.

Colours of soft parts. "Irides very pale yellow" (Rippon).

Bill livid at the base, turning to yellow at the middle and tip, sometimes tinged with green on the cere; irides pale to bright yellow; legs and feet dull purplish-red, or deep dull coral-red, the claws horny-brown and the soles a paler red.

Measurements. About 15 in. in total length. Wing from 7.65 in. (= 194.3 mm.) to 8.50 in. (= 216.3 mm.), the first measurement being that of an abnormally small bird, the next smallest in the British Museum Collection being 7.85 in. (= 199.4 mm.); average of forty-two specimens: 8.24 in. (= 209.7 mm.); bill at front .65 in. (= 16.5 mm.) and from gape 1.05 in. (= 26.6 mm.); tarsus between .9 in. (= 22.8 mm.) and 1 in. (= 25.4 mm.). Tail about 5.0 in. (= 127 mm.).

"Length 13½ to 14 in.; wing 8½ to 9 in.; tail 4¾ to 5 in." (Jerdon).

THE ASHY WOOD-PIGEON—*ALSOCOMUS PULCHRICOLLIS*

(½ Nat. Size.)

PLATE 17

Adult female. Similar to the male.

Colours of soft parts. The same as in the male.

Measurements. There are, unfortunately, practically no sexed birds in the British Museum Collection, and it is therefore impossible to say whether the female is smaller than the male, though this is very probably the case. Twice when I obtained pairs of this bird I found the female on each occasion smaller and much slighter in build than its companion.

Young male. Similar to the adult, but with practically no gloss, the collar less developed and the general tone of the plumage more brown than in the old bird.

Distribution. This Pigeon is found in Nepal, Sikhim, and Tibet at elevations between 7,000 and 10,000 ft., possibly descending a good deal lower than this in winter. It occurs throughout the hills south of the Brahmapootra River from 4,000 ft. upwards; Osmaston found it not uncommon between 7,000 and 8,000 ft. near Darjiling, and Messrs. Thompson and Craddock obtained a single specimen at Loi Maw in the Shan States at 7,200 ft. Harington also records it from the Shan States, but did not apparently meet with it himself anywhere in Burma. The only other place from which it has been recorded is Formosa.

Nidification. There is nothing on record about the nidification of this bird beyond Osmaston's and my own notes on the subject. In the *Ibis* for 1896, p. 155, I wrote as follows: "Two nests of this Pigeon, taken at Hungrum, about 5,000 ft. elevation, were of the ordinary Wood-Pigeon type, mere rough platforms of small twigs coarsely, but strongly interlaced with one another; but they had one very distinctive and unexpected feature, namely a sparse lining of feathers. The nests were rather large, nearly 9 in. in diameter; there was little or no depression for the eggs, these laying among the feathers and prevented from falling out by some of the twigs projecting beyond the others, and by the numerous interstices and small hollows in between them, in which the eggs would have caught had they moved about. Each nest contained a single egg, perfect ellipses in shape, rather coarse and stout in texture, with a dull surface and measuring 1.55 in. by 1.15 in. and 1.50 in. by 1.17 in. Both nests were found on the same date, 22nd June, 1891."

These two nests were placed in the beautiful stunted-oak forest growing between 5,000 and 6,000 ft. on the Barail Range, beautiful not so much because of the picturesque oak-trees as on account of their beautiful surroundings and the wonderful growth under and around them. Each tree stood in a growth of bracken, caladiums, jasmine, begonias, and maidenhair fern, and all over the tree itself was a wondrous wealth of orchid-life, the orchids, many of the greatest beauty, peeping out from amongst a mass of pendant green moss which swayed to and fro in every breath of wind.

On such a tree, and partly resting on a dense mass of *Dendrobium chrysotoxicum* and *Dendrobium dalhousianum*, one pair of Pigeons had placed their nest whilst the other pair were content to build on a small branch about 15 ft. from the ground, unadorned by any orchids, but almost hidden in a mass of vivid green moss and hart's-tongue fern.

In 1897 and 1898 I again took nests of this Pigeon, both in the same kind of forest and in the same month, and each containing a single egg. The nests were similar to those described above, and like them had quite copious linings of feathers, most of which seemed to have belonged to the birds themselves, though there were one or two barbet and other feathers also.

Osmaston, writing in the *Journal* of the Bombay Natural History Society, says that he found this Pigeon " fairly common in the dense oak and chestnut forests between 7,000 and 8,000 ft. I found two nests in small trees about 6 ft. and 10 ft. respectively above the ground on the 21st June. They were of the ordinary platforms of sticks, and contained each one young bird. These I brought up by hand, and they are now denizens of the Calcutta Zoological Gardens."

The eggs seem to me to be rather small for the size of the bird: my biggest egg measures 1.56 by 1.18 in. (= 39.6 by 30 mm.), and the smallest 1.46 by 1.06 in. (= 37 by 26.9 mm.).

Two of the eggs are curiously coarse in texture for a Pigeon's egg, and are probably abnormal in this respect as two others in my collection are as smooth as any other Pigeon's or Dove's egg, though with a very stout and strong shell.

In Sikhim this Pigeon seems to be comparatively plentiful, and Osmaston has found it to be " fairly common " round about Darjiling, where it kept to the dense oak and chestnut forests. Elsewhere, all over its range, it appears to be very rare, though this may be partly due to its very shy, retiring habits.

In North Cachar it only occurred as a quite rare straggler; some years I would see it half-a-dozen times during the whole twelve months, at other times a couple of years would pass without a single bird being noted. In the Naga Hills, adjoining the North Cachar Hills, the Darjiling Wood-Pigeon was less uncommon, but there the ranges run from 6,000 to 10,000 ft., whereas in North Cachar there are few over 6,000 ft., an elevation which is too low for the bird to frequent in any numbers. In the Khasia Hills I never came across it, and I do not think it ever enters these hills, nor would the pine-forests, the usual forest over 4,500 ft., hold out any inducement to the birds to visit them.

From the little I saw of them in North Cachar, I came to the conclusion that when not nesting they were the hardest of all the Pigeons to get close to. They used to sit in the denser foliaged parts of the oak-trees, never moving or uttering a sound until they thought I had got too near to be safe, when they quietly dropped, if I may use such an expression, out of the tree on the side opposite to me and wended their way to safety through the tree-tops. Even their flight was singularly quiet, and beyond an occasional "flip-flap" of their wings as they started, or again as they made some extra effort in twisting and turning in and out of the trees, I heard no sound. Never did I hear them make the loud clapping with their wings indulged in by most Pigeons at the start of their flight, this probably because they *descended* when first leaving the tree instead of springing into the air with an extra effort, as so many of their relations do.

Although so noiseless, their flight is just as powerful as that of any other of the bigger Pigeons, and the way they dodged in and out of the trees when going at speed was really astonishing.

The first time I ever saw this Wood-Pigeon was when finding one of the Pigeon's nests referred to above. I saw the parent bird slip over the side, fired a snap-shot at it and missed. I had a good glimpse of the bird, however, and saw that it was something quite new to me, so lying full-length and well hidden in the bracken I waited until the bird returned, when I again fired and again missed. Hiding again, I once more waited in hopes they would return, but it was not until over two hours had passed that at last both birds appeared and perched on the tree close to the nest and then, after knocking over one as it sat, I was lucky enough to get the other as it flew off.

Both these birds had been feeding on a small berry, growing on a tiny creeping-plant which is entirely terrestrial in its habits, so they must have descended to the ground to get them. They also eat all fruit, acorns, etc., especially the blackberries and raspberries which grow in great profusion over the higher hills. The Nagas also tell me that they sometimes come into their patches of Indian corn, but that they are never numerous enough to do any real damage. I have also, on one occasion only in November, seen them walking about in the rice-stubble on a hill-side, evidently picking up the rice which lay about in considerable quantities. Another bird I shot had been eating wild cardamum berries, and yet another had its crop full of tiny snails—little things, none of them as big as a green pea.

They go about in very small flocks and sometimes singly or in pairs. I have never seen a flock of more than five, but it must be remembered that my district was only on the fringe of their normal habitat, and in more favoured regions the flocks may number more.

I have seldom heard their note, which is very like that of the English Wood-Pigeon—a deep, sonorous "coo," but I think it is deeper still, and it is certainly more abrupt and less soft.

(34) ALSOCOMUS PUNICEUS Tickell.

THE PURPLE WOOD-PIGEON.

(PLATE 18.)

Alsocomus puniceus Tickell, in Blyth's J.A.S.B., XI p. 461 (1842); Blyth, Cat. B.M.A.S.B., p. 233; Layard, Ann. and Mag. N.H., XIV p. 58; Jerdon, B.I., III p. 469; Ball, Str. Feath., II p. 424; Blyth and Wald., B. Burma, p. 145; Godw.-Aus., J.A.S.B., XLIII pt. 2 p. 171; Armstrong, Str. Feath, IV p. 337; Hume and Dav., ib., VI p. 418; Ball, ib., VII p. 224; Hume, Str. Feath., VIII pp. 109, 157; id., Cat. no. 782; Oates, Str. Feath., VIII p. 167; Bingh., ib., p. 196; Legge, B. Cey., p. 696; Hume and Inglis, Str. Feath., IX p. 258; Oates, ib., X p. 235; id., B. Brit. Burma, II p. 289; Hume, Str. Feath., XI p. 296; Oates, in Hume's Nests and Eggs, 2nd ed., II p. 345; Blanf., Avi. Brit. I., IV p. 38; Stuart Baker, J.B.N.H.S., X p. 359; Inglis, ib., XI p. 474; Stuart Baker, ib., XIII p. 568; Hopwood, ib., XVIII p. 433; Harington, ib., XIX p. 365; id., B. Burma, p. 67.

Columba punicea Blyth, J.A.S.B., XIV pp. 867, 878; Salvadori, Cat. B.M., XXI p. 306; Sharpe, Hand-List, I p. 71.

Vernacular Names. *Lali Pagooma*, Assamese; *Daohukuruma Korogophu*, Cachari.

Description.—*Adult male.* Whole upper part of head from fore-head to nape, together with a narrow line below the bare orbital skin, greyish-white; sides of head and neck dull, rather pale chestnut-brown, greyish next the base of the lower mandible, and with the black bases of the neck-feathers often showing through on the upper-neck; back and scapulars rich, deep chestnut, the feathers broadly edged with brilliant green and amethyst, the former predominating on the shoulders where their broad edges cover the whole of the visible plumage, and the amethyst covering the upper-back and interscapulars and showing as bars on the lower-back; rump and upper tail-coverts deep slaty-grey, almost black, and margined with amethyst, except on the longest tail-coverts; tail blackish-brown. Whole of the visible portion of the wing-coverts rich chestnut-brown, the lesser and median-coverts narrowly edged with metallic amethyst; edge of wing and greater primary-coverts blackish-brown; quills blackish-brown, the second primary narrowly edged with pale brown, this edging decreasing in extent until it disappears on the 5th or 6th primary. Innermost secondaries like the back. Breast, abdomen, flanks, axillaries and under wing-coverts a pale and rather vinous-chestnut, darker about the vent and tibial plumes; the breast is overlaid with a faint iridescent green sheen; under tail-coverts brownish-black, paler than the tail itself.

Colours of soft parts. Irides creamy-yellow, orange-yellow to orange-red, the eyelids bright, almost carnation-red and the orbital skin a duller purplish-pink. Bill greenish or bluish-horny from tip to nostril and the angle of the gonys, and thence to the fore-head and lores, including cere, a sanguineous-pink. Legs and feet purple-red, the soles paler and the claws horny-white.

"Iris bloodshot amber; bill vinous-purple at base, remainder greenish white; legs carnation, claws white" (Wardlaw Ramsay). "Claws pale yellow" (Jerdon).

Measurements. Total length about 16 in. (= 406 mm.); wing from 8.3 in. (= 210.8 mm.) to 9.3 in. (= 236.2 mm.) with an average of 8.8 in.

THE PURPLE WOOD-PIGEON—*ALSOCOMUS PUNICEUS*

(½ Nat. Size—Male above, female below.) PLATE 18

(= 224 mm.); bill at front .65 in. (= 16.5 mm.) and from gape 1.1 in. (= 27.9 mm.); tarsus rather under 1.0 in. (= 25 mm.); tail 6 in. (= 152.4 mm.) to 7 in. (= 177.8 mm.).

Tenasserim birds do not appear to be any smaller than those from north-east India, one of them having a wing measuring 9.25 in. (= 234.9 mm.), but in the Hume collection there is a rather large percentage of obviously young birds from this part of Burma, and it may be on this account that Blanford has recorded his opinion to the effect that birds from this district are smaller than from elsewhere.

Davison has only given the weight of one bird, and this as but 8 oz. On the other hand, the only two I have weighed were 14 and 14½ oz. respectively, and 8 oz. seems very little for so big a bird so it may have been a mistake for 18 oz. Cripps records the weight of six males as varying between 12.75 and 18 oz.

Adult female. Similar to the male, but slightly smaller. The head is as pure a grey and the purple-chestnut as rich and glossy in the *fully* adult female as it is in the male, but from the large percentage of dull coloured females in collections it may be that females take six months or a year longer than the males in obtaining their full splendour.

Measurements. The female is decidedly smaller than the male, being about 14 in. (= 355.6 mm.) in total length and with a wing-average of 8.44 in. (= 214.3 mm.) and a range in extremes of 8.0 in. (= 203.2 mm.) and 8.85 (= 224.8 mm.); the measurements of the other parts are correspondingly slightly smaller. Two females weighed by Cripps were 13.60 and 14 oz. respectively.

Young in first year's plumage (? females in second year also) are generally much duller in coloration and with the under-parts from chin to vent a dull pale brown only suffused here and there with chestnut; the head is the same coloration as the neck, and the upper-parts are more brown.

Young in first plumage are still browner and duller and have the wing-coverts and interscapulars brown margined with rufous and submargined with darker.

Distribution. In the heavily-forested parts of Eastern Bengal, Singhbhum, Manbhum, Purulia, Sunderbunds, Dacca and Mymensingh and thence throughout the districts of the Assam Valley into Burma. South and east of Assam it is found in Cachar, Sylhet, Tipperah and Chittagong, and through all the damper wooded parts of Burma, Cochin China, and Siam into the Malay Peninsula. There is a single specimen of this species in the Poole Museum, which was procured by Layard in Ceylon, and Legge himself thought he saw a flock of them near Borella in 1869. Since then no one has again met with this Pigeon, and it can only occur in that island as a very rare straggler. It has never been found in southern India.

Nidification. There are only two notes recorded on the breeding of this Pigeon. Oates, the first to discover its nests and eggs, writing to Hume from Pegu recorded: "Kyeikpadein, 27th July.—Nest in fork of horizontal bamboo-bough, about 10 ft. from the ground, composed of a few twigs woven carelessly together. Male bird sitting. One egg quite fresh. Colour white, very glossy. Size 1.47 by 1.15 in. Probably only one egg laid."

The first eggs seen by myself were taken by my collectors on the 1st and 2nd of June, 1889, and were brought to me a few days later. The two nests from which they were taken were described as rough structures of sticks through which the eggs were visible from below, and in both cases they were said to have been placed in small saplings five or six feet from the ground. These two eggs measured 1.65 by 1.28 in. and 1.63 by 1.25 in.

Since 1889 I have taken about a dozen nests of this Pigeon in North Cachar, Assam, and in the Khasia Hills. The nest is the usual Pigeon's nest of twigs and sticks, and measures about 8 or 9 in. in diameter by about 2 to 4 in. deep. The materials of which it is composed appear to have been picked up dead from the ground and not torn from the living tree; the depression is hardly visible and the twigs are put together in the roughest manner imaginable.

In most cases the nest is placed in a small tree or tall bush at no great height from the ground, generally between 5 and 10 ft., but occasionally it is placed higher up in a tall tree and still more seldom in a bamboo-clump. In the latter case, however, the bamboo-clump selected appears to be always one standing in mixed tree and bamboo forest, and not in jungle composed of bamboo only.

Normally the number of eggs laid is one only, but more than once I have taken two from the same nest, and the bird probably lays two eggs in about once in every five instances.

The eggs are of the ordinary *Columba* type, pure white, long ellipses in shape or long ovals, abnormal eggs tending towards pointed ovals. The texture is hard and close but not very fine, and, even when first laid, they are not highly glossed.

They vary extraordinarily in size, the largest egg in my collection being 1.65 by 1.28 in. (=41.8 by 32.5 mm.) and the smallest 1.40 by 1.10 in. (=35.5 by 28 mm.); the average of fifteen eggs is 1.48 by 1.15 in. (=37.6 by 29.2 mm.).

They seem to be late breeders, all my eggs having been taken in the last few days of May, in June, or in early July. Both birds take a share in the duties of incubation, and I have taken more males than females on the nest, but this is possibly due to the fact that, as is the case with many other Pigeons and Doves, the male bird seems to take up his duties during the daytime, whereas the female sits principally at night.

The tree, bush, or bamboo-clump selected as a site for their nest is one almost always within easy reach of water, often on the bank of some small forest-stream or pool and, equally invariably, it is one standing in fairly thick forest.

The Purple Wood-Pigeon is a bird more of the plains than mountains, but ascends the latter regularly to a height of some 2,000 ft., and is sometimes found up to about 4,000 ft. At whatever height it is found, it seems essential that there should be both ample evergreen or shady forest and a certain amount of cultivation. Over the greater part of its range it appears to be a decidedly rare bird. In the plains of Cachar and Sylhet it is commonly met with, and both Messrs. Vernon Woods and W. Cathcart, C.I.E., tell me that they have frequently shot this Pigeon in the rice-fields when out snipe-shooting at the end of the season after the rice has been cut. About the foot-hills of the Sylhet and Khasia Hills it is even more numerous, and Harington says that in the Myitkina district and round about Rangoon it is very fairly plentiful. Bingham also found them by no means rare in the Sinzaway Forest Reserve, in Tenasserim, but everywhere else, though widely distributed, it is only to be found in very small numbers.

I have never seen this Pigeon in flocks, nor have the numerous observers and collectors who have worked for me ever seen them except singly or in pairs, or perhaps a pair of old birds accompanied by their young one on its first leaving the nest. Colonel Tickell, however, the discoverer of the bird, found them in small parties of four or five along the banks of rivers shaded by large forest-trees in Singhbhum.

This fine Wood-Pigeon has hitherto been considered to be entirely frugivorous, but this is by no means the case, as it eats grain of almost any kind quite as freely as fruit. When the rice has been harvested and the fields have all dried up, this bird is a regular visitor to those fields which border or intersect the forest-lands, and may be met with in the very early mornings or late afternoons walking about in the stubble picking up the rice which has been left behind. So also, the Sylhetees inform me, it frequents the fields of Indian corn and "Bajra," a species of millet, eating both these kinds of grain from the crop itself as it ripens or from the gleanings after the crop has been reaped.

I do not think it is ever found feeding very far from forest, but it will traverse considerable extents of open country in order to get from one feeding-place to another, and I have had several reports sent me of birds killed in wide open plains whilst thus crossing it from one forest to another. It is a strong, swift flier, very direct in its movements and proceeding with the typical, rather deliberate wing-beats of the Common Wood-Pigeon. On the ground it is a decidedly active bird, moving about well and freely with action similar to, but less clumsy than, that of our European bird.

I have never heard the call of this Pigeon, but Bingham describes it as "a soft mew, not unlike that of *Carpophaga aenea*, only not half so loud or booming."

The plumage of the Purple Wood-Pigeon is just as thick as that of the other species of the genus, whilst it seems to be also closer together and better attached to the skin, so that it offers an even greater resistance to shot than the others do, and it is consequently a very difficult bird to bring down at long range. On the other hand, when falling from a height it does not get so dreadfully knocked to pieces as do most Pigeons, and, consequently, good skins are more easily obtained, or rather, more frequently in proportion to the number of birds killed.

(35) ALSOCOMUS PALUMBOIDES (Hume).

THE ANDAMANESE WOOD-PIGEON.

(PLATE 19.)

Carpophaga palumboides Hume, Str. Feath., I p. 302 (1873); id. ib., II pp. 53, 263 and 498; id. ib., III p. 327; id. ib., p. 292; id. ib., VIII p. 109; id., Cat. no. 781, quat.

Ianthoenas palumboides Walden, Ibis 1873, p. 315, pl. XIII.

Ianthoenas nicobarica Walden, Ann. and Mag. N.H., XIV p. 157; Hume, Str. Feath., III p. 327.

Columba palumboides Salvadori, Cat. B.M., XXI p. 308; Sharpe, Hand-List, I p. 71.

Alsocomus palumboides Blanf., Avi. Brit. I., IV p. 39; Butler, J.B.N.H.S., XII p. 690.

Vernacular Names. None recorded.

Description.—*Adult male.* Whole head a beautiful pearl-grey or pearl-white, showing a faint iridescent sheen of emerald-green on the crown and nape; upper-neck a little darker and with the sheen showing more definitely, lower hind-neck the same but with the dark bases of the feathers showing through and the metallic lustre rather a darker green, getting quite a dark metallic green on the shoulders. Remainder of upper-parts and wing-coverts a deep slaty-grey, almost black, all the feathers with a broad metallic border, amethyst or copper-purple in most lights, green in a few, except on the median wing-coverts on which the margins are very narrow and appear to always show green; quills and greater coverts of primaries blackish-brown, the 2nd, 3rd, and 4th, and sometimes the 5th, primary with a narrow edge of grey-brown to the outer web. Tail blackish brown; lower part from neck to vent light slate-grey with a faint sheen of emerald-green; under wing-coverts, axillaries, flanks and under tail-coverts a rather darker grey.

Colours of soft parts. "Back and sides of tarsi and toes pale fleshy-pink, front of tarsi bright but light red, soles whitish, claws white. Upper mandible and lower mandible to tip of gonys pale whitish-yellow, cere and rest of lower mandible lake red. Irides orange near pupil, darkening to light red on posterior margins" (Davison).

"Iris reddish-yellow; feet pink, claws white; bill pinkish-lilac at base and white at tip" (Wardlaw Ramsay).

Measurements. Length about 17 in. (= 432 mm.); wing average 9.95 in. (= 252.7 mm.), and with extreme measurements of 9.50 in. (= 241.3 mm.) and 10.15 in. (= 257.8 mm.) respectively. Bill at front about .85 in. (= 21.6 mm.), and from gape about 1.4 in. (= 35.5 mm.); tarsus about 1.2 in. (= 30.5 mm.).

"Weight 1 lb. 2 ozs." (Davison).

THE ANDAMANESE WOOD-PIGEON—*ALSOCOMUS PALUMBOIDES.*

(½ Nat. Size.) PLATE 19

Adult female. "In the female the head and neck is slightly greyer than in the male" (Blanford).

I cannot see that this difference is constant, and there is one female in the British Museum Collection with a head as pure a grey-white as it is in any of the males. The difference noted by Blanford is probably only due to immaturity.

Colours of soft parts are the same as in the male.

Measurements. From the small series available for comparison it would appear that the female is slightly smaller than the male. Excluding an abnormally small, poor-conditioned female with a wing of only 8.5 in. (=215.9 mm.) the remaining four females in the Museum Collection vary in wing-measurements between 9.5 in. (=241.3 mm.) and 9.95 in. (=252.7 mm.), with an average of 9.70 in. (=246.3 mm.). Measurements of bill and tarsus are also slightly smaller on an average than the male.
"Weight 1 lb. 2 oz." (Hume).

Young in first year. Have the head a much darker grey than in the adult and with no green sheen, the wider parts are a duller, browner grey, also without sheen, and the back and wing-coverts are browner and less glossy.

Distribution. The Andaman and Nicobar Islands.

Nidification. Nothing has as yet been discovered as regards the breeding of this fine Pigeon.

The Andaman Wood-Pigeon is a bird concerning which practically nothing has been recorded since its discovery, in 1873, by Hume and Davison.

It appears to be closely similar to the Fruit-Pigeons in its habits, and Hume, writing about a bird which he then had alive in Calcutta, says: "In its mode of holding itself and its broad substantial body it is a typical *Carpophaga* and not at all like the more slender and pigeon-like *Metallica.*" Butler, however, does not agree with this, for he writes (l.c.): "I only shot it once on Car Nicobar, and unfortunately the bird went bad before I could preserve it. It seemed to me more of a Wood-Pigeon than a Fruit-Pigeon; my bird rose either from the ground or from a low branch within a foot or two from it—far lower than I have seen a *Carpophaga* settle." This settling on low branches would, however, appear to be exceptional, for Hume thus describes one of their favourite resting-places: "About midway in the Straits is a conical rocky islet, perhaps half an acre in extent, rising to an elevation of 70 or 80 ft., and crowned by trees of an equal or greater height; these trees seemed to be a favourite half-way house of the Fruit-Pigeons. During the half-hour that we hung about and remained on the island we must have seen a couple of hundred. They were always perched on the tops of the highest trees; we could see them perfectly well from a boat at a distance of 150 yards, and examine them with binoculars almost as well as if they were in the hand, but directly we landed they became invisible. With my half-broken back I could not climb, but my companion crawled up to the summit. There, at the very roots of the trees, on which they were sitting in dozens, though he could hear their deep coo, their clattering amongst the leaves as they alighted, their fluttering and the whirr of their wings as they flew off, he could *see* nothing. He fired once or twice by the sound, but I do not believe the shot ever got through the dense, unbroken, massive sheet of foliage that protected them."

Davison, like Butler, shot the first bird he obtained seated quite close to the ground; he says: "I know nothing special of the habits of this fine species, which seemed to me in every respect an Imperial Pigeon. I found the one I shot at Port Moriat sitting on a low branch by the side of a forest path; it was not at all shy, and allowed me to get close enough to shoot it with a walking-stick gun. It had swallowed several fruits about the size of a walnut, two of them with stalks, about two inches long and as thick as a goose quill, attached."

Hume seems to have found it comparatively common in Macpherson's Straits, where he saw "numerous small parties . . . which repeatedly passed over us, flying from the tops of the trees on the hill-slopes on one side to similar positions on the other, and, of course, well out of shot. One party settled on Bird Island, a tiny precipitous wooded islet, and though we could hear their loud deep coo, and from the water's edge watch them feeding, scuffling and making love on the branches of the highest central trees, we could see nothing of them, when, with infinite trouble we worked a way up to the base of these trees, though we could still hear them.

"I have no doubt that this species is a permanent resident of the Andamans and Nicobars, moving, as *Nicobarica* does, from island to island, as the different fruits and berries, which constitute the sole food of these large Pigeons, ripen."

DOVES.

GENUS STREPTOPELIA (Bp.).

The generic-name by which this the best known group of Doves has been known until recently is *Turtur*; but unfortunately, as Hartert has shown (*Hand-List of British Birds*, p. 161), Selby's name, which was instituted in 1835, was preoccupied by Boddaert in 1773 for a totally different form of Pigeon, and the name *Turtur* must therefore be suppressed. The next oldest name which can be applied to the group is *Streptopelia* of Bonaparte, published in 1857.

Sharpe in his Hand-List divides the genus *Turtur* as it originally stood, into many genera of which *Turtur*, *Streptopelia*, *Onopopelia*, and *Spilopelea* are all represented in India, but with the exception of *Onopopelia* (= *Oenopopeha*), in which the sexes differ in plumage, I see no valid reason for dividing the others and, therefore, retain them under the title and genus *Streptopelia*.

According to Blanford, in the genus *Streptopelia* (= *Turtur*) there are seven species of Doves occurring within Indian limits, but of these I reduce *orientalis* and *ferrago* to the rank of subspecies of *Streptopelia turtur turtur*, and *tigrinus* to be a subspecies of *suratensis*. There are therefore still four species retained as such in the genus and, on the other hand, besides the above three subspecies, I accept in addition *arenicola* and *meena* as two more subspecies of *S. turtur turtur*.

In general features the birds of the genus *Streptopelia* may be known by their small size, comparatively small head and slender neck, weak narrow bill, and by their comparatively long and narrow wing, of which the 2nd and 3rd primary is the longest. The tail exceeds two-thirds the length of, but is never longer than, the wing itself, and it is considerably graduated. The feet and tarsi are formed for walking, the toes being narrow, and the legs strong though short.

The sexes are similar in colour and all the species are birds of grey or brown plumage, and are decorated with a demi-collar or a patch on either side of the hind-neck.

They are sociable but not gregarious birds, and some of the species are resident whilst others are migratory.

Key to the Species.

A. A patch of black feathers tipped with white or grey on either side of the neck but divided down the nape ... *S. turtur.*

B. A collar of black feathers each ending in a double white spot *round back of neck* ... ... *S. suratensis.*

C. A collar of black feathers with rufous tips *round front of neck* ... ... *S. cambayensis.*

D. A collar of plain black feathers *round back of neck* ... ... *S. risoria.*

STREPTOPELIA TURTUR.

Key to the Subspecies.

A. Tips to feathers of neck-patch white :
- *a*. Darker and duller and with more vinous on the under-parts ... ... *S. t. turtur.*
- *b*. Paler and brighter and with the abdomen more extensively white ... ... *S. t. arenicola.*

B. Tips to feather of neck-patch grey :
- *c*. Vent, flanks, and under tail-coverts dark grey ... *S. t. meena.*
- *d*. Vent, flanks, and under tail-coverts pale grey ... ... *S. t. orientalis.*
- *e*. Vent and flanks very pale grey and under tail-coverts white ... ... *S. t. ferrago.*

Unfortunately it is quite impossible to give any key which will render it easy to discriminate these races one from another, as all the differences are ones of comparative depth of colouring only, although typical specimens are easily separable when laid alongside one another.

Roughly speaking it may be said of the five subspecies that—

Streptopelia turtur turtur is a very rare straggler from north Persia and Asia Minor.

S. turtur arenicola is an equally rare straggler into north-west India from southern Persia and Arabia.

S. turtur ferrago is a migratory bird, breeding in the Himalayas and visiting almost every part of India in the cold weather.

S. turtur meena is the common resident form over Continental India, eastern India, and Burma.

S. turtur orientalis is the resident species in the extreme north.

From the key it is seen that I consider all the above birds to be subspecies of *Streptopelia turtur*, whilst Hartert and others consider *S. orientalis orientalis* and *S. orientalis meena* form another group. To me, however, they all appear to be geographical races of the same species, and if it is correct to say that *turtur turtur* grades into *turtur arenicola*, and that again into *turtur ferrago*, so it seems to me that *turtur arenicola* grades into *turtur orientalis*, and there are a few birds in the British Museum Collection which form an excellent connecting link between the two subspecies.

(36) STREPTOPELIA TURTUR TURTUR (Linn.).

THE TURTLE-DOVE.

Columba turtur Linn., Sys. Nat., I p. 284 (1766) (India); Latham, Ind. Orn., II p. 605.

Turtur communis Selby, Nat. Lib., Orn., V pp. 153, 171 (1835), *descr. nulla*; Blanf., Avi. Brit. I., IV p. 42.

Turtur vulgaris Eyt., Cat. Brit. B., p. 32 (1836).

Turtur migratorius Sw., Classif. B., II p. 349.

Turtur auritus Gray, List Gen. B., p. 38 (1840); Blyth, Cat. B.M.A.S.B., p. 237 (Hume, Lah. to Yark., p. 278; Blanf., E. Persia, II p. 270; Scully, Str. Feath., IV p. 177; id., J.A.S.B., VI p. 86. All these latter references apply more properly to the bird which Hartert has separated as *arenicola*).

Columba afra Webb and Beth., Orn. Can., p. 28.

Turtur turtur Salvadori, Cat. B.M., XXI p. 397; Sharpe, Hand-List, I p. 77; Oates, Cat. Eggs B.M., I.

Streptopelia turtur Bonaparte (1857); Hart., Jour., Tice., and With., Hand-List Brit. B., p. 161.

Vernacular Name. *Turul-ghu* (Turki).

Description.—*Adult male.* Upper portion of head from fore-head to base of hind-neck ashy-grey; a patch of black feathers on either side of the base of the neck, each feather edged with white, the white and black forming regular streaks in the living bird; upper-back pale brown, but varying much in tone and with the grey of the neck sometimes encroaching into the inter-scapulars; lower-back, rump, and upper tail-coverts ashy-brown, in some cases more grey than in others, more especially on the lower-back and sides of the rump. Central tail-feathers brown, very narrowly tipped with white or fawn-white; remaining tail-feathers slaty-black with a broad terminal band of white and the outermost pair with the whole outer web white also. Scapulars, lower and inner median coverts and innermost secondaries brownish-chestnut or cinnamon, with bold black centres divided from the outer colour by faint intermediate lines of grey; remaining coverts grey; quills brown, narrowly edged with whitish and the outermost secondaries more ashy at their bases; chin, sides of head and throat pale vinous, albescent on the chin and often rather fulvous on the throat, gradually changing to deep vinous on the breast, and again changing to white on the centre of the abdomen, vent, and thigh-coverts; under tail-coverts pure white. Under wing-coverts, axillaries, and flanks dark dove-grey. Under aspect of tail black with broad terminal band of white.

Colours of soft parts. Iris orange, orange-red, red or orange-brown; eyelid reddish-brown and orbital skin still more purple; legs and feet purple or reddish-purple, paler on the soles and with the claws horny-black; bill greyish or slaty-black, the edge of the gape purplish-red.

Measurements. Length about eleven inches or rather over. Wing 6.5 in. (= 165.1 mm.) to 7.2 in. (= 183.9 mm.); bill at front about .65 in. (= 16.5 mm.), and from gape about .85 in. (= 21.6 mm.); tail 4.5 to 5 in. (= 104.3 to 127.4 mm.); tarsus about .75 in. (= 19 mm.).

Female. "The plumage less bright and pure" (Salvadori).

I cannot discriminate in any way between the two sexes in plumage, and much the highest coloured bird in the British Museum Collection is sexed as a female.

The male is, however, a rather heavier-built bird, though it has no greater average wing-measurement and is no longer in total length.

Colours of soft parts are the same as in the male.

Young male is generally, but by no means invariably, a good deal browner than the adult on the upper-parts; the black patches at the base of the neck are absent, or only show as faint black bases to the feathers of that part; the bold black centres are absent from the scapulars and much less developed on the wing-coverts and innermost secondaries. The lower-back, and often also the rump and upper tail-coverts, have narrow edges of rufous-white, these white bars sometimes extending to the scapulars; wing-coverts narrowly edged with pale rufous, and the quills more broadly margined and also tipped with rufous. The under-parts are more grey and less vinaceous, and in very young birds the breast-feathers are very narrowly and faintly edged with rufous.

Colours of soft parts. Bill slaty-black, tipped paler on the lower mandible, and with the gape more strongly marked with purple. Iris dull pale-brown, becoming reddish-brown after the first moult.

Distribution. Within Indian limits the European Turtle-Dove is only a very rare straggler into the extreme north-west, and in the British Museum Collection I can find but one specimen, an adult female obtained by Lieutenant-Colonel Swinhoe in Quetta on the 7th May, 1881. The other specimens hitherto shown as of this subspecies are all undoubtedly *arenicola*. In the *Hand-List of British Birds*, by Hartert, Jourdain, Ticehurst, and Witherby, the range of this Dove is given as "Europe from Scandinavia and north Russia to Mediterranean and westernmost Asia; in winter in north Africa, south to Abyssinia and Red Sea. Replaced by allied races in north Africa, Persia and probably other parts of western Asia." I think, however, it is probable that typical *turtur turtur* extends a good deal further east than these writers give it credit for. The bird obtained by Colonel Swinhoe in Quetta is a quite typical European bird and can be matched by many birds shot in Great Britain, and I have seen other specimens killed in northern Persia and Afghanistan which cannot possibly be divided from it. Admitting that it breeds in "westernmost Asia," there is nothing very astounding in stragglers being obtained in the winter months as far south as north-west India.

Nidification. There is, of course, nothing on record of this bird breeding within our limits. According to Seebohm (vide *Eggs of British Birds*, p. 159), "The nest is sometimes built in a tall, dense hedge, sometimes in an evergreen bush, or in the branches of a pine-tree; as a rule, however, it is much nearer to the ground than that of the Ring-Dove, sometimes within easy reach of the hand. It is usually a slight, flat structure, made of slender twigs, but I have occasionally found it to be more substantially made.

"The eggs are two in number, creamy-white in colour, like those of the Stock-Dove, and oval in form, both ends being almost equally pointed; they vary in length from 1.25 to 1.1 in., and in breadth from .94 to .86 in. The small size of the eggs of the Turtle-Dove prevents them being confused with those of any other British species of Pigeon."

Seebohm's reference to the creamy tinge of these eggs presumably refers to those unblown, as the eggs otherwise are absolutely pure white.

They breed principally in the end of April and May—Morris gives May as the chief month in which most eggs are laid—but I have myself taken eggs in the second week in April, and again late in June, this probably being a second brood.

Morris states the period of incubation to be sixteen or seventeen days.

(37) STREPTOPELIA TURTUR ARENICOLA (Hartert).

THE PERSIAN TURTLE-DOVE.

Turtur turtur arenicola Hartert, Nov. Zool., I p. 42 (1894).

Turtur auritus Hume, Lah. to Yark., p. 278; Blanf., E. Persia, II p. 270; Scully, Str. Feath., IV p. 177.

Turtur turtur Salvadori, Cat. B.M., XXI pt. I (part); Sharpe, Hand-List, pt. I, p. 77 (part); Oates, Cat. Eggs B.M., pt. I, p. 94 (part).

Vernacular Name. *Tarul-ghu*, Turki.

Description.—*Adult male.* Similar to the adult male of *S. turtur turtur*, the European Turtle-Dove, but much paler and brighter in colour. The upper-back, scapulars, and wing-coverts bright pale cinnamon, the head paler and more ashy and the under-parts very much paler, with the extent of white greater and the vinaceous less as well as being brighter and more pink. The edges to the feathers of the black patches on the neck are wider and at the same time less pure a white than in *turtur turtur*, this being especially noticeable in the Yarkand, Persian, and Afghanistan specimens.

Measurements. "The dimensions of the type of *Turtur turtur arenicola* in the Tring Museum are as follows: Total length about 11 in., wing 6.45, tail 4.4, culmen 0.68, tarsus 0.8. English Turtle-Doves have the wing larger." (Hartert.)

The series in the British Museum have wings measuring from 6.40 in. (= 161.5 mm.) to 7.15 in. (= 181.6 mm.), so that it does not appear that in a large series the wing of the European bird would average any larger than that of the Persian.

"Weight 4.4 oz." (Scully).

Colours of soft parts. "Bill greyish black, edge of gape and orbital space purple; irides orange yellow; legs and feet purple, claws black" (Scully).

"Iris orange, legs and feet lake red" (Forsyth).

Female. Similar to the male.

Young. Differs from the adult in the same way as the young of *turtur turtur* differs from the adult male of that subspecies.

This bird was originally described by Hartert in *Novitates Zoologicae* from a specimen obtained at Fao in Persia, and he there notes "those from Yarkand are different from the European bird and brighter cinnamon on the back, scapulars, and upper wing-coverts." I cannot, however, separate the birds from Afghanistan, Yarkand and Gilgit from the south Persian birds, and these again seem to me to be identical with birds from Palestine. They are very close to, barely separable indeed, from the North African birds, but are perhaps a trifle brighter and more cinnamon in tint above and paler and less vinous below.

Distribution. Persia in the south—but replaced in the extreme north and Trans-Caucasia by the true *turtur*—Arabia and Palestine, Afghanistan,

Yarkand, and wandering into Gilgit, whence there are two specimens in the British Museum Collection.

If *arenicola*, the Persian Turtle-Dove, is considered identical with the north African Turtle-Dove, then its range must be further extended to Algeria in the east and Shoa in the south.

Nidification. In *Stray Feathers* Scully gives an interesting account of this Dove's nesting. He writes: "The Turtle-Dove is a seasonal visitant to the Plains of Eastern Turkestan, arriving in May and migrating towards the end of September or beginning of October; it was never observed in winter. This Dove frequents trees and orchards; and in May and June its beautiful, soft, musical note could be heard every day about the neighbourhood of Yarkand. It lays in May and June, and on the 15th of the latter month I saw two very young nestlings of this species. I found a nest of this species; it was a loose kind of cup, composed of twigs and placed in the fork of a willow-tree about seven feet from the ground. It contained only one egg, the contents of which were found to be quite fluid; the female bird was sitting on the nest at the time and only flew away when I got close to it. On the 12th June a nest of the Turtle-Dove, containing two eggs, was placed in a thorn-bush. On the 25th June I found another nest, containing one egg—much incubated to judge by the colour. A thick main branch of a willow-tree had been cut off, and on the horizontal face of this cut stump, which was slightly concave, a few twigs were arranged in a concentric manner forming a thin shallow cup in which the eggs rested. The twigs of this bedding were so loosely put together that the wood of the tree could be seen through them.

"The three eggs of this Dove, which I have, are pure white and glossy. They may be described as a regular oval, a somewhat pointed oval, and a longish narrow oval. They measure 1.36 by 0.91; 1.28 by 0.9; and 1.18 by 0.89. Average of the three eggs, 1.27 in length by 0.9 in breadth."

There are a good many eggs of this subspecies from Persia in the British Museum Collection, taken by W. Cumming at Fao in the Persian Gulf on the 16th and 22nd of May. They cannot be in any way distinguished from the eggs of the Common Turtle-Dove.

The habits, flight, voice, and food of the Persian Dove do not appear to differ in any way from those of the European Dove but, owing to its not being differentiated from that bird, little has been placed on record concerning it.

(38) STREPTOPELIA TURTUR MEENA (Sykes).

THE INDIAN RUFOUS TURTLE-DOVE OR SYKES'S TURTLE-DOVE.

(PLATE 20.)

Columba orientalis Lath., Ind. Orn., II p. 606 (1790).

Columba meena ♀ Sykes, P.Z.S. 1832, p. 149 (Dukhan).

Columba agricola Tickell, J.A.S.B., II p. 581 (1833).

Columba gelastis Temm., Pl. Col., pl. 550 (1835).

Turtur meena Gray, Gen. B., II p. 472; Blyth, J.A.S.B., XIV p. 875; Jerdon, B.I., III p. 476; Godw.-Aus., J.A.S.B., XXXIX pt. 2, p. 272; Hume, Lah. to Yark., p. 277; id., Nests and Eggs, p. 501; id., Str. Feath., III p. 163; Blyth and Wald., B. Burma, p. 146; Fairbank, Str. Feath., IV p. 262; Anders., Yun-nan Exp., Aves, p. 665; Hume and Dav., Str. Feath., VI p. 420; Davidson and Wend., ib., VII p. 86; Ball, ib., p. 224; Cripps, ib., p. 296; Hume, ib., VIII p. 110; id., Cat. no. 793; Vidal, Str. Feath., IX p. 74; Butler, ib., p. 420; Oates, ib., X p. 235; id., B. Burma, II p. 292; Barnes, B. Bom., p. 290; Hume, Str. Feath., XI p. 298; Oates, in Hume's Nests and Eggs, 2nd ed., II p. 350; Barnes, J.B.N.H.S., V p. 330; Stuart Baker, ib., X p. 360; Inglis, ib., XI p. 474.

Turtur orientalis Blyth, J.A.S.B., XIV p. 876; Anders., Yun-nan Exp., Aves, p. 666; Hutton, J.A.S.B., XVII pt. 2, p. 13; Salvadori, Cat. B.M., XXI p. 403 (part); Blanf., Avi. Brit. I., IV p. 40 (part); Sharpe, Hand-List, I p. 78 (part); Oates, Cat. Eggs B.M., I p. 95 (part); Inglis, J.B.N.H.S., XVI p. 73; Macdonald, ib., XVII p. 496; Stuart Baker, ib., p. 971; Mears, ib., XVIII p. 86; Harington, ib., XIX p. 309; id. ib., XX p. 1010; D'Abreu, ib., XXI p. 1167; Hopwood, ib., p. 1214.

Columba rupicola Adams, Str. Feath., I p. 390.

Vernacular Names. *Kala fakhta, Basko fakhta*, Hin.; *Sam ghughu, Ram ghughu*, Beng.; *Yedrupoda guwa*, Tel.; *Daotu gajao*, Cachari; *Paho*, Assamese; *Inruiku*, Naga.; *Vohgura*, Kuki.

Description.—*Adult male.* Whole head and neck reddish-vinous, paler on the sides and palest on the chin; the crown is often tinged with bluish-grey which sometimes extends to the fore-head; a patch of black feathers on either side of the neck, each feather edged with silvery-grey, this colour disposed in regular lines; upper-back brown, the feathers often edged with rufous and sometimes almost wholly of this colour and tinged with vinous; lower-back and rump slaty-grey with dark centres, sometimes concealed sometimes showing distinctly; upper tail-coverts and central rectrices dark brown, faintly tipped paler; outer rectrices almost black, broadly tipped with pale grey, and with the outermost greyish-white on the outer-web also. Scapulars, inner wing-coverts and inner secondaries dark brown with broad ferruginous borders; outer median wing-coverts and greater coverts dark

SYKES'S TURTLE-DOVE—*STREPTOPELIA T. MEENA*

(½ Nat. Size.) PLATE 20

slaty-grey, primary-coverts blackish; quills brown, edged and tipped with pale brownish-white; lower-throat, breast, and abdomen vinous-red, the breast generally rather darker than elsewhere and sometimes tinged with greyish; vent, flanks, tibial plumes, and under tail-coverts rather dark slate-grey.

Measurements. Length about 13 in. (= 330 mm.); tail 4.6 to 5.2 in. (= 116.8 to 132 mm.); wing 6.40 to 7.20 in. (= 162.5 to 182.8 mm.); average 6.92 in. (= 175.5 mm.); bill at front .60 in. (= 15.2 mm.) and from gape about 1 in. (= 25.4 mm.); tarsus about .8 in. (= 20.3 mm.).

Colours of soft parts. Bill pale to dark horny-brown, basal half reddish or purplish; irides golden-yellow, orange-yellow, orange-red to red; eyelids and very narrow orbital skin pale bluish or lead-colour with the edges of the eyelids red; legs dull coral, purple-red, or dull brick-red, the soles paler and the claws nearly black.

Female similar to the male, but is perhaps less vinous and more brown on the upper-parts on an average.

Measurements. The same as in the male. In the British Museum Collection there are females with wings of 7.10 in. from Burma, 7.05 in. from Assam, and 7.30 in. from Darjiling.

Young. The whole upper-parts where reddish-brown in the adult are a dark earth-brown in the young bird, and the feathers of the lower-back, the scapulars, coverts, and inner secondaries are boldly edged with pale rufous and the quills are broadly tipped with a darker, richer tint of the same colour; the dark grey lower-back and rump are narrowly edged with pale grey, and there are also indications of pale bars on the head. Below, the breast is suffused with smoky-brown, and the feathers of this part are narrowly edged with pale rufous.

Colours of soft parts. The same as in the adult, but duller, and the iris is a dull whitish-brown.

Still younger birds have the whole upper-parts a paler, duller brown, this colour replacing even the grey on the rump and upper tail-coverts. Everywhere from fore-head to tail-coverts the feathers are narrowly edged with dull rufous, these bars being almost obsolete on the centre of the back. The coverts and quills of the wing are still more freely edged with pale rufous. Beneath, the throat, breast, and upper-abdomen are pale smoky-brown, each feather narrowly edged with pale yellowish-rufous; the under wing-coverts, axillaries, and flanks are mixed grey and rufous, the former colour predominating on the posterior flanks. The under tail-coverts are grey as in the adult, but there are two or three very fine bars of black near their ends, and the tips are narrowly edged with rufous. This is the plumage of the young bird on leaving the nest.

Nestling, in down, is covered with a pale buff down.

Distribution. Bengal, from as far west as Manbhum, Purulia, and Chutia Nagpur, throughout eastern Bengal, Assam, Cachar, and Sylhet, the Bhutan Dooars and Terai south of it; and to the east throughout Burma as far as the south of Tenasserim. East of Bengal it has been obtained in Central India, the Deccan north of about 15° N. lat., and has been obtained as a rare straggler in the Central Provinces. There are two specimens in the British Museum Collection from Mahabaleshwar in the Bombay Presidency. Outside India to the north and east its place is taken by *Streptopelia turtur orientalis*, the next bird.

Nidification. Almost wherever found the bird is resident and breeds, and its breeding-season practically lasts for the greater part of the year, though the principal breeding-months in the north-east of India and in Burma would seem to be April and May, and in southern and Central India January to March.

In North Cachar, where the bird was not very common, I have seen their nests containing either eggs or young in every month from March to November, and have no doubt that they occasionally breed in the other months also. They certainly have two broods in the year and many probably have three. The second brood may be reared either in the old nest or in a new one, in most cases perhaps the latter. I have often noticed when nests are taken late in the year that a short search often produces another and older nest in the immediate vicinity, sometimes in the same bush or cane-brake; at the same time, I have more than once known two broods reared in the same nest. Their nests may be found in bushes, cane-brakes, small saplings, or clumps of bamboo, generally fairly low down between 5 and 10 ft. from the ground, now and then higher up than this, and still more rarely 3 or 4 ft. only from it.

There has been little or no attempt to conceal such nests as I have found myself, or which have been pointed out to me. A few, from their positions in the interior of a thick bush, bamboo-clump or dense cane-brake, may have been hard to detect at first, but the majority were in quite conspicuous positions, often on a bare branch or cluster of twigs, and quite visible yards away.

The normal nest is no better made or shaped than is usual with this family; the twigs and short bents of which it is composed are roughly, though fairly strongly, interlaced so that they form a rough circular platform some six or seven inches in diameter by an inch or two in depth. As a rule the material is so scanty that the eggs or young can easily be seen through the bottom of the nest. When a second clutch is laid in the same nest as the first, there are always a few feathers and a good deal of the yellow down from the previous young adhering to the nest, and the materials, as a whole, get matted, and present a more solid appearance than is the case with fresh nests.

Irwin, it should be noted, described a nest of this bird as being "neatly constructed of twigs, circular in shape, with the egg cavity somewhat deep, certainly unlike the platform nest described by Capt. Hutton."

The bird is a very close sitter, and I have stood within a yard or two of a nest with eggs upon which the bird has sat, its eyes steadily fixed upon me, but making no attempt to fly off until my hand was actually raised towards the nest. Both birds take an equal share in all the labour appertaining to a family: the male collects the material for the nest which the female constructs, both attend to the incubation, and the male does at least as much of the feeding as the female.

The eggs are invariably two in number, and of the usual description of Doves' eggs, i.e. white in colour and broad ovals in shape, the ends equal. The texture is fine and close and there is a fair gloss on the surface.

A very large series of these eggs which have passed through my hands, or are now in my collection, vary in length from 1 in. (= 25.4 mm.) to 1.37 in. (= 34.8 mm.) and in breadth from .82 in. (= 20.3 mm.) to .97 in. (= 24.6 mm.). The egg measuring 1.37 by .97 in. is one of a pair of quite abnormally large eggs, and eliminating these, the average size of eighty eggs is 1.12 in. (= 28.4 mm.) by .88 in. (= 22.4 mm.).

Although the bird is, as I have said above, a resident form over the whole of its breeding-area, they appear to wander considerably further afield during the winter, more especially in the extreme west. These local migrations are probably due to the migratory instinct inherited from the parent stock being still not quite exhausted. The original bird, probably *Streptopelia t. turtur*, the European Turtle-Dove, from which all our Indian subspecies are descended, must have been a migratory bird, breeding possibly in the far north and migrating, more or less, over the whole of India during the winter. In time a few birds remained behind in the lower hills of the Himalayas and developed into our *ferrago*, the Indian Turtle-Dove, which has greatly restricted its migrations, and now goes no further north than the Himalayas to breed. Next, yet other birds settled in the plains of India, and from these has come the non-migratory form *meena*, Sykes's Turtle-Dove. In the hills of Nepal and eastwards, yet another set of birds settled down and developed the small changes in plumage which constitute the subspecies *orientalis*.

It is, therefore, probable that on the western coasts this bird is only a visitor in the cold-weather months, during which fewer birds are breeding.

It is a very sociable bird and is often seen consorting in large numbers when feeding in rice and wheat fields, etc., and some writers consider it actually gregarious. Thus Jerdon says it is often seen in large flocks, and Blewitt writes that his experience leads him to suppose "that this species congregates in flocks after the breeding-season." Personally, I have never seen a flock of these Doves, either in the plains or hills, for though many have often been together in the same field, their actions, except in pairs, have always seemed to me quite independent of the rest of the birds. When they are disturbed they fly off in pairs or singly, and in all directions—some only to the nearest tree, others to a considerable distance, and some quite out of sight.

They are often found in very great numbers picking up the fallen rice after the fields have been cut and, shocking as it may appear to shoot Doves, they really give one many an afternoon's very pretty sport, and shooting quite difficult enough to satisfy even a good shot. After the first cartridge or two has been fired, they get up at thirty yards or so and get away very quickly, twisting and doubling as they rise, so that it is no tyro's work to drop them right and left in a satisfactory manner. The only point against them is that at first a good many birds *will* seek refuge in the nearest tree, and then think they are safe, but the sportsman can well afford to leave these alone and pursue the others.

For the table they are delicious, and excel any of the Pigeons in delicacy of flavour, whilst they equal them in plumpness and general condition.

It is not a bird of heavy forest and jungle, keeping much to thin scrub and patches of light jungle round about villages and cultivation, and feeding almost entirely in the open. It is more of a bird of the plains than of the hills, but ascends the latter certainly up to 4,000 ft. and commonly up to about 2,000 ft.—in Burma possibly a good deal higher. It is principally a grain and seed eater, but will also devour most fruit obtainable when hungry. They are very active on their feet and get their food for the most part from the ground, spending the greater portion of their time upon it when not sleeping during the heat of the day or roosting during the night. Their note is a thrice-repeated, very deep "coo," of the same nature, yet quite distinct from, that of most Doves, and easily recognizable.

It is a favourite cage-bird, very easily tamed and very easy to feed and keep, for no matter how small the cage, this fleet-winged and wide-ranging bird does not appear to suffer from confinement. In captivity it becomes very lethargic and silent, except during its selected breeding-months, when it wakes up, displays, "coos," and makes love to its companions should it be lucky enough to have any. Blewitt writes of a pair kept by him: "The pair I have are very tame, and the coo of the male (I have not heard the female) is far oftener heard of a morning and evening than during the day. When irritated they utter a peculiarly loud hissing kind of note."

It must, however, be remembered that they are quarrelsome birds, and though doubtless they would be much more interesting pets in a fair-sized aviary than they are in the tiny native cages, they cannot be kept in company with other birds.

Nearly all Doves are thirsty birds, and whilst the majority drink every morning early and every evening before retiring to rest, all, I think, do so regularly and deeply before they take their mid-day siesta, and many again before commencing to feed.

As a rule they take a few long sips, run about on the bare sand or shingle, picking up scraps of it as they go, and then take another drink. This process may be repeated several times before they eventually fly off. The pebbles they swallow are sometimes of comparatively large size, and I have taken round stones from some Doves' crops and stomachs almost as big as a small pea.

(39) STREPTOPELIA TURTUR ORIENTALIS (Lath.).

THE RUFOUS TURTLE-DOVE.

Columba orientalis Lath., Ind. Orn., II p. 606 (part), 1783 (ex Sonnerat).

Columba rupicola Pall., Zoogr. Rosso-As., I p. 566.

Columba agricola Tickell, J.A.S.B., II p. 581 (1835).

Turtur orientalis Blyth, ib., XIV p. 876; Hutton, ib., XVII 2nd pt. p. 13 (?); Scully, Str. Feath., VIII p. 340; Dresser, J.B.N.H.S., XVI p. 729; Ward, ib., XVII p. 943; Salvadori, Cat. B.M., XXI p. 403 (part); Blanf., Avi. Brit. I., IV p. 40 (part); Sharpe, Hand-List, I p. 77 (part); Oates, Cat. Eggs B.M., I p. 94 (part).

Turtur rupicolus Jerdon, B.I. (part), III p. 477.

Vernacular Names. None recorded which really refer to this form of *Streptopelia*.

Description.—*Adult male.* Differs from the Rufous Turtle-Dove (*meena*) in being much paler-coloured below, the centre of the abdomen is albescent, and the feathers of the vent and tibial plumes are practically white; the under tail-coverts, flanks, and under wing-coverts are a paler dove-grey, and the fore-head, chin, and throat are also decidedly paler. The differences pointed out are sufficient to distinguish this race at a glance from its southern prototype, and in addition to this it is a considerably larger bird.

Measurements. About 14 in. (= 345.6 mm.) in total length; wing 7.50 (= 190.5 mm.) to 7.85 in. (= 199.4 mm.) and averaging 7.70 in. (= 195.5 mm.); tail 5.2 to 6 in. (= 132 to 152 mm.); bill at front about .7 in. (= 17.7 mm.) and from gape about 1.1 in. (= 28 mm.); tarsus rather over .90 in. (= 22.8 mm).

"Weight 6 oz." (Davison).

"Length 12 to 12.9; expanse 21.7 to 23.7; wing 7.3 to 7.95; tail 5.0 to 5.6; tarsus 1.0; bill from gape 0.9 to 0.95; bill at front 0.65 to 0.71; closed wings short of tail 1.5 to 2.5; weight 6.5 to 7.5 oz." (Scully).

Colours of soft parts. "Irides orange; bill dusky leaden; cere at base, gape, and margins of eyelid, purple; eyelid plumbous; tarsi purple, toes livid purple, claws dusky" (Davison).

"Iris pale red; bill dusky horny, skin purplish; legs and feet pale lake red" (Walton).

Female resembles the male in all respects.

Scully considers the female to be smaller than the male and gives the following measurements of six birds: "Length 11.75 to 12.5; expanse 20.5 to 22.8; wing 6.85 to 7.6; tail 5.0 to 5.6; tarsus 0.97 to 1.13; bill from gape 0.87 to 0.95; bill at front 0.6 to 0.75; closed wings short of tail 2.0 to 2.6; weight 6 to 7.5 oz."

Young. Exactly like that of *meena*, but rather paler below.

Distribution. Sikhim, Tibet, Nepal, and thence into China and north to Manchuria, Corea, and Japan.

There is a very typical specimen from Darjiling in the British Museum Collection, but most birds from this district, at least all those from low elevations, are typical *meena*; the Nepal birds are without exception true *orientalis*, as are those from Sikhim and Tibet.

Owing to *Streptopelia turtur ferrago*, the Indian Turtle Dove, migrating over so large an area throughout India during the cold-weather months, and to the present bird also in some cases meeting the last bird, Sykes's Turtle-Dove, and intergrading with it—it is not always easy to decide into which of the three subspecies some specimens may belong. Thus Davidson says: "Now in Western Khandesh I have shot right and left specimens, one of which had white under tail-coverts and the other grey, and I have seen others that I could hardly say whether the coverts were pure white or greyish-white. . . . I would add to this that I have shot moulting birds, with the new under tail-coverts white and the old ones grey." This, however, does not, as Hume points out in *Stray Feathers*, mean that they are one and the same form, and though one may, as Davidson did, shoot the two forms out of the same tree, it merely shows that the migratory form has visited the district in which the other form is resident.

Nidification. The Nepalese Rufous Turtle-Dove breeds throughout the area it inhabits, but it moves higher up or lower down the mountains according to the season of the year.

I can find absolutely nothing on record about the breeding of this Dove either in China or India, although its eggs are not very rare in collections.

I have its eggs from Nepal, Tibet, and native Sikhim, but never having taken its eggs myself can only put on record the notes of my collectors, both European and Indian. According to these it builds a nest just like that of its European cousin—a flimsy flat construction of twigs, very carelessly and very untidily put together and measuring anything between 6 and 8 in. in diameter.

The site selected seems to be in some high thick bush, small sapling, or a tangle of briers, and I have had no account of any nest taken at more than some ten or twelve feet from the ground. In Sikhim and Tibet the nests were taken in very open country, sometimes in quite isolated bushes and trees, but in Nepal my informants tell me that they took the nest *generally* in well-wooded ravines and sometimes in the inside of quite extensive forests. All the nests, as far as I am aware, were taken at over 8,000 ft. elevation, and some up to 12,000 ft.

The few eggs I have vary in length between 1.16 in. (= 29.4 mm.) and 1.36 in. (= 34.5 mm.), and in breadth between .90 in. (= 22.8 mm.) and 1.10 in. (= 27.9 mm.), whilst they average 1.28 in. (= 32.5 mm.) by 1.03 in. (= 26.1 mm.)

In shape they are the usual ovals, practically equal in form and size at the ends, but I think on an average they are rather longer in proportion than are most Doves' eggs. The texture and surface are as usual.

My eggs from Tibet were all taken in July, and those from Sikhim and Nepal in the end of May and June.

Scully says that: "This Dove is fairly common in one part or another of the Nepal Valley throughout the year. In May, June, and July it is only found in the forests, at elevations of from 7,000 to 8,000 ft.

where it breeds. From August to September it is plentiful in the central woods of the valley. From January to March only a few birds are to be found in the central part of the valley, the majority having moved down to warmer regions; and in the latter part of March and throughout April it is again common in the central woods. I also found it common in the Nawakot district in November and in the plains of Nepal in December. It is usually seen in parties of from six to ten, high up in trees; and its note is a low, deep, *kur-kur-ku.*"

(40) STREPTOPELIA TURTUR FERRAGO (Eversm.).

THE INDIAN TURTLE-DOVE.

Columba meena ♂ Sykes, P.Z.S. 1832, p. 149.

Turtur auritus Vigne (nec Auct.), P.Z.S. 1841, p. 6.

Columba ferrago Eversm., Add. ad Zoogr. Rosso-As., fasc. III p. 17 (1842).

Columba pulcrata Hodg., in Gray's Zool. Misc., p. 85 (1844).

Columba orientalis Layard (nec Lath.), Ann. Mag. N.H. (?), XIV p. 62.

Turtur ferrago Wardl. Ramsay, Ibis 1880, p. 68; Salvadori, Cat. B.M., XXI p. 401; Blanf., Avi. Brit. I., IV p. 41; Sharpe, Hand-List, I p. 78; Oates, Cat. Eggs, B.M. I p. 95; Wilson, J.B.N.H.S. XII p. 639; Inglis, ib., XIV p. 562; Foulton, ib., XVI p. 60; Inglis, ib., p. 73; Rattray, ib., p. 663; Ward, ib., XVII p. 943; Magrath, ib., XVIII p. 298; id ib., XIX p. 155; Perreau, ib., p. 919; Whitehead, ib., XX p. 967; id. ib., XXI p. 161.

Turtur vitticollis Hume, Lath. to Yark., p. 274.

Turtur pulchrata Hume, Nests and Eggs, p. 500; Butler and Hume, Str. Feath., IV p. 3; Hume, ib., VI p. 421; Butler, ib., IX p. 420; Reid, ib., X p. 60; Davidson, ib., p. 315; Davison, ib., p. 407; Barnes, B. Bom., p. 290.

Turtur pulchratus Hume, Str. Feath., VIII p. 110; id., Cat. no. 792; Legge, B. Cey., p. 711; Barnes and Davidson, J.B.N.H.S., V p. 330.

Turtur pulchrala Oates, in Hume's Nests and Eggs, 2nd ed., II p. 349.

Vernacular Names. *Koin*, Chamba; *Hulagud*, Mahr.; *Powari*, Marie Gond.; *Kullah*, Bohari; *Lal Punduk*, Hin.; *Pahari Perki*, Lucknow; *Ram Ghaghu*, Bengali; *Lali Kopu-hu*, Assamese; *Hagrani Daotu*, Cachari.

Description.—*Adult male.* Similar to *Streptopelia turtur orientalis*, but differs in being still paler below; the chin and centre of the throat are albescent, the whole of the abdomen from the breast downwards is white or nearly so, the under-tail coverts are white and the tip of the tail and edge of the outer-web of the outermost feather are either pure white or very pale-grey; the under wing-coverts and flanks are a paler, purer grey also than in either Sykes's or the Rufous Turtle-Dove.

Dimensions. About 13.5 in. (= 343 mm.); wing 6.65 in. (= 169 mm.) to 7.85 in. (= 199.4 mm.), average about 7.50 in. (= 190.5 mm.); tail 5 in. (= 127 mm.) to 5.75 in. (= 146 mm.); bill at front about .65 in. (= 16.5 mm.), and from gape about .95 in. (= 24.1 mm.); tarsus .85 in. (= 21.6 mm.).

Colours of soft parts. Bill dusky-horny, reddish on base and on cere, and quite a purple on the latter in some cases; irides bright cinnamon-brown, orange, reddish-orange or golden-yellow; feet dull red, lake-red, or reddish-purple, the soles paler and the claws blackish-horny.

The female does not differ from the male in coloration or size or in the colour of the soft parts.

Young birds differ from the adult in the same way that the young of *orientalis* differ from the full-grown birds.

Distribution. Western Central Asia, Turkestan, Persia, Afghanistan and the Himalayas as far east as Sikhim, migrating in the cold weather over practically the whole continent of India and Ceylon.

It is not very uncommon in the Deccan and occurs as a straggler into Gujerat, near Sambhur, but does not appear to be ever found in Sind. To the south, Hume gives about lat. 15° as its usual limit; Davidson obtained it in western Khandesh, and Davison in Mysore, and it probably occurs practically over the whole of southern as well as northern India, for it has twice been recorded from Ceylon. So far, however, it seems to have escaped observation in the Nilgherries, Palnis, Shevaroys, and many other places in southern India where it must occur occasionally. North of the Madras Presidency it is very common in the cold weather, and is numerous throughout Orissa, west Bengal, and thence less common in east Bengal and Assam, but not in the extreme east of the latter province. I have not met with it in Dibrugarh, Sibsagar, or Tezpur, but it is said to occur in Goalpara, and is certainly an occasional straggler into Dhubri.

Nidification. Hume thus sums up the breeding-range of this bird: "Our Indian Turtle-Dove breeds throughout the lower ranges of the Himalayas, from Afghanistan to Sikhim at any rate, at elevations of from 4,000 to 8,000 ft. It is for the most part only a summer visitant to these hills.

"*Turtur pulchrala*" (=*ferrago*) "lays throughout the summer. I have found eggs early in May and late in August, but the majority lay in June. It makes a loose, but rather more substantial, twig nest than many of its congeners, placed on some horizontal branch of a large tree, usually not far from the extremity."

In and about Murree, Mussoorie, and Kashmir it breeds in great numbers, and its nests and eggs have been taken by many collectors. It appears to build at all heights, as Hutton says "that it makes its nest on tall forest trees," whilst Captain Cock recorded it as building "on trees and bushes at no great height from the ground in May and June."

Normally this bird is a resident of the hills and the hills alone during the breeding-season, but in 1901 Inglis found it breeding in the plains of Behar, and in the *Bombay Natural History Journal* thus records his find: "This year I was successful in securing this bird's eggs for the first time. I shot a male in March, which was evidently breeding, and so had a good look-out kept wherever any of these birds frequented; it was not, however, until the 25th of May that the first nest was secured at Jainagar; it contained a single egg. On the 20th June, near Baghownie, a second nest was found containing two eggs. Both nests were on mango trees."

This is an extraordinary extension of this Dove's breeding-range, and looks as if the subspecies *ferrago* was gradually also becoming a non-migratory bird, in which case we should eventually have those settling in the plains merging into *meena* and those settling in the hills reverting to *orientalis*, or differentiating themselves yet again.

A very curious instance of this bird's nesting, or rather non-nesting, has been observed by Mr. C. S. R. Pitman, who writes to me that he "took a fresh egg at Nathea Gali, on 10/5/12, but the bird had not troubled to make a nest, the egg being laid on some dry earth which had accumulated in an open hollow in the side of a trunk of a large tree. Altitude about 8,500 ft."

It probably has two, or perhaps even three, broods during the year, though there is as yet no direct evidence on this point.

The eggs, which are the usual two in number, do not differ in any respect, except size, from other Doves' eggs. Oates gives the average of twenty-one eggs as 1.22 in. by .93 in. (= 30.9 by 23.5 mm.), and the extremes in length as 1.1 in. to 1.34 in. (= 27.9 to 34.0 mm.), and in breadth .85 to 1 in. (= 21.6 to 25.4 mm.).

The eggs in my own collection come within the above measurements.

This Dove breeds principally between 3,500 and 8,000 ft., whereas the Rufous Turtle-Dove breeds exclusively over the latter height, and generally between 8,000 and 12,000 ft. altitude.

The Indian Turtle-Dove seems to keep, both in its breeding haunts and those visited on migration, much to well-forested and well-watered tracts, and to prefer such as are a combination of cultivated areas and patches of jungle or orchard. At the same time, provided the water supply is ample, they may be found in considerable numbers in stretches of rice and wheat country where there is no real jungle, though there may be plenty of mango and other orchards.

They are almost entirely grain and seed feeders, though doubtless they also feed on fruit to some extent, and also at odd times on tiny snails though, it always seems to me, these may have been picked up by the birds in mistake for seeds. Like most Doves they drink regularly morning, noon and evening, and seem to take a lot each time they drink. When there is sand or grit and small pebbles close by, they generally pick some up during the intervals of drinking.

They are very active on foot, and obtain most of their food on the ground, running in and out of the wheat or rice stubble with considerable speed.

Their flight is in no way distinct from that of the other subspecies, and their note is a loud deep "coo," trisyllabic like that of the rest.

During their migrations, and shortly before they commence, the Indian Turtle-Doves collect in very large flocks, often numbering a hundred or more individuals, but at other times, though very sociable, the flocks break up and the birds go about either in pairs or singly, generally the former.

Species SURATENSIS.

This species, and the Burmese form *tigrina*, have been placed by Sharpe in a different genus—*Spilopelia*, but I cannot see that there are any differences sufficiently pronounced to make it either necessary or convenient to divide our Indian Doves into different genera, and I therefore retain them under the name *Streptopelia* together with those Turtle-Doves in which the male and female are similarly plumaged.

Key to the Subspecies.

A. Back distinctly and boldly spotted with pale rufous ... *S. s. suratensis*.

B. Back spotted very indistinctly or not at all ... ... *S. s. tigrina*.

Well-marked specimens of these two subspecies are very easily discriminated, and even where the two meet the area over which the intermediate form prevails is very small, and in nearly all cases birds can be assigned to one or the other of the two.

(41) STREPTOPELIA SURATENSIS SURATENSIS (Gm.).

THE SPOTTED DOVE.

Columba suratensis Gm., Syst. Nat., I p. 778, no. 48 (1788); Lath., Ind. Orn., II p. 609.

Columba tigrina (part) Temm.; Pig. et Gall., I pp. 317, 481 (1813).

Turtur vitticollis Hodg., in Gray's Zool. Misc., p. 85 (descr. nulla).

Turtur suratensis Strick., P.Z.S. 1842, p. 168; Blyth, J.A.S.B., XIV, 2nd pt., p. 874 (part); id., Cat. M.A.S.B., p. 236; id., J.A.S.B., XXIV p. 263; Jerdon, B.I., III p. 479; Stoliczka, J.A.S.B., XXXVII pt. 2 p. 67; Godw-Aus., ib., XXXIX pt. 2 p. 112; Hume, Str. Feath., I p. 218; Adam, ib., p. 390; Ball, ib., II p. 425; Hume and Butler, ib., IV p. 3; id., Nests and Eggs, p. 504; Fairbank, Str. Feath., IV p. 262; id. ib., V p. 409; Hume and Bourd., ib., VII p. 39; Dav. and Wend., ib., p. 86; Ball, ib., p. 224; Cripps, ib., p. 297; Hume, ib., VIII p. 110; id., Cat. no. 795; Scully, Str. Feath., VIII p. 341; Vidal, ib., IX p. 75; Butler, ib., p. 420; Legge, B. Cey., p. 705; Reid, Str. Feath., X p. 60; Dav., ib., p. 408; Barnes, B. Bom., p. 291; Hume, Str. Feath., XI p. 298; Oates, in Hume's Nests and Eggs, 2nd ed., II p. 353; Sharpe, Yarkand Misc. Av., p. 119; Salvadori, Cat. B.M., XXI p. 444; Blanf., Avi. Brit. I., IV p. 43; Barnes, J.B.N.H.S., V p. 331; Butler, ib., X p. 310; Inglis, ib., XI p. 474; id. ib., XIV p. 502; Bourdillon, XVI p. 3; Fulton, ib., p. 60; Ward, ib., XVII p. 943; Stuart Baker, ib., p. 971; Magrath, ib., XIX p. 155; Perreau, ib., p. 919; Moss-King, ib., XXI p. 99; Whitehead, ib., p. 167; D'Abreu, ib., p. 1167; Dewar, Birds of the Plains, p. 124.

Spilopelia suratensis Sharpe, Hand-List, I p. 80; Oates, Cat. Eggs B.M., I p. 99.

Vernacular Names. *Chitroka fakhta, Chitta fakhta, Perki, Chitla, Kangskiri, Panduk*, Hin.; *Chaval ghughu, Telia ghughu*, Bengali; *Kawala*, Mahr.; *Bode*, Gond.; *Powari*, Marie Gond.; *Poda-bella-guwa*, Tel.; *Puli-pora*, Tamil; *Mani-praa*, Tam. Ceylon; *Kobeyu, Allikobeya*, Cing.; *Ku-po-hu*, Assamese; *Kodaya punduk*, Behari; *Daotu*, Cachari; *Inruigu*, Naga.; *Vohkurup*, Kuki.

Description.—*Adult male.* Upper portion of head and nape vinous, more grey on the fore-head and often also above the eye; a small spot or streak of black between the eye and base of bill; a demi-collar on back and sides of neck of black feathers, bifurcate and with two white spots at the tip; on the upper-back the feathers gradually change from the rich velvety-black to brown, and the spots from pure white to rufous; the bifurcations become less pronounced and cease on the lower-back where the spots become narrow terminal bars; lower-back and rump brown with narrow rufous fringes; upper tail-coverts slaty-brown, bifurcated and tipped narrowly with brown and still more narrowly subtipped rufous, the latter bar sometimes obsolete. Central tail-feathers brown obsoletely barred darker; the next pair almost black with broad terminal band of dark slate, each succeeding pair has the slate-colour darker and the band of grey paler and wider until on the outermost the basal half is quite black, and the terminal half and a narrow edge down the other web practically pure white; scapulars and innermost secondaries brown like the back, but with larger, paler spots tinged with vinous; lesser and median wing-coverts grey-brown with large terminal spots of vinous, divided by a streak of deep brown, broadest terminally and narrowest towards the base; towards the shoulder of the wing the spots fade and the grey increases, making this part look grey streaked with brown; greater-coverts grey; edge of wing, primary-coverts and quills dark brown, outer primaries and outer secondaries narrowly edged with grey. Below, chin white and centre of throat albescent, changing into the vinous-pink on the sides of the head, throat, and breast; centre of abdomen, vent, and under tail-coverts white, the latter often having a small V-shaped spot of black or dark brown at the tip.

Some birds, irrespective of age, have a few fine bars on the lower-plumage formed by the feathers of the breast, abdomen and shorter tail-coverts being fringed with dark brown.

A few other birds, all of which seem to be very old males, have the lower-back and rump a slaty-grey, the feathers more or less edged with rufous.

Measurements. "Length about 11 inches, wing 5.5, tail 5.5, bill 0.55, tarsus 0.9" (Salvadori).

This little Dove varies very considerably in size, not only in different localities, but individually.

The following is a resumé of the wing-measurements of the very large series in the British Museum, to which are added a few others:—

	Wing.	Average.
North-west India	5.25 to 5.80 in. = 134.3 to 147.3 mm.	5.55 in. = 141.0 mm.
North-east India	5.35 to 5.70 in. = 135.9 to 144.8 mm.	5.55 in. = 141.0 mm.
Southern India ...	5.05 to 5.65 in. = 128.3 to 143.5 mm.	5.35 in. = 139.9 mm.
Ceylon	4.85 to 5.10 in. = 123.2 to 129.5 mm.	4.98 in. = 126.5 mm.

Colours of soft parts. Irides bright reddish-hazel and of two rings, the outer redder and the inner more hazel; eye-lids and narrow orbital bare space red; bill dark horny-brown or horny-plumbeous; legs and feet dull red, lake-red, or purplish-red, never very bright; claws dark horny-brown.

Female. Similar to the male. but I have seen no specimen with the pure slate-grey rump sometimes acquired by old males.

Measurements. The female is slightly smaller than the male on an average, the wing being about ¼ in. less, but the largest females considerably exceed in size the smallest males from the same locality.

Colours of soft parts as in the male.

Young birds are browner and paler on the head and have no nuchal collar of black and white, the upper-parts are paler and are barred instead of spotted with rufous and vinous, the black streaks are entirely wanting at first and the markings on the wing-coverts and inner secondaries are pale sandy-rufous instead of vinous; the primary-coverts are narrowly and the secondaries broadly tipped with rufous, a considerable portion of the inner webs of the inner primaries being of this colour. The under-parts are pale fulvous-brown instead of vinous, and the breast-feathers are fringed with narrow edges of pale fulvous.

Colours of soft parts. Same as in the male, but the irides are pale brown and the feet a paler duller red.

Young, after the first moult, acquire a certain amount of vinous tinge on the breast and flanks, and have the neck-patch represented by a few feathers with black bases which show through; the scapulars and outer lesser wing-coverts become streaked with dark brown and occasionally the vinous spots begin to appear.

The Ceylon bird, as may be seen from the measurements given above, is very much smaller than the northern bird and somewhat smaller even than the southern Indian one, but I can trace no difference between the two forms in plumage.

If divided from the northern form on account of the smaller measurements the Ceylon form would bear the name *Streptopelia suratensis ceylonensis* (Rchnb., *Syn. Av., Columbariae, Novit.*, t. 253B (1851).)

Birds from Cachar Plains and Sylhet are intermediate between the Indian Spotted Dove and the Burmese form, whilst those from the North Cachar Hills and Manipur are almost typical *tigrina*. Birds from Gilgit are very pale in their plumage both above and below.

Distribution. There is little to add to Blanford's summary of this bird's habitat. He says that it is found "throughout the whole of India and Ceylon; most common in well-wooded countries, rare in drier regions, and wanting in desert tracks. This Dove is found throughout the Himalayas up to 7,000 ft. and in Gilgit and Ladak. (The statement in the British Museum Catalogue that it inhabits Yarkand is a mistake). To the eastward it is found in Assam, Cachar, and Manipur, but is replaced in Burma by *T. tigrinus*."

Throughout Assam Dr. H. N. Coltart and myself found only *suratensis*, and never came across *tigrina*, yet in North Cachar I found this latter to be the common form, whilst some birds sent me from Manipur were intermediate but leaning more to the Burmese than the Indian form. In Chittagong and the Chittagong hill-tracks also the former is the one met with.

Captain Malden reported it as "pretty common in the south of Sind," but it probably only enters this part of India in exceptionally wet seasons as no one else seems to have noticed it there. Both "Eha" and Dewar state that this Dove is never found on the island of Bombay though both the Little Brown Dove and Ring-Dove swarm.

Nidification. The Spotted Dove breeds from the level of the plains up to at least 8,000 ft. in the Himalayas and possibly even at higher elevations than this. In the plains it breeds practically all the year round, and in the higher portions of its hill-range from March to September. In Bengal undoubtedly March to June and, again, September and October, are the principal breeding-months, but Cripps found them breeding in Furredpore from November to May also. I think, however, that during the height of the rainy season most birds stop breeding, though I once found a Spotted Dove seated on her very exposed nest in August, during unusually heavy rain which had soaked her, the nest, and all its surroundings through and through. In Kumaon, Thompson found them breeding from February to October; in the Konkan, Vidal got nests from October to April, and Cardew says that it nests in the Neilgherries from February to September.

It would appear therefore that it breeds in the hills during the whole time of its visit to them, and that in the plains it only stops breeding during the height of the rains in the rainy climates and during the season of extreme drought in the drier climates.

It does not breed in the interior of heavy forests and not often in open country which is devoid of a plentiful growth of trees; short of this it may be found breeding anywhere and everywhere. In gardens, and even in verandahs and outhouses; in small trees growing in rice, wheat, or other grain-fields; in orchards, in bushes, in scrub-jungle, or in uninhabited tracts on the borders of forests or thinly-wooded plains.

Mr. R. Thompson, writing from Kumaon, gives the following very interesting note on the breeding of this Dove: "The Spotted Dove is the most common and abundant of the family in the lower Himalayas, remaining on the lower hills throughout the winter.

"The nest is composed of from about fifty to one hundred and fifty small twigs and roots laid loosely together, that portion of a bush or tree being selected for the purpose which will give the broadest foundation, no matter whether it be the intertwining of many slender branches or a hollow in a thicker one.

"The breeding-season commences as early as February in the warmer valleys and continues to the end of October. Two or even more broods are reared during the season.

"The eggs are pure white and two in number and nearly perfectly oval. The young remain in the nest until able to fly, when they come out and perch on the branches, but are easily frightened out of the nesting-tree by the approach of a person, and not being able to sustain a protracted flight can easily be taken if followed up.

"The female sits very close on her nest, but if forced from it she will at times fly, or in fact throw herself down upon the ground in front of the intruder, and will then mimic before his astonished gaze all the actions and efforts of a wounded bird trying to escape its pursuers, and thus endeavour to turn him from its nest.

"In their selection of sites for their nests these birds show very little intelligence, suiting themselves to the first place they find handy, often amongst old furniture in the verandah of a house, cornices of old buildings, low hedges and bushes, or even the lopped trunk of a tree if a flat surface is left sufficient to place the nest on, and often in the most exposed situations, when the wretched birds are sure to pay the penalty of their imprudence."

Many people, when they notice in what exposed positions the nests are placed, have wondered at the great abundance of this little Dove, but though only two eggs are laid at a time, the hen-bird invariably has two or three broods in the year and often five or six, so that if but one pair escape final destruction in every two or three years it is enough to replace the deaths amongst adult birds, whilst if but one pair escape every year there would very soon be no room for any other species of bird in India.

The Spotted Dove is one of those birds which often makes its nest close to that of the nest of some bird of prey—a most curious trait; and as neither themselves nor their young are ever molested it would really seem as if there was some law of nature governing this habit and protecting the weaker bird from the normal habits of the stronger. The nest of this Dove has been found in the same tree as that of the Laggar, a Falcon which preys more upon Pigeons and Doves than any other bird. It has also been found breeding either in the same tree or close beside one occupied by the

Turumpti (*Falco chiquera*), by the Fish-Eagles (*Poliaetus ichthyaetus* and *humilis*), and also in a bush under a tree in which a family of young Black-winged Kites (*Elanus coeruleus*) were being brought up.

Whatever this law may be, however, it is not obeyed by the Crow, who is a law unto himself, or the Magpie (*Dendrocitta*)—an outcast amongst birds and a destroyer of all life feebler than himself, and one of the worst egg-thieves in India.

The eggs are, of course, only two in number although, long ago, Tickell recorded them as numbering "two to six." Equally of course they are pure white and the normal Dove-shaped oval.

Oates, in Hume's *Nests and Eggs*, gives the average of thirty-three eggs as being 1.06 by .82 in. (= 26.9 by 20.8 mm.), the extremes in length as .95 and 1.17 in. (= 24.1 and 29.7 mm.), and in breadth .75 and .95 in. (= 19.0 and 24.1 mm.).

Mr. C. R. S. Pitman sends me the measurements of a large series which averaged the same as Oates's in length but measures .85 in. in breadth (= 21.6 mm.). His extreme measurements are, however, well within those given by Oates. A hundred eggs measured by myself give the same average in size as given by Mr. Pitman and does not extend the maximum or minimum given by Oates.

The Spotted Dove is one of the most familiar and widespread of birds in India over all but the most bare and desert portions, such as parts of the Deccan and Sind. It is a bird that is very intolerant of thirst, so that a plentiful supply of water is an absolute necessity, and, given this, it will be found practically everywhere, plains and hills alike, at any rate up to some 8,000 ft. Where water is plentiful there also will be found trees and vegetation in sufficiency, for the Spotted Dove does not require heavy forest in which to hide, and though it does not shun the vicinity of such, it will be met with more frequently in cultivated country, especially if this be well supplied with groves and trees.

If not persecuted it is a most confiding little bird, and will run about on the ground close to human beings without taking fright. It is much given to haunting roads and village-paths, and one can hardly travel many hundred yards along such without coming across one or more pairs searching for grain in the droppings and dust. They are nearly always in pairs and, though the two birds may keep some little distance apart, their constant sweet "coos" are uttered and answered every few minutes; and when they do fly away it is always together, the nearest tree generally offering them a convenient perch where they can sit side by side until the interloper has passed and they can once more return to their quest for food. Their "coo" is a very soft melodious tone, difficult to set forth in writing, but which Blyth has tried to express by the words "oot-raow-oo oot-raow-oo," and others by the syllables "ku-krroo-ku," repeated two or three times.

During the heat of the day and also in the early mornings and evenings in Bengal they resort much to the mango-groves which are to be found in the vicinity of most villages, and during these hours the place is full of the melody of their calls, for they are by no means sparing of their voice. When disturbed on the ground they rise very straight into the air for a few feet, making a great fluster and clapping of wings in so doing, and then flap quickly away with tail widespread so as to show the white on each side. Once well off the wing-beats are few and the tail-feathers less spread, but the flight is seldom continued far.

A pair of these Doves once built in the verandah of my house, selecting the top of one of the verandah pillars for their nesting-site, and soon became so tame that they would not move more than a foot or two out of the way of the servants and others using the verandah. Both birds would come down to the table when the dish-washer was carrying on his work, and feed on any of the scraps thrown to them as his duties proceeded. I noticed then that these Doves, by nature almost entirely grain and seed feeders, would eat almost anything thrown to them—bread, potatoes, cabbage, and indeed almost anything but meat and fish.

They were a most loving little couple, and in the rare intervals when they had no eggs to hatch or greedy young ones to attend, they always roosted close side by side on the top of the pillar next the one on which was their nest.

Cripps and others say that this bird never uses the same nest twice, but this pair used the same many times, of course repairing it on each occasion, but never starting a new one, though there were many other verandah pillars quite as convenient. As parents both birds were equally excellent and attentive, sharing all duties fairly, in addition to which the cock-bird was very attentive to his little wife, often taking her up special dainties from the table below.

They are very easy birds to keep in confinement, and though they quarrel very badly amongst themselves or with other Doves, are not so pugnacious with other birds. They are also much more active and interesting than the Green Pigeons, and breed freely, even if kept in comparatively small cages.

The Indians feed them principally on *suttoo*, a mixture of meal and water, and on rice, both husked and unhusked; but they will eat any grain freely, and should also be given any fruit which may be obtainable. Above all, however, they should be supplied with an ample bath daily, for they love splashing and washing in a shallow pan with about an inch of water in it. When wild they seem to relish alike a dust-bath or a swill in some shallow streamlet.

They are extremely good to eat, and, in India, where it is so often hard to get a change from the ubiquitous fowl, many a Spotted Dove goes into the pot, and having regaled the eye and the ear of the camper-out in the morning, ministers to his wants in yet another way in the evening.

(42) STREPTOPELIA SURATENSIS TIGRINA (Temm.).

THE MALAY OR BURMESE SPOTTED DOVE.

(PLATE 21.)

Columba tigrina Temm. and Knip, Pig., I pl. 43 (1808-11).

Columbina inornata Gray, List Gallinae B.M., p. 13 (1844).

Turtur chinensis Gray, Gen. B., II p. 472 (1844).

Columba chinensis Thienem, Fortplf., p. 59.

Turtur suratensis Blyth, J.A.S.B., XV p. 372; Stuart Baker, J.B.N.H.S., X p. 360; Venning, ib., XXI p. 631.

Turtur tigrinus Blyth, J.A.S.B., XXIV p. 480; id. ib., XXXIX pt. 2, p. 332; Ball, Str. Feath., I p. 80; Hume, Nests and Eggs, p. 506; id., Str. Feath., II p. 269; Blyth and Wald., B. Burma, p. 145; Hume, Str. Feath., III p. 164; Armstrong, ib., IV p. 337; Oates, ib., V p. 164; Hume and Dav., ib., VI p. 422; Anderson, Yun-nan Exp., Av., p. 665; Hume, Str. Feath., VIII p. 110; id., Cat. no. 795, bis; Bingh., Str. Feath., IX p. 194; Hume and Inglis, ib., p. 258; Oates, ib., X p. 235; id., B. Burma, II p. 290; Hume, Str. Feath., XI p. 299; Oates, in Hume's Nests and Eggs, 2nd ed., II p. 356; Salvadori, Cat. B.M., XXI p. 440; Blanf., Avi. Brit. I., IV p. 44; Harington, B. Burma, p. 68; Macdonald, J.B.N.H.S., XVII p. 496; H. R. Baker, ib., p. 760; Mears, ib., XVIII p. 86; Harington, ib., XIX pp. 306 and 365; Allan, ib., p. 523; Harington, ib., XX p. 1010; Hopwood, ib., XXI p. 1214; Robinson, J.F.M.S. 1905, p. 57.

Turtur tigrina Hume, Str. Feath., I p. 461.

Spilopelia tigrina Sundev., Méth. Nat. Av. Disp. Tent., p. 100 (1872); Sharpe, Hand-List, I p. 80; Oates, Cat. Eggs B.M., I p. 99.

Vernacular Names. *Tekukor*, Malayan; *Gyo, Gyo-lĕ-byouk*, Burmese; *Daotu*, Cachari; *Inruigu*, Naga.; *Vohkurup*, Kuki.

Description.—*Adult male.* Similar to *S. s. suratensis*, but differing in the following respects: The rufous spots on the upper-back are absent, and those on the wing-coverts, scapulars, and innermost secondaries are either wholly wanting or are only faintly shown; the vinaceous spots on the wing are absent, though the outer webs of the median coverts are more or less a pale vinous-brown. The grey greater coverts of *suratensis*, are replaced by pale vinous-brown with merely grey edges in *tigrina*.

Below the chin is less albescent and often almost concolorous with the breast; there is less albescent on the abdomen, which with the under tail-coverts is often a fulvous-vinous with no white at all.

Measurements. On an average the Burmese Spotted Dove is decidedly bigger than the Indian bird. Total length about 13 in. (= 330 mm.), wing 5.40 in. (= 137.1 mm.) to 6.05 in. (= 155.1 mm.), and with an average of

THE MALAY SPOTTED DOVE—*STREPTOPELIA S. TIGRINA*

($\frac{1}{2}$ Nat. Size.)

PLATE 21

5.70 in. (= 144.8 mm.), as against an average of 5.55 in. (= 141 mm.) in the largest local form of the Indian bird.

The bill is also slightly larger, being .65 in. (= 16.5 mm.) from the front against .55 in. (= 14 mm.) in the Indian Spotted Dove, and about .9 in. (= 22.8 mm.) from the gape.

Colours of soft parts. Iris reddish-brown, or bright hazel with a reddish outer-ring; bill dark horny or slaty-brown, sometimes nearly black; edges of eyelid and narrow bare orbital-skin reddish-lake; legs and feet dull red, reddish-purple, or deep coral-red.

The Sumbawa birds are said to have the irides pale bright yellow (Guillem, *P.Z.S.* 1885, p. 510) and the birds from Menado and Talisse islands brown ones (Buttik., *Notes Leyd. Mus.*, IX p. 76).

Female. Similar to the male.

Measurements. A trifle smaller than the male with an average wing-measurement of about 5.55 in. (= 141 mm.) and the other measurements in proportion.

Young differ from the adult in the same way as the young of the Indian Spotted Dove differ from the adult of that subspecies; but, judging from the few young specimens in the British Museum Collection, the young of the Burmese bird are far more rufous in their upper-plumage than are the young of the Indian one.

Nestling. At first a naked black-skinned object, with sparse yellow-buff down here and there, gradually becoming thicker as the bird grows older.

Distribution. From Chittagong, Looshai Hills, Manipur, and North Cachar, through Burma, Yun-nan, Siam, Cochin-China, the whole of the Malay Peninsula, and Sumatra as far south as Timor and the Moluccas, where Salvadori considers it a winter-visitor only.

The birds from Chittagong, the Chittagong Hill Tracts, and the Looshai Hills are all typical *tigrina*, but as I have already shown, the birds from Manipur are intermediate though the majority are nearer the Burmese than the Indian form, whilst those from the North Cachar Hills are either typical Burmese birds or very nearly so.

The birds from the Sunda Islands and especially from Java, Lombock, and Timor, are said to be somewhat larger, with a wing averaging 5.9 in. (= 150 mm.), but with the large amount of material available for examination in the British Museum I cannot differentiate between the birds of these islands and further north.

Nidification. All writers agree that this bird breeds practically all the year round. Macdonald, Major H. R. Baker, Oates, and Harington say that this is the case, and no one seems to have selected any special months as the ones in which most eggs may be taken.

Oates, writing from Upper Pegu, remarks that this Dove "is common everywhere except on the hills, where I did not meet with it. It seems to breed all the year round." Again, writing from Wau in Lower Pegu, he adds: "The nest of this bird is to be found all the year through."

The nest is like that of the Indian Spotted Dove, a very flimsy concern made of fine twigs and coarse grasses, with occasionally a few roots and weed-stems added to the others. These are all interlaced to form a rough and very transparent platform 5 or 6 in. in diameter, which is placed in any shrub, bush, sapling, clump of bamboos or cane-brake a few feet from the ground, never over some 20 ft. or so, generally lower and sometimes as low as 3 ft. At this height Mr. J. Darling found a nest built on the upper surface of a large-leaved tree growing on a range of hills east of Tavoy.

More curious even than this is the finding of two nests of the Malayan Turtle-Dove on the ground by Mr. C. W. Allan. Writing from Henzada in Burma, he says: "Yesterday, the 3rd March, I found two nests of the Common Dove (*Turtur tigrinus*) built on the ground.

"The first I found in the morning whilst inspecting a timber cutting in the Kyangin forest reserve. It was on the ground, right out in the open, under a teak tree and was of the ordinary kind, just a few twigs collected on some fallen leaves. There was no attempt at concealing the nest. There were two eggs in this nest, freshly laid.

"The second nest I found the same evening. It was placed at the foot of a catechu (*Acacia catechu*) tree not far from my camp. The bird flew off as I approached the tree. There were two eggs in this nest, also freshly laid.

"In all my wanderings in Burma and India I have never before come across Doves nesting on the ground and cannot account for these, as there were lots of bushes and trees about to build on."

The eggs of this bird cannot be distinguished from those of the Indian Spotted Dove.

The eggs recorded in Hume's *Nests and Eggs* varied in breadth from .76 in. (= 19.3 mm.) to .88 in. (= 22.3 mm.), and the series in the Museum average 1.18 by .86 in. (= 30 by 21.8 mm.) whilst the extremes in length are 1.05 and 1.25 in. (= 26.6 and 31.7 mm.) and in breadth .8 and .9 in. (= 20.3 and 22.8 mm.).

Macdonald's eggs average a good deal smaller than this and he records the measurements as 1.05 by .88 in. (= 26.6 by 22.3 mm.), but it will be noticed that his eggs are broader than those in the Museum series.

The eggs in my collection all come within the limits given above.

The Malayan Turtle-Dove differs but little in its habits from its Indian cousin. It is perhaps on the whole more of a jungle and forest-bird, and it certainly does not seem to ascend the hills to so great a height, not commonly being met with much above 4,000 ft. At the same time it does not haunt jungles and forests unless these are broken up with open land, either cultivated or barren, for it is a bird which generally seeks its food on the ground and the greater part of this consists of grain and seeds which are obtained in the cultivated areas.

Robinson's remarks on this bird's habits in the Malay States are worth quoting. He writes: "This bird is found in much the same situations as the Barred Ground Dove, but is less tied to cultivation than that species. It is widely distributed throughout the Peninsula, and is particularly abundant in the sandy wastes and casuarinas that fringe large portions of the East Coast. It is also very common in Negri Semlilan, especially in the Linggi district, but is rarer in Selangor and Perak. In habits it is less terrestrial than *Geopelia striata* and is much shyer. It is also more gregarious, and at certain times of the year is found in flocks that may number as many as thirty or forty individuals, though this is exceptional. It is a common cage-bird with all classes of natives."

Over the whole of its range this character for shyness given it by Robinson seems to hold good, and nowhere do I find any record of its being the familiar village-bird that the Common Spotted Dove so often is. At the same time in some parts of northern Burma, in the more populous, cultivated areas, it is comparatively tame and confiding.

It has the same habit of frequenting roads and village-paths in search of food as has the previous bird, and, like that, when disturbed, gets up with the same fluster of wing and expanded tail, and also like that bird makes for the nearest tree for refuge. Both these subspecies have a predilection for sitting on dead trees or on dead branches of live ones, and may often be seen in cultivated clearings, in which the few trees left standing are all ringed and dead, perched in numbers high up on their leafless boughs.

As a rule they go about in pairs, and though sociable and fond of collecting in numbers in their feeding-haunts, they are not generally considered gregarious in the true sense of the word.

(43) STREPTOPELIA CAMBAYENSIS (Gm.).

THE LITTLE BROWN DOVE.

(PLATE 22.)

Cambayan Turtle Lath., Syn., II 2, p. 652, no. 47 (1783).

Columba cambayensis Gm., Syst. Nat., I 2, p. 779, no. 49 (1788); Lath., Ind. Orn., II p. 609.

Turtur senegalensis Blyth, J.A.S.B., XIV p. 873 (part) (1845); id., Cat. B.M.A.S.B., p. 237; Jerdon, B.I., III p. 479; Blanf., E. Persia, II p. 276; Davidson and Wen., Str. Feath., VII p. 86; Hume, ib., VIII pp. 66, 110, and 463; Vidal, ib., IX p. 74; Barnes, ib., pp. 219 and 408; Butler, ib., p. 420; Reid, ib., X p. 60; Davidson, ib., p. 320; Dav., ib., p. 408; Barnes, B. Bom., p. 291; Oates, in Hume's Nests and Eggs, 2nd ed., II p. 351; Sharpe, Yarkand Misc. Av., p. 118; Barnes, J.B.N.H.S., V p. 331.

Turtur cambayensis Bp., Con. Av., II p. 62; Jerdon, B.I., III p. 478; Stoliczka, J.A.S.B., XXXVII pt. 2 p. 66; id. ib., XLI pt. 2, p. 248; Hume, Str. Feath., I p. 218; Adam, ib., p. 390; Butler, ib., IV p. 3; Fairbank, ib., p. 262; id. ib., V p. 408; Ball, ib., VII p. 224; Salvadori, Cat. B.M., XXI p. 45; Blanf., Avi. Brit. I., IV p. 45; Marshall, J.B.N.H.S., XV p. 352; Bourdillon, ib., XVI p. 3; Fulton, ib., p. 60; Osmaston, ib., XVII p. 489; Ward, ib., p. 943; Perreau, ib., XIX p. 919; Fenton, ib., XX p. 221; Whitehead, ib., p. 967; Moss-King, ib., XXI p. 100; Whitehead, ib., p. 168; D'Abreu, ib., p. 1167; Dewar, Birds of the Plains, p. 125; Aitken, Com. B. Bom., p. 151.

Stigmatopelia cambayensis Sharpe, Hand-List, I p. 80; Oates, Cat. Eggs B.M., I p. 100.

Vernacular Names. *Chota fakhta, Perki, Tortra fakhta, Panduk*, Hin.; *Chitti bella guwa, Sowata guwa*, Tel.; *Touta-pora*, Tamil.

Description.—*Adult male.* Whole head and neck a beautiful lilac-pink, darkest on the crown and fore-head, and palest on chin and throat; a patch of black feathers on either side of the neck, meeting in a narrow gorget below the throat, each feather bifurcate and broadly tipped with bright rufous; back, scapulars with lesser and median coverts adjoining them, innermost secondaries, rump, upper tail-coverts, and central rectrices pale earthy-brown, sometimes slightly rufous; the two pair of feathers next the central rectrices greyish-brown with small white tips, the remaining pairs black at the base and white on the terminal half, the white also extending on the outermost pair down the outer web; remaining wing-coverts french-grey, the greater edged slightly paler; edge of wing and winglet blackish-brown; primaries brown, three or four of the outer ones edged pale; outer secondaries dark slaty-brown, a fine narrow brown edge to some of them; breast, shading from the chestnut of the collar to a vinous-pink, and from

THE LITTLE BROWN DOVE—*STREPTOPELIA CAMBAYENSIS.*

(½ Nat. Size—Male on left, female on right.)

PLATE 22

that into white on the abdomen and under tail-coverts; under wing-coverts, axillaries, and flanks dark dove-grey.

Measurements. Length 10 to 11 in. (= 254 to 280 mm.); wing from 4.75 in. (= 120.6 mm.) to 5.15 in. (= 130.8 mm.) and averaging about 4.95 in. (= 125.7 mm.); tail 4.5 in. to 5.2 in. (= 114.3 to 132.1 mm.); bill at front .5 in. (= 12.7 mm.) and from gape about .7 in. (= 17.7 mm.), tarsus about .8 in (= 20.3 mm.).

Colours of soft parts. Irides dark hazel-brown with an inner conspicuous ring of white; bill dark horny-brown, often nearly black; legs and feet pink-lake, pale scarlet or deep flesh-colour, the claws black.

Female. Similar to the male.

Measurements. According to Salvadori the female of this and the closely allied *senegalensis*, from Africa, are a trifle smaller than the male, but I cannot discover any such difference from the large series I have examined, though probably the female is more slender and lighter.

Colours of soft parts, as in the male.

Young are similar to the adult, but have no signs of the gorget of black-and-red feathers; the head is duller, more brown, and less vinous-pink, and the scapulars and wing-coverts are narrowly tipped with pale dull rufous and subedged with a black band; the feathers of the upper-back are also obsoletely barred with darker. The breast is duller and less vinous-pink and the grey feathers of the wing are margined with rufous and submargined with dark grey.

Young at an older stage than this have narrow whitish-rufous bars showing on wing-coverts and back, and also sometimes show the faintest indications of narrow bars on the breast. After the autumn-moult these all disappear and the gorget appears first in blackish spots, the black base of the feathers showing through the plumage before the rufous spots are developed.

Nestling, in down. A dirty yellowish-fawn above and below.

Distribution. Practically the whole of India west of Calcutta and a line drawn thence west of the rivers Hugli, Ganges, and Kosi. But even west of these rivers the Little Brown Dove is rare in all the very wet districts of eastern Bengal, and I believe only wanders into these during the dry months. Inglis does not report it as occurring in the Madhubani district of Behar, but it certainly occurs in other districts of that province, and it is found in Chutia Nagpur, though not commonly except in the comparatively dry districts of Hazaribagh and Ranchi. It is generally said to be absent from the Malabar coast, but Bourdillon notes that it is to be found in the dry region of the extreme south, not far from Cape Comorin, though by no means common even there. It is not found in Ceylon, but occurs in the Andamans, according to Osmaston, though he himself did not meet with it there, and it is probably extremely rare, or possibly the occurrences are only individuals which have escaped from captivity. It is not recorded thence by Hume, and Kloss and Butler also did not meet with it. Outside India it is found in Turkestan, Arabia, south Persia, Baluchistan, and Afghanistan.

Nidification. Over the greater part of its range the Little Brown Dove breeds throughout the year, the months February to April, and again September to November, being, perhaps, more favoured than the rest. In the hills, to which this bird is only a summer-visitor in the higher parts, it breeds more or less continuously from April to October. How many times a year these little Doves indulge in a family it is impossible to guess; all have two or three broods, and some of them probably have as many as five or six, for, with strict attention to business, there is time for this each year. On an average the nest may be said to take a week to build, the eggs a fortnight to hatch, and the young ones a month to bring up and turn into the world to fend for themselves, so that in a couple of months the parent birds are quite ready to start their domestic cares once more. For the second brood the old nest suffices, and in some instances even a third is brought up in it after which, if the female is still intent on laying, she usually turns to another site.

As regards the site itself, the bird is not hard to please. Most nests are placed in bushes, small saplings, tangles of cane, briers, or creeping plants; some rest on boughs open to all the world to inspect, and many are placed somewhere or other inside human habitations. Nests on the tops of masonry pillars of verandahs are common, others are placed on the walls or on beams across the ceiling. Mr. A. Anderson had a pair build on the corner rope of his tent whilst in camp; the rolled up blinds—or "*chics*" as they are called in India—used to keep the sun out of the verandahs are favourite sites for their nests, and I have even heard of one pair who built their nest in a dining-room of a big house between a picture and the wall from which it was hanging.

The history of a pair of birds who built their nest on the top of one of these "*chics*" is told by Dewar in his *Birds of the Plains*. This little pair built their first nest, and reared two young, on the top of a "*chic*" whilst it was rolled up, and when it was let down in the hot weather they stuck to the site and actually built another nest and hatched out three more broods of young ones, and after this a pair of domestic Pigeons, whose eggs had been substituted for a pair of their own.

Perhaps more strange than any of the above nests are some which have been found actually on the ground. The first record of this kind is that of a nest found by Mr. B. Aitken "on the ground, at the top of a ditch, in a plain covered with short grass, either spear-grass, or some very fine sort like spear-grass. Not a stick or straw had been carried to the spot, but the grass, as it grew, had been worked into a very neat nest."

More recently Mr. Fenton has recorded in the Bombay Natural History Society's *Journal*, that he "found, some years ago at Chorwar in Khatiawar, the nest of *Turtur cambayensis* (the Little Brown Dove) placed on the ground, on a large bare plot surrounded by the ordinary Indian Cactus. The nest contained two young birds."

Considering the amount of vermin, winged and four footed, which swarms everywhere in India, it seems incredible that any birds could ever reach maturity under such circumstances, for most ground-birds are adepts at concealing their eggs, or these latter are adaptive in coloration.

Needless to say, the eggs are always two in number. It may be that on rare occasions three are laid (*vide* Jerdon and others), and sometimes but one is laid when the birds have already reared two or three broods. They are white, smooth in texture, with a slight gloss, a stout shell for their size, and in shape they are a regular oval, both ends subequal in size and shape and often somewhat lengthened.

All the eggs I have seen come within the dimensions given by Oates in Hume's *Nests and Eggs*, and their average is the same as his. The measurements he gives are as follows: "In length the eggs vary from 0.88 to 1.18 in. (= 22.3 to 30.0 mm.) and in breadth from 0.75 to 0.90 in. (= 19.0 to

22.8 mm.)"; but the average of forty eggs is 1.01 in., barely, by 0.86 in. full (= 25.6 by 21.9 mm.).

They breed up to at least 5,000 ft. in the Himalayas.

The Little Brown Dove is a resident, non-migratory bird, but like many others of this family, moves about locally according to the abundance or otherwise of its food-supply, and also up and down the mountains to some extent under the influence of the various seasons.

On the whole, it is a bird of drier climates than is the Spotted Dove, far more tolerant of heat and drought combined and also more restricted to open country. In its habits it is just as confiding and tame as the last bird, and resorts regularly to gardens and compounds and the immediate vicinity of villages, where it runs about on the ground picking up grain and the various seeds upon which it chiefly feeds. If not harassed or frightened it will hardly move out of the way of the children as they play about, and when forced to move, merely flies to the nearest bare branch of a tree, where it sits and "coos" until it once more returns to the ground to feed.

Its flight is much like that of the Spotted Dove: they rise with a clatter and much flapping of the wing straight up from the ground for two or three feet, and then more quietly fly straight away. Once on the wing they are capable of flying with great speed, but normally fly rather leisurely and with slow beats, alternating with short sailing movements.

When courting, their actions on the wing are very pretty: as a rule they perch high up on some bare branch, and after much billing and cooing to his little mate, the male suddenly launches himself high into the air, his wings meeting over his head in loud claps as he mounts higher and higher, and then there is a sudden stoppage of the noise and he sinks slowly with widespread wings in gradually lessening spirals back to the side of his wife.

These birds probably pair for life and are most affectionate to one another and very faithful. They are also excellent parents and share all duties between them, the hen generally sitting by day when they have eggs, and the cock by night, and the latter also constantly feeds and attends to his wife when she is thus employed. But though in their own family circle they show such admirable traits, outside they share in full with the other members of their tribe the faults of greediness and quarrelsomeness.

They are favourite cage-birds and constantly utter their soft *kroo kroo* in captivity. Their voice has been well described as "low, subdued and musical, a dissyllabic sound, repeated four or five times successively."

They drink regularly in the mornings and possibly also at midday before their siesta, and again in the evenings, but there seems to be no evidence on this point.

They are excellent eating, but are sometimes said to be rather more dry than the Spotted Dove, though similar to it in taste.

(44) STREPTOPELIA RISORIA RISORIA (Linn.).

THE INDIAN RING-DOVE.

Turtur indicus Aldrovandus, p. 510 (1637).

Columba risoria Linn., Syst. Nat., I p. 285 (1766).

Turtur douraca Hodg., in Gray's Zool. Misc., p. 85 (1844) (descr. nulla); Salvadori, Cat. B.M., XXI p. 430; Newman, Avi. Mag. 1896, p. 321.

Turtur risorius Strick., Ann. and Mag. N.H., XIII p. 38; Blyth, J.A.S.B., XIV p. 870; id., Cat. B.M.A.S.B., p. 235; id., J.A.S.B., XXIV p. 261; Jerdon, B.I., III p. 481; Stoliczka, J.A.S.B., XXXVII pt. 2, p. 67; id. ib., LXI pt. 2, p. 248; Godw-Aus., ib., XXXIX pt. 2, 272; Hume, Str. Feath., I p. 218; Adam, ib., p. 390; Hume, Nests and Eggs, p. 506; Blanf., E. Persia, II p. 270; Butler, Str. Feath., IV p. 3; Fairbank, ib., p. 462; id. ib., V p. 409; Butler, ib., VII p. 171; Ball, ib., p. 224; Cripps, ib., p. 297; Hume, ib., VIII p. 110; id., Cat. no. 796; Vidal, Str. Feath., VIII p. 173; Scully, ib., p. 342; Vidal, ib., IX p. 75; Butler, ib., p. 420; Barnes, ib., p. 458; Legge, B. Cey., p. 702; Reid, Str. Feath., X p. 60; Davison, ib., p. 408; Oates, in Hume's Nests and Eggs, 2nd ed., II p. 357; Barnes, B. Bom., p. 291; Hume, Str. Feath., XI p. 299; Aitken, Com. B. Bom., p. 152; Dewar, Birds of the Plains, p. 124; Blanf., Avi. Brit. I., IV p. 46; Barnes, J.B.N.H.S., V p. 332; Stuart Baker, ib., X p. 360; Inglis, ib., XI p. 474; Wilson, ib., XII p. 639; Inglis, ib., XIV p. 562; Marshall, ib., XV p. 353; Bourdillon, ib., XVI p. 3; Fulton, ib., p. 60; Dewar, ib., p. 495; Nicol Cumming, ib., p. 691; Ward, ib., XVII p. 943; Perreau, ib., XIX p. 919; Whitehead, ib., XX p. 967; Moss-King, ib., XXI p. 100; Whitehead, ib., p. 168; D'Abreu, ib., p. 1167.

Turtur stoliczkae Hume, Str. Feath., II p. 519; id. ib., III pp. 217 and 415; Scully, ib., IV p. 178; Sharpe, Yarkand Misc. Av., p. 117.

Streptopelia dourica Sharpe, Hand-List, I p. 79; Oates, Cat. Eggs B.M., I p. 96.

Vernacular Names. *Dhor fakhta, Perki, Punduk, Gugi*, Hin.; *Daola* or *Doula*, Hin. Behar; *Kalthak, Kakalaki, Pankghugu*, Bengali; *Pitha hola*, Mahr.; *Pedda-bella guwa*, Tel.; *Cally-praa*, Tamil, Ceylon; *Daotu gophu*, Cachari; *Jungle Kapoth*, Biluchi; *Pakktah*, Turki.

Description.—*Adult male.* Whole head and neck lilac-grey, the throat paler and the chin sometimes albescent; in some birds the fore-head is paler than the crown, as are also the sides of the head; a narrow collar of white succeeded by a broader one of black, a few of these latter feathers being very narrowly edged with white, forming a third very narrow and indefinite band, which extends with the others to form a nuchal collar about two-thirds round the neck; upper-parts from shoulders to tail and including inner wing-coverts pale brown, varying from fawn-brown to pale earthy according to state of plumage. Central tail-feathers pale brown, but often more or less suffused with ashy-grey; succeeding pair of feathers more grey and with narrow white tips, the outermost pair black at the base and white on the terminal half and edge of outer web, intermediate feathers grading from one to the other. Outer wing-coverts pale grey, gradually changing into the colour of the back; primaries dark brown edged pale whitish-brown, secondaries more grey, finely edged with whitish. Breast lilac like the head, gradually changing to pale dove-grey on the abdomen and to darker french-grey on the under tail-coverts; flanks, axillaries and under wing-coverts pale silver-grey; under aspect of primaries light brown and of secondaries greyish-white.

Measurements. Total length about 13 in. (= 330 mm.); wing 6.25 in. to 7.10 in. (= 158.7 to 180.3 mm.) and averaging 6.65 in. (= 168.8 mm.) in Indian birds; bill at front about .7 in. (= 17.8 mm.) and from gape nearly 1 in. (= 25.0 mm.); tarsus about 1 in. (= 25.4), and tail varying from 4.6 in. (= 116.8 mm.) to 5.5 in. (= 140.0 mm.).

Colours of soft parts. Irides lake-red, red, or crimson; bill almost black; edge of eyelid red, and narrow orbital skin round eye white, pale livid, or pale slaty-grey, *never* yellow; legs dark pinkish-red, crimson-red, or dull purple, the claws almost black.

Female. Similar to the male.

Measurements. From the series I have examined it is impossible to determine that the female is any smaller than the male, but aviculturists claim that the female is distinctly the lighter build of the two sexes and easily recognizable.

Young are browner and less vinaceous below; the wing-coverts are edged with pale sandy-brown, and there are narrow dark bars on the breast.

Nestling, in down. A dirty pale yellowish-white.

Birds from China would seem to run very large, a male in the British Museum series having a wing of no less than 7.40 in. (= 188 mm.); a female, however, from the same place has one of only 6.75 in. (= 171.4 mm.), a size exceeded by several unsexed Indian birds. Again, a female from Japan has a wing of only 6.30 in. (= 160 mm.), which is practically the same in size as that of our smallest Indian specimen.

The colour does not seem to vary geographically, though bleached birds are, of course, much paler than those in freshly-moulted plumage.

As regards the name which the Indian Turtle-Dove must bear, there has been a great deal of discussion and many opinions given. In 1903 Dresser, referring to the synonymy of certain Palaearctic birds, attempted to show that neither the name *douraca* of Hodgson nor *risoria* of Linnaeus could be used for this bird—*risoria* presumably on the strength of the oft-repeated assertion that Linnaeus only intended this name to apply to the domestic bird, and *douraca* because that name is a later one than *decaocta* of Frivaldsky, who gave the Balkan bird this name in 1838.

An examination of Linnaeus, however, shows that the bird he calls *risoria* is that which Aldrovandus named *Turtur indicus* in 1637. On p. 510 of Vol. 15 of the *Works of Aldrovandi* there is an excellent plate of the Turtle-Dove, and on pp. 511 *et seq.* there is the usual full account of habitat, habits, etc. etc. Here Aldrovandus gives India as the country from which it comes, adding many other places, and amongst other items observing that it is most common amongst the Tartars.

Further Linnaeus quotes Albin and Brisson, both of whom give India as the bird's habitat, and finally Linnaeus himself simply states "Habitat in India."

There cannot, therefore, be the slightest doubt that Linnaeus meant the name *risoria* to be applied to the wild Dove which had the headquarters of its habitat in India.

In the *Aviculturist Magazine* Newman again refers to the name by which this Dove should be known, and after showing why *decaocta* must be accepted for the Balkan bird named by Frivaldsky, proceeds to show that *douraca* must stand for our Indian bird. He does not, however, attempt any reference to Aldrovandus, Brisson, and Linnaeus, but merely states as a fact that *risorius* can only be applied to the domestic form. I cannot, myself, find any constant distinguishing characteristics between the east European and the Indian bird, but if the former is worthy of separation it will stand as *Streptopelia risoria decaocta* whilst our bird will remain *S. r. risoria*.

Distribution. The Indian Ring-Dove is found practically throughout India and Ceylon except in the wettest, most heavily-forested portions of the eastern Himalayas, and from parts of the Malabar Coast. It is common in eastern Bengal in the open country and is fairly so in western Assam in the cultivated plains portion, but becomes much more rare in the extreme east and in Cachar and Sylhet. In Chittagong, I think, but am not sure, that it is replaced by the Burmese Ring-Dove. The exact dividing line between the two subspecies, of which the latter has but recently been distinguished, has not yet been definitely settled either in regard to the Indian or the Chinese borders. It is quite certain, however, that the Indian form does not occur in Burma.

This bird is probably entirely absent from the greater part of the Malabar Coast, as Davidson only once met with it in the extreme east of Kanara, and Bourdillon says it is only found in the dry stretch of country near to Cape Comorin. In Cachar and to the east of this I think it is but a rare straggler; Inglis hardly ever saw it in the plains, and I do not think I saw a dozen specimens in the hills in as many years.

It ascends the Himalayas up to some 8,000 to 9,000 feet, but is not resident in the higher hills much over 4,000 ft. Outside Indian limits it extends as far as Turkey in Europe and throughout the intervening countries, being replaced in Palestine, Egypt, and northern Africa by other subspecies.

Nidification. The Indian Ring-Dove breeds throughout the year in the plains portion and lower hills of its habitat. To mention but one or two of its collectors, Inglis says that he has taken its eggs in every month of the year except February; Bingham says they breed practically all the year round, and Hume took the eggs in every month from December to August. In eastern Bengal very few birds breed during the most rainy months, July, August, and September, most of them nesting in the two or three months immediately preceding and succeeding the rains.

In the higher hills the breeding-season is considerably curtailed, few eggs will be found before April, or after September, and the principal months are May and June. Each pair of birds, like most other Doves, are responsible for at least two broods a year, and many of them doubtless have four or five. As a rule, I think, they generally build a new nest for each brood, but sometimes they rear two or even more in the old one, merely repairing this sufficiently for the time being.

The nest is the usual Dove's structure of sticks made into the roughest of platforms, with but little or no depression in the centre for the eggs.

Occasionally, however, it is rather better made, more cup-shaped, and with other materials, such as grass, roots, tendril and moss roots intermixed, and, according to Hume, it is sometimes *lined* regularly with grass. In diameter it may be anything between some five and seven inches, but the shape is very irregular and often a couple of inches longer one way than the other.

The nest is placed, in most cases, in thick bushes—prickly ones are especially affected—cane-brakes, bamboo clumps, or small saplings. Hume says: "The nest is placed in any bush or tree, prickly and thorny sites, such as are afforded by the *Ziziphus*, wild date, babool, *Euphorbias*, etc., being often, but by no means universally selected. Generally the nest is within 15, not very rarely within 5 ft. of the ground, but again, I *have* found it 30 or 40 ft. up in a large tree."

Mr. A. Anderson, who found the nest of the Spotted Dove on the ground, also found a nest of this bird in a similar position. He remarks: "I have discovered a curious nesting site for *Turtur risorius*, viz. *the bare ground*. On the 20th November (of the present year) whilst drawing sandy downs, covered with a low flowering grass, such as the Desert Fox delights in, a Dove was flushed from off her nest which contained a pair of fresh eggs. These clearly belonged to *T. risorius*, but not having seen the bird myself, and identification in a matter of this sort being an absolute necessity, I replaced the eggs and subsequently shot one of the parent birds.

"The nest, if such it can be styled, consisted of a few dry twigs which rested on the bare sand. There was no tree nearer than a mile, but the ground on all sides was covered with grass seeds, which constitutes the chief food of these birds; and this pair were evidently sensible enough to adapt themselves to the force of circumstances."

The site selected is generally a bush or tree in quite open country, or such as is only thinly covered with trees, never, as far as I am aware, is it placed inside heavy forest. Although not actually entering buildings for nesting purposes, as both the Spotted and Little Brown Doves do, they will often select a bush within gardens and compounds or the environment of a village. They do not take much care to place their nests in concealed positions, although they certainly, as Hume says, prefer thorny trees to others. I have seen a nest so placed in a small babool tree, standing quite by itself, that it was visible from at least two hundred yards away in every direction, yet in spite of this and of the fact that kites, crows, magpies, and other egg devourers swarmed on all sides, they had managed to hatch and rear two young ones.

Scully says that in Turkestan they often make their nests on the tops of walls.

The eggs, two in number, are of the regular smooth, rather glossy texture of all Dove's eggs; the shell rather stout in proportion to its size, and in shape the normal oval, the two ends almost equal, whilst abnormal eggs tend to be rather lengthened, and often somewhat pointed at both ends.

There is a big series of these in the British Museum Collection, of which Oates writes: "The eggs of the Indian Ring Dove in the collection possess a comparatively small amount of gloss, and measure from 1.05 to 1.25 in length, and from .85 to 1 in breadth."

My own eggs come within the extremes given by Oates, and these together with the Museum eggs average 1.16 in. by .93 in. (= 29.4 by 23.5 mm.).

The Indian Ring-Dove is an extremely common bird over the greater part of its range, but is rather capricious in its tastes, and is rare in some districts which would seem suitable for its habitat, and common in a few others which appear to be quite the reverse. On the whole, this Dove seems to require ample open country, and to dislike heavy forests and jungle and, whilst being able to stand in comfort the drought and heat of the hottest and most desert places, such as Sind, the Deccan, etc., is unable to endure a very heavy rainfall such as occurs in the Assam Valley or in the district stretching from Cachar and Sylhet towards Burma.

It is not a migratory bird in the true sense of the term, but moves about locally, according to the seasons and the food-supply obtainable, probably wandering a good deal further east during the cold weather and dry season than in the rains.

Vertically it moves upwards with the advent of the hot months, being found up to at least 8,000 ft. in the western Himalayas, probably a good deal higher, and in October it returns to the lower hills and plains. Ward speaks of it as common in Kashmir, but does not say up to what height it is found, nor unfortunately do Colonel Wilson, Davidson, and others who have so industriously worked this State.

In its habitat and haunts the Indian Ring-Dove is almost as confiding and tame as the Spotted Dove and Little Brown Dove, and it may be seen feeding round about the villages in any open patch of cultivation, whilst it constantly enters the compounds and gardens of the European houses. It runs about the ground much in the same way as do the Doves just referred to; perhaps they are not quite so tame as those Doves are, and perhaps also they are not quite so exclusively ground-birds. Besides resting on trees during the heat of the day and roosting thereon at night, they perch a good deal at odd times, and occasionally feed on fruit-trees.

Their diet is, of course, principally grain and seed, which they obtain from the cultivated country and grass-land, but they are also fruit-eaters when necessity compels.

In Turkestan, Afghanistan, etc., it appears to be quite as fond of the vicinity of human habitation as it is in India. Scully writes of it in Turkestan: "It is always to be found near villages and houses: perching on trees, or running about on the ground picking up grain and seeds. The birds are very tame, and in winter they would come right up to the door of my room at Yarkand to be fed. A regular colony of these Doves lived about the compound of the Residency at Yarkand.

A favourite trick of the Yarkand boys is to capture one of these Doves and smear its feathers all over with soot mixed up with oil. The bird is then allowed to fly away, and after a few days, when the feathers have shaken into their ordinary position, the Ring-Dove presents quite a natural appearance, only as it moves about with its fellows it looks truly a Dove in mourning."

It is a very sociable bird, and is generally found feeding in some numbers together, but it, strictly speaking, keeps more in pairs than in flocks, only collecting in these latter prior to indulging in one of their local migrations when, according to some writers, they assemble in very large numbers, often of a hundred or so more individuals.

Their flight is much the same as that of the Spotted Dove, but stronger and quicker; they rise off the ground in the same noisy manner, but, when disturbed, generally fly further before re-settling.

Their note is a trisyllabic "coo," repeated softly two or three times, and is very melodious and sweet. According to Blyth it "is quite different from that of the domestic Turtle-Dove, and may be expressed by *kookoo-koo, kookoo-koo.*"

(45) STREPTOPELIA RISORIA XANTHOCYCLA (Newman).

THE BURMESE RING-DOVE.

Turtur xanthocycla Newman, Avi. Mag. 1896, p. 321; Mears, J.B.N.H.S., XVIII, p. 86; Harington, B. Burma, p. 68.

Turtur douraca Salvadori, Cat. B.M., XXI p. 430 (part).

Turtur risorius Blanf., Avi. Brit. I., IV p. 46 (part); Anderson, Yunnan Exp., p. 666; Hume, Str. Feath., III p. 165; Wald., in Blyth's B. Burma, p. 146; Oates, Str. Feath., X p. 235; id., B. Brit. Burma, II p. 293; Hume, Str. Feath., XI p. 299 (part); Macdonald, J.B.N.H.S., XVIII p. 496.

Streptopelia dourica Sharpe, Hand-List, I p. 79 (part); Oates, Cat. Eggs B.M., I p. 96 (part).

Vernacular Name. *Gyo-lin-bya*, Burmese.

Description.—*Adult male.* "In general appearance like *T. decaocta decaocta*" (*Streptopelia risoria*), "but easily distinguished by broad yellow bare rings round the eyes" (Newman).

"The colour generally is darker and more vivid than in Indian specimens of this species, and the collar is larger and more crescentic than in ordinary *T. risorius*, and if Jerdon's measurements are founded on fresh specimens, this bird is decidedly larger. He gives 13 in. as the extreme length, but my specimen measures 14 in., its wing 7 in., and its tail 6 in." (Anderson's *Report* on the Expedition to Western Yunnan.)

There is little on record about this Dove except what has been written by Mr. Newman in the *Avicultural Magazine* already referred to; he there sums up as follows the evidence to show that the Burmese and eastern bird is different to the Indian: "The Burmese bird possesses most remarkable yellow rings of bare skin round its eyes, which are most conspicuous in the living bird. I do not know any other Turtle-Doves of any species whatever that has yellow round the eye. I had hoped to have been able to compare the plumage with birds from India, etc., which the lamentable destruction of the specimen now renders impossible. I am informed by those who know the Collared Turtle-Dove well in India, where it is a common bird and frequently kept in cages, that there it has no such yellow bare skin, in fact, in this respect it seems to resemble the domestic Barbary Dove. I have also looked up numerous references, and in every case when the colour of the orbital skin is given (excluding the two localities Burma and China mentioned below) it is described as 'Lower eyelid slaty-grey' (this is the typical form from Yarkand), Scully, *Stray Feathers*, IV p. 178; 'orbital skin bluish-white' (Eastern Bengal), Cripps, ib., VII p. 297; and again 'orbital skin bluish-white' (Ceylon), Legge, *Birds of Ceylon*, p. 702; also 'orbital skin whitish' (Palestine), Dresser, *Birds of Europe*, VII p. 51. In the original drawing from which fig. 2 in the plate has been traced, which was taken from the type of *Turtur douraca*, the skin round the eye is coloured greyish-white, with no sign of yellow. This is a native drawing, and great care has been taken, in this wonderful series of drawings of the Birds of India, bound in six large folio volumes, collected by the late Mr. B. M. Hodgson, to get the soft parts of his birds correctly coloured. Oates, in his *Handbook to the Birds of Burmah*, writes: 'Eyelids and skin of face yellow'; Swinhoe writes, in *Proceedings* of the Zoological Society for 1870, p. 446, on a bird from China, 'its eyelid is pale yellow.'"

Distribution. Burma to the extreme south of Pegu, and extending thence to the countries in the east and north-east into China. Whether it is this bird which spreads through south central China and into Japan there is at present nothing on record to show, but this seems very likely to be the case. Harington only records it as occurring in the dry zone in Upper Burma and the Chindwin. It has, however, also been found in Arrakan, Pegu, Yun-nan, Cochin China, and the north-east Shan States.

Nidification. Macdonald reports this bird as common all over the Myingyan District, and breeding principally during the latter end of the rainy season.

I have had a fair series of its eggs sent me from Burma, and these cannot be in any way distinguished from those of the Indian Ring-Dove. The notes accompanying the eggs also show that the nest is, as one would have expected, of precisely the same description, and the only thing necessary to say about it is that it seems to be more often found in comparatively thickly-wooded country or even in thin forest.

In habits this bird takes in Burma exactly the same position as the Indian Ring-Dove does in India. It haunts open spaces and cultivation near villages, and also the more open but uninhabited uplands in the Chin Hills and Shan States, though even here it would seem to be more common round about villages than in the wilder parts.

Oates merely says that it is found round about villages in cultivated parts, either singly or in pairs, or else in small flocks.

Harington says that it is a very common bird in the dry zone, and that it is a larger and heavier bird than the Indian one. He also remarks that its notes are deeper and that it has "as it flies an almost hawk-like call quite different to its ordinary notes."

It appears to be rather less intolerant of wet than is the Indian bird and, probably because of this, to be found rather more frequently in the better-forested parts of the country.

In some notes sent to me, Major Harington says: "It is very partial to thorny scrub jungle, feeding in the fields morning and evening, but I have never seen them actually in the villages. Like *Turtur tigrinus* it is essentially a jungle bird. It is very fond of soaring, when it utters a hawk-like cry."

GENUS OENOPOPELIA.

This genus is one created by Blanford for two birds, subspecies, which differ from other Doves, as shown by him in the *Avifauna of British India*: "The little Ruddy Ring-Dove is distinguished from all other species by its long wing, with its first primary nearly or quite equal to the second, and by having the sexes dissimilar in plumage." He then adds: "Two species are generally attributed to this group, but I cannot see that they are sufficiently distinct to deserve separation." There certainly is not enough difference between them to form two species, nor would it be correct to do so for the two intergrade and the Burmese form is but a geographical race, or subspecies, of the Indian bird. At the same time they are distinct enough to make it an easy matter to at once pick out specimens of either race from amongst a series of the two races mixed together, with the exception of a certain number which are to be found in the area where the two forms meet.

Key to the Subspecies.

A. Paler, more especially on the lower-parts; under wing-coverts, axillaries, and flanks very pale-grey ... *O. t. tranquebarica.*

B. Darker and more red, especially on the lower-parts; under wing-coverts, axillaries, and flanks dark grey ... *O. t. humilis*

(46) OENOPOPELIA TRANQUEBARICA TRANQUEBARICA (Herm.).

THE INDIAN RED TURTLE-DOVE.

Columba tranquebarica Herm., Obs. Zool., p. 200 (1804).

Columba humilis Step. (nec Temm.), Gen. Zool., XIV p. 280 (1826).

Oena murwensis Hodg., in Gray's Zool. Misc., p. 85 (1844).

Turtur humilis Blyth, J.A.S.B., XIV p. 872; id., Cat. M.B.A.S.B. p. 236; id., J.A.S.B., XXIV p. 261; Jerdon, B.I., III p. 482 (part); Hume, Str. Feath., I p. 218; Butler, id., II p. 424; Hume, Nests and Eggs, III p. 507; Butler and Hume, Str. Feath., IV p. 3; Fairbank, ib., p. 262.

Streptopelia humilis Bp., Con. Av., II p. 66.

Turtur tranquebarica Wald., Trans. Z.S., IX p. 219; Hume, Str. Feath., IV p. 292; Davidson and Wen., ib., VII p. 86; Ball, ib., p. 224; Cripps, ib., p. 297; Hume, ib., VIII p. 110; Scully, ib., p. 342; Doig, ib., p. 371; Hume, Cat. no. 797; Legge, B. Cey., p. 708; Vidal, Str. Feath., IX p. 75; Butler, ib., p. 421; Reid, ib., X p. 61; Barnes, B. Bom., p. 292; Oates, in Hume's Nests and Eggs, 2nd ed., p. 359; Salvadori, Cat. B.M., XXI p. 437; Barnes, J.B.N.H.S., I p. 55; id. ib., V p. 332; Stuart Baker, ib., X p. 360; Rattray, ib., XII p. 345; Inglis, ib., XIV p. 562.

Turtur humilior Hume, R.A.S.B. 1874, p. 241; id., Str. Feath., IV p. 279; id. ib., IV p. 292.

Oenopopelia tranquebarica Blanf., Avi. Brit. I., IV p. 47 (part); Inglis, J.B.H.N.S., XIV p. 562; Ward, ib., XVII p. 943; Whitehead, ib., XX p. 967; Moss-King, ib., XXI p. 100; Whitehead, ib., p. 168; D'Abreu, ib., p. 1167; Oates, Cat. Eggs B.M., I p. 97.

Onopopelia tranquebarica Sharpe, Hand-List, I p. 79.

Vernacular Names. *Seroti fakhta, Ghirwi fakhta, Biki*, Hin.; *Golabi ghugu, Ithuiya ghugu, Tuma khuri*, Bengali; *Itoo-ah*, Behari; *Rak-guwa, Periaripu guwa*, Tel.; *Powari*, Marie Gond.

Description.—*Adult male.* Upper part of head and neck dark ashy-grey, the fore-head and lores sometimes, and the sides of the head invariably, rather pale; a black collar across the sides and back of neck, a few birds also showing the faintest indications of grey fringes to the lowest feathers; back, scapulars, wing-coverts, and innermost secondaries on visible portions vinous red, tinged with brick-red everywhere except, sometimes, on the back and scapulars; lower-back, rump, and upper tail-coverts dark slaty-grey; central tail-feathers light greyish-brown, the amount of grey varying in different individuals, succeeding two pairs dark grey at the base, pale grey on the terminal third, remaining three pairs dark slate-black on the basal two-thirds, white on the terminal third, and white also on the outer web of the outermost pair; primary-coverts and edge of wing greyish-black, quills blackish-brown very narrowly edged with whitish. Below, chin and centre of the throat albescent, remainder of lower-plumage to the vent vinous-red; vent, and feathers of tibia white, tinged with vinous, and under tail-coverts nearly pure white; under wing-coverts, axillaries, and flanks very pale grey, the latter often being pure white; under aspect of the tail black at the base, pure white on the terminal third.

Measurements. Length about 9 in. (= 228.6 mm.); wing 5.15 (= 130.8 mm.) to 5.7 in. (= 144.8 mm.), with an average of 5.4 in. (= 137.2 mm.); tail 3.75 (= 95.2 mm.) to 4.20 in. (= 106.7 mm.), generally about 4 in. (= 101.6 mm.) ; bill at front .52 in. (= 13.2 mm.), and from gape about .75 in. (= 19 mm.); tarsus about .7 in. (= 17.8 mm.).

The bird with a wing measuring 5.7 in. is a specimen from Nepal where the birds are intermediate between *tranquebarica* and *humilis*.

Colours of soft parts. Irides hazel-brown to dark brown; edge of eye-lid plumbeous; bill black, rather leaden on the cere and gape; legs dull red, dull purplish-red, or brownish-lake; claws black.

Female. The grey of the head and the vinous-red on the upper-parts of the male are replaced by pale earthy-brown, generally paler on the head, which is often more or less tinged with grey; rump and tail as in the male; chin and centre of throat albescent, lower-throat and breast light earthy-brown, paler than the back and generally with a certain amount of vinous-red suffused over it; abdomen paler, and under tail-coverts and vent white; wing-coverts the same colour as the back, the outer lesser and median coverts often much more grey, rarely a pure grey; quills as in the male, except innermost secondaries, which are the same colour as the back.

The black collar on the female is sometimes edged above with grey.

Measurements. The female is slightly smaller than the male on an average : the wing runs from 4.80 in. (= 122 mm.) to 5.35 in. (= 135.3 mm.) with an average of 5.15 in. (= 130.7 mm.), and the other measurements vary correspondingly.

Colours of soft parts as in the male.

Young in first plumage resemble the female, but the feathers of the upper-plumage, wing-coverts, and breast are narrowly edged with very pale fulvous, scarcely noticeable on the breast and most distinct on the scapulars. The iris is a pale dull brown.

Young male after autumn-moult assumes in part the plumage of the adult, the black colour of the collar appears in a patch on either side of the neck, the breast becomes more distinctly vinous-red, and the same colour appears in patches on the wing-coverts, scapulars, and upper-back; the grey head is one of the last characteristics to be developed, and at this stage of the plumage the innermost-secondaries and outer-coverts are tipped pale and subtipped with a bar of blackish-brown.

Nestling, in down, is yellowish-white, the upper-parts darker than the lower and rather buff in tint.

Distribution. Practically throughout India from the extreme west in Sind and the North-west Provinces, as far east as Bengal and Behar in the plains, and the west of Nepal in the hills. In the south of India it is rare in the wet, forested portions of Malabar and Travancore, but extends to the drier area in the latter country. Throughout south-east India it is found as far north as Orissa, being rare in the forested portions of that province. In Bengal it is common in the west, rare in the east, and in Assam and the

Surrma Valley is replaced by the Burmese form, though birds in the west of the former valley are intermediate. Birds from the Nepal Terai are intermediate, but nearer the Burmese than the Indian form, whilst those from east Nepal proper are true, or nearly true, *humilis*.

It has once been found in Ceylon by Layard, who obtained it one year in some numbers in the dry portion of the north, where they were breeding in coconut gardens.

Nidification. The Red Turtle-Dove breeds throughout the year over the greater portion of its habitat, but only from April to September in the hills, and after the rains break in those parts which are subject to the greatest droughts.

The sites they select for their nests are generally at a little distance from human habitations, and often in thin forest, big groves, or similar places, but they occasionally build round about villages and in gardens and compounds. The sort of tree selected varies greatly in different places. Hume "always found the nests at or near the extremities of the lower boughs of very large trees, at heights of from 8 to 15 ft. from the ground, and laid across any two or three convenient branchlets." In Sind, Butler "noticed nests innumerable on the *babool* trees below the camp." Cripps once found a nest in a clump of bamboos near a cultivator's house, and they have also been taken from bushes, especially thorny ones, palms, cacti, cane-brakes, and saplings. Barnes, however, adds yet other and more curious places. He writes: "I have taken nests both before and after the rains, but I think the majority of them breed just after the rains. I have always found the nests in small trees, well in the jungle—acacia trees for preference. The nest is very frail, and the eggs are usually visible from beneath. I have taken the eggs from old Crow's nests, and once found a nest built in the foundation of a Tawny-Eagle's nest, which had on the opposite side a nest of the Common Munia."

The nest is a very flimsy, roughly-built one, even for a Dove's, and looks as if it would be blown away by the smallest gust of wind, yet it often stands severe storms and lives through bad weather long enough for the brood it contains to be hatched and reared.

As a rule the nest is made of twigs, bents, and pieces of grass very roughly put together and without lining of any sort; but Mr. C. R. S. Pitman writes me that he found a nest "in the branch of a 'Bolass' tree, about 12 ft. from the ground, with a lining of dead grass."

As a rule the eggs are two in number, but curious to relate this Dove appears not uncommonly to lay three eggs in a clutch. Hodgson says that in the Nepal Terai—this, as I have said above, is nearer the Burmese form—*it lays two or three eggs.*

Colonel Butler found a nest on the 6th June at Deesa, containing *three eggs*, and writing of Sind says: "On several occasions I have seen three eggs in a nest, and once or twice three young birds."

The eggs are said by nearly all writers to be more often than not an ivory-white rather than a pure white, a tint which is quite discernible when the eggs are placed alongside truly white eggs, such as those of the Wood-Pigeon, Rollers, etc. Many eggs, however, have not got this ivory tinge, and I cannot say that I remember this characteristic in the few eggs of the species taken by myself in Bengal.

In texture they are smooth and slightly glossy, and perhaps rather finer in grain than most Doves' eggs—much like the eggs, in fact, of *Streptopelia cambayensis.* They about equal these eggs also in size, but in shape are generally a little longer in comparison with their breadth.

The series in the British Museum Collection, and the others which I have measured have averaged 1.05 by .81 in. (= 26.7 by 20.6 mm.), whilst the greatest and least in length were 1.12 and .97 in. (= 28.4 and 24.6 mm.) respectively, and in breadth .87 and .75 in. (= 22.1 and 19.0 mm.)

Although the Red Turtle-Dove is a very common, familiar bird in many parts of the wide area over which it is distributed, it cannot be said anywhere to be quite so confiding in its habits as either the Little Brown Dove or the Spotted Doves. It frequents the outskirts of villages and may, on rare occasions, even be found in gardens of European houses, but it only enters these latter in search of food, and when disturbed is not content with flying up on to the nearest tree like the other Doves, but clears out altogether.

It feeds almost entirely on the ground, and its main articles of diet are grass and other seeds and various kinds of ripening grain; it also, however, eats a certain amount of green food and buds of plants, for I have shot them with their crops full of young mustard-leaves.

It is generally to be found where there is a certain amount of forest or jungle of some kind, rather than in the more open country; but it is very capricious in its choice of haunts, and it is not always easy to say why it selects one particular piece of country for a home and rejects apparently similar places close by. It must have water somewhere near, for it is as thirsty a bird as are the other Doves, and drinks morning, noon, and evening.

Mr. C. R. S. Pitman, writing to me about this Dove, says: "I found it plentiful in the Chanda District of the Central Provinces, and generally well distributed throughout the jungle and forest tracts, but, like all other Doves, it is dependent on the water-supply, and whilst I failed to meet with it in some places, in others which seemed to me to be no more suitable, it simply swarmed. . . In one of these latter places the dry, bare paddy fields, shorn of their crops, looked a rich magenta-colour in patches from the number of male Red Turtle-Doves which were feeding there. It was curious to see these vast flocks which were composed entirely of males, whereas one generally sees them going about in pairs.

"I found these Doves much more shy than the other species, and they were very wary whenever I was out with a gun in my hand."

The flight of the Red Turtle-Dove is extremely fast, as one would imagine from the shape of the wing, and it probably covers as much ground per second as any of the Pigeons. It also gets up from the ground quicker and " jumps into its stride " at once, so they make very good shooting, and after but a very few shots have been fired, it is really quite hard to get within killing distance of them. Of course, as food they are excellent, and being almost invariably very plump and well-conditioned, form a savoury dish to the camper when other game fails him.

Its note can hardly be called a " coo," as it is very short and deep, more a monosyllabic grunt, repeated at distinct intervals.

(47) OENOPOPELIA TRANQUEBARICA HUMILIS (Temm.).

THE BURMESE RED TURTLE-DOVE.

(Plate 23.)

Columba humilis Temm., Pl. Col. 259 (♂) (nec pl. 258) 1824.

Turtur humilis Gray, Gen. B., II p. 472 (1844); Jerdon, B. I., III p. 482 (part); Hume, Str. Feath., II p. 269; id., Nests and Eggs, p. 507 (part); Wald., in Blyth's B. Burma, p. 145; Hume, Str. Feath., III p. 165; id. ib., IV p. 292; Armstrong and Hume, ib., p. 338; Hume and Davidson, ib., VI p. 423; Hume, ib., VIII p. 210; id., Cat. no. 797, bis; Bingham, Str. Feath., IX p. 194; Oates, ib., X p. 235; id., B. Brit. Burma, II p. 294; Hume, Str. Feath., XI p. 299; Salvadori, Cat. B.M., XXI p. 434.

Streptopelia humilis Bp., Con. Av., II p. 66.

Turtur humilior Hume, P.A.S.B. 1874, p. 241; id., Str. Feath., III pp. 279, 280.

Turtur tranquebarica Blyth, B. Burma, p. 145; Stuart Baker, J.B.N.H.S., X p. 360; Inglis, ib., XI p. 474. Oates, in Hume's Nests and Eggs, 2nd ed., II p. 359 (part); Harington, B. Burma, p. 69.

Oenopopelia tranquebarica Blanf., Avi. Brit. I., IV p. 47 (part); Osmaston, J.B.N.H.S., XVII p. 489; Macdonald, ib., 496; Mears, ib., XVIII p. 86; Harington, ib., XIX pp. 309 and 365; id. ib., XX p. 1010; Hopwood, ib., XXI p. 1214.

Oenopopelia humilis Sharpe, Hand-List, I p. 74.

Vernacular Names. *Gyo-ni-bu,* Burmese; *Daotu kashiba gajao,* Cachari; *Lali Pohu,* Assamese.

Description. — *Adult male.* Similar to *O. t. tranquebarica,* but is, generally speaking, a darker bird. The vinous-red is darker, more especially on the lower-parts, and the feathers about the vent are more grey. The under wing-coverts, axillaries, and flanks are a much darker grey, and the axillaries are never white. Typical birds from Burma can be separated from birds from continental India at a glance, but birds from the intervening countries are intermediate.

Measurements. The Burmese Red Turtle-Dove is a rather larger bird than the Indian, with a wing averaging 5.55 in. (= 141 mm.) and varying from 5.4 (= 137.1 mm.) to 5.8 in. (= 147.3 mm.).

Colours of soft parts. Similar to the same parts in the Indian bird. "Bill black; irides dark brown; eyelids plumbeous; legs vinaceous brown; claws black; the joints of the scales on the legs white" (Oates).

Female differs from the male in the same way as the last bird, and can be distinguished from the previous subspecies by its generally darker plumage, the dark grey of the under-wing coverts and flanks, and by its slightly larger size.

THE BURMESE RED TURTLE-DOVE—*OENOPOPELIA T. HUMILIS.*

(½ Nat. Size—Male on left, female on right.) PLATE 23

Young birds are similar to those of the same age in the last subspecies; differing in the same degree as do the adults.

Distribution. Cachar, Sylhet, and the districts east to Chittagong, the Assam Valley from Sibsagar eastwards and back west through the Darjiling Terai and eastern Nepal, where the two forms meet and birds are more or less intermediate. The birds of the Khasia, North Cachar, Naga, Manipur, and Looshai Hills are all of this form, and it extends throughout the Andamans, the Chin Hills, Shan States, Yun-nan, Cochin-China, Siam, China, and the Phillipines.

As regards the Malay Peninsula, Robinson, in his *Hand-list of the Birds of the Malay Peninsula*, says: "The only specimens recorded from the Malay Peninsula are those in the British Museum obtained at Malacca by Wallace and Maingay. The bird is imported from South China to Singapore as a cage bird, and I am inclined to think that these birds were escapes from captivity, as the species is one that is not at all likely to be overlooked, and no recent collector has met with it."

Nidification. Curiously enough there is practically nothing on record concerning the breeding of this extremely common Dove. Harington writes in the Bombay *Journal* that it was very plentiful at Maymyo, 3,500 ft., and was breeding there; again, in his *Birds of Burmah*, he notes that "they generally breed in trees, placing the nest in a big branch so that it is invisible from below, and can only be found by seeing the bird fly out and leave two creamy-white eggs."

In Volume X. of the Bombay *Journal* I also recorded the fact that I had taken many eggs of the Red Turtle-Dove, though by a slip I am credited with saying that the eggs are *larger* than those of *Steptopelia t. meena.* Of course, it should be smaller.

In North Cachar I found it exceedingly common up to about 2,500 ft., but rare over 3,500 or 4,000 ft., and in the plains in the Lakhimpur district it was also very common, and both Dr. Coltart and I took many nests and eggs.

There is little about the nests and eggs to distinguish them from those of the previous bird, but I think the Burmese Red Turtle-Dove is even more exclusively a forest-bird than the Indian form, and many of our nests were taken in comparatively heavy forest. Some were in the secondary growth, which so soon grows up over areas which have been cultivated and abandoned, and others were in trees in more open country or thin scrub and tree jungle.

On the whole, also, this bird builds its nest at greater elevations than do any of the other Doves whose nests I have taken. Not a few may be found at twenty to twenty-five feet or greater heights even than this, up to some forty feet or so. They also frequent big trees for nesting purposes rather than bushes and saplings, and the nest itself is often difficult to find owing to its being placed in thick foliage.

In size and construction the nest is just like that of the Indian Red Turtle-Dove, and calls for no remark.

Harington, in a letter to me, says that he took this Dove's eggs at both Kindat and Maymyo in April and May, and, he adds, "I found several nests built close to those of Drongos, both *Dicrurus ater* and *Dicrurus cinneraceus*" [probably *nigrescens*] "and also *Chibbia*, evidently built in these positions for the sake of the protection given by these pugnacious little birds. The first nest I found was in a leafless tree in which there was also a nest of the Black

Drongo; it, the Dove's nest, was very high-up and in a most exposed situation, but I spotted the bird in the first instance and it was not until I drew nearer that I saw it was sitting on a nest. The eggs seem to be creamy and not quite a pure white."

The eggs cannot be distinguished from those of the Indian Red Turtle-Dove, but average a trifle larger, viz. 1.08 by .83 in (= 27.4 by 21.1 mm.).

In habits this bird seems to be even more strictly confined to the better-wooded districts than is its Indian cousin, but it certainly prefers such districts when they also contain plenty of open spaces and cultivation. In Assam and the Surma Valley they were equally common all the year round, but Harington thinks that in Burma they are locally migratory and that they only visit the dry zone in the cold weather. During that season he found them in large flocks, whilst in other parts they were nearly always to be seen in pairs, or less often singly.

Even in Assam, however, after the rice and other crops have been cut, they desert the cover to some extent and feed in very great numbers in the fields, when they offer very good sport indeed. They are magnificent little fliers and rise and get away like lightning, seldom allowing one to get within thirty yards or so before they take to wing. If the food is tempting, the stubble fairly long, and the open country extensive, they will fly half a mile or more before again alighting, but when flushed a second time leave for the forest and do not return to feed that evening. I have, however, known bags of twenty and thirty couple of this little Dove shot in a couple of hours in an evening, and though the birds may swarm and keep rising all round, not one in twenty comes within shot, so that this toll on their numbers has little or no effect in checking their increase.

They are delicious eating, though it takes a good many to make a square meal, and they seem always to be in splendid condition.

Their note is the same single, abrupt grunt as that of the Indian bird, and is rather freely indulged in in the mornings and evenings, each utterance being accompanied by a funny little bob, as if the sound had to be jerked out.

I have seen them drinking at all times of the day, and they are fond of bathing as well, or dusting themselves in dry earth.

Genus MACROPYGIA.

The genus *Macropygia* is included by Salvadori in his family *Columbidae*, but, together with three other genera, is placed in a subfamily, *Macropygiinae*, whilst Blanford retains it with the Wood- and Rock-Pigeons and the true Doves in his *Columbinae*. It is a very well-marked genus, with a long tail exceeding the wing in length and having the feathers very much graduated, in both these respects differing from all our other genera of this subfamily. The bill is small and weak, the tarsus short and feathered for the greater part of its length, the toes long, and the soles broadened. The feathers of the rump are spinous, and the tail-coverts elongated.

One of the most remarkable features in the plumage of this genus, in so far as it is found within Indian limits, is in regard to the barring found on the plumage of the adult male or female. Thus, in one species, *tusalia*, the lower plumage is barred throughout in the adult female and not at all in the male, whereas in the next species, *rufipennis*, the male bird is barred and the fully adult female is entirely without barring on the lower-plumage; and yet again in the third species, *ruficeps*, there is no barring on the breasts of either sex when adult, but the breast is mottled with black in the female and with white in the male.

As it is to be presumed that all these three species have descended from one ancestor, it is interesting to try to work out which is the primitive type of plumage, and if, as would probably be held to be the case, the barred plumage is the earliest type of colouring, why has this persisted in the male in one species, in the female in another, whilst it has practically disappeared in a third?

In the *Ibis* for April, 1890, Wardlaw Ramsay dealt at some length with the genus *Macropygia*, in which he recognized twenty-six species, including the above three species, but not including *assimilis*. The questions of differentiation in sex he considers, in this article, very carefully, and it will be seen that on the whole I agree with the conclusions at which he arrives, but that I do not consider the males and females of *rufipennis* are entirely alike when fully adult.

Although Wardlaw Ramsay does not divide *assimilis* from *ruficeps*, he appears to consider that the Tenasserim bird is larger than the latter and should be divided, but I have gone very carefully into the question and cannot agree with him on this point.

Key to the Species.

A. Tail banded throughout on the central rectrices with alternate black and rufous ... ... *M. tusalia.*

B. Tail plain brown with no bands :
  a'. Wing exceeding 7 in. ... ... *M. rufipennis.*
  b'. Wing under 6.5 in. ... ... *M. ruficeps.*

(48) MACROPYGIA TUSALIA (Hodg.).

THE BAR-TAILED CUCKOO-DOVE.

(PLATE 24.)

Coccyzura tusalia Hodg., J.A.S.B., XII p. 937 (1843).

Macropygia leptogrammica Blyth, J.A.S.B., XIV p. 809; id., Cat. B.M.A.S.B., p. 235; Oates, B. of Brit. Burma, II p. 295.

Macropygia tusalia Blyth, J.A.S.B., XII p. 936; Jerdon, B.I., III p. 473; Godw.-Aus., J.A.S.B., XXXIX pt. 2, p. 112; Hume, Nests and Eggs, p. 500; Wald., in Blyth's B. Burma, p. 146; Hume and Dav., Str. Feath., VI p. 419; Hume, ib., VIII p. 110; id., Cat. no. 791; id., Str. Feath., XI p. 297; Oates, in Hume's Nests and Eggs, 2nd ed., II p. 362; Salvadori, Cat. B.M., XXI p. 338; Blanf., Avi. Brit. I., IV p. 49; Sharpe, Hand-List, I p. 73; Oates, Cat. Eggs B.M., I p. 91; Stuart Baker, J.B.N.H.S., X p. 361; Osmaston, ib., XV p. 515; Stuart Baker, ib., XVII p. 971; Mears, ib., XVIII p. 86; J. P. Cook, ib., XXI p. 675; Venning, ib., p. 632; Robinson, ib., p. 261; Harington, B. Burma, p. 69; Robinson, J.F.M.S. 1905, p. 54.

Vernacular Names. *Tusal*, Nepalese; *Ka-er*, Lepcha; *Daotukuntlaima*, Cachari.

Description.—*Adult male.* Fore-head, lores, cheeks, chin, and throat buff, faintly tinged with lilac; crown, hind-neck, and sides of neck behind the ear-coverts metallic lilac-purple, this colour not contrasting with, but changing gradually from, the buff of the face; rest of upper-surface from the back to the tail barred black and rufous, the black bars being boldest on the upper tail-coverts and most narrow on the upper-back and shoulders where they are overlaid with a beautiful green, purple, or copper-sheen, all these tints being visible in certain lights and varyingly dominant in others. Tail dark brownish-black, narrowly barred with rufous, the rufous disappearing on the outermost rectrices, which are dark grey with a broad band of black about one-third of their length from the tip; the intermediate feathers are

THE BAR-TAILED CUCKOO-DOVE—*MACROPYGIA TUSALIA*

(½ Nat. Size—Male on right, female on left.)

PLATE 24

also intermediate in colour, grading from one extreme to the other. Upper-breast lilac like the shoulders, but the bars of black always less apparent and in old birds often entirely absent, and with the metallic sheen covering this portion of the plumage as on the upper-back; lower-breast more dull in tint and with no gloss, gradually changing into buff on the abdomen and under tail-coverts. Wing-coverts and innermost secondaries like the back, primaries and outer secondaries dull deep brown.

Colours of soft parts. Bill deep lead-colour, almost black; irides pink, with an inner ring of very pale blue, eyelids fleshy-purple and narrow orbital-ring grey; legs dull purplish-red, with the claws black.

"Legs and feet are pinkish-brown or brownish-red" (Davison).

Measurements. About 16 in. (= 406.4 mm.); wing 7 in. (= 177.8 mm.) to almost 8 in. (= 203.2 mm.), and averaging about 7.6 in. (= 193 mm.); tail about 8 in. (= 203.2 mm.); bill at front 0.55 in. (= 13.9 mm.), and from gape 1.0 in. (= 25.4 mm.); tarsus about 0.66 in. (= 16.7 mm.).

This species varies a good deal in size, and young birds probably do not attain their full dimensions until well into their second year.

Weight of old male in fat condition 12 oz., average weight about 10 oz., or rather less than this. A male weighed by Hume was only 9 oz.

Adult female. The upper-plumage like that of the male, but lighter, and the upper-surface of the central rectrices much more boldly barred with rufous; the sheen on the shoulders is less, and that on the head very slight, and the crown itself is more a brown than lilac-grey; the fore-head, cheeks, and sides of the throat are more or less barred with dark brown, the bars sometimes extending on to the throat in the younger birds, and much fainter everywhere in very old individuals. The rest of the plumage below is barred buff and dark brown or brownish-black, the latter colour being the prevailing one on the breast and flanks, but the buff increasing gradually in extent until the abdomen and under tail-coverts are almost entirely of this colour. The under aspect of the tail is, like that of the male, a dull brown-grey, with curious bars of rufous, looking as if a thick pigment had been laid on with a paint-brush.

Very old females often have a pronounced gloss on the breast, this showing most as a beautiful green on the dark bars when held facing the light.

Colours of soft parts. The same as in the male.

Measurements. The female is slightly smaller than the male, the average wing-measurements of twenty-seven individuals being 7.3 in. (= 185.4 mm.). They are also considerably lighter, weighing only from 8 oz. to 10 oz., and averaging about 9 oz., or rather less. Davison gives the weights as 7 oz. only in *Stray Feathers*, but his data tickets give heavier weights.

Young male. Like the female but with no gloss, and barred throughout on head and nape.

When nearly adult the males are still heavily barred on the chest, and do not appear to lose this barring until the autumn of their second year. There is also a considerable amount of rufous edging to the wing-coverts until the bird is in its second year.

Distribution. The Bar-tailed Cuckoo-Dove is found throughout the Himalayas from Simla in the west, through Kashmir, Nepal, Bhutan, and all the Mishmi and Abor ranges north of the Brahmapootra River into Burma. South of the Brahmapootra it is exceedingly common from the Khasia and Garo Hills in the extreme west to the various Naga ranges in Dibrugarh on the east. Thence it is found through the whole of the hill country of Burma, Chin Hills, and Shan States into southern Burma, where it meets *M. leptogrammica*, its southern representative in the Malay Peninsula.

Davison records it as very rare in Tenasserim.

There are two races of this Dove, *M. tusalia leptogrammica* found, as already mentioned, in the Malay States, and in Java and Sumatra, and *M. tusalia swinhoei*, which occurs in Hainan. The former race, or subspecies, which may possibly enter the extreme south of Tenasserim, is a smaller form with its plumage generally more rufous and less glossy. The latter subspecies is about the same size as our bird, but is darker in general tint.

Nidification. I found this bird breeding in great numbers in North Cachar, where I took many nests. The nest is typical of the Order, but is perhaps rather more stoutly built than most: the twigs of which it is composed are nearly always torn from the living tree, and are thus pliant and easy to manipulate when first used, and therefore interwoven with one another very compactly. Another curious feature is that the birds sometimes use grass or, still less frequently, moss as a rough lining to the nest. This lining I saw in several nests taken at Hungrum, a place some 6,000 ft. up in the Barail Range in Cachar, but in the nests taken in the adjoining Khasia Hills, where it was equally common, I only saw about two nests with a lining of this description.

The greater number of nests found by myself and my collectors were placed in small saplings, or in small stunted oak trees at any height between six and sixteen feet from the ground, but a few were found on high, thick bushes, and a good many on taller trees, thirty feet or more above it. Mr. S. M. Robinson (l.c.), however, records finding a nest of this species "placed on bracken leaves not far from the ground in dense bamboo and undergrowth."

The majority of birds lay but one egg; but in a certain number of nests two eggs will be found, and, strange to say, in North Cachar the single eggs were generally of a different type to those taken in pairs. I remarked on this long ago in the *Journal* of the Bombay Natural History Society, where I wrote of these two types: "The first (those laid in pairs) is a long oval decidedly pointed at one end, though not much compressed, and the second is the normal Doves' egg shape, only being of a rather longer oval than usual. The colour ranges from a buff, so pale as to appear white unless contrasted with real white, to a rather warm tint of *café-au-lait*. Curiously enough, too, the first type of egg mentioned is almost invariably darker than the second." The eggs, however, bleach and fade so quickly that in a year or two after they are taken they are all much of a muchness in tint.

Mr. B. B. Osmaston took a number of the Cuckoo-Dove's eggs round about Darjiling, but in no case found more than a single egg in the nest, though he, too, remarks on the two different types of egg laid. He gives the average of his eggs as being :—

> "Large pointed ovals—average 1.44 in. × 1.00 in.
> Small ellipsoid ovals—average 1.25 in. × 0.96 in."

The average of 200 eggs measured by myself is 1.39 in. (= 35.3 mm.) by 1.0 in. (= 25.4 mm.), and the extremes in length are 1.20 in. (= 30.4 mm.) and 1.52 in. (= 38.1 mm.), and in breadth 0.87 in. (= 19.8 mm.) by 1.09 in. (= 27.6 mm.). Their texture is very fine and close even for a Dove's egg, and the surface often has a considerable gloss when the eggs are first laid.

though this wears off to a great extent after they have been kept a few years. The shell is very strong and rather thicker in proportion than most Doves' eggs, and the inner lining is not quite so pure a white, being faintly tinged with buff or cream.

They are late breeders as a rule, a few birds start in April, but not many will be found laying until late in May, and most birds in June and July, though I have taken eggs as late as the 15th of September in the Khasia Hills. They breed from 3,000 ft. upwards, most frequently between 5,000 and 7,000 ft., but up to nearly 9,000 ft.

Both birds assist in incubation, and they are very close sitters, for though I have never actually touched a bird whilst on its nest, I have more than once stood within two or three feet of a bird so engaged, and it has not stirred until I put out my hand to the nest.

The Bar-tailed Cuckoo-Dove is normally a bird of considerable elevations, seldom remaining during the breeding-season much below 2,500 ft., but in the cold weather they wander a short distance into the plains and are very common in the broken ground and foot-hills all along the Terai of the Himalayas and their various branches. Wardlaw Ramsay describes the bird as "a Ground-Dove of a tame nature, very partial to open glades and clearings in dense forest, especially when covered with a secondary growth of low scrubby jungle." I have quoted this in full as it does not quite agree with my own experiences. All through the hot weather and rains I have found the Cuckoo-Dove to resort principally to dense evergreen or oak forest where it leads a life that is far more arboreal than terrestrial. Its deep booming "coo" calls one's attention from far away, and when the bird is finally located it is almost certain to be seated high up on some tree which stands well above those surrounding it. This trait is such a constant one in the bird's character, that when I wanted specimens my procedure was always to make for any conspicuous clump of lofty trees, and if not already made aware of the Dove's presence by its call, I would generally find it there on my arrival.

The note consists of a single "coo," ending up in a sort of boom, difficult to syllablize, but perhaps it may be represented by the word "croo-omm," the two syllables running into one another, and the tone very deep and vibrating, so that it can be heard at a great distance.

They feed both on trees, on acorns, berries, etc., and on the ground on seeds, grain and shoots of young crops, and they are particularly fond of the tender young shoots of the mustard-plant.

They are *not* one of our sporting-birds, being easy to kill in every way. In the first place they are so tame that anyone can get near enough for a shot, and secondly their flight is slow when they first take to wing, and their plumage does not resist shot like that of the Green Pigeon, so that they do not carry away or resist shot as the latter birds do. Nor when killed are they of much use, unless wanted for a museum, as their flesh is generally very hard and dry, and only palatable when made into stew with claret and vegetables.

The male bird has a curious habit during the breeding-season, not uncommon amongst members of the family, of perching on the top-most twig of some tree and then launching itself high into the air with vigorous clappings of its wings until it has risen some 50 ft. or so, when it spreads its wings out straight, puffs out its feathers, especially the long spiny ones of the rump, and sails slowly down in a spiral to its former perch. There it rests a few moments, booming at intervals of two or three seconds, and then once more parades in the air before its lady-love. At these times it is a very noisy bird and, where it is common, its deep call may be heard resounding in every direction, but, at times other than the breeding-season, it is very silent.

This bird is not gregarious in its habits, but where one is met the pair to it will assuredly not be far off, for the male and female seem to mate for life, and will be found together in breeding and non-breeding season alike.

When shooting Jungle-fowl, Doves, etc., in the mustard-clearings in North Cachar, I almost invariably put up great numbers of these birds, and out of small patches, perhaps fifty yards wide by less than half a mile long, must often have disturbed over a hundred Cuckoo-Doves. These mustard-fields are generally clearings made along the banks of some hill-stream and, more often than not, have dense forest on all three of the other boundaries away from the stream, so that they form favourite resorts for all kinds of game, from Doves to Hornbills, and from squirrels to buffaloes and elephants, whilst the mustard, when full grown, provides cover so high and dense that even big deer can lie close in it without being detected. Out of cover of this description the Cuckoo-Doves flush in quick succession a few paces in front of one, rising straight up until they are six to ten feet in the air and then sailing away quite slowly to a distant part of the clearing, or to some tree upon which they sit until the intruder has passed by. Of course, these birds, like all other Doves and Pigeons, when frightened or otherwise urged to exertion, are capable of flying at great speed, and during the breeding-season I have often seen them chasing one another in and out of the trees with wonderful activity.

(49) MACROPYGIA RUFIPENNIS Blyth.

ANDAMAN CUCKOO-DOVE.

(PLATE 25.)

Macropygia rufipennis Blyth, J.A.S.B., XV p. 371 (1846); id., Cat. B.M.A.S.B., p. 234, no. 1422; Ball, J.A.S.B., XXXIX p. 32; id. ib., XLI p. 287; id., Str. Feath., I p. 80; Hume, ib., II p. 266; id. ib., VIII p. 110; id., Cat. no. 721, bis; Salvadori, Cat. B.M., XXI p. 344; Blanf., Avi. Brit. I., IV p. 50; Sharpe, Hand-List, I p. 73; Butler, J.B.N.H.S., XII p. 690; Osmaston, ib., XVII p. 489.

Vernacular Names. None recorded.

Description.—*Adult male.* Whole head and hind-neck chestnut-purple, chin and throat very pale rufous-white, upper-back dark brown, the feathers minutely stippled with pale rufous; in some specimens, not quite adult, these frecklings develop into small bars; the remainder of the upper-parts dark brown, becoming more chestnut on the upper tail-coverts. Central rectrices chestnut-brown, the outermost bright chestnut with an oblique subterminal dusky band; lesser wing-coverts and scapulars brown, more or less edged with chestnut, median wing-coverts still more distinctly edged with chestnut; greater wing-coverts and quills dark brown, the primaries more or less cinnamon on the inner webs, and innermost secondaries rufescent-brown on the inner webs. Whole of the lower surface light rufous-brown, darkest on the breast, and palest on the abdomen, barred throughout with narrow wavy lines of black; under tail-coverts, under aspect of the wings, and axillaries ferruginous-red; under aspect of tail pale grey-brown, the chestnut on the upper surface of the tail feathers showing through strongly and the dark bar also visible, but to a less extent.

Colours of soft parts. "Legs dull pinkish-red in front, bright but pale pink behind, soles whitish, claws horny; bill dull horny-red, tinged near gape with pink; irides violet" (Davidson).

Weight, according to Davison, from 8 to 10 oz.

"Iris light blue, encircled with a ring of carmine; orbital ring leaden-blue; bill and legs purplish-pink" (Wardlaw Ramsay).

Measurements. "Total length about 15.5 in.; wing 7.3 to 7.7 in.; tail 8.0 in.; bill 0.9 in.; tarsus 1.0 in." (Salvadori).

The series in the British Museum gives a wing-length from 7.1 in. (= 180.3 mm.) to 7.6 in. (= 193 mm.); bill at front about 0.5 in. (= 12.7 mm.) and from gape 0.9 in. (= 22 mm.).

Richmond gives the total length as 394 to 425.5 mm.

Adult female. General colour like that of the male, but the stipplings on the back are very much more pronounced, and nearly always developed into small bars, which, in all but very old birds, are continued to some extent on the lower-back. In practically every bird of this sex a certain amount of black mottling shows through the chestnut feathers of the head. The lower

THE ANDAMAN CUCKOO-DOVE—*MACROPYGIA RUFIPENNIS.*

(½ Nat Size—Male on right, female on left.) PLATE 25

surface of the body is much more of a *chestnut*-brown than it is in the male; the bars on this part of the plumage are either entirely wanting or they are represented by a faint stippling of blackish-brown on the abdomen and lower-breast.

In old birds the feathers of the lower-neck and upper-breast are edged with black, giving a somewhat striated appearance to this part of the plumage.

According to Wardlaw Ramsay the adult female is similar to the adult male, but this does not appear to be the case. In the British Museum Collection there is not a single specimen of a female which is anything like the adult male. In both sexes in old birds in perfect plumage there is a faint lilac sheen on shoulders or breast or both, but the females which possess this sheen—never present in young birds—are all as described above. Moreover, as is shown below, immaturity is quite distinctly shown by definite markings, and the adult female cannot well be confounded with immature birds.

Colours of soft parts. As in the male.

Measurements. The females are, perhaps, a trifle smaller than the males, the average wing-measurements of seventeen birds being 7.25 in. (= 184 mm.). In bulk they are decidedly less, weighing, according to Davison, from 6 to 8 oz., only one bird attaining the latter weight.

Richmond gives the length of the female as 390.5 mm.

Young males differ from the adult female in being more rufous in their general tone of coloration; the wing-quills are broadly edged and tipped with this colour, the innermost secondaries being almost entirely rufous.

The chestnut feathers of the head and neck are edged with black, and the barring on the upper- and lower-back is much more distinct, the bars being both wider and darker. The feathers of the rump, and to a less extent those of the upper tail-coverts, are also much more chestnut than in the adult male.

Distribution. The Andaman and Nicobar Islands.

Nidification. The nest and eggs of this Cuckoo-Dove have not yet been discovered with any certainty, though Davison found a nest which, at the time he found it, he believed to have belonged to this species. He says: "I have never found the nest of this bird, nor could I obtain any authentic information as to its nidification beyond that it breeds about May, building among the mangroves on the island of Trinkut. I found a nest, and from the sight I got of the bird as she left the nest I put it down at once as that of the present species; but a few days afterwards I found a nest exactly similar, and containing exactly similar eggs, and off this nest I shot the female, which proved to be *Chalcophaps indica*, so I infer that the first nest was also one of *C. indica*."

From what we know now of the eggs of the two allied species, *tusalia* and *ruficeps*, they only differ from the eggs of *Chalcophaps* in that those of *tusalia* are much bigger, and in the case of both birds are somewhat differently shaped *as a rule*, though I have eggs of *ruficeps* which could not possibly be distinguished from those of the Emerald Dove. In his identification of the bird which left the nest it would be utterly impossible for Davison to have made a mistake, and it seems certain, therefore, that his first identification was correct, and that the nest was that of the Andaman Cuckoo-Dove.

Davison, as quoted by Hume in *Stray Feathers* (l.c.), says: "This Dove is very abundant at the Andamans, but somewhat less so at the Nicobars; it frequents gardens, clearings, the secondary jungle, etc., retiring to the forest during the heat of the day. As far as I have observed, and I have examined a great many of these birds, I find that they live exclusively on the Nepal or bird's-eye chilli.

"This plant grows abundantly all over the Andamans and Nicobars, especially in the secondary jungle, and on the edges of clearings. I was informed, when at the Andamans, that the flesh of this bird was quite pungent from feeding on these chillies, but I tried several, having had them cooked without even the usual adjuncts of pepper or salt, and although the flesh had a somewhat peculiar, but not unpleasant, flavour, I could not detect the slightest trace of this attributed pungency. "The amount of chillies consumed by these Doves must be enormous. I have often shot them with their crops so distorted that, falling from a moderate height, they have burst."

In regard to this quaint diet, Messrs. Abbot and Kloss record that they found the bird on all the islands except Car Nicobar, and most common on Katchal, where all those they shot were found to have been feeding on chillies. Butler, however, though he also examined the contents of the stomachs of nine dozen birds, never found a chilli in any of them. He notes the contents of four birds' stomachs as follows: "(1) Crop full of a small, hard, round, black seed, about the size of No. 1 shot. I bit open one or two of these and they had a white nutty kernel, which caused a slight but distinct irritation in the mouth, lasting for some moments. (2) Crop contained 39 green berries, looking very like large boiled peas. (3) Had been feeding on a long green fruit, an inch in length, with another inch of stalk attached. (4) Same as (2)."

Like their bigger relative the Bar-tailed Cuckoo-Dove, they are both arboreal and terrestrial in their habits, feeding, as is shown in the notes quoted above, freely both on trees and on the ground. Their flight is said to be quick and powerful, and Butler describes them as flying at a very great height when flighting to and from their feeding-grounds.

Their plumage, like that of all others of this genus, is very lax, and seems to be loosely attached to the skin, so that when shot, and on falling to the ground, they lose so many feathers that it is very difficult to procure good specimens for museums.

There appears to be nothing on record in regard to their voice beyond Osmaston's note in the Bombay Natural History Society's *Journal*, where he states that it is very peculiar and somewhat resembling that of *Cuculus c. canorus*, the common Cuckoo.

(50) MACROPYGIA RUFICEPS (Temm.).

THE LITTLE MALAY CUCKOO-DOVE.

Columba ruficeps Temm., Pl. Col., pl. 561 (1835).

Macropygia amboiensis (?) Raffl., Trans. L.S., XIII p. 318 (1822).

Macropygia ruficeps Stoliczka, J.A.S.B., XXXIX pt. 2 p. 331; Blyth, B. Burma, p. 146; Hume, Str. Feath., VI p. 420; Everett, J.S.B.A.S. 1899, p. 103; Salvadori, Cat. B.M., XXI p. 360; Blanf., Avi. Brit. I., IV p. 51; Sharpe, Hand-List, I p. 73; Robinson, J.B.N.H.S., XX p. 261; Cook, ib., p. 675; Robinson, J.F.M.S. 1905, p. 55.

Macropygia assimilis Hume, Str. Feath., II p. 441; Wald., in Blyth's B. Burma, p. 146; Hume and Dav., Str. Feath., VI p. 420; Hume, ib., VIII pp. 68, 110; id., Cat. no. 791, ter; Oates, B. Burma, II p. 296.

Macropygia ruficeps assimilis Streseman, Nov. Zool., XX p. 312.

Vernacular Name. *Tekukor api*, Malay.

Description:—*Adult male.* Upper part of the head, lores, cheeks, ear-coverts and anterior of sides of neck cinnamon-rufous, darkening posteriorly and changing gradually into purple-brown on the lower-neck and upper-back, the purple tint being generally most distinct on the sides. The shoulders and sides of the extreme lower-neck are more or less glossed with lilac, and, except in very old birds, there are always faint indications of dark bars on these parts and sometimes also a little pale-rufous barring as well. Back, rump, and upper tail-coverts brown, the latter more or less rusty in tint, and the scapulars the same as the back, but rather darker. Wings deep brown, the coverts edged with rufous, least heavily so in the oldest birds, and in such practically not at all on the greater coverts; primaries and outer secondaries very finely edged with rufous, and the innermost secondaries with broader rufous edges, and with a considerable amount of rufous at the bases of the inner-webs. Tail, central feathers dark red-brown, in freshly-moulted birds showing very faint obsolete dark bars in a good light; outermost rectrices chestnut, a broad black or dark brown bar across the teminal third, the tips being broadly rufous of a paler tint than at the base, the intermediate feathers grading gradually from the central to the outermost in coloration. Below, chin and centre of throat whitish, varying greatly in purity in different individuals; remainder of plumage below pale cinnamon-rufous, darkest on the upper-breast, flanks and under tail-coverts, and palest on the abdomen. The feathers of the breast are tipped with dull white, giving a mottled-white appearance to this part of the plumage, whilst the purple of the sides of the neck is sometimes extended so as to form a faint collar above the white mottling.

Colours of soft parts. Legs and feet vary from brownish-pink or red, through a lake-brown to a dark purplish-brown; bill pale horny-brown, sometimes suffused with pink, more especially at the base. Irides pearl-white or grey, occasionally pinkish-white and sometimes grey with an inner ring of blue; orbital skin and eyelids pale bluish.

Measurements. Length 12 to 13 in. (= 305 to 330 mm.); wing from 5.3 to 5.95 in. (= 134.6 to 151.1 mm.); tail 6.3 to 7.0 in. (= 160.0 to 177.8 mm.); bill at front, about .5 in. (= 12.7 mm.), and from gape about .9 in. (= 22.8 mm.); tarsus .75 in. (= 19.0 mm.).

"Weight 3.5 to 4 oz." (Davison).

Males not quite adult. The amount of rufous edging to the feathers of the wing and back is greater in extent, and a certain amount of black mottling shows on the breast; the dark barring on the neck and upper-back is more pronounced and the sheen less distinct.

Female. Differs from the male in being duller and darker above; the rufous of the head is well defined from the brown of the back and neck, and there is no purple tint or lilac sheen on these parts; below also the colours are generally darker and duller, and the mottlings on the breast caused by the black bases and edges of the feathers is very pronounced, this mottling often extending up on to the neck and even on to the sides of the throat. The feathers of the upper-back and neck are also minutely freckled with pale brown.

Colours of soft parts. As in the male.

Measurements. I cannot see that the female is any smaller than the male, though it is generally credited with being so. The largest bird in the British Museum Collection is a female from Flores, with a wing 6.3 in. (= 160 mm.), whilst the smallest is a bird of the same sex from Kina Balu, with a wing of only 5.15 in. (= 130.8 mm.).

Young males are like the female, but with the black mottling on the breast still more extensive, and with the whole of the upper-parts barred with black and rufous; the feathers of the rump are more vermiculated than barred and have rufous fringes to the longer feathers, whilst the upper tail-coverts are broadly edged with rufous.

As long ago as 1874 Hume (*Stray Feathers*, II p. 441) separated the Burmese form of *ruficeps* from the Javan bird, giving the former the name of *assimilis*, and very recently Streseman (*Nov. Zool.*, XX p. 312) has again gone very carefully into the question of dividing *ruficeps* into local races. Hume divided his bird on account of three details in which, he said, the Burmese form differed from the southern: (1) Back of neck and interscapulary region dark brown, with scarcely any metallic gloss; (2) breast conspicuously mottled with dark brown; (3) chin and throat pale rufescent-white. As regards these differences—(1) is worthless, as the three most highly-glossed and palest-coloured birds I have ever seen are three fine males from Tenasserim; (2) is only a question of age; (3) is partly a question of age and also partly a question of how a skin is made up. A series of skins, well made with the feathers lying flat, will show much whiter chins and throats, on an average, than will a series in which these parts are badly made. Also a series of very old birds will show up much whiter than a series of young. Now the skins Hume dealt with were Davison's well-made adult skins from Tenasserim, and a series not nearly so well made, and averaging much younger, from the Malay Peninsula and elsewhere, hence his third characteristic is also valueless. Streseman has divided this species into four subspecies: *ruficeps ruficeps*, *ruficeps orientalis* (Hartert), *nana* (Streseman), and *assimilis* (Hume).

Streseman relies principally upon average measurements on which to base his subspecies, and to this adds: (1) amount of dark spotting on crop;

(2) green reflection on nape-feathers; (3) white tipping on feathers of breast. All three of these characteristics are those of age alone, not of locality; and, age for age, I can see no difference in the races from any of the localities whence the bird is obtained, which would permit of their being separated into local subspecies. As I have already said, the series from Burma have a larger percentage of adult birds than the series from Malay, Borneo, Sumatra, and the other islands, and hence, as a series, show whiter throats (Streseman does not refer to this), breasts less marked with black and more with white, and comparatively a higher gloss on the nape, neck, and upper-back.

It is, however, on the variation in size principally that Streseman relies as a reason for separating the four forms he recognizes. These are:—

Macropygia ruficeps ruficeps from Java, Bali, and Lombok, with an average wing-measurement of 144.5 mm. and extremes of variation in eight birds between 140-150 mm.

Macropygia ruficeps nana from Borneo, Sumatra, and Malacca, with an average wing-measurement of 137.7 mm. and extremes of 127 and 148 mm.

Macropygia ruficeps orientalis from Pantar, Flores, and Sumbawa to Lombok, with a wing averaging 157.0 mm. and ranging between extremes of 146 and 167 mm.; and finally—

Macropygia ruficeps assimilis from Burma, with an average wing of 146.6 mm. and extremes of 139 and 153 mm.

To some extent these figures are borne out by measurements taken by myself, which read as follows:—

Java	average	wing	142.7	mm.	extremes	139.1	and	149.3	mm.
Sumatra	,,	,,	140.4	mm.	,,	139.7	,,	140.9	mm.
Borneo	,,	,,	137.9	mm.	,,	131.8	,,	147.3	mm.
Flores	,,	,,	154.9	mm.	,,	146.0	,,	160.0	mm.
Malay	,,	,,	136.6	mm.	,,	135.1	,,	139.7	mm.
Burma	,,	,,	145.2	mm.	,,	140.9	,,	150.3	mm.

If we examine these figures carefully we find we have fairly well-defined groups—Java, Sumatra, etc., with a wing of about 140-142 mm., Borneo and Malay States with a wing of about 137 mm., and Burma with a wing of about 145 mm. Outside these three groups we have Flores, with a very big bird having a wing of 155 mm. But unfortunately the series from Borneo, chiefly from Mount Dulit and Kina Dalu, consists almost entirely of young birds, the same with those from the Malay States, whereas the Burmese series contains a high percentage of adult birds, and those few I have been able to examine from Flores are all adults. Thus it is more than possible that, though individuals from all localities vary very greatly in size, if there were equal series of adult specimens from each locality the differences would disappear.

The alleged differences in coloration, on the evidence obtainable, appear to be entirely due to age and sex, and in the absence of better proof of a definite difference in size, I must retain the Indian form under the original name of *ruficeps*; at the same time, it is more than probable that the bird from Pantar, Flores, and Sumbawa will turn out to be a good subspecies, greatly exceeding in size birds from other localities. Hartert (l.c.) separated the Sumbawa bird not only on account of its greater size, but by reason of its supposed darker, deeper rufous tail-coverts. The latter character, however, is only individual, and some birds from Borneo, and others again from Burma, are as dark as those from Sumbawa, and throughout its area of habitation it will be found that young birds are darker on this part of their plumage than are adults.

Distribution. Burma, throughout the Malay States, Siam, Borneo, Sumatra, and Java.

Within Indian limits it is found throughout Tenasserim in suitable localities, in southern Pegu, and at least as far north as Shandoung, about latitude 19°, in the Bré country, south of Karennee, where it was obtained by Messrs. S. M. Robinson and J. P. Cook. Davison also obtained it at Kolidoo, and Colonel (then Captain) Wardlaw Ramsay in the Karen Hills, east of Tonghoo, whence also Mr. de Wet sent specimens to Oates.

Nidification. The first record of this little Dove's breeding is that of Mr. S. M. Robinson in the *Journal* of the Bombay Natural History Society. Whilst bird-nesting in Shandoung on April 19th, 1911, he came across its nest, and thus records his find: "Higher up the hill, after the undergrowth had ceased, in bamboo jungle consisting of separate clumps of six, eight or ten bamboos and quite open, I saw a pad of moss where the bamboo shoots take off in a cluster. On going up, a long-tailed Dove flew off. I waited twenty-five minutes and shot it practically on the nest. This consisted of a flat pad of moss, almost quite hard, about 12 ft. up the bamboo. It was difficult to get the egg, as I expected it would roll off every minute as we telescoped the bamboo.

"The egg measured 1.26 by .84 in., a perfect ellipse, and cream tinted with very faint coffee-colour."

On April 25th of the same year and at the same place Mr. J. P. Cook found a second nest containing one hard-set egg. The nest, like the last, was placed high up in a single bamboo, but unlike that taken by Mr. Robinson, was of the usual type and "composed of a very scanty collection of twigs." The egg unfortunately got broken in getting it down from the nest. I have had several eggs sent me by Mr. W. A. T. Kellow taken in the hills near Perak and also by my collectors in Tenasserim.

The nests are described as the usual Dove's nests of sticks, but often with a base of moss and sometimes composed almost entirely of this material. Generally they are placed on bamboos, either singly or in clumps, at anything from six to fifteen feet from the ground, but a few nests were taken from small saplings or high bushes, and in these latter cases no moss was ever used in their construction.

The breeding-season seems to be an early one. In the extreme north of their range in the Karen Hills they lay, as we have seen, in April. Further south, my men took their eggs in February and March, and in Perak and the surrounding country they appear to lay in January and February, whilst some eggs I have received from Borneo have also been taken in February. On the other hand, eggs I purchased from the Waterstradt Collection, also taken in North Borneo, were all laid in July, and I have also one or two eggs from Perak laid in May, so it seems probable that they have two broods in the year.

They lay either one or two eggs, generally I believe the former, but my North Bornean eggs are all in pairs, and I have likewise had pairs from the Malay States and Tenasserim.

The eggs in my collection vary very greatly in size, the biggest, possibly an abnormal egg, measuring 1.32 by .90 in. (= 33.5 by 22.8 mm.), and the smallest 1.10 by .80 in. (= 27.9 by 20.3 mm.), whilst the average of sixteen eggs is 1.17 by .83 in. (= 29.7 by 21 mm.).

They are in appearance very much like big eggs of the Emerald Ground-Dove, but average longer and narrower in proportion and are also a somewhat paler cream or *café-au-lait.* In fact, they are miniatures of the eggs of *Macropygia tusalia*, and like them are of two types and sizes, the single eggs being bigger than those laid in pairs, and also, as a rule, less true ellipses.

The Little Malay Cuckoo-Dove is a bird of high elevations and seems never, even during the cold weather, to descend to the level of the plains, or, indeed, much below 2,000 ft. Robinson and Cook found it at about and over 4,000 ft., and my men reported it as very rare below this height.

Hume states that in the Karen Hills about 3,000 ft. is its normal altitude.

There is practically nothing on record about this little bird beyond what is noted by Davison, in *Stray Feathers*, to the following effect: "This bird is not very rare, but is still most difficult to obtain. It is extremely shy, and keeps to the densest parts of the forests; on Mooleyet in the mornings and evenings I used to hear numbers calling. The note is very peculiar, and sounds like Oo-who-who-oo, repeated quickly several times. The birds keep in small parties of four or six. They live on small fruits, and the stomachs of some I examined contained what looked to me like buds or tender undeveloped leaves."

Subfamily GEOPELIINAE.

The family *Geopeliinae* contains, according to Salvadori, three genera, but two of these are decidedly atypical, having twelve tail-feathers, whereas the first genus, *Geopelia*, has fourteen.

The birds of this subfamily have no ambiens muscle or caeca, in these respects agreeing with the Green Pigeons : but it has no oil-gland, differing in this both from the Doves and the Green Pigeons.

The bill is small, tail long and well graduated as in *Macropygia*, and the general form is that of a *Turtur*.

The legs are devoid of feathering on the tarsi, which are rather long, and the feet and toes are built for running about on the ground.

The only genus represented in India is *Geopelia*.

Genus GEOPELIA.

This genus contains five species, of which but one is represented in India, *Geopelia striata*.

This little bird is in all its external characters, as well as in its voice, habits, etc., very closely allied to the true Doves, and it is well placed by Blanford after the Barred Cuckoo-Doves, with which it has many external characters in common.

It is a small bird with partly barred plumage. The first quill is greatly attenuated over the terminal third, and the third quill is longest, the wing itself being short and well rounded. The sexes are alike.

(51) GEOPELIA STRIATA (Linn.).

THE BARRED GROUND-DOVE.

(PLATE 26.)

Turtur sinensis striatus Briss., Orn., I p. 107 (1760).

Turtur indicus striatus Briss., Orn., I p. 109 (1760).

Columba striata Linn., Syst. Nat., I p. 282 (1766); Lath., I. Orn., II p. 608.

Columba sinica Linn., Syst. Nat., I p. 284.

Columba malaccensis Gm., Syst. Nat., II p. 788 (1788); Lath., I. Orn., II p. 612.

Columba bantamensis Sparm., Mus. Carl. (1788).

Columba lunulata Bonn. Enc. Méth., p. 251 (1790).

Geopelia striata Gray, List Gen. B., p. 58 (1840); Blyth, Cat. B.M.A.S.B., p. 235; Jerdon, B.I., III p. 486; Hume, Str. Feath., III p. 323; Hume and Dav., ib., VI p. 423; Hume, ib., VIII p. 110; id., Cat. no. 797, ter; Oates, B. Brit. Burma, II p. 298; Salvadori, Cat. B.M., XXI p. 458; Blanf., Avi. Brit. I., IV p. 52; Sharpe, Hand-List, I p. 80; Oates, Cat. Eggs B.M., I p. 101; Harington, B. Burma, p. 118. Finn, J.B.N.H.S., XIV p. 576; H. R. Baker, ib., XVII p. 760.

Vernacular Names. *Merbok, Ketitir*, Malayan.

Description.—*Adult male.* Fore-head and crown as far back as the centre of the eye ashy-grey; cheeks, chin, and throat the same but paler; crown from the centre of the eye and nape light rusty-brown; hind-neck, sides of neck, and throat and sides of breast barred blackish-brown and white, the pale bars on the upper-neck generally more or less tinged with fulvous; whole upper-plumage from neck to tail earthy-brown, each feather edged with a black bar; tail a darker brown on the central feathers which are obsoletely barred darker, the adjoining pair of feathers blackish-brown and the remaining four pairs black on the basal half and white on the terminal half, the white also extending some way down the edge of the outer web. Breast a beautiful vinous-pink, gradually changing to pale fulvous-white on the abdomen and to pure white on the under tail-coverts; flanks barred brown or black, and vinous- or fulvous-white. Wing-coverts like the back, but with a silvery tinge; quills a darker brown, except the innermost tertiaries which are like the back, and with the basal half of the inner webs chestnut; under wing-coverts barred chestnut and black.

Measurements. Total length 8.25 to 9 in. (= 209.4 to 228.6 mm.); wing 3.75 in. (= 95.2 mm.) to 4 in. (= 101.6 mm.), with an average of 3.90 in. (= 99.0 mm.); tail 4 in. (= 101.6 mm.) to 4.6 in. (= 116.8 mm); bill at front about .48 in. (= 12.2 mm.), and from gape about .7 in. (= 17.7 mm.); tarsus about .7 in. (= 17.7 mm.).

"Length 8.35 to 9.25; expanse 11.75 to 12.62; tail from vent 3.62 to 4.55; wing 3.75 to 4.1; tarsus .75 to .8; bill from gape .7 to .75; weight 2.0 to 2.25 oz." (Davison).

Female. Similar to the male.

Measurements. The same as in the male, the largest and smallest birds in the Museum Collection are both females, the former with a wing of 4.1 in. (= 104.1 mm.), and the latter of 3.70 in. (= 92 mm.).

Hume, it should be noted, makes out the female to average a good bit larger than the male: "Length 8.62 to 9.5; expanse 12.25 to 12.62; tail from vent 4.0 to 4.45; wing 3.75 to 4.5; tarsus .7 to 1.76; bill from gape .65 to .75; weight 1.75 to 1.25 ozs."

Colours of soft parts. "Irides bluish-white; orbital skin pale bluish-grey; bill dull, pale plumbeous; front of tarsus dull pale purple; back dirty pink" (Davison).

"Iris white; legs dull purple; bill dull blue; orbital skin ultramarine" (Everett).

A bird from Java, unsexed but probably a female, has the whole head reddish-brown, the fore-head more brightly rufous, and the feathers about the vent are broadly splashed with the same. This colour may be due to a stain from some fruit getting on to the bill and fore-head and thence to the other feathers on the bird preening itself.

Young. Similar to the adult, but the banding on the sides of the breast and flanks is continued quite across the breast and abdomen; the pink tint on the former part of the plumage is absent, being replaced by dull pale rufous on the pale bars.

Distribution. This little Ground-Dove is found in the extreme south of Tenasserim, whence it ranges south throughout the Malay Peninsula and Archipelago, as far east as the Phillipines and the west of New Guinea; it is also found in Siam, but is apparently rare there and was never met with by Count Guildenstolpe during his expedition in 1911-12.

It is not indigenous to, but has been introduced into, Seychelles, Madagascar, Mauritius, Round Island, Réunion, and St. Helena, and appears to thrive in these various climates.

Nidification. There is practically nothing on record in regard to the nesting of this little Dove. The British Museum Collection contains only one egg which is described by Oates as "slightly glossy," and measures .82 by .64 in. (= 20.8 by 16.3 mm.).

My own collectors in Tenasserim failed to obtain the nest and eggs, but I have received the latter from Mr. W. A. T. Kellow, from near Perak, and from other collectors in the Malay States. All the eggs in my collection are very regular ovals, equal at both ends. The texture is fine, but not very glossy, and the shell very stout for so tiny an egg. The extremes in length are .93 and .78 in. (= 23.6 and 19.8 mm.), and in breadth .70 and .56 in. (= 17.7 and 14.2 mm.). The difference in size between the largest and smallest egg is very remarkable, and I am inclined to think my smallest pair must be quite abnormal. The average is .87 by .65 in. (= 22.1 by 16.6 mm.).

The nest is said to be a tiny platform of thin twigs and bents, only about four inches in diameter, and most flimsy in character, placed on low scrubby bushes.

The eggs in my collection were taken in January, February, and June.

THE BARRED GROUND-DOVE—*GEOPELIA STRIATA*

(½ Nat. Size—Male on left, juvenile on right.)

PLATE 26

Although this is such a very common little Dove, notes on its habits are very meagre. Davison says: "The general habits of this little Dove are the same as those of *tigrina*, except that it never occurs in flocks, being always found singly or in pairs. It keeps about cultivation and feeds on the ground, walking about here and there and picking up seeds. Its note is quite unlike that of any of the other Doves that I am acquainted with, and sounds like 'kok-akurr-kurr,' soft, but repeated several times. It is very common about cultivation in the Wellesly province."

Robinson, in the *Journal* of the Federated Malay States Museums, notes: "The Barred Ground Dove is generally distributed throughout the Peninsula, but is never found in high forest and but rarely in Bluker (?). It is perhaps commoner in the East than in the West, and in the coastal districts rather than the more inland ones. It is usually very common in coffee cultivation, where it is found singly or in pairs, searching the ground for seeds, etc. It is a very favourite cage bird amongst the Malays, and high prices are paid for 'lucky birds,' lucky or the reverse being diagnosed by counting the number of scales on the toes."

It is regularly imported also into India as a cage-bird, where it is equally popular. I have often seen it in large cages with numerous other kinds of birds, and it appeared to live with them in perfect amity, so that it cannot be as quarrelsome a Dove as most of its kind.

They build and lay freely enough in captivity and are hardy little birds, thriving in almost any climate, feeding on any grain or seed, or quite content with bread and milk, *suttoo*, or other substitute for their proper diet.

INDEX.